Paul K. Moser is Professor and Chair of Philosophy at Loyola University Chicago. He is author of *Philosophy After Objectivity* (1993) and *Knowledge and Evidence* (Cambridge University Press, 1989). He is co-editor of *The Rationality of Theism* (2003) and *Divine Hiddenness* (Cambridge University Press, 2002). He is editor of *Rationality in Action* (Cambridge University Press, 1990), *The Oxford Handbook of Epistemology* (2002), the *Oxford Handbooks of Philosophy* book series, and the journal *American Philosophical Quarterly*.

D1157048

THE ELUSIVE GOD

Three questions motivate this book's account of evidence for the existence of God. First, if God's existence is hidden, why suppose that God exists at all? Second, if God exists, why is God hidden, particularly if God seeks to communicate with people? Third, what are the implications of divine hiddenness for philosophy, theology, and religion's supposed knowledge of God? This book answers these questions on the basis of a new account of evidence and knowledge of divine reality that challenges skepticism about God's existence. Its central thesis is that we should expect evidence of divine reality to be *purposively available* to humans, that is, available only in a manner suitable to divine purposes in self-revelation. This lesson generates a seismic shift in our understanding of evidence and knowledge of divine reality. The result is a needed reorienting of religious epistemology to accommodate the character and purposes of an authoritative, perfectly loving God.

Paul K. Moser is Professor and Chair of Philosophy at Loyola University Chicago. He is author of *Philosophy After Objectivity* (1993) and *Knowledge and Evidence* (Cambridge University Press, 1989). He is co-editor of *The Rationality of Theism* (2003) and *Divine Hiddenness* (Cambridge University Press, 2002). He is editor of *Rationality in Action* (Cambridge University Press, 1990), *The Oxford Handbook of Epistemology* (2002), the *Oxford Handbooks of Philosophy* book series, and the journal *American Philosophical Quarterly*.

The Elusive God

Reorienting Religious Epistemology

PAUL K. MOSER
Loyola University Chicago

CAMBRIDGE
UNIVERSITY PRESS

CAMBRIDGE UNIVERSITY PRESS
Cambridge, New York, Melbourne, Madrid, Cape Town, Singapore, São Paulo, Delhi

Cambridge University Press
32 Avenue of the Americas, New York, NY 10013-2473, USA

www.cambridge.org
Information on this title: www.cambridge.org/9780521889032

© Paul K. Moser 2008

First published 2008

Printed in the United States of America

A catalog record for this publication is available from the British Library.

Library of Congress Cataloging in Publication Data
Moser, Paul K., 1957–
The elusive God : reorienting religious epistemology / Paul K. Moser.
p. cm.
Includes bibliographical references and index.
ISBN 978-0-521-88903-2 (hardback)
1. Knowledge, Theory of (Religion). I. Title.
BL51.M743 2008
212′.6–dc22 2007045452

ISBN 978-0-521-88903-2 hardback

For Linda,
with gratitude

Nothing is concealed except for the purpose of becoming revealed.

Mark 4:22

Contents

Preface

For better or worse, reflective people eventually face the question of whether God exists. Aside from one's preferred answer to that question, the immediate follow-up question concerns what *evidence*, if any, is available regarding God's existence. Undeniably, the divide between theists and atheists, past and present, has been deep and wide. It suggests, at a minimum, that God's existence isn't transparent to all reflective humans. The relevant available evidence is, it seems, less than obvious to all reflective people, or at least it doesn't make God's existence obvious to all such people. We might thus say that God's existence is at best elusive, subtle, or incognito.

God's existence is *incognito*, according to standard English dictionaries, if it is *concealed* or *hidden* from some people at some time for whatever reason. The term derives from the Latin *incognitus*, meaning "not known or not recognized." If God exists, according to many able-minded adults, God's existence is concealed or hidden at least from them at some times. At those times, God's existence, we're told, isn't obvious to them or even beyond reasonable doubt for them. If God exists, then, God's existence is elusive, and disputable as well.

Three questions arise immediately. First, if God's existence is concealed or hidden, why suppose that God exists at all? Specifically, what are the prospects in that case for *human knowledge* that God is real? Second, if God exists, *why* is God's existence incognito, particularly if God seeks to communicate with people in some way? Third, what are the implications for philosophy and religion as they bear on talk of God and of knowledge of God? This book answers these questions on the basis of a new account of conclusive evidence and knowledge of God's reality, and it does so in a way that challenges skepticism about God's existence. Given the proposed account, the urgent cognitive problem is not so much in the available evidence itself as in the *people* capable of receiving that evidence. We shall find, accordingly, that there's no cogent inference from divine hiddenness to the conclusion that God doesn't exist.

The heart of the book's account is that we should expect evidence of divine reality to be *purposively available* to humans, that is, available in a manner, and only in a manner, suitable to divine purposes in self-revelation. The latter purposes, we'll see, would mirror God's morally perfect character, and aim noncoercively (that is, in a manner that can be humanly rejected) but authoritatively to transform human purposes to agree with divine purposes. We thus should expect a distinctive kind of *authoritative* evidence rather than spectator evidence that fails to challenge humans to yield their wills to a perfectly authoritative agent.

We should, the book contends, look for authoritative evidence that is *person-involving* and even *life-involving* in identifying and challenging *who we are* and *how we live* as morally responsible personal agents indebted to a perfectly authoritative and loving personal God. Philosophers, theologians, and others have generally overlooked this crucial lesson about authoritative evidence of divine reality, but this book identifies the central significance of this lesson for knowledge of God's existence. Indeed, the book shows how this lesson generates a seismic shift in our understanding of conclusive evidence and knowledge of divine reality. The result will be a needed reorienting of religious epistemology to accommodate the character and self-manifestation of a perfectly authoritative and loving God.

The book offers, on the basis of purposively available authoritative evidence, a distinctive *argument from volitional transformation* for God's reality. The argument has the special virtue of involving *all* of one's life, including its most profound features and its most troubling features. It thus avoids the abstract and speculative character of many familiar (but ultimately unconvincing) arguments for God's existence. In particular, the argument has *existential* clout in highlighting and challenging the motivational core of one's existence. The argument acknowledges a role for purposively available evidence of God's reality in *all* occasions of life, and not just in the gaps where we otherwise lack understanding. It thus yields illumination of all aspects of human life, while acknowledging that one's clearly apprehending the illumination will depend on one's volitional tendencies.

The book draws from revised parts of some of my recent publications in philosophy of religion: "Cognitive Idolatry and Divine Hiding," in Daniel Howard-Snyder and Paul Moser, eds., *Divine Hiddenness* (New York: Cambridge University Press, 2002); "Religious Skepticism," in John Greco, ed., *The Oxford Handbook of Skepticism* (New York: Oxford University Press, 2008); "Cognitive Inspiration and Knowledge of God," in Paul Copan and

Paul Moser, eds., *The Rationality of Theism* (London: Routledge, 2003); "Jesus and Philosophy: On the Questions We Ask," *Faith and Philosophy* 23 (2005); "Reorienting Religious Epistemology," in James Beilby, ed., *For Faith and Clarity* (Grand Rapids: Baker, 2006); and "Divine Hiddenness, Death, and Meaning," in Paul Copan and Chad Meister, eds., *Philosophy of Religion: Classic and Contemporary Issues* (Oxford: Blackwell, 2008). The Appendix draws from my essay "Skepticism Undone?" in John Greco, ed., *Ernest Sosa and His Critics* (Oxford: Blackwell, 2004). I thank the publishers for permission to draw from these essays.

I have benefited from comments, suggestions, and questions from many people, too many to name all of them here. I thank, however, the following for help with one or more parts of the book: Jason Baehr, James Beilby, Peter Bergeron, Thomas Carson, Paul Copan, Andrew Cutrofello, Stephen T. Davis, Garrett DeWeese, Blake Dutton, Evan Fales, Doug Geivett, John Greco, William Hasker, Pamela Hieronymi, Daniel Howard-Snyder, Keith Kenyon, Mark McCreary, Chad Meister, Linda Moser, Tim O'Connor, Gary Osmundsen, Alan Padgett, Alvin Plantinga, J. L. Schellenberg, Brad Seeman, Blaine Swen, J. D. Trout, Arnold vander Nat, Bernard Walker, Jonathan Westphal, Gregory Wolcott (with special thanks for help with the index), Tom Wren, David Yandell, Keith Yandell, and two anonymous referees for Cambridge University Press. I also thank audiences at various meetings of the American Philosophical Association, the Evangelical Philosophical Society, the Society of Christian Philosophers, and my graduate seminars on the philosophy of religion at Loyola University Chicago. Thanks also to Nancy Tuchman for support from the Loyola University Office of Research Services. Andy Beck has been altogether helpful as the Commissioning Editor for this project at Cambridge University Press. In addition, Ken Karpinski at Aptara and Lee A. Young have been very helpful in the production process.

Paul K. Moser
Chicago, Illinois

Introduction

1. QUESTIONS

According to Blaise Pascal's *Pensées*, any religion denying that God's existence is concealed is false (1670, sec. 275, Sellier ed.). The same holds for any philosophy, science, or other theory that denies divine concealment. Let's say that God's existence is concealed, hidden, or *incognito* for a person at a time if and only if at that time God's existence fails to be not only obvious but also *beyond cognitively reasonable doubt* for that person. Many psychologically normal adults hold that God's existence is hidden from them at least at some times. At those times, they report, God's existence isn't obvious or even beyond cognitively reasonable doubt for them.

Here and throughout we'll use the overused term "God" as a maximally honorific *title* that connotes an authoritatively and morally perfect being who is inherently worthy of worship as wholehearted adoration, love, and trust, even if God doesn't actually exist. This title, in keeping with titles generally, is intelligible even if it lacks a titleholder. We'll use "authoritative" to signify *worthiness* of an executive decision-making status in some area, and "perfectly authoritative" to connote such *inherent* worthiness regarding every relevant area. So, one doesn't become authoritative just by amassing clout.

It seems undeniable that God's existence is hidden at least from some people at some times. The theme of divine concealment is endorsed, in one form or another, by many influential proponents of Jewish and Christian monotheism, including Isaiah, Jeremiah, Ezekiel, Jesus, Paul, Augustine, Maimonides, Aquinas, Luther, Pascal, Kierkegaard, Buber, Barth, Brunner, Bonhoeffer, Rahner, and Heschel. (For references and an extensive bibliography, see Howard-Snyder and Moser 2002.) The theme receives further support from many proponents of Islamic monotheism. Very few writers, however, have developed an account of human knowledge of God's reality in

1

relation to divine concealment. This book contends that, despite being concealed at times, the reality of the God of traditional monotheism is knowable firsthand by humans on the basis of salient and conclusive, if elusive, evidence. "Conclusive" evidence, in my taxonomy, is well-founded undefeated support suitable for (fulfilling the justification condition for) knowledge; it may or may not be logically, or deductively, demonstrative.

The conclusive evidence suited to one's knowing God's reality firsthand is, we'll see, profoundly challenging for humans and significantly different from our familiar evidence for the reality of, say, pomegranates or kitchen appliances. *Person-intended* evidence is typically influenced, if not controlled, by the *purposes* of a personal agent, and such purposes may be elusive and subtle, and leave us with correspondingly elusive and subtle evidence. Conclusive firsthand evidence for divine reality is, I'll contend, *purposively available* to humans, that is, available in a way, and *only* in a way, that accommodates the distinctive purposes of a perfectly loving God. The latter purposes, we'll see, would aim noncoercively but authoritatively to transform human purposes to agree with divine purposes, despite human resistance of various and sundry sorts. In addition, those purposes would mirror God's moral character, and thus be constrained by what it would take for a being of that character to be self-revealed. They would, accordingly, be anchored in God's character, and would not be at all arbitrary or whimsical.

We'll consider purposively available evidence that is both *person-involving* and *life-involving* in its identifying and challenging both *who we are* and *how we live* as morally accountable personal agents under the authority of a perfectly loving personal God. Such purposively available evidence would seek whole-hearted transformation of humans toward God's character via volitional fellowship with God, where such fellowship between God and a human requires sharing in each other's concerns guided by love. The relevant evidence, then, wouldn't assume that humans are just spectators in need of further information or intellectual enlightenment. It would thus contrast sharply with any kind of *spectator evidence* that fails to challenge humans to yield their wills to a perfectly authoritative agent. We'll have to attend, then, to cognitive problems arising from *potential human knowers*, including the direction of their wills, beyond any problems with the relevant available evidence. Many philosophers, including many skeptics about God's existence, can benefit from attention to such problems.

One's willingly *receiving* evidence that makes a demand on one doesn't entail one's willingly *conforming* to (the demand of) that evidence. One would willingly conform fully to the available divine evidence in question if and only if, in response to that evidence, one willingly satisfied fully God's demands and purposes involved in that evidence. The latter purposes may include (a) God's revealing to a person the adequacy or inadequacy of that person's moral and cognitive standing before God, (b) God's entering into full volitional (that is, will-oriented) fellowship with a person on God's terms, and (c) God's transforming a person whole-heartedly from any selfishness to God's perfectly loving moral character. The notion of willing conformity to purposively available divine evidence has been neglected in philosophical and theological treatments of knowledge of divine reality. It can shed significant light, however, on the problem of divine elusiveness and firsthand evidence and knowledge of God's existence. Henceforth my talk of evidence and knowledge of God's reality concerns *firsthand* evidence and knowledge, that is, evidence and knowledge directly from its source. Accordingly, we'll bracket the ins and outs of secondhand testimonial evidence and knowledge, which depend ultimately for their cognitive grounding on firsthand evidence and knowledge.

This book will identify purposively available evidence that underwrites a new *argument from volitional transformation* for God's reality. The evidence involves an inquirer's core motivational attitudes, and thus sidesteps the abstract and speculative matters characteristic of traditional philosophical arguments for God's existence. The book's treatment of purposively available evidence of divine reality seeks, accordingly, to reorient not just beliefs but also *readers themselves* as personal agents, in terms of their motivational core. The reorienting involves a change of intentional attitudes beyond one's assenting to information. In particular, it primarily involves one's *will*, and not just one's intellect. It mainly concerns what one *intends to be and to do*, and not just what one believes about the world. The proposed reorienting of religious epistemology will show that some cognitive questions about (human knowledge of) God's existence aren't purely intellectual but irreducibly involve matters of the human will. We'll see how this works, in detail.

Beliefs do indeed matter, in many important ways, but reality doesn't consist of beliefs all the way down. The same holds for human reality, as there's more to human persons than their beliefs. Morally responsible personal agents aren't just belief-holders, since they *intend to act* and even do intentionally act at times. They thereby move themselves and the world too. Whether they also move Heaven remains to be seen. In effect, this book will contend that they do, and that this bears on relevant evidence of divine reality.

In light of the distinctive purposively available evidence to be identified, the primary cognitive issue about (human knowledge of) God's reality, at least from an authoritative divine perspective and perhaps from a judicious human perspective too, would be not so much

(a) Do we humans know that God exists?

as

(b) *Are we humans known by God* in virtue of (among other things) our *freely and agreeably being willing* (i) to be known by God and thereby (ii) to be transformed toward God's moral character of perfect love as we are willingly led by God in volitional fellowship with God, thereby obediently yielding our wills to God's authoritative will?

The shift of primary focus from question (a) to question (b) gives *divine authority* a central cognitive role, and changes virtually everything in inquiry about knowledge of God's existence. It yields, as the book will show, a Copernican Revolution in cognitive matters about God's existence, and it can thereby awaken us from dogmatic slumber regarding divine reality. We'll see that question (a) is fruitfully approached via question (b), given that a perfectly authoritative and loving God would be distinctively purposive in relating to humans, cognitively (in terms of evidence and knowledge provided) and otherwise.

God, if real, would seek to have humans answer question (a) affirmatively by means of answering question (b) affirmatively, in order to have humans become freely and agreeably willing to be led by God in volitional fellowship and transformation toward God's morally perfect character. Philosophers and others have generally missed this crucial lesson about knowledge of God's reality, perhaps owing to an inadequate notion of divine authority, but we'll give this lesson a properly central role in cognitive inquiry about God's existence. The result will be a needed reorienting of religious epistemology in a manner appropriate to the character and self-manifestation of a perfectly authoritative and loving God. (The proposed shift is suggested, in passing, in some of Paul's undisputed epistles, for example, Galatians 4:9 and 1 Corinthians 8:3; cf. Forsyth 1913.)

Question (b) hides a prior noteworthy question:

(c) Are we humans known by God in virtue of (among other things) our freely being willing to receive an authoritative call to volitional fellowship from a God of perfect love that is presented to us in order to reveal, at least to us, the adequacy or inadequacy of our moral and cognitive standing before this God?

Question (c) is less demanding of humans than question (b), because its affirmative answer, unlike that of (b), doesn't require one's being willing to be transformed toward God's character of perfect love. I could answer yes to (c) but refuse to allow myself to be transformed toward a perfectly loving character; indeed, I could even hate and vigorously oppose God in that case. The call in question could come in various forms, and in subsequent chapters we'll explore its central content and purposes. We'll assume, in any case, that perfect love requires one's sincerely intending what is morally good for all people, beyond what people actually "deserve" by familiar retributive standards.

Neither my freely being willing to receive nor my actually receiving a divine call to volitional fellowship (for what it actually is intended to be) entails my *conforming to or accepting what the call offers or commands* (namely, volitional fellowship with God). Analogously, my receiving an invitation to a celebration party (for what it actually is intended to be) doesn't require my attending the party or even my intending or being willing to attend. In contrast, an affirmative answer to question (b) entails one's being willing to be transformed by God toward a character of perfect love. A perfectly loving God could, however, use question (c) as a preliminary means to the more demanding question (b).

We are morally responsible for the questions we willingly pursue, just as we are similarly responsible for everything else we intentionally do. The typical focus on question (a) to the exclusion of questions (b) and (c) tends to place the sole responsibility on *God* for supplying the desired knowledge to humans, as if humans were just spectators who need only to open their eyes to see the relevant evidence. In contrast, this book's focus on questions (b) and (c) as means to answering question (a) directs us to ask whether *we humans* are well-positioned to receive any purposively available evidence and knowledge of God's reality. Perhaps we aren't thus well-positioned, because our wills have gone awry and thus need attunement to reality, including divine reality. This book contends that this is indeed so, and redirects the epistemology of God's reality accordingly. We'll see how this change puts human inquirers themselves under challenging examination.

A rough, inexact visual analogy may be helpful as a familiar starting place. A volitional commitment to redirect visual focus can bring a new perspective either on an ambiguous visual figure, such as the famous duck–rabbit figure, or on an autostereogram where a three-dimensional visual image is "hidden" (or incognito, we might say) in a two-dimensional pattern, such as the images at http://en.wikipedia.org/wiki/Autostereogram or at http://www.magiceye.com/. The new visual perspective in such cases yields access to available visual evidence that wouldn't be received at all apart from the volitional commitment to redirect visual focus. (This rough illustrative analogy concerns the role of the will in the *reception* of some available evidence, *not* the ultimate *accuracy* or truth-conduciveness of the evidence.) Analogously, as we'll see, the redirection of one's will can contribute to one's receiving otherwise overlooked but nonetheless purposively available evidence regarding divine reality. The point, of course, isn't that I'll get firsthand visual evidence of, for instance, what is behind my desk only if I decide to look behind my desk. It's rather that some evidence is made available with a definite *purpose regarding how the evidence is to be acquired*, and recipients must receive the evidence, if they receive it at all, in keeping with that purpose.

Another rough analogy comes from our offering a person an unselfish friendship guided by mutual respect, genuine care, and edifying fellowship in keeping with a morally good relationship. The person's receiving some important components of the available evidence of our offer of friendship would require her willingly attending to the available evidence of our offer in a way that allows it to be salient for what it actually is intended to be in her experience: an evident offer of unselfish friendship that shows genuine care for her. The person's attending to the evidence in that way would contribute to her receiving available evidence regarding us, including our intentions and moral character, that she would otherwise miss. Evidence regarding our offer would be *available* to the person at the start and could even impinge rather vaguely on her awareness, but in the absence of her attending to it in the manner indicated, that evidence (in any ordinary situation) would fall short of being salient for what it is intended to be in her experience. It wouldn't then be received by her for what it is intended to be, regardless of whether she is willing to receive *what* is being offered.

If God as authoritative and perfectly loving invites people into morally caring and edifying fellowship with God on God's terms, via human conscience, we have a rough analogy here. In order to receive the relevant available evidence of God's invitation for what it is intended to be, we would need to attend to available evidence of God's invitation, in our conscience, in a way that allows it to be salient for what it actually is intended to be: an evident invitation to morally caring and edifying fellowship with God. This would contribute to our *receiving* available evidence regarding God's reality (including evidence regarding God's intentions and moral character) that we would otherwise miss. It would change the evidence from being *merely* available to us to being received by us as salient for what it actually is intended to be in our experience. We do well, then, to acknowledge a crucial role for one's will in receiving some purposively available evidence.

One's firsthand knowledge of God's reality requires, of course, that purposively available evidence of divine reality become more than *merely* available for one. It requires one's attending to the available evidence in a way that allows it to *attract one's attention* and become saliently experienced by one for what it actually is intended to be. In that case, the relevant evidence would be revealed to one as including a divine *authoritative call, or invitation,* to let God know oneself and thereby transform oneself toward God's moral character in virtue of one's being led by God in volitional fellowship with God. This divine call to such fellowship would be a natural expression of perfect love, and would come with definite expectations of humans. Our attending to one's allowing for this distinctive evidence in one's experience would fit with the proposed shift in focus from question (a) to questions (b) and (c) above. In addition, this shift would be advisable if the problem in our knowing a perfectly authoritative God's reality lies primarily in *us* rather than in God, even if at times God's existence is concealed, hidden, or incognito. We'll proceed with careful attention to this shift, and ask whether, and if so how, human wills can influence divine concealment.

The previous discussion recommends that we distinguish between three different kinds of human reception of the evidence in question: *conforming* (or, obedient) reception, *indifferent* reception, and *negative* (or, disobedient) reception of available evidence indicating a divine call to human transformation. The adjectives *conforming, indifferent,* and *negative* concern one's *attitude to the divine call,* beyond one's simply receiving (evidence of) the call for what it is intended to be. One's conforming reception of a party invitation, for instance, will include one's *satisfying* the invitation by one's willingly attending the party and perhaps thereby receiving otherwise unavailable evidence regarding the host of the party, including the host's moral character. Likewise, one's conforming reception of purposively available evidence of divine reality can lead, as we'll see, to otherwise unavailable evidence regarding the divine evidence-giver. One's conforming reception of evidence, however, doesn't entail one's *deserving* reception of evidence; obedient recipients of divine evidence, in particular, may actually be *un*deserving and *un*worthy of it, relative to divine moral perfection. We have intentionally moved from simple talk of a divine call or invitation to talk of (defeasible and possibly misleading) *evidence* of a divine call or invitation in order to join epistemological disputes in a manner that avoids begging controversial questions.

Our focus on human willing, in connection with received purposively available evidence and knowledge of divine reality, is for a good reason. Human diseases can run deeper than physical and intellectual diseases, and can bear on our intentional make-up too, including on our wills. We can be diseased morally responsible intentional *agents*, not just diseased bodies or minds. Our *intentions* can go astray, even in morally accountable ways. Can they (and we ourselves) be brought back in line with reality and with what's truly good for us? If so, how? We'll consider a widely neglected affirmative answer that puts the spotlight on our ways of willing, including our intentions. (On the causal role of intentions, beyond desires and beliefs, in actions in general, see Mele and Moser 1994.)

This book's account of purposively available conclusive evidence and knowledge of divine reality focuses on a distinctive kind of evidence available in experience: evident authoritative divine love expressed via human conscience, including an evident invitation to repentance and volitional fellowship with God. Such experiential evidence differs significantly from the mystical, spectacular, or fantastic religious experiences reported by many proponents of religious belief (on which see Wiebe 1997, 2004). In addition, it differs from what some call "numinous" religious experiences, if being numinous entails "being overwhelmingly powerful" (cf. Yandell 1993, p. 236). Religious experiences of a mystical, spectacular, fantastic, or numinous kind are, according to this book's account, not only unnecessary but also dangerous for experientially well-founded theistic belief. Their danger arises from their easily diverting human attention from what would be crucially important in a divine self-revelation to humans: namely, the purportedly redemptive manifestation of a divine authoritatively loving character worthy of worship and thus of obedient human submission. Such an evident divine manifestation via human conscience would be humanly suppressible, and thus not "overwhelmingly powerful." Even so, such human suppression of divine evidence could leave salient experiential evidence of its own, including human restlessness (lack of peace), joylessness, selfish fear, and a dearth of unselfish love.

Three main questions will occupy us throughout this book. First, if God's existence is concealed, hidden, or incognito, why should we hold that God exists at all? More specifically, what is the potential in that case for *human knowledge* of God's reality based on genuine conclusive evidence? Second, if God exists, *why* is God's existence hidden *at all*, particularly if God aims to communicate with people in some way and to lead them into better lives? Third, what are the implications of God's concealment for philosophy and religion as they concern talk of God and of knowledge of God? This book answers these questions with due aversion to fideism and due attention to conclusive purposively available evidence that can challenge skeptical doubts about God's existence. Careful attention to skeptical qualms will keep us honest in our inquiry, and save us from any uncritical or cognitively arbitrary dogmatism. Chapters 1–3 take up the first two main questions, and Chapter 4 treats the third question. Chapter 5 outlines the aftermath of the proposed cognitive reorientation as it concerns the human predicament of destructive selfishness and impending death. The book's Appendix defuses any remaining general skeptical worries. The overall result is a new, skeptic-resistant understanding of purposively available evidence and knowledge of God's reality as incognito. This result, we'll see, yields an effective new challenge to skepticism about the reality of God.

2. PLANS

Chapter 1, "Doubting Skeptics," begins with an ageless question kicked around by all age groups. Does our available evidence entitle us to acknowledge a God who can deliver us from the human predicament of destructive selfishness and impending death? The underlying issue: *is there* really a God who can save us and even cares to save us from our fatal problems? (If a person sincerely holds that we have no fatal problems, that person may benefit from consultation with a psychiatrist.) If the God in question actually exists, how is this God to be flushed out of hiding into plain view? We want plain view, because plain view seems to be *easy* view for us. Plain view evidently won't ruffle our feathers. What if, however, a perfectly loving God wants to ruffle our feathers, and even needs, as God, to ruffle dangerous, life-threatening features of ours? How then would God relate to humans? We'll consider a challenging answer that bears directly on how a worship-worthy God who hides would be known by humans. Realities intrude in our lives in various ways, and we'll attend to a kind of intruding, and corresponding available evidence, often neglected by philosophers, theologians, and others.

Skeptics about God's reality, otherwise known as "agnostics," propose various doubt-raising questions about God's existence. They contend that some questions of theirs decisively resist answer, owing to inadequate available evidence concerning divine reality. In particular, skeptics about God's reality contend thus regarding the question of God's existence, and therefore recommend on evidential grounds that people withhold judgment on the claim that God exists: that is, neither affirm nor deny the claim. Agnostic skeptics, then, aren't atheists, given that the latter actually deny that God exists.

Skeptics about God's reality, according to Chapter 1, have overlooked an important kind of purposively available evidence for divine reality. One will receive this available evidence firsthand, as suggested above, only via one's allowing the evidence to attract one's attention in such a way that it becomes saliently experienced by one for what it actually is intended to be: an evident divine authoritative call to volitional fellowship whereby one allows one's volitional attitudes to be conformed to divine perfect love. Chapter 1 calls this *perfectly authoritative evidence* of divine reality. This is the kind of evidence characteristic of a God worthy of worship.

In contrast with *spectator evidence*, perfectly authoritative evidence of divine reality makes an authoritative call on a person's life, including a person's will, to yield wholeheartedly to divine perfect love, in fellowship with God. It thereby treats the person as something other than a neutral spectator or self-sufficient cognitive judge. (Among humans, there are no neutral spectators or self-sufficient cognitive judges anyway, even if we sometimes pretend otherwise in classrooms, labs, courtrooms, and philosophy discussions.) Is the perfectly authoritative evidence in question real and, if so, where is it to be found? In addition, where is the corresponding personal authority to be found? Who has the needed road map to this authority, and what is the price of this map?

Part of the price to be paid, in accordance with question (c) above, is that we must be freely *willing to be known* by God in virtue of our allowing a divine authoritative call to volitional fellowship to be saliently presented to us in such a way that it judges us in terms of our moral and cognitive standing before God. This involves the aforementioned decisive shift in focus from asking simply, "Do I know that God exists?" to asking "Am I *willing to be known* by God in virtue of being authoritatively challenged by God for the sake of my being transformed toward God's moral character via my being led by God in volitional fellowship?" The latter question looms large in this book, and, as suggested, yields a seismic shift in issues concerning human knowledge of God's reality. It makes, as we'll see, all the difference in the world, and in *us* too, regarding knowledge of God's existence.

Chapter 1 introduces a widely ignored notion of *volitional knowledge* of God's reality that would be suited to a purposive authoritative God who seeks to transform people noncoercively toward God's moral character of perfect love. Such knowledge involves perfectly authoritative evidence demanding that humans yield their wills to the morally perfect authority offered as the source of the evidence, that is, God. To the extent that a person is unwilling to be led by God in transformation toward God's moral character, a demand of the authoritative evidence would be violated by that person. For instance, if a person opposes the unselfishly loving ways of God, that person would be in volitional conflict with a demand of the evidence in question.

The demands of the perfectly authoritative evidence would be fully satisfied only by one's actual volitional fellowship with God whereby one allows oneself to be transformed wholeheartedly toward divine perfect love. The unselfish love inherent to a morally perfect God's character would be *person-relational* in that it would be genuinely received only via volitional fellowship of the recipient with the divine giver of this love. Whereas some evidence is sensitive to intellectual or sensory reception, the evidence appropriate to volitional knowledge of divine reality is sensitive to *volitional* reception of unselfish love. So, we'll base the needed account of purposively available authoritative evidence and knowledge of divine reality on the character of the perfect love required for worthiness of worship. We thus won't allow for any *ad hoc* cognitive exception for belief in God's existence, with regard to needed supporting evidence. Fideism, as suggested, will find no foothold here. Instead, a distinctive version of volitional theistic evidentialism will emerge and flourish in subsequent chapters.

A perfectly loving God would want to influence not just our thoughts but our *wills* as well, in order to lead us noncoercively to love as God loves, in volitional fellowship with God. For the sake of philosophical and theological pertinence, skeptics and others need to attend to this live option. It figures directly in the crucial shift regarding knowledge of God's reality developed in this book. The shift moves such knowledge beyond the merely intellectual domain to the domain of one's will, involving what one loves and hates. At that volitional level, a person intends to act and even brings about actions that directly involve other people and the nonpersonal world too. We are, of course, *agents* as well as thinkers, and our thinking itself often rests on our intentional activity.

Chapter 1 asks how skeptics about God's existence aim to *underwrite their skepticism* with adequate evidential support. Turnabout is fair game when it comes to demanding evidence. How, then, can skeptics actually reach a cognitive position where they can reasonably report on *all* available evidence regarding God's existence for *every* person? Do they have access to the evidence available to every person? If so, how did they achieve such rare cognitive access? Most of us, in any case, seem to be excluded from access to all available evidence regarding God's existence for every person. Why do some skeptics assume that they are exceptional in this regard? What's a skeptic to say, given a daring commitment to skepticism about God that supposedly bears on all available evidence regarding God for every person?

We'll see that skeptics about God's reality may not be as impartial and trustworthy as they have supposed. They actually have a lot of difficult explaining to do, since we'll identify reasons to doubt that they are in a good cognitive position to assess all available evidence of God's reality for every person. In challenging skeptics, we'll make good use of a cognitive analogue of Aristotle's insight, in the *Nicomachean Ethics*, that an educated person looks for precision in each class of things just so far as the nature of the subject matter admits. Correspondingly, we'll consider what kind of purposively available evidence one should expect regarding the reality of a perfectly authoritative and loving God. We'll contend that skeptics not only have neglected to consider such evidence but also lack the cognitive resources to mount a decisive challenge to such evidence. In particular, we'll identify a neglect by skeptics of purposively available authoritative evidence of God's reality.

Chapter 2, "Knowing as Attunement," pursues issues about why and where God might hide from humans at times. We'll face an idea that is startling at least initially: *God as incognito*. We'll thus ask about God's *hiding place*. Can we find it, however strange the very notion? Equally importantly, are *we willing* to look seriously, even in ways and in places that could end up reorienting us ourselves, if we are willing, by means of volitional transformation at our motivational core? Or, alternatively, do we uncritically assume that divine hiding would be the cognitive equivalent of child abandonment without a safe haven? Many philosophers assume just that, and then summarily dismiss the whole matter of God's existence. At a minimum, then, we need to make some sense of the very idea of divine hiding. We'll do so with help from the idea of purposively available authoritative evidence of divine reality.

Perhaps God hides from us, at least at times, because we aren't *willingly ready* to be led noncoercively by God on the basis of our recognizing our grave inadequacy in living on our own, apart from God's authoritative guidance and fellowship. (It doesn't follow, of course, that one who is thus ready is morally better, in terms of lifestyle and conduct, than someone who isn't ready.) Perhaps, in other words, divine hiding aims to challenge us to become willing to be known and led by God *on God's terms* and thereby transformed noncoercively, in volitional dependence on God, toward God's unselfish moral character. This wouldn't be surprising given the approach to knowledge of God's reality advanced in this book: an approach grounded in the distinctive moral character of an authoritative God who perfectly loves people noncoercively and seeks what is morally perfect for them and from them. Such a God would want to know people in ways that lead them to undergo transformation toward God's unselfish moral character, in volitional fellowship with God. This, we'll see, calls for purposive elusiveness on God's part in relating to wayward humans. As suggested, we aren't inquiring about a pomegranate or a kitchen appliance. The stakes are now much higher.

Chapter 2 acknowledges human cognitive commitments that obstruct our apprehending purposively available authoritative evidence of God's reality. We'll call these obstructions *cognitive idols*. We rarely criticize or even consider idols in the *cognitive* domain, because they are too close to us and too protective of our closely held preferences. Still, they flourish in the cognitive domain with real harm to their owners. We all set up or otherwise adopt, if only implicitly, cognitive standards for what is (reasonably) to count as real. There's no problem here in principle, but we thereby may obscure or otherwise damage our perspective on significant features of reality. For instance, if we require that available evidence of reality be *reproducible* in ways we can control, we will potentially obscure for ourselves available evidence for the reality of any being that doesn't leave such reproducible evidence. Alternatively, if we require that all available evidence of reality be *sensory*, we will exclude (at least from our acknowledgment) available evidence for any being that doesn't leave sensory evidence. Our cognitive standards thus matter significantly, and may obstruct our apprehension of reality. Bad epistemology can cloud what's real. We do well, then, to have our standards conform to reality rather than to obstruct or to distort reality on the basis of our antecedent standards.

Regarding self-revelation, a morally perfect God would be at least as subtle as a discerning human being. So, we may expect God to be purposively elusive or incognito at times, given the corrective challenges needed by wayward humans. Contrary to popular wishes, God wouldn't be at our beck and call, and this would be in our best interest after all. We'll explore what a morally perfect God would seek from humans in response to divine elusiveness. Perhaps humans need to learn to put their true *needs* first, ahead of their casual or selfish wants. Purposive divine elusiveness, we'll see, can contribute to our learning this, although the very idea of divine elusiveness offends many. Its offensiveness may actually be part of its intended benefit for us.

If a perfectly loving God is indeed for us, then why would God be coy or elusive at all? Shouldn't God show up, blazingly clear, for all to see, including even those out to disregard or even to demote God? Shouldn't God wear divine reality on God's sleeve? Perhaps God should show up on the evening news too, for good measure, or at least God should somehow make divine reality beyond reasonable doubt for all concerned. God, however, might think otherwise, for various morally perfect purposes. In any case, we'll flush out some whys and hows of purposive divine elusiveness. We'll see that such divine elusiveness doesn't supply a decisive reason for everyone to doubt God's existence. On the contrary, it should be expected of a perfectly loving God seeking to challenge humans for a redemptive purpose of noncoercive (that is, humanly rejectable) volitional transformation of willing humans toward God's moral character, in fellowship with God.

Given purposive divine elusiveness, we'll have to explore the idea of our becoming *attuned* to God's reality and moral character. Our *conformingly* (or, obediently) receiving available evidence of God's reality requires our becoming thus attuned, at least to a certain extent, at the level of our will as well as our beliefs. The relevant idea of attunement fits well with the cognitive shift promoted throughout the book, since the idea connotes our allowing ourselves to be transformed volitionally in a way that gives us reception of otherwise missed available evidence of divine reality. Chapter 2 clarifies such attunement, and offers a new argument from volitional transformation for God's existence that sums up the proposed cognitive shift and highlights its importance regarding purposively available evidence and knowledge of divine reality. The argument captures the central way a perfectly loving God would purposively give self-revelation and conclusive evidence of divine reality. It also supplies, as we'll see, a cognitively robust alternative to skepticism about God's reality.

Chapter 3, "Dying to Know," considers what is at the heart of the book's argument from volitional transformation for God's reality: purposively available evidence of the *transformative gift of fellowship* with God in perfect love. We'll see that the relevant volitional change from selfish tendencies to default unselfish love comes not by divine coercion or intimidation but rather by the power of an authoritative divine invitation to transforming fellowship conformingly received by a person. The invitation is to ever-deepening fellowship with an authoritative God who, in sustaining and enriching life, makes selfishness unnecessary and even self-thwarting. Reportedly, the God in question testifies to having demonstrated divine unselfish love on our behalf, redemptively in the life, death, and resurrection of Jesus as divinely appointed Lord, and elsewhere too. Things become potentially offensive here but nonetheless inviting at the same time. This feature of constructive offensiveness may be characteristic of the ways of a perfectly authoritative and loving God relative to wayward humans. At a minimum, we should give this option a fair hearing.

How could the God we allegedly need now have demonstrated divine love *for us here and now* in an obscure, outcast first-century Galilean? This seems, at least at first glance, too provincial and insufficiently universal for a God who is perfectly loving toward all people. The geography-free god of deism seems less offensive and more cosmopolitan, and thus we might prefer that god on simple psychological and geographical grounds. In any case, we naturally prefer to rarefy, or to attenuate, God, and much religion is in just that domesticating and trivializing business. We'll see, however, that we do well not to attenuate a God who is morally unique in terms of authoritative perfect love.

The true God may indeed be troublesome rather than convenient by our preferred standards, and may need to be thus, given our dire predicament of destructive selfishness. If God seeks to rescue us convincingly from our predicament, God would need to convince us of our need of rescue and of God's reliability in the rescue effort. In addition, God would have to challenge and then noncoercively transform our deadly selfishness. A God of perfect love, as suggested, would aim to elicit not just new beliefs in us, but also new *volitional attitudes*, including unselfish intentions and desires. That's no small task, of course, and it may succeed rarely if at all. As indicated, however, we shouldn't assume that divine intervention is *just* in the life of Jesus; it may be wherever God is at work, regardless of geography, even if Jesus is the authoritatively and morally perfect exemplar of divine revelation in a human.

A perfectly loving God, according to Chapter 3, would work by *killing* attitudes obstructing life in order to bring life. We thus have: God as *killer*. This may seem strange and even perverse at first blush. If, however, we must *die (to selfishness) into* the new life of unselfish love and fellowship with God we arguably need, we should expect *a lot* of internal killing of attitudes to be needed. God would be out to kill whatever attitudes put our lives at risk. (Note well the critical difference between "whatever" and "whoever"; attitudes, of course, aren't persons.) Our selfishness would top the list of obstacles, as it blocks us from volitional knowledge of, and fellowship with, a God of unselfish love. It's a killer that needs to be killed relative to needed knowledge of, and life in fellowship with, a God of perfect love. Hence, we need, in keeping with the chapter's title, to be "dying to know" the true God's reality.

Chapter 3 considers two species of life from death: *spiritual* and *bodily*. Clearly, bodily resurrection is not (yet) with us, as we remain subject to bodily aging, failure, and death. *Spiritual* resurrection, however, could come now via volitional fellowship with a perfectly loving God who can underwrite and empower unselfish love in place of selfish human tendencies. Given our ensconced selfishness, we would have to die to deep-seated tendencies in order to realize spiritual resurrection into unselfish love in fellowship with God. Such resurrection life wouldn't be an easy add-on to what we have competitively and selfishly made of ourselves, but instead would call for the death of our selfishness in order to create room for new lives that flourish and last in unselfish love. Chapter 3 characterizes spiritual resurrection accordingly, and identifies how we can know that it's genuine on the basis of distinctive purposively available evidence. In doing so, the chapter extends the argument from volitional transformation in Chapter 2. Chapter 3 also asks whether *we humans are willingly ready* for the kind of resurrection in question, in keeping with the promised cognitive shift regarding human knowledge of God's reality.

If we are genuine candidates for resurrection life, on the basis of an authoritative divine call, what would, or at least should, happen to the longstanding human pursuit called "philosophy"? Would it be business as usual in that quarter, or, alternatively, would resurrection life bear significantly even on our philosophical and other intellectual pursuits? Chapter 4, "Philosophy Revamped," raises such questions in the light of what a God of authoritative perfect love would require of people and noncoercively empower people to do. It identifies some divine love commands that bear directly on philosophical and other intellectual inquiry in a universe governed by a perfectly authoritative and loving God. We'll see that, given these commands, it's a new day indeed in philosophy and related truth-seeking disciplines. These disciplines will still be robustly cognitive, and conceptually rigorous too, but they will be guided by purposively available authoritative evidence that permeates all areas of truth-seeking in challenging ways. Philosophy itself will then become inherently kerygmatic, or at least kerygma-oriented, in a manner to be identified.

Chapter 4 contrasts two modes of being human: a *discussion mode* and an *obedience mode*. Divine love commands would call for an obedience mode that fulfills and moves beyond discussion. They would demand that reflection and discussion lead to love *in intentional attitude and action*, on the basis of the kind of purposively available authoritative evidence mentioned above. Truth-seeking would be commendable so long as, and only so long as, it conformed to the love commands in question. Truth-seeking would thus be *very* distinctive when undertaken from this perspective, given that a perfectly authoritative and loving God would then guide our ways, including our cognitive ways. We would then become morally accountable to God for the truths we pursue, and even use of our time would become subject to divine love commands. It may be initially difficult to imagine this, since it's foreign to our daily routines, but we'll redouble our efforts to portray this scenario vividly.

Intellectual inquiry of a certain morally responsible sort becomes, as we'll see, a central part of an accountable response to divine love commands. We'll identify how this change of perspective redefines philosophy and related disciplines, making them inherently person-oriented, morally accountable, and directly relevant to human life's most important opportunities and needs. The proposed change in focus bears on intellectual and practical life, and on *us as moral agents*. Given the book's proposed epistemological shift, we'll have to ask whether we are willing to face and to undergo the change in question.

Chapter 4 outlines how philosophy in the obedience mode, relative to divine love commands, would become service to the genuine needs of others, and thus would no longer be *just* philosophical *truth-seeking*. Some philosophers may balk, but we know that old habits die hard, if at all. As noted above, we face a seismic cognitive shift if a perfectly loving God intrudes in and authoritatively governs our lives. The urgent matter, for cognitive and practical purposes, is whether *we humans are willing* to allow for such divine intrusion. We'll keep this matter front and center throughout, because, as the book contends, it's the hinge on which we turn to life or turn to death. Chapter 4 portrays how intellectual pursuits would change decisively if we turn to life offered by an authoritative God of perfect unselfish love. The change would be dramatic indeed, worthy even of the bold term "revolution."

Chapter 5, "Aftermath," identifies how the human predicament of destructive selfishness and impending death fares in the wake of Chapters 1–4. Its thesis is that special *power* is needed to overcome our predicament, and that the needed power is not supplied by humans on their own. The elusive God portrayed in Chapters 1–4 would have the needed power and be eager to share it for the good of all humans, but this God would refuse to flaunt it in a manner that enables it to become a selfish commercial or entertainment commodity for humans. The reality of this God would be, at least at times, incognito for people looking for a worldly power that can be exploited for selfish ends, because this God would have purposes antithetical to selfishness. Accordingly, as indicated, the relevant evidence of divine reality would be purposively available to humans in a manner suited to the distinctive unselfish purposes of a perfectly loving God.

The divine power of perfect love would be conformingly received by humans only as they freely willed to participate in the requirements of that love manifested by God. Accordingly, Chapter 5 shows that the aftermath of the book's proposed cognitive shift offers unmatched benefits to humans, even in connection with suffering, dying, and death, but that we humans need a suitable volitional orientation to receive the benefits and the evidence thereof agreeably. More accurately, we need to become volitionally attuned to the powerful divine reality in question that (or better, who) noncoercively intrudes on our wills (in terms of testing without coercing their direction regarding God's will) purportedly for our own good. In doing so, we'll see firsthand how the human predicament of destructive selfishness and impending death can yield to a greater personal power after all. Since the power in question is inherently purposive and thus personal, we need to attend to the purposes at work in this power, cognitively and otherwise. The final chapter outlines some unsurpassed benefits of doing so in connection with a God who is at times incognito but nonetheless real and authoritative.

The book's Appendix, "Skepticism Undone," undermines any remaining general skeptical worries about the proposed account of evidence and knowledge of divine reality. It removes some confusions common to skeptical worries, and shifts a difficult explanatory burden to skeptics. The result is removal of any serious skeptical threat to the book's central thesis.

3. GOD UNDERCOVER

The otherwise slippery word "God," when used carefully in exchange with skeptics, is a maximally honorific *title*, and not a proper name. It signifies an authoritatively and morally perfect being who is inherently *worthy of worship*, that is, worship as wholehearted adoration, love, and trust. Worship and worthiness thereof shouldn't be taken lightly or excluded from consideration in the epistemology of theism. They call for an authoritatively and morally perfect character in any qualified being, and this character must not depend on the status of others. It must be self-possessed, not borrowed from another being; otherwise, the candidate for God wouldn't be *inherently* worthy of worship. Worship calls not only for wholehearted veneration, adoration, and reverence, but also for full love and trust toward the perfectly authoritative character being worshiped. Morally deficient beings don't merit worship, then, because their moral deficiency recommends against full trust in them. A worshiped being should thus be without moral deficiency, and, therefore, we ourselves are immediately disqualified as candidates for (worthiness of) worship. That shouldn't come as breaking news to anybody.

Adoration, as I use the term, is maximally exalting. Let's say that I adore a being if and only if I glorify, or honor, that being as self-sufficiently authoritatively and morally perfect. (We shouldn't assume that moral perfection requires that a divine being *can't* act wrongly; otherwise, God wouldn't be morally praiseworthy for morally good choices, and thus wouldn't be morally perfect after all.) Self-sufficient authoritative and moral perfection is rare stuff, and thus beings who are worshiped should be correspondingly rare. Polytheism suffers gravely from the fact that it's difficult to find even *one* being worthy of worship. People may, of course, use the term "God" however they wish; so, we won't haggle over the term here. I'll use the term as a title in the manner just outlined, since this fits well with the problems occupying traditional monotheism, including cognitive problems raised by skeptics and the twofold human predicament of destructive selfishness and impending death. The cognitive matter of available *evidence* of divine reality, however, goes beyond any proposed semantic usage, and remains to be treated carefully in the subsequent chapters.

Moral perfection has a moral depth that exceeds performing only right actions. It bears on *intentions* as well as actions, and thus a morally perfect being must have morally perfect intentions. If I intend to bring needless harm to another person, I thereby disqualify myself as morally perfect. More generally, if I intend to bring about any evil, I fail to be morally perfect. In addition, if I fail to intend to bring about what is good for any other person (when I can bring this about), I fail to be morally perfect. A being worthy of worship must be perfectly loving toward *all* people in virtue of being morally perfect. So, a being who hates or otherwise fails to love another person falls short of being worthy of worship. The title "God," then, connotes a self-sufficiently authoritative being who is perfectly loving toward all people, even enemies. Universal enemy-love is, we may say, a litmus test (as a logically necessary condition) for one's being God. If we omit this requirement, we end up with a morally domesticated god who, like us, falls far short of moral perfection and thus of worthiness of worship.

Forgiveness fits in straightforwardly but demandingly. Morally perfect love is perfectly merciful, that is, perfectly forgiving. Such merciful love entails love, including willing what is good, toward *all* people, even toward one's enemies. Specifically, morally perfect love, being perfectly merciful, entails *a sincere offer* of forgiveness to *all* people, even to enemies. Indeed, a sincere offer of enemy-forgiveness is a litmus test (as a logically necessary condition) for being a God worthy of worship. Many philosophers and theologians have overlooked or rejected this requirement, but, as we'll see in Chapter 3, it merits acceptance as central to being a morally perfect God. At any rate, in requiring enemy-love and enemy-forgiveness, divine love would be starkly different from much familiar human "love," and would even be inherently offensive to many humans. Such love would be a real stumbling-block, even a scandal, for people who want to continue with selfish or vengeful business as usual, including toward their enemies.

Since worthiness of worship requires moral perfection, only a perfectly loving being is worthy of worship. This considerably narrows the field of viable candidates, even among all the world's religions. The ideal candidate would be a God who *lovingly promises human redemption*, in other words, a God who promises reliably to give humans an opportunity to be saved, in a loving relationship with God, from the human moral and mortal predicament, including ethical deficiency and impending death. A perfectly loving God would seek what is morally perfect for us as persons, and thus would give us an opportunity for such redemption, at least as long as there's hope for us. Owing to the crucial role of human free will, however, the divine project of redemption could fail, given that people could ignore it and even reject it. Genuine love as a response to love offered can't be coerced (that is, made unrejectable), even by God. The needed redemption, in any case, would be redemption of *us*, thereby preserving our status as persons and preserving us ourselves, not just something else closely related to us. *We* would not be redeemed if we no longer survived as personal agents.

We can use the title "God" intelligibly without begging a sober doubter's question whether God actually exists. A title (say, "King of North Dakota" – no, they don't actually have one there) can have semantic significance owing to its connotation, even if it lacks denotation and thus doesn't refer to an actual being at all. So, our use of the term "God" as a title doesn't automatically ignore the qualms of atheists and agnostics. It is, in fact, logically compatible with atheism and with agnosticism. This is altogether fitting for our use of the term "God," given that we should take coherent skeptical qualms seriously, and not dismiss them by linguistic fiat. Some skeptical concerns can't be defined out of existence.

If God exists, God is hidden, at least from some people at some times. As cited above, Pascal was dead right, but Jesus evidently went further, and *thanked* God for hiding. After giving his disciples instructions regarding their proclaiming the arrival of God's kingdom, Jesus prayed as follows: "I thank you, Father, Lord of heaven and earth, because you have hidden these things from the wise and the learned, and you have revealed them to infants. Yes, Father, this seemed good in your sight" (Lk. 10:21; cf. Matt. 11:25–26, Isa. 45:15). (Translations from the Greek New Testament are my own unless otherwise noted.) If a perfectly loving God aimed to help us to overcome selfishness and death, wouldn't we all get a clear revelation of God's reality that is beyond reasonable doubt for us? Wouldn't a perfectly loving God appear convincingly in order to dispel doubts, or at least reasonable doubts, about God's reality and about God's help available to humans? One might think so, at least on initial reflection. A perfectly loving God whose reality is incognito: that seems farfetched, if not incoherent. So, proponents of God's reality have some careful explaining to do.

We think we readily know what we *should* expect of a perfectly loving God. As a result, we confidently set the parameters for God's reality as if our favored parameters were decisive. This is a careless move, if bold, common, and apparently self-serving. We seldom ask, however, what *God* would expect of *us*. We'll raise this issue in the following chapters, for lack of any better question. A perfectly loving God would promote unselfish love, of course, and thus wouldn't settle for our simply *knowing that* God exists. I could know that God exists but resolutely and demonstrably hate God and others while promoting my own selfish interests (not to be confused with interests actually good for me). Indeed, my hate toward God could increase as my evidence of God's reality increased. As I got more evidence of God as a genuine moral authority over me, I could easily deepen my hate toward God. This could come, out of resentment, from willful insistence that I be my own moral authority at least in certain areas of my life.

Hate toward God wouldn't be intrinsically good for anyone, even for the one who hates God. It would block a congenial relationship between the one who hates God and the only One who could overcome death and supply lastingly good life for willing humans. So, a perfectly loving God wouldn't promote hate toward God as an ultimate end for any human. (We'll thus set aside, as dangerously confused, any prospect of such divine undermining behavior, even if it's in the name of divine "sovereignty" or "power.") For the person resolutely opposed to God, more evidence of God's reality could be genuinely harmful, because it could intensify and solidify opposition to God. Such opposition would be intrinsically good for no one, given its conflict with the source of what humans need.

A perfectly loving God would seek to break down self-destructive opposition to God (at least in cases where there's hope for correction), but not by means of a counterproductive direct assault. Instead, God would invite us in various more promising ways to come to our senses and to renounce our selfishness, including our destructively selfish fears, for the sake of fellowship with God. Since people aren't coerced pawns of God in terms of the direction of their wills (even if some misguided souls think and even wish otherwise), we shouldn't expect universal success in terms of everyone's accepting the divine invitation. If humans were just coerced pawns of "God" in terms of the direction of their wills, then "God" would be causally and morally responsible for human evil, and thus wouldn't be God after all. However crudely powerful and frightening, such a "God" wouldn't be morally perfect and thus wouldn't be worthy of worship, although a perfectly loving God as creator would have a right to take a human life and thus terminate the exercise of a human will, in accordance with moral perfection. People could thus freely reject an invitation to fellowship from a perfectly loving God, given that the invitation wouldn't be coercive of the direction of human wills. So, some people might not come around to love or even to acknowledge God, despite God's best efforts on their behalf. Genuine love toward the people of this world, including us, may be a recipe for suffering and frustration for the one who loves, even for God.

What of agnostics, otherwise known as "skeptics" regarding divine reality? They withhold judgment regarding God's existence on the basis of allegedly counterbalanced, or at least inadequate, evidence regarding divine reality. They reportedly endorse agnosticism "for reasons of evidence." Typically, however, skeptics overlook the most important evidence of God's reality:

namely, the reality of God's genuinely unselfish love manifested in the life of a person who yields obediently to the same transforming God who called Jesus to offer up his life to God for others. This kind of love prompted the apostle Paul to make the following *cognitively* relevant point: "[Christian] hope does not disappoint, because the love of God has been poured out within our hearts through the holy Spirit who was given to us" (Rom. 5:5). Paul thus suggests a kind of purposively available conclusive evidence that would save one from disappointment in hoping in God: the obediently received transforming presence of God's Spirit characterized by God's unselfish love. For the sake of assessing such evidence, Chapter 1 will give careful attention to skeptics about God's reality, and Chapters 2 and 3 will explain in detail purposively available conclusive evidence of divine reality. The result will be a challenge to skeptics regarding divine reality.

Self-avowed friends of God, including followers of Jesus as divinely appointed Lord, often fail to live up to the high authoritative calling to live in divine unselfish love, in fellowship with God. Indeed, few things are more obvious in this morally troubled world. This, however, doesn't undermine the distinctive evidence just noted. Such evidence could be genuine but come to *defective* recipients, and, in any case, it wouldn't immediately make them morally perfect, given that it's noncoercive of the direction of human wills (that is, rejectable with regard to what it demands). The recipients in question are best regarded as works in progress, often slow and difficult progress. The analogy of raising a selfish child can highlight the slowness and the difficulty of the kind of transformative progress in question. Still, a change of life-direction for a person toward manifesting unselfish love even for that person's enemies merits careful attention as salient evidence of divine intervention. We'll give it such attention, because the needed power for the change in question is no mere self-help or peer-help program. Chapter 2 will make the latter point clear.

A perfectly loving God would seek to be known *as perfectly authoritative God*, for the good of humans and the rest of creation. So, God would seek to be known as *our* perfectly authoritative God. Reportedly, God sent Jesus as living human evidence that God is for us, and not against us. The self-giving sacrifice of Jesus, we are told, manifests God's redemptive intervention on our behalf when we ourselves couldn't meet God's standard of unselfish morally perfect love. (Chapter 3 will return to this offensive idea, and give it a fair hearing as a pointer to purposively available evidence of divine intervention.) In his intentional journey from Gethsemane to Calvary, Jesus resists ("dies to") selfishness in order to live in obedient fellowship with a morally perfect God regarded as his Father. To that end, he avowedly and resolutely subjects his will to the unselfish will of his divine Father. This subjection of a human will to a divine will is cognitively as well as morally significant, as we'll see in detail. It highlights autobiographical volitional factors in one's receiving purposively available conclusive evidence of God's reality.

Perhaps *I myself*, in terms of the direction of my will, am the biggest obstacle to my receiving purposively available conclusive evidence of God's reality. This kind of autobiographical evidential consideration will figure centrally in the cognitive shift mapped and measured in this book. This makes perfectly good sense, given that an immediate concern is whether *I* am in a good cognitive position to receive purposively available evidence of divine reality. A similar cognitive concern applies to every other person as well. So, in this context at least, we shouldn't remove volitional autobiography from epistemology.

By way of summary, we can sketch a rough cognitive portrait at this point. Conclusive evidence of God's existence would be purposively available to humans, given God's purpose to engage humans in terms of what they truly need and thus to avoid trivializing (evidence of) divine reality as a matter of casual human speculation. The relevant evidence of God's existence would thus be available to humans in keeping with God's vital purpose in making it available, and this purpose would reflect God's morally perfect character. In particular, God would have a significant, morally relevant purpose regarding how humans are to receive the evidence, and this purpose would set requirements for human reception of the evidence. A central divine purpose, characteristic of a perfectly loving God, would aim noncoercively but authoritatively to transform human purposes to agree with divine purposes, including a goal of divine–human fellowship in perfect love. God would aim, accordingly, to have us willingly attend to the relevant evidence in such a way that it would emerge saliently for what it is intended to be: an evident authoritative call to volitional fellowship with God.

Three crucial divine purposes, as indicated above, include (a) God's revealing the adequacy or inadequacy of one's moral and cognitive standing before God for the sake of inviting one into fellowship with God, (b) God's entering into volitional fellowship with one on God's morally perfect terms, and (c) God's transforming one noncoercively toward God's perfect moral character. As I experience via conscience, if vaguely at first, God's evident authoritative call to volitional fellowship and I attend to it in a way that allows it to become a salient challenge to my life relative to God's perfect love, I then face a volitional crisis, and must respond in one way or another. Of course I might refuse to attend at all to the experienced call (in any way that allows it to become salient in my experience), and that would be a response with potentially obstructing consequences.

My main options would be

(i) I subsequently ignore the evident authoritative call to volitional fellowship, perhaps with intentional diversion of my attention toward something else, maybe even something rigorously philosophical or theological;

(ii) I dismiss it as ultimately fraudulent, perhaps with help from an alternative explanation of my experience, say one from clinical psychology or psychiatry;

(iii) I withhold judgment on its reality, perhaps with the accompanying proposal that my evidence for its reality is too mixed and thus inconclusive;

(iv) I decide to disobey what it asks of me, while granting the call's reality, perhaps with the judgment that what it demands of me is too inconvenient given my own purposes;

(v) I willingly conform to its demand, if imperfectly, and welcome the anticipated change in me, in volitional fellowship with God.

Each of these options enjoys support among some people, and we would be accountable to God for how we settle on an option. In each of options (i)–(iv), I would choose not to obey the evident authoritative call, and I would do well to make such a choice carefully, given the significant consequences if I'm wrong.

In taking option (v), I would follow the volitional attitude of Jesus in Gethsemane. I would then reasonably expect a perfectly loving God to continue noncoercively, in terms of the direction of my will, with self-revelation and to emerge as *my* authoritative God, in virtue of my obeying God's evident authoritative call to volitional fellowship. I thereby would become God's willing servant in virtue of God's authoritative call to reconciliation in volitional fellowship. Only in such volitional yielding on my part would God become *my* authoritative God, as I obediently receive purposively available conclusive evidence of, and even know, God's reality firsthand. A perfectly loving God would desire this for every willing person, as each person willingly yields to God's perfectly loving will. As a result, God would supply purposively available evidence to humans that includes an authoritative call via conscience to yield to God's will. Any less demanding evidence of divine reality would be relatively incidental and certainly inadequate to guide a life or a death in fellowship with God.

A perfectly loving God would, as a matter of moral character, call others to fellowship with God in perfect love, and obedient acceptance of this authoritative call would require volitional fellowship between a human recipient and the divine giver. The alleged evidence of much traditional "natural theology," including first-cause, design, and ontological arguments, is at best incidental, even a dispensable sideshow, in comparison, given its relative laxness in supplying evident divine volitional demands on recipients. We can't, in any case, adequately live and die by such alleged evidence. So, it usually ends up as just a speculative discussion topic, if not a theoretical swamp, for philosophers and theologians, among others. We need not, at any rate, be distracted by it, given our more robust cognitive goals. (For a survey of notable additional problems facing traditional natural theology, see Gale 1991, 2007, Oppy 2006; cf. Parsons 2007.)

We'll give due attention to options (ii) and (iii) above: namely, the option of dismissing any apparent divine call as ultimately fraudulent (perhaps with help from an alternative explanation of my experience) and the option of withholding judgment on its reality (perhaps with the accompanying proposal that my evidence for its reality is too mixed and thus inconclusive). We'll see that undefeated defeaters of the purposively available evidence in question aren't at all easy to come by, contrary to suggestions from many proponents of options (ii) and (iii). We'll give special attention, however, to an alleged defeater in the elusiveness of evidence for divine reality. This alleged defeater will turn out, in the end, *not* to be an undefeated defeater of evidence for divine reality.

Many people have testified to their exemplifying options (i) and (iv), and it's doubtful that we have decisive reasons to contest all such reports. We need not pursue those options here, but we should note that those options (especially option (iv)) speak against any overdrawn view implying that one's *having conclusive evidence* of God's reality requires one's *obediently yielding* to God's will in terms of volitional fellowship. At any rate, I reject any such view on the ground that it's clearly too demanding of one's having conclusive evidence of divine reality. One could have conclusive evidence of God's existence but resolutely hate and consistently oppose God. In particular, one could acknowledge and receive God's call to fellowship, on the basis of conclusive evidence, but intentionally disobey the call. I find no convincing reason of any kind to suggest otherwise.

As perfectly loving, God would seek to transform my will from selfishness to God's unselfish love, and would offer purposively available conclusive evidence of divine reality accordingly, rather than for my selfish entertainment or speculation. We may tell ourselves that *if* God appeared to us in an astonishing manner (in a way to be judged ultimately by us, of course), *then* we would obediently yield to God as God. This, however, is doubtful, because we then would have set *ourselves* up as dubious cognitive judges over God, and in doing so, we would have excluded ourselves from God's cognitive authority. We are, of course, in no position to serve as cognitive judges over a perfectly loving God, despite our uncritical assumptions to the contrary. (Chapter 2 will return to this matter in connection with human cognitive idolatry, while avoiding fideism and embracing evidentialism.)

Even if initial evident divine interventions in human conscience would be rather vague and elusive without our willing reception of them for what they are intended to be, we would be responsible to God for how we handle those initial interventions. As we willingly attended to them as what they are intended to be, and thereafter obediently yielded to them, we could acquire less vague, even salient, interactive evidence of divine reality. Such interactive diachronic evidence, involving evident interaction between God's will and human wills, could then be saliently experienced and received by us as compelling and conclusive. Chapter 2 will use the idea of "volitional attunement" to capture such interactive evidence. It will contend that a perfectly loving God would aim to have human knowledge of divine reality be not just propositional knowledge *that* God exists but also volition-conforming knowledge *of God* as one's perfectly loving Lord and God. My talk of knowledge of "God's reality," accordingly, is more demanding than familiar talk of propositional knowledge that God exists. Chapter 2 will clarify this important distinction.

The interactive diachronic evidence in question would amount to evidence by *volitional fellowship* with God, and would figure in conclusive evidence and knowledge of God's reality by such fellowship with God. God's reality would ideally be known in divine–human volitional fellowship, given that God would seek to be known ideally by obedient human reception of, and participation in, unselfish divine love. A perfectly loving God would seek such *fellowship-based* evidence and knowledge as the conclusive ideal cognitive means of advancing divine love among humans and between God and humans. Resolute opponents of fellowship with God would thus risk excluding themselves from some very significant evidence and knowledge of God's reality. Subsequent chapters will explore the widely neglected phenomena of conclusive evidence and knowledge of God's reality by volitional fellowship with God. In omitting attention to the role of volitional fellowship in knowledge, philosophers and others have neglected some important epistemological lessons.

Affirmation of the existence of a perfectly loving God can yield significant explanatory value, at least in certain areas of inquiry. Such an affirmation, we might argue, makes the best sense available of who we are as moral agents and of why we as moral agents have come into existence at all. The overall cognitive reasonableness of theistic belief would thus be underwritten in part by an inference to a best available explanation of our overall experience. (We'll return to this topic in Chapters 1 and 2, which avoid any dubious commitment to so-called "self-authenticating" religious experiences.) Even so, the basic firsthand experiential evidence of God's reality would be found in one's willingly experiencing the evident presence of God's potentially transforming perfect love. This experienced evident presence of divine love wouldn't itself be an argument of any kind, but it would include an evident authoritative and loving divine call to a person to enter volitional fellowship with God. Such a call, when genuine, would be a direct manifestation of divine love; in experiencing it for what it is intended to be, one would experience divine love. One would also be accountable to God for how one handles this call, but one would nonetheless be free to reject it or to ignore it. If a call promotes hate toward any people, then it is, by definition, *not* from a *perfectly loving* God. False gods would compete on all fronts with a perfectly loving God, and would be identifiable relative to their violating the morally perfect standard of unselfish love even toward enemies. We thus can readily eliminate many imposters, despite their having deceived or at least attracted many "religious" people.

For a person willing to yield to God's perfectly loving ways, the purposively available evidence would be, if subtle or elusive, arguably conclusive (being unhindered by defeaters) and thus adequate to satisfy the justification condition for genuine knowledge that God exists. It would be subtle or elusive perhaps in order to keep people humble, in particular, free of prideful triumphalism of the kind that destroys loving relationships and community. In our pridefulness, we would readily turn a conveniently available God into a selfish commodity or sledgehammer and thus a destructive idol of our own making. The elusive evidence available to us arguably fits with the reality of an elusive God who aims to teach us to trust fully (that is, to entrust ourselves wholeheartedly to) the One who alone can save us from destructive selfishness and impending death. This book will explore, clarify, and defend this thesis in detail.

The proposal under consideration is that we gain *evidentially* and thus *cognitively* as we turn from (that is, "repent" of) our selfish ways in order to get in line with a perfectly loving God and to get further purposively available evidence of this God's reality. This may seem to be difficult news, because old habits die hard, and we have a hard time trusting a God we cannot see, handle, control, buy, outsmart, or market. Still, as we experience a perhaps vague evident divine call in conscience, we may do well to call for divine help to yield to God's evident call and to renounce old habits of selfish behavior. The transformation thus begun wouldn't be just a self-help or peer-help program, given its anchor in an evident divine call to volitional fellowship. We fear, of course, that our well-being and our rationality, if not our public or academic reputation, will be at risk if we trust an invisible God. The fact of the matter, however, is that our well-being and rationality are at risk already and even doomed if we fail to have a perfectly loving God to trust. Death serves as a vivid reminder, even a loud shout, of potentially irreversible trouble at hand. Without a perfectly loving God as our trustworthy savior, final death awaits us, and only a dark grave then remains for us. There's no hope for well-being or rationality, or even worthwhile reputation, in that vicinity. Still, we do well not to confuse a notion of what we need and a notion of what is supported by our available evidence.

Perhaps as we begin to die to our selfish ways, with invoked divine help, in order to live to a perfectly loving God, we can obediently receive God as our known savior from death and selfish corruption. Nothing could then extinguish us, not even death. Death leaves us, in any case, either with lives that are *ultimately* an empty tragedy (if everyone shares this fate) or with a God subjecting this world to futility in order to save it on God's distinctive and challenging terms. In sincerely hoping for the latter, on the basis of initial purposively available evidence, we may become open to a kind of interactive purposively available evidence that will change us forever, even from death to life. If we have the courage to hope in God, on the basis of elusive evidence, we may see that Plato was correct: philosophy done right prepares us for dying and death. This evidence may also lead to the One we truly need in our human predicament. In that case, philosophy would be not just preparing ourselves for death but mainly pointing reasonably, and kerygmatically, to the One who offers perfect love in a life of fellowship beyond death. Chapters 4 and 5 will return to this widely neglected ideal of philosophy done right. We turn now to some skeptical doubts about divine reality and to some cogent but neglected doubts about those skeptical doubts.

1

ᏰᏗ

Doubting Skeptics

Many philosophers contend that any acknowledgment of a perfectly loving God who cares for people is just wishful thinking, and not sound judgment at all. Their skepticism about God's reality colors their whole conceived universe, even darkly as far as lasting hope for human life goes. Whether they *know* that we have mere wishful thinking in acknowledgment of God's reality remains to be seen. In any case, we need to face such skepticism head on. It has remarkable staying power among philosophers, whatever its standing regarding truth and available evidence.

In keeping with philosophical positions generally, skepticism comes in many different versions. Skeptics have doubted the reality of the external world, (other) minds, abstract objects, physical objects, history, the future, causation, God (of course), evil, goodness, and so on. In addition, skeptics have disavowed various cognitively important states: certainty, knowledge, justified belief, and reliable belief, among others. Skepticism also comes in different strengths of doubt. *Modal* skeptics disavow that a cognitive state, such as knowledge, is even *possible*. *Actuality* skeptics disavow that a cognitive state, such as knowledge, is *actual*. This is just the beginning of distinctions about skepticism, but we won't delay with elaborate taxonomy. Instead, we'll turn directly to religious skepticism and its prospects regarding God's existence.

Religious skepticism, we'll see, is not as compelling from a cognitive point of view as many philosophers have supposed, and is in fact open to serious challenge. In particular, we'll see that we have no easily generalizable support for religious skepticism about the reality of God. Even if an individual person were to lack adequate available evidence for God's reality, this person would have no ready way to generalize to the truth of religious skepticism *for people in general*. This chapter reaches this conclusion after identifying what motivates influential religious skeptics and what confounds them.

1. SKEPTICISM

Religious skepticism is, unsurprisingly, skepticism about religion. What, however, is *religion*? The question appears simple enough, but this appearance is
illusory, because the term "religion" is as unclear as any in the English language. When is something a religion, and when not? The answer is certainly
not easy, and rarely comes with adequate precision. English language-users
sometimes call even a sport or a hobby a "religion": "Baseball is his religion,"
or "Knitting is her religion." How, then, could all of the following coherently
qualify as religion: Judaism, Christianity, Islam, Buddhism, Hinduism, Confucianism, Taoism, Shinto, Bahaism, baseball, and knitting? They clearly lack
a common goal or object. Perhaps, however, they sometimes share an underlying human *attitude*. That is, a distinctive kind of human *commitment* may
be common to these diverse phenomena: namely, a *religious* commitment.

We now shift our slippery question. When is a human *commitment* religious, and when not? Whatever the answer, this shift redirects skepticism to
consider a particular kind of human commitment. In doing so, the shift has
religious skeptics question something about a psychological attitude. Let's
suppose, if only for the sake of discussion, that a commitment is religious
for a person if and only if the commitment is intrinsic (that is, not *merely*
instrumental toward something else) and is intended to be life-defining (that
is, intended to be constitutive of living) for that person. We can imagine a
person for whom baseball or knitting is, however strangely and sadly, an
object of religious commitment in this sense. (In reality, for what it's worth,
there are purchasable T-shirts in Chicago and elsewhere boldly proclaiming,
"Baseball is Life"; see also Evans and Herzog 2002.) Religious skeptics, in this
case, would express doubt about a religious commitment among humans.
Their doubt could stem from this issue: is the commitment *ill-advised* rather
than *well-advised*? This is a question about value, in effect: is the religious
commitment in question *bad* rather than *good*?

Goodness and badness, like many normative realities, come in different
species. We can distinguish *moral* goodness, *cognitive* goodness, *prudential*
goodness, *aesthetic* goodness, and so on. (For details see Moser 1989, chap.
5, Moser 1993, chap. 4.) Taxonomy for value theory, however, isn't our topic.
Religious skepticism is our quarry, and thus we won't digress. We'll make
do with just the distinctions we need for an adequate assessment of religious
skepticism.

Religious skeptics can disavow various species of value with respect to
religious commitment. A religious commitment could be *factually* bad with
regard to capturing reality; in that case, it would fail to capture reality as

indicated. We may say that it lacks "factual" goodness in that case. A religious commitment could also be *cognitively* bad by virtue of lacking the status of knowledge or of justified belief, owing perhaps to inadequate evidential support, even if it happens to turn out to be factual, that is, true. In addition, a religious commitment could be *morally* bad by virtue of bringing about moral harm, such as social injustice or individual selfishness and harm. (Imagine, for instance, hijacked commercial jet airliners, loaded with innocent passengers, flying into skyscrapers in New York City on September 11, 2001, allegedly for the vindictive cause of some viciously militant god; or, sadly, read about it in any major newspaper published the next day; cf. Juergensmeyer 2003.) Religious skepticism regarding *factual* goodness and *cognitive* goodness has dominated philosophical discussion, and such skepticism will occupy our attention in this chapter.

We may plausibly jettison *semantical* religious skepticism, the position that dismisses religious claims on the ground that they are semantically meaningless. Nothing credible speaks in favor of such semantical skepticism regarding prominent religious claims. One could, with as much plausibility, reject religious *skepticism* on the ground that it is itself semantically meaningless. On the most charitable diagnosis, a certain lack of imagination underlies semantical religious skepticism regarding prominent religious claims. Skeptics who reportedly can't imagine, for instance, that the God of traditional monotheism exists need remedial work in the area of imagining circumstances. The real deficiency here lies with the semantical *skeptics*, not with the semantical status of monotheism. Sometimes this deficiency is accompanied by a dubious general approach to semantical meaning, such as Humean empiricism or positivist verificationism about meaning. In that case, semantical skeptics appear to be caught in both the frying pan and the fire, without any imagination of a line of escape. We are, in any case, well-advised to move on, to less desperate positions.

The *factuality* of the object of a religious commitment serves as a common target for religious skeptics. In the case of baseball or knitting, skeptical doubt would be strange indeed, since people involved in modern society don't usually doubt the reality of baseball or knitting. When they do doubt such reality, we are inclined to question their sanity or at least their sense of humor, if only because those "religions" allegedly offer so much to so many. Going to the extreme, ardent skeptics might introduce *global*, or *comprehensive*, doubt that bears on baseball, knitting, and everything else, but that would be a dramatic move well beyond religious skepticism. We won't wander now into that far-flung region where anything whatever seems to go in the area of doubt (see this book's Appendix and Moser 2004a for a challenge to global

skepticism). Our topic is much closer to home, where our decisions typically
make important differences and even bear on our lives.

For our purposes now, a certain irrelevance characterizes skepticism
about religious commitments that have no supernatural object. Consider,
for instance, a morality-focused *non*theistic religious commitment held by
some contemporary proponents of Confucianism. Their religious commitment focuses on moral virtues, and has no role for a personal God or any
other such supernatural object. (This was evidently *not* the attitude of Confucius himself, for what it's worth, but that's beside the point at hand.) Suppose
that a skeptic questioned the factuality of the objects of these Confucianists'
religious commitment. This would amount to *moral* skepticism, and not
skepticism about supernatural phenomena. Our topic, however, is *religious*
skepticism that does not reduce to moral skepticism. The most common
target of such skepticism is *theistic* religious commitment. As a result, we'll
focus on skepticism about theistic religious commitment, in particular, skepticism about its supernatural object: God. This focus includes doubt about
the reality of God and doubt about *the positive cognitive, or epistemic, value*
of affirmations of God's reality. If religious skeptics are correct, we shouldn't
be confident about God's reality, at least from a cognitive point of view. We
should, instead, withhold judgment. Is their skeptical advice credible, from
a cognitive point of view?

2. DIVINE EVIDENCE

The term "God" is, unfortunately, as unclear as the term "religion." At times
it seems that each person has his or her own distinctive understanding of
the term, but in reality the situation is not quite so fractured. Along with
many other people, I use the term "God" as a supreme *title* that connotes
an authoritatively and morally perfect being inherently worthy of worship –
worship as wholehearted adoration, love, and trust. The holder of this title,
as the Introduction noted, must be perfectly loving toward all people, even
toward enemies, and, as perfectly authoritative, must be inherently worthy of
an executive decision-making status regarding every relevant area. Plausible
candidates seem few and far between, if there is any worthwhile candidate
actually available.

As a title, the term "God" can be fully intelligible to us even if there is
no titleholder, that is, even if God doesn't exist. This use of the term thus
allows for the intelligibility of familiar skeptical questions and doubts about
the existence of God, and it fits with some prominent understandings of
monotheism in Judaism, Christianity, and Islam. Let's continue, then, to use

the term in that manner, as a preeminent title that may or may not be satisfied by an actual titleholder. To avoid even the appearance of begging the main question against skeptics about God's existence, I shall typically talk of what God *would* do or be like, where this is short for *would if God actually exists*. We'll thus give skeptics a fair hearing, but still offer a serious challenge to their skepticism about God's reality.

True to their cause, skeptics about God's existence usually raise doubt that there is a titleholder for the supreme title "God." Their familiar allegation is that people lack *adequate evidence* (for cognitively reasonable belief) that God exists. This charge is, of course, cognitively bold if it concerns *all* people, given the wide scope of potentially relevant evidence for all people. The skeptical allegation is *cognitive* in that it concerns *evidence*, and the alleged lack of adequate evidence underlies skeptical doubt regarding *the reality* of God, that is, doubt that God exists. These skeptics assume that if we lack adequate evidence of the reality of God, then we should, from a cognitive point of view, doubt (that is, suspend judgment) that God exists. If we define "adequate evidence" broadly enough, this assumption among skeptics is true and even cognitively compelling. We won't join fideists, then, in opposing skeptics on this front, since fideism implausibly entails that theistic commitment need not rest for its cognitive status on supporting evidence. In any case, we have more difficult opponents than fideists to face.

Belief that God exists would be *evidentially* arbitrary and thus *cognitively* irrational in the absence of supporting evidence, even if it's *true* that God exists. Mere factuality, or truth, in a person's belief doesn't necessarily yield evidential merit for that belief; many claims are true but still altogether without supporting evidence. Lucky guesses, say at the racetrack or on Wall Street, supply good examples of truth without supporting evidence. The requirement of adequate evidence for cognitively rational belief is impeccable, if its notion of adequate evidence is suitably broad and free of unduly narrow empiricist, rationalist, and deductivist strictures. Since a concern about adequate evidence for theism drives and defines mainline religious skepticism, we'll attend to that concern. We won't be concerned, then, with the question whether theistic belief makes believers *feel better*. I, for one, am largely indifferent to that question, but even if theistic belief did make that difference in feeling, it could still lack a good evidential status and thus be cognitively deficient and unreasonable in that regard.

How should we understand the slippery demand for adequate evidence? Many skeptics set the standard very high. One very high standard demands *cognitive reproducibility*. Given this standard, adequate evidence of God's reality must be reproducible either for a single person or for a group of people. If someone asks, for instance, whether I know English as a spoken language, I can supply the needed evidence *by speaking English*, loud and clear, in the person's presence. In addition, I can straightforwardly reproduce this evidence for myself and for the person in question. I can simply speak English again, and again, until my interlocutor yields or departs. I have control over the production of the needed evidence. Given such control over evidence, I can meet a skeptic's demand of cognitive reproducibility in that particular case. *Some* evidence thus meets the suggested standard.

Must evidence be under our control? Certainly not, contrary to what many religious skeptics uncritically assume. Much of the inferred original evidence in cosmology, astrophysics, and geology, among other natural sciences, is neither under our control nor reproducible by us. Even if we can supply helpful analogies regarding some inferred original scientific evidence, that evidence itself is directly available to us only "in principle." We can't control or reproduce, for instance, the inferred original evidence of the big bang origin of the universe that occurred many billions of years ago. We lack the sheer power to do so; the inferred original evidence is, literally, beyond our powers of actual reproduction, and we obviously can't change this. Still, given our best science in cosmology and astrophysics, the original evidence was part of reality and is available to us indirectly and inferentially.

If the relevant science is deemed unconvincing by a skeptic, we can make the suggested point from ordinary perceptual experience. For instance, if I whisper a secret to you in an ordinary situation, you have salient evidence from your experience of hearing my whisper. Even so, you can't thereby control or reproduce the original evidence, given the following considerations: you can't control my utterances; you have no recording of my whisper; and I refuse to repeat my whisper. The original evidence in your experience of hearing in this case is real indeed but definitely beyond your control. There's no big surprise here, since much of what impinges on us perceptually (including some sensory pressures and some perceptual distractions) is beyond our control.

We should reject without hesitation any requirement that genuine evidence must be under our control or reproducible by us. As a result, we should reject any skeptical argument that assumes the following: if evidence of God's reality isn't reproducible by us, then it isn't genuine evidence. Our receiving evidence can be independent of our being able to reproduce that evidence, and, on reflection, it's amazing that any reflective adult would think otherwise. Still, hasty generalization does its damage in this quarter, inspiring and reproducing many wayward religious skeptics. The best antidote comes, as suggested, from familiar cases where we have genuine evidence but that evidence is beyond our control.

In popular, and even unpopular, discussions of theism, some skeptics demand "proof" of God's existence, even without clarification of what they mean by the ambiguous word "proof." In these discussions, "proof" is a fighting word, pure and simple. Let's define "proof," for the sake of clarity, as a deductively valid argument with true premises. Must adequate evidence of God's reality, sufficient for the justification condition for propositional knowledge, include such an argument? Certainly not.

Very little of the evidence for propositions we know includes deductively valid argument. Most of our empirical (including perceptual) knowledge, for instance, rests on evidence free of deductively valid arguments. Likewise, most of my knowledge about myself and about other people doesn't arise from proof. Typically, proof resides in the domains of logic and mathematics, but the claim that God exists is definitely not a claim of logic or mathematics. God, if real, is a personal agent, not an axiom, a theorem, or an argument; it would be a serious category mistake to suppose otherwise. In keeping with these plausible considerations, Michael J. Buckley observes:

> ... [deductive or inductive] inference [to God] simply cannot substitute for experience [of God]. One will not long believe in a personal God with whom there is no personal communication, and the most compelling evidence of a personal God must itself be personal. To attempt something else as foundation or as substitute, as has been done so often in an attempt to shore up the assertion of God, is to move into a process ... of which the ultimate resolution must be atheism (2004, p. 138).

The history of philosophy of religion bears out this observation. In addition, we lack not only proof but also adequate evidence of any kind for thinking that adequate evidence of God's existence must include deductive proof as just defined. Let's not be hindered, then, by any skeptical demand for deductive proof of God's existence. Instead, we'll let the relevant *notion* of God guide the suitable cognitive parameters, including the kind of evidence to be reasonably expected if God is real. Otherwise, we would risk begging some important questions about God's reality and evidence thereof, regardless of whether God actually exists.

Evidence available to a person, characterized broadly, is a *truth-indicator* available to that person. Evidence thus indicates, even if fallibly and non-deductively, that a proposition is true. Clearly, evidence can be misleading, with regard to what is actually true, as the history of scientific evidence amply illustrates. Truth-indicators, as just suggested, come in various forms. Some indicate a truth *deductively*; others indicate a truth *nondeductively*. In addition, some truth-indicators are *propositional* in virtue of expressing a proposition; others are *non*propositional, such as those from perceptual experiences that don't depend on our categorization or judgment but just on suitably determinate attention-attraction. Some truth-indicators can be controlled and reproduced by us; others can't. In all cases, however, a truth-indicator indicates for a person, in some way or other, that an identifiable proposition is true. The phrase "for a person" captures that justification, unlike truth, is *perspectival* in being relative to one's evidential perspective consisting of one's truth-indicators. (For elaboration on the idea of a truth-indicator and its central role in an account of evidence and knowledge, see Moser 1989, 1993.)

We can portray a person's *actual* evidence, beyond *merely* available evidence, in terms of a truth-indicator that has intruded in that person's awareness, even if that truth-indicator is fallible and thus potentially misleading. (We thus do well to distinguish between a person's *actually acquired* evidence and evidence *merely available*, in a modal sense needing specification, to that person but not actually acquired by that person.) Of course, not all intrusions are bad; some are good, even cognitively good, and needed too if humans are to grasp reality aright. Some evidential intrusions come through sensory awareness; others come through merely reflective, or intellectual, awareness. Still others intervene in one's will, intruding in one's willing in certain ways.

An adequate account of evidence and knowledge will characterize the various kinds of truth-indicators that intrude in a person's awareness. In addition, such an account won't confuse the notion of evidence *acquired* and the notion of evidence *willingly received*. Some evidence can intrude in one's awareness without one's willingly receiving it; such evidence is involuntary, as it coercively attracts one's attention, at least momentarily. Even so, such evidence often doesn't constantly coerce one's attention, and when it doesn't, one can decide to attend to something else instead. We'll see that purposively available evidence of divine reality doesn't constantly coerce one's attention or coerce the direction of one's will, even if it attracts one's attention momentarily.

An inadequate approach to evidence and knowledge will risk epistemological dogmatism by excluding some intruding truth-indicators, perhaps owing to an excessive and thus misguided quest for simplicity in kinds of evidence. (Cavalier use of Ockham's razor has misled many a philosopher throughout history.) Both thoroughgoing empiricism and thoroughgoing rationalism about evidence fall prey to such epistemological inadequacy. A similar inadequacy marks the deductivist view that all intrusions by truth-indicators include deductively valid proof. Deduction has no monopoly on truth-indicators; in fact, an endless regress of needed truth-indicators threatens if we suppose otherwise (on which, see Moser 1989, chap. 2).

We should embrace a cognitive analogue to Aristotle's wise advice, in his *Nicomachean Ethics* (Book I, chap. 3), to look for precision in each class of things *just so far as the nature of the subject matter admits*. The analogue is that we should let our understanding of evidence, and thus of knowledge, be guided by the actual features of the truth-indicators that intrude in our awareness rather than by some dubious antecedent cognitive standard, such as deductivism, thoroughgoing rationalism, or thoroughgoing empiricism. In doing so, we'll characterize evidence in a manner true to the reality of our actual truth-indicators, even if, in keeping with fallibilism, some truth-indicators are ultimately misleading regarding reality.

Evidence of God's reality is, by definition, a truth-indicator for the proposition that an authoritatively and morally perfect agent worthy of worship actually exists. Where might we find such evidence? In nature? In history? In books? In ourselves? People have looked far and wide for evidence of God's reality, even in their valuable spare time, but religious skeptics remain unconvinced about claims to success. For instance, Bertrand Russell (1970) anticipated his response if he were to meet God after death: "God, you gave us insufficient evidence." Insufficient for *what*? For Russell's highly questionable expectations of God? In any case, Russell's charge against God sounds blaming, to put it mildly. Russell might have considered a bit more modesty in the presence of an authoritatively and morally perfect God. In that case, a humbled Russell, unlike the actual Russell, would have asked: "God, what purposes of yours led to your being subtle and elusive in the purposively available evidence of your reality?" It's astonishing, and regrettable too, that Russell as a self-avowed rational truth-seeker gave no indication of being aware of such a compelling and important question for a rational truth-seeker.

We now face a question widely but unduly neglected by skeptics about God's existence. If a perfectly loving God would choose to give humans evidence of God's reality, what parameters or defining features for the evidence would God observe? God as perfectly loving toward all people would seek to communicate with people if this was in their best interest, and thus God would offer in that case some kind of evidence of God's reality. The key cognitive issue is: exactly what *kind* of evidence? It seems safe to say that God as morally perfect wouldn't necessarily be bound by the kind of evidence *we humans* happen to prefer. Instead, we should expect to have to conform our cognitive expectations to *God's* preferred evidence. On reflection, we shouldn't be surprised by this cognitive order of priority, given divine supremacy and human inferiority.

Clearly, the evidence of God's reality would have to be suitable to God's character as morally perfect and worthy of worship. So, contrary to some versions of fideism, we shouldn't hold that the claim that God exists is in principle beyond the threat of disconfirming evidence. If, for instance, we were to face a world of *nothing but* unrelenting pain and suffering, we would have significant evidence against God's reality. We would then have significant evidence against the reality of a God who truly cares for all humans, and we would have no positive indication of the reality of such a God. The actual world, though obviously deeply troubled, is clearly *not* a world of nothing but unrelenting pain and suffering. It has its silver, if subtle, lining of good, even when its evil *seems* to have triumphed. Consider, for instance, a volunteer rescue worker unselfishly and eagerly caring for an injured stranger. That's a silver lining indeed, if anything is. Consider also Mother Teresa and her friends reaching out to aid the poorest of the poor in Calcutta. That's another bright silver lining, among many others. We need to ask whether the available good in this world is of the right kind for the reality of a morally perfect God who has created free agents.

What would evidence suitable to God's character look like? In other words, what kind of evidence of God's reality would fit with the reality of a morally perfect God worthy of worship? Here's a vague answer: any kind of evidence indicating that God, as an authoritatively and morally perfect being worthy of worship, is real. Although true, this answer doesn't help much at all. Let's consider a more specific question: what kind of evidence of God's reality would be given to us by a morally perfect God worthy of worship who finds it in our best interest to receive evidence of God's reality? The answer depends on what God would intend to do with this troubled world, including us, and this would involve divine knowledge of how the world actually stands in relation to God. For instance, God would know whether this world has become altogether hopeless relative to what God desires of it.

God would have the cognitive and moral authority to reveal the things of God *in God's preferred ways,* in keeping, of course, with God's morally perfect character. We must beware, then, of uncritically demanding that evidence of God's reality must meet *our* preferred standards of evidence (in the way Russell did). Instead, as suggested, our evidential demands must be attentive to what would be a morally perfect God's character and corresponding purposes. Russell and many other religious skeptics have overlooked this basic cognitive lesson. As we'll see, it's an uncomfortable lesson indeed for such skeptics. One result is that the view that conclusive evidence of divine reality *must* conform to a (nontrivial) deductive proof is misguided. An even more demanding view is that conclusive evidence of divine reality must be undeniably obvious, that is, obvious in a way that undeniably dominates one's attention. Both views are excessively demanding for the purposes of a perfectly loving God.

A perfectly loving God may offer a nondemonstrative and even nondominating, or rejectable, truth-indicator of divine reality, in order to allow people either (a) to know God's reality noninferentially or (b) to ignore or to reject freely God's intervention and any awareness of God. A "nondominating" truth-indicator may involve modest attention-coercion as a rejectable intrusion in one's attention, but it wouldn't involve strong attention-coercion as a dominating, nonrejectable takeover of one's attention. Given divine use of nondemonstrative and nondominating evidence, some familiar deductivist and skeptical demands regarding theistic evidence would be misguided. We need to be open, then, to God's offering rejectable noninferential evidence of divine reality. Otherwise, we'll be guilty, as are many religious skeptics, of harmfully misleading cognitive dogmatism regarding evidence of divine reality.

3. JUDGMENT

Let's move further away from theological abstractions to conceptual specificity, so as not to languish in cognitively sterile generalities about divine reality (an occupational hazard in academic, especially philosophical, discussions of "God"). The God of Jewish and Christian monotheism is widely and explicitly disavowed by religious skeptics, including many philosophers (see Martin 2007 for abundant examples and references). Even so, many Jews and Christians regard this God as worthy of worship and thus as morally perfect and inherently trustworthy. In the absence of a better candidate, we'll give some attention to the nature of this alleged God and the corresponding cognitive lessons about divine reality.

The God in question, we're told, seeks to redeem (that is, to reconcile to God) a world of people alienated from fellowship with their creator and thereby gripped by selfish fear, moral failure, and personal dying and death. The alienation of humans supposedly arises, at least in part, from their selfish willfulness, that is, their asserting their own wills in conflict with what is willed by a perfectly authoritative and loving God. Such selfish willfulness may stem from human fear of personal loss and destruction, in the absence of reliance on divine aid. In any case, all of human life is allegedly surrounded by this alienation and deeply infected by it too. We'll pursue this approach to divine and human reality, and ask whether it can answer and even challenge religious skeptics. We'll have to leave it as unfinished business to consider exactly how the God of Jewish and Christian monotheism relates to the versions of monotheism in Buddhism, Hinduism, Islam, Bahaism, and other traditions. Clearly, there's no plausible story of full agreement or even full consistency to tell regarding their approaches to God. The relevant historical and theological details, however, would demand extensive discussion, well beyond the scope of this book.

We won't simply assume, of course, that the God of Jewish and Christian monotheism exists. Fideism about commitment to God's existence, in disregarding a need for evidence of divine reality, gains nothing of stable value in an exchange with skeptics or in a quest for well-grounded truth regarding the reality of God. Instead, we'll ask what we should expect by way of evidence regarding the reality of a morally perfect God *if* this God exists. In addition, we'll examine whether the characteristic features of the alleged God of Jewish and Christian monotheism illuminate our understanding of a morally perfect God. We can then ask if our world and our experience fit well with our cognitive expectations suited to a morally perfect God. We'll then be able to tell where our overall evidence actually points. Skeptics about God, then, will receive a fair hearing, but it doesn't follow that all skeptics will be convinced. People typically can ignore or disregard available evidence, and sometimes will do so if the evidence challenges them to change the direction of their lives. There's a lot at stake regarding one's life, as we'll see, in one's sincerely affirming, denying, or withholding judgment that a perfectly loving God exists.

Cognitively discriminating religious skeptics are very rarely, if ever, seriously challenged by an evidential case for the attenuated God of deism or minimal theism. (Minimal theism, for our purposes, affirms that God exists but refrains from claims about God's redemptive purposes.) We'll move beyond consideration of deism and minimal theism, then, and look for the consequences for religious skepticism from the more robust Jewish and Christian monotheism. If we ignore robust Jewish and Christian monotheism, for the sake of deism or minimal theism, we'll fail to appreciate the bearing of robust theism on skepticism about God's existence. Settling for deism or minimal theism, philosophers often miss this opportunity, but we'll seize it here. At least we'll then apprehend what kind of robust theism is in question or, instead, what kind of robust theism is putting *us* as cognitive agents in question. Such a reversal regarding who is judging and has a right to judge is characteristic of robust Jewish and Christian monotheism. It removes any sophomoric easiness from skepticism about God's existence, and it fits with the seismic cognitive shift promised in the Introduction. For now, however, we are exploring a *notion* of God found in Jewish and Christian monotheism; we are not assuming the existence of this God. This conceptual exploration is fitting, because we need a notion of God even to deny God's existence or to withhold judgment, at least intentionally, about God's existence.

Humans generally seek their main security and contentment, as an alternative to fear of personal loss, from things other than God, typically from things in the world that seem to offer safety and satisfaction. This, of course, is a confirmable empirical truth. (See Kasser 2002 for empirical evidence on some of the unhappy consequences.) The familiar list of apparent sources of human security goes on and on: health, wealth, longevity, education, family, reputation, physical appearance, entertainment, selfish religion, sexuality, human friendship, self-protective plans, and so on. Anything other than the true God could take on the role of a supposedly satisfying idol for a person, and then leave the person unsatisfied and insecure. Honesty about the inadequacy of idols is difficult, however, in the absence of a stable replacement. Insecurity and despair then become a painful threat, and it can even seem easier to change the subject altogether.

In perfect love, God would place the world under judgment to try (perhaps among other things) to save people from dying with their idols, their ultimately insecure replacements for God. A perfectly loving God would try to lead people noncoercively (that is, in a manner that can be rejected, in terms of the direction of their will) not only to *recognize* the ultimate futility of the idols offered by the world apart from God, but also to *let go* of such idols in order to make proper room for God as authoritative Lord. This would be integral to any attempted divine redemption, or reconciliation, of humans to God, in volitional fellowship with God. It would also highlight that, contrary to various ancient and modern gnostic writers, humans need more than cognitive enlightenment for their lasting security or salvation. Apart from cognitive and intellectual matters, human *volitional reliance* on idols needs an antidote, even corrective judgment, in a world governed by God as authoritative Lord.

The theme of divine *judgment* is Christian as well as Jewish. For instance, the apostle Paul (a Christian Jew) echoes a theme from Ecclesiastes: "... the creation was subjected to futility, not by its own will, but by the will of the One who subjected it, in [this One's] hope that the creation itself will be liberated from its bondage to corruption and brought into the glorious freedom of the children of God" (Rom. 8:20–21; cf. Eccl. 1:2–11, 2:1–24). Many skeptics have raised doubts about God's existence on the basis of the obvious reality of extensive pain and suffering in our world. They doubt that a perfectly loving God would allow the horrifying pain and suffering in this world, and thus they offer this world's pain and suffering as supplying a defeater of any evidence for God's existence. Matters are, however, more complex than this move suggests. We humans, of course, aren't (and shouldn't expect ourselves to be) in a position to explain why all the pain and all the suffering in this world occur, or (if God exists) are allowed to occur. Our explanatory and cognitive resources are much too limited for this difficult explanatory task. Even so, we can consider that pain and suffering result, at least in part, from the way that creation has been "subjected to futility" for the sake of corrective divine judgment.

The created world, according to a prominent strand of Jewish and Christian monotheism, was subjected to breaking down by a perfectly loving God, as in the case of physical entropy or atrophy, *for a hopeful divine purpose.* The overarching purpose is, according to the divine hope in question, that all willing humans would learn that their lasting security and contentment won't be found in any part of the created world apart from God. Karl Rahner (1983a) has called this "Christian pessimism" about the created world by itself (cf. Rahner 1978, pp. 403–5, Niebuhr 1949, pp. 151–70, Crowley 2005.) Lasting security and contentment need to be found elsewhere, and, according to the apostle Paul, "the children of God" will find it in *God* rather than in the created world apart from God. They will then be liberated from their deadly idols of insecure replacements for God found in this dying world. They will then have the personal life Preserver they need to overcome the human predicament of destructive selfishness, tragic suffering, and impending death. They will then trust (that is, have faith in) God above all else, rather than some inadequate, deadly alternative. We need to characterize the cognitive basis for such bold trust, because without such a basis the trust in question will risk becoming wishful thinking and thus cognitively irrational.

We can make some sense, in Paul's wake, of why a perfectly loving God would allow certain kinds of pain and suffering. This God, as perfectly loving, would be after something more valuable than human sensory pleasure and the satisfaction of worldly human wants. God would hope that people be liberated from deadly idols in virtue of trusting God as the authoritative Lord who provides genuine human security and contentment, come what may in this world. This divine hope could thus make good use of allowing pain and suffering among us rather than protecting us from all pain and suffering. This would be part of God's redemptive judgment of human idols, by bringing them to noticeable futility, for the sake of reconciliation of humans to God in volitional fellowship with God. It would be judgment intended, at least characteristically, to correct humans from their reliance on futile idols and to restore them to their creator and sustainer in volitional fellowship.

Regarding divine redemption of humans from deadly idols, one maxim seems clear: *no pain, no gain.* A perfectly loving God, in any case, wouldn't settle for maximizing sensory pleasure for wayward humans. Sensory hedonism wouldn't capture or even approach the solution needed by selfish humans.

A serious, even painful, challenge may be better for us than quick and easy protection from our pain. Such a challenge may be integral to divine *perfect love* toward us that seeks to transform us to love as God loves, in volitional fellowship with God. A rough analogy: our intentionally prying a dangerous tool (say, a razor-blade knife) from the playful but clenched hands of a child for the child's well-being may bring some pain to the child but would nonetheless be good, wise, and loving. In fact, the child may later, upon reflection, thank us for such uncomfortable but obviously good and loving intervention. (On the kind of corrective judgment in question, see Meadors 2006 and Buttrick 1966.)

The prospect of divine redemptive judgment is *cognitively* important, although widely ignored in that regard. It bears importantly on the nature of purposively available evidence of God's reality, that is, evidence available to humans in a manner, and only in a manner, that serves God's perfectly loving purposes, including any redemptive purposes. The latter purposes would represent God's moral character, and seek noncoercively but authoritatively to align human purposes with divine purposes, for the sake of divine–human volitional fellowship. Given a perfectly loving creator, wayward humans, as part of creation, would be under divine judgment for their selfish, anti-God ways. So, we should expect that our coming to know God's reality, in virtue of our receiving purposively available evidence of divine reality, would have an important place for divine perfectly loving judgment of us and our selfish ways.

Politeness aside, we selfish humans are ourselves our most common destructive idol, even though we *obviously* can't supply lasting security and contentment for ourselves. We can't even supply lasting subsistence for ourselves, and our limitation here is painfully obvious, if anything is. A short visit to any funeral home, cemetery, or obituary section of a newspaper will confirm this truth in sad but compelling detail. Many humans thus prefer to change the subject altogether, to something more polite and affirming. Life then seems easier, or at least less painful.

A perfectly loving God would demand that we move beyond our selfishness to characteristically divine unselfish love toward all people, but we obviously fail repeatedly and persistently on this front. This is failure in what we may call *Love's Demand*. If unsuppressed, our conscience, as an inner source of moral conviction, convicts us of this failure, and we then experience guilt, shame, and judgment. Our self-centeredness leaves us with a troubled conscience, at least in the absence of our fully suppressing our conscience. We thereby may be challenged and judged, for the purpose of reorientation, by a divine standard of love represented in conscience. Reinhold Niebuhr has remarked in this connection: "... it is a fact that man is judged [in conscience] and yet there is no vantage point in his own life, sufficiently transcendent, from which the judgment can take place" (1941, p. 129). Vantage points aside, moral honesty about ourselves requires that we acknowledge the *propriety* of judgment relative to Love's Demand, regardless of our view of the judgment's actuality or source. It requires candor from us about our violating Love's Demand, even intentionally at times. Our self-defense runs thin in this connection.

Human moral pride boldly but mistakenly resists honesty about our flouting Love's Demand. It offers a cover-up story instead, to try to salvage our moral honor, including our good civic standing. Our moral pride suggests, contrary to what is actually the case, that we have no need of moral guilt or shame, on the ground that we are morally in the clear on our own, even if morally imperfect. So, according to our moral pride, we aren't deserving candidates for moral judgment. Instead, we merit moral approval, even from God, by the lights of our pride. Our moral pride thus opposes any place for judgment of us from Love's Demand. In keeping with this, according to sociological surveys, most people think of themselves as morally better than most other people. Something, of course, is wrong with that moral self-portrait, and undue moral pride is the stubborn culprit.

Our moral pride emerges as a frayed paper-thin veneer in the presence of Love's Demand. We violate Love's Demand regularly, and we have salient available evidence for this, particularly regarding our treatment of socially neglected people, including the poor, the elderly, and the disabled. Any diversionary efforts on this front won't change the available vast evidence for this at all, but will simply lead us deeper into the dishonesty of moral pride. Our most dangerous failures before a perfectly loving God who issues Love's Demand would include a failure of moral honesty.

Our moral pride may stem largely from fear of judgment owing to moral failure and fear of not being in charge morally. Even so, dishonesty about our unloving ways is among our most harmful failures before Love's Demand, because such dishonesty will lead us to resist, or at least to fail to see our need of, a perfectly loving God who issues Love's Demand. It will obscure, at least in our own minds, how far we have departed from Love's Demand and thus from any volitional agreement with its divine source. It will therefore also obscure not only our need of repentance relative to the standard of divine love, but also the suitability of any divine call to human repentance. A perfectly loving God who issues Love's Demand and an authoritative call to human repentance couldn't transform us noncoercively toward divine love as long as we cling to moral dishonesty about our unloving ways. We would have to acknowledge our need for such transformation in order to yield to it freely, willingly, and gratefully.

In purposively redemptive love, a perfectly loving God would subject *us* to futility with regard to our aspirations and pretensions toward selfishness and self-reliance. This futility would include our impending physical death (facing *each* of us, despite energetic diversions), when we will meet our end in this tragic dying world. A perfectly loving God's hope, out of redemptive love, would be that we see the futility of our intended self-reliance and come to our senses, thereby turning to trust wholeheartedly in God as authoritative Lord. Conclusive purposively available evidence of God's reality would fit with such divine hope. We'll examine how and why, and see how epistemology and philosophy undergo dramatic change.

The notorious God of deism, the cosmic watchmaker on the lam, would perhaps settle for providing us with evidence that the God of deism exists. This God, however, would have no message of reconciliation in volitional fellowship and certainly no redemptive judgment for humans. Instead, this God would be content to have people acknowledge, on the basis of empirical evidence from creation, that a creator (probably) exists, or at least *did* exist at the time of creation. Who's to say that the God of deism hasn't died, whether recently or long ago? We may simply not have been on the guest list for funeral announcements, and deists evidently weren't either. A mere creator, in any case, gives no guarantee or even assurance of being a *lasting* creator. Deists rarely acknowledge this truth, but it's hard to challenge this truth on traditional deist assumptions.

The God of deism would be the classic underachiever in heaven. Having created with a blazing flourish, even with light and heat effects, this God would refuse to follow up in any direct way, despite the tragic predicament of a dying creation. Such behavior won't win any contest for unselfish caring for creation. Indeed, it won't even show in the local or state contest rankings, let alone national benchmarks, and friends of the environment should be especially disappointed. The God of deism is truly the absent, AWOL God, guilty of felony child abandonment. So far as that God goes, we weren't left with even a clue of safe haven in this cosmic debacle. Indeed, this God is no God at all, if we retain "God" as a title for one worthy of worship in virtue of self-sufficient authoritative and moral perfection. Moral indifference obviously robs one of perfect love and thus of moral perfection and deity. Deism suffers accordingly, despite its initial appearance of desirable religious inclusiveness.

The Jewish and Christian God wouldn't be identifiable with the God of deism. This God would, in redemptive love, intervene too much for the carefree purposes of the God of deism, and thus they wouldn't even be coworkers.

In addition, the Jewish and Christian God wouldn't be impressed at all with mere human belief, even mere reasonable human belief, that God exists. The Epistle of James, one of the most Jewish writings in the New Testament, makes a related point regarding mere belief that the God of Jewish and Christian monotheism exists: "Even the demons [God's archenemies] believe [that God is one reality], and shudder" (2:19). For the sake of reconciling humans to God, the Jewish and Christian God would seek a human response that goes beyond belief, and even knowledge, that God exists. The distinctive purposively available evidence offered by this God would contribute to that conciliatory redemptive goal. We'll see what such evidence and such a goal would include. Philosophers and religious skeptics typically miss this crucial lesson, but we'll give it full attention. Otherwise, we would fail to give robust monotheism a fair hearing, and it rarely does get a fair hearing from skeptics or from philosophers generally. In the interest of a fair hearing, we'll make things morally uncomfortable for ourselves. The result will be well worth the moral discomfort.

4. UNDER AUTHORITY

The Jewish and Christian God, perhaps unlike the casual God of deism, wouldn't approach us as people who fully welcome evidence of the reality of God that challenges and judges our selfish ways. This God, in addition, would know better than to pander to humans, and we should too. The evidence in question concerns a God who, out of unselfish love, would challenge our selfish, deadly ways. Contrary to much popular marketing, teaching, and preaching about God, we wouldn't start out as friends of this God. We rather would be at odds with this God, owing to our selfish attitudes, actions, and habits. The notion of "enemies" of God readily comes to mind, but this differs from a notion of "condemned" enemies.

We shouldn't confuse divine corrective judgment with merely destructive *condemnation*, since there's a big difference between the two, a difference between potential life and final death. The Jewish and Christian God, given any hope for humans, would come to us with redemptive judgment of us and our selfish ways, for our own good. So, this God shouldn't be expected to come to us with *spectator evidence*, that is, evidence pointing to some truth but *not* demanding that its recipients yield their wills to (the will of) the source of the evidence. This God would have no interest in playing such an intellectual game.

The God in question would come to us with *authoritative evidence* of divine reality, that is, evidence demanding that we yield our wills to (the will of) the divine source of the evidence in question. Indeed, this God would come with *absolutely perfectly* authoritative evidence of divine reality: evidence demanding that we yield our wills to the *self-sufficiently perfect source* of the evidence in question, that is, God. A merely human moral leader might offer us authoritative evidence by making a demand on our wills, but this would fall short of *absolutely perfectly* authoritative evidence; the source, being merely human, wouldn't be self-sufficiently perfect. (Hereafter our talk of perfectly authoritative evidence of divine reality will concern absolutely perfectly authoritative evidence.) The God in question, then, would be no friend of human cognitive voyeurism regarding divine reality, given the authoritative demand, based on human redemptive need, that we yield our wills to God's morally perfect will. So, this God would be at odds with familiar philosophical and skeptical approaches to evidence of God's existence that focus on spectator evidence. This God would recognize that merely human inquirers suffer *volitional* (will-related) as well as cognitive impediments and deficiencies, and thus need corrective authoritative evidence of divine reality. This theme very rarely gets attention from philosophers and theologians, but we'll correct this neglect straightaway.

For purposes of cognitively rational belief that God exists, skeptics and philosophers generally demand that God provide us with spectator evidence of divine reality. In doing so, they miss what would be the main redemptive and cognitive aim of the Jewish and Christian God. They overlook that, faced with our dying selfish world, the morally perfect titleholder of "God" would be (*if* God still has hope of redeeming humans) a God of intended redemption as reconciliation of humans to God. (On the significance of reconciliation to the God in question, see Farmer 1935, 1966, Martin 1981, Stuhlmacher 1986, and Chapter 3 below.) Such a God would come to us, not with spectator evidence, but rather with perfectly authoritative evidence of divine reality. Spectator evidence from God would allow God to be inculpably domesticated and taken for granted by us in our selfish ways, because it would lack corrective judgment toward us and our selfishness.

Given spectator evidence, the topic of divine reality would readily become a matter for casual, speculative discussion, and thereby would be trivialized with regard to God's authoritative character. In that case, we might hear familiar echoes of traditional natural theology, with its endless haggling over alleged spectator evidence of attenuated first causes, intelligent designers, and the like. In neglecting a divine authoritative call to humans, spectator evidence of God's existence would thus risk serious harm to us and fail as a means of genuine redemption. It would enable undue comfort in our destructive ways, allowing us to suppose that we are prepared on our own to face cognitive matters of divine reality. Spectator evidence, in keeping with traditional natural theology, would fail to challenge humans in the ways needed, particularly regarding the inadequacy of human moral and cognitive standing before a perfectly authoritative and loving God.

Some philosophers and theologians seek to recruit the apostle Paul as a proponent of natural theology and spectator evidence, in light of his remarks in Rom. 1:19–20. Careful attention to his remarks, however, reveals that (a) he does *not* propose that nature *alone* reveals divine reality, but that (b) he explicitly claims that "God has manifested" divine reality to people. Given an intention to redeem us, a perfectly loving God would be a God of perfectly authoritative evidence for humans. So, this God would have a definite purpose different from our casually knowing that God exists: the purpose of bringing humans into lasting reconciliation with God, in loving and obedient fellowship with God. We should thus expect the titleholder of "God" to offer purposively available evidence of God's reality (if divine hope for human redemption remains) that advances this redemptive purpose. Divine redemption, we've suggested, need not be comfortable for us in order to be good for us. On the contrary, we should expect it to challenge our morally dubious comforts as long as we're selfish in any way. If we suffer from selfishness, we'll be inclined to be selfish in protecting our selfishness. We thus should be prepared to be discomforted by anyone challenging our selfishness. A perfectly loving God, then, would bring needed correctively good discomfort in order to bring good comfort. We might thus look for a rough analogy in a benevolent surgeon who brings discomfort to a person in order to bring something good to that person.

A central problem of divine redemption would be that we need to be saved from ourselves in our selfishness, because we ourselves would be at odds with God's perfectly loving character and redemptive plan. We would need to be saved from (a) our deadly quest for self-reliance into (b) obedient trust (on God's terms) in the God who could save us from our destructive selfishness and impending death. (Chapter 5 will return to the latter twofold predicament.) Unlike spectator evidence, perfectly authoritative evidence of divine reality would attend to resolving this predicament by seeking human volitional transformation toward divine perfect love.

Opposing selfish human pride, authoritative divine evidence would work by *cognitive grace*, a free, unmerited gift from God, rather than by any human earning that supposedly obligated God to redeem a person or to give divine self-revelation to a person. Such divine evidence would counter our supposed powers of intellectual earning in order to deflate intellectual pride, and would thus demonstrate our weakness, including our self-*inadequacy*, regarding finding the true God on our own. The God of perfectly authoritative evidence would therefore not fit well with the docile gods of the philosophers and natural theologians. The latter gods offer no authoritative challenge to our being pridefully puffed up in our supposed special knowledge or argumentation regarding divine reality; nor do they call us into divine–human fellowship via human repentance. Authoritative evidence from an authoritative perfectly loving God, in contrast, would build up rather than puff up humans. (Chapters 2 and 3 will return to the widely neglected theme of cognitive grace.)

We have no conclusive evidence for thinking that *by our own resources* we can reason our way to, or otherwise achieve, knowledge of the reality of the Jewish and Christian God. At least, I know of no such evidence, and the alleged evidence from traditional natural theology falls short of conclusive evidence for the reality of a perfectly authoritative and loving God of redemption. Instead, we evidently need a *self-revelation* from God as the source of the needed conclusive evidence of divine reality. A God who is worthy of worship and thus morally perfect would, of course, be significantly different from us humans in terms of moral character and cognitive subtlety and depth. In addition, it's doubtful that such a God would be at our convenient cognitive disposal, as if we either had the authority or were well-positioned on our own to gain access to this God. Otherwise, we would be left with a God whose authority could be overridden or at least compromised by humans.

We should contrast (a) the attempt to reason our way to, or otherwise achieve, knowledge of God's reality by our own resources and (b) our need to receive purposively available conclusive evidence as a gift from a perfectly loving God who calls us to live as God's dependent obedient children, even in the cognitive domain. The relevant divine call, I've suggested, would itself be a manifestation of divine love; in experiencing it in one's conscience for what it is intended to be, one would experience divine love. This approach is foreign to how philosophers, including skeptics, typically think of evidence, but this doesn't count against it at all. It identifies a kind of experienced theistic evidence that would be cognitively more basic than any argument for God's reality. We'll see that this approach yields a new challenge to skeptics about God's reality.

Ultimately, humans would need to depend on God to supply conclusive evidence of divine reality via self-revelation, and God, of course, wouldn't expect humans to be cognitively in charge of the nature of divine revelation for humans. God alone would be absolutely perfectly authoritative and thus have the prerogative to decide, in keeping with God's morally perfect character, what exactly the divine revelatory evidence would be for humans and when it should emerge. This fact alone should keep humans cognitively modest regarding divine revelatory evidence, but it rarely has, especially among philosophers and skeptics.

According to many first-century Jewish Christians, God chose to supply perfectly authoritative evidence of divine reality through Jesus of Nazareth as God's perfectly obedient Son. This evidence, according to these Christians, was ratified by God's intervening Spirit, the "holy [that is, distinctively righteous] Spirit" of God. We'll consider this cognitive approach, because it purports to identify the evidential ways of a perfectly authoritative and loving God. In addition, we would gain nothing by pretending that this approach doesn't exist or by brushing it aside as a lost cognitive cause from the start. We need, instead, to determine what kind of cognitive status it actually has. (Chapter 3 will return to the cognitive role of God's intervening Spirit in detail.)

Steeped in epistemological concerns, the Gospel of John portrays Jesus as characterizing the cognitive and moral role of God's intervening Spirit as follows:

> When [the Spirit] comes, he will convict the world of guilt regarding sin, righteousness, and judgment ... [w]hen ... the Spirit of truth comes, he will lead you into all truth. He will not speak on his own, but will speak only what he hears, and he will announce to you what is yet to come. He will bring glory to me, because he will take from me and announce this to you (Jn. 16:8, 13–14).

God's intervening Spirit, according to this first-century portrait, has the cognitive role of making things known regarding God and Jesus. Jesus emerges as God's unique revealer who calls humans (a) to receive God's Spirit of redemption through trust (that is, faith) in God, in response to God's call, and (b) thereby to live as God's dependent obedient children in fellowship with God. This theme captures what Jesus sought to manifest, according to the New Testament Gospels, and it has, as we'll see, distinctive cognitive implications. In any case, we've entered strange cognitive territory, where the true God may lurk incognito. We'll do well to linger here a bit, in order to examine the peculiar evidential situation.

God's intervening Spirit, on the portrait under review, would noncoercively (that is, in a rejectable manner) "lead" people to Jesus and his Father as their Lord and their God, and the experience of "being led" in this way would be cognitively significant. It would include the perfectly authoritative divine call, via human conscience, to relinquish our own selfish willfulness for the sake of living for the unselfish perfectly loving will of God. This elusive wake-up call would aim to work, if painfully, through human conscience in order to reach us at our internal moral center, where one could "know reality together" with God, as the etymology of "conscience" suggests. It wouldn't be reducible to spectator evidence, but would come instead with a moral challenge to us to be awakened from our selfishness to the moral primacy of divine love, even if we dislike and dismiss the challenge. We would, in any case, be accountable to God for how we respond to such a life-or-death challenge to be transformed toward God's character. Our lives would show how we respond, even if we change the subject to something less challenging and more selfish. (On the central role of conscience in a call from a perfectly loving God, see Forsyth 1913, Hallesby 1933, Rahner 1983b, and Grave 1989; for a misguided approach, influenced by Luther on the bondage of the human will, that eclipses the crucial role of the human will in suppressing or enabling conscience, see Thielicke 1966, pp. 298–331.)

Our failure to apprehend God's authoritative call saliently may result from *our preferring not* to apprehend it on God's terms of unselfish love for all people. We often prefer, for instance, *not* to have to forgive or to love our enemies, and we act accordingly toward our enemies. For decisive confirmation of this preference, we may check any daily newspaper or ask any honest observer of human interactions. It *seems* easier, or at least more in our own interest, to suppress or to ignore any call from God for us to live as dependent obedient children of God who reflect, if imperfectly, perfect divine love. God's authoritative call toward perfect love would be anything but comfortable, given our selfish ways, particularly if we resolve to obey, come what may. This fits with the fact that genuine goodness doesn't guarantee convenient comfort, and we do well not to confuse the two. As I suggested, we won't let selfish comfort, at least for current purposes, drive our moral and cognitive deliberations about divine reality.

In our skeptical moments, we may ask: God, are You there at all? Are You truly *with us* at all? If so, why must You be so very elusive, often to the extent that You seem nonexistent? Instead, in redemptive love, God would ask us: Are you truly *with Me*, in your *will* as well as in your thought? If we aren't, spectator evidence of God's reality would only domesticate or otherwise devalue God's authoritative reality, because it wouldn't challenge us to submit to God as the Lord of our lives. The providing of such spectator evidence would be akin to what Jesus bluntly called "casting pearls before swine." Harm would be done, because God would be recast as a cognitive idol for us, specifically as an object of cognitive voyeurism, apparently to be used by us as *we* wish. We have enough such harmful idols, and a perfectly authoritative and loving God wouldn't be one of them. As a result, God would elude our demeaning and domesticating ways, for our own good, even in the cognitive domain. Any resulting discomfort for us would also be for our good.

For the sake of upholding redemptive love toward humans, God wouldn't trivialize knowledge of God's reality by offering spectator evidence, as if knowing God's reality were an optional spectator sport. A perfectly loving God wouldn't be after mere spectators or even mere speculators, including mere philosophers. As a result, in redemptive judgment, God would hide God's ways from those who are "wise and intelligent" on their own terms in a way that devalues God's cognitive authority and supremacy (cf. Matt. 11:25–27, 1 Cor. 1:19–21). Given people who aren't ready, owing to whatever deficiency, for authoritative divine self-revelation of perfect love, God would hide on occasion from those people to avoid their harmfully trivializing divine self-revelation. Clearly, God wouldn't be obligated to give divine self-revelation to prideful supposed cognitive superiors who are resolutely and irredeemably opposed to God's ways. Even so, a perfectly loving God would work noncoercively to undo such opposition as long as there's hope for human redemption.

Perfectly authoritative evidence of divine reality, as noted above, would demand that we yield our wills to the perfect source of the evidence in question, namely, God. Such demanding would include an authoritative but noncoercive (that is, rejectable) *call* to us to yield to God's will in fellowship with God. It would require a personal source, an intentional agent, who has a will and a purpose to promote morally perfect love for and among all people. More specifically, a central purpose would be to have us freely yield to God's life-giving perfectly loving will as opposed to our own selfish wills. So, nonpersonal evidence, such as that from pomegranates, clouds, mountains, and cellular complexity, can't be perfectly (or even imperfectly) authoritative evidence; it lacks the needed will and call from a personal agent.

The kinds of "evidence" proposed in traditional first-cause, design, and ontological arguments for God's existence are logically independent of a personal authoritative call (for example, to divine–human fellowship) and thus aren't authoritative evidence. They lack an authoritative demand, or call, to us to yield our selfishness to the unselfish will of a perfectly loving God for the sake of divine–human fellowship. They thus offer at best spectator evidence, and leave us with no fitting challenge from the authoritative will of a perfectly loving God. This is not the kind of purposively available evidence a perfectly loving God of redemption would give to humans, because this is extraneous to what would be God's redemptive purpose to reconcile wayward humans to God.

Spectator evidence in its various manifestations would allow people to persist without challenge in their selfish anti-God ways, and thus would seriously misrepresent the character and reality of a perfectly authoritative and loving God. So, as promised, we won't be distracted by such proposed evidence that is at best incidental to the question of God's existence. We do well instead to move on to purposively available authoritative evidence that promises to settle our urgent questions about divine reality in relation to our dire human predicament. Traditional natural theology and philosophy of religion have simply neglected such authoritative evidence for divine reality, for the sake of more comfortable, less challenging spectator evidence. As a result, skeptics about God's existence haven't been adequately challenged by the relevant evidence. We are now in the process of correcting this deficiency.

A central challenge for us from a perfectly loving God would be an authoritative call to *repent* and to *obey faithfully and wholeheartedly*: that is, to turn our wills, with divine aid, to fully obedient submission to God's unselfish, perfectly loving will that offers a lasting life of fellowship with God. In receiving God's will as preeminent, we would acknowledge God as *our* God, as Lord of *our* lives. We would thereby acknowledge our status as beings dependent on a perfectly loving God. In that case, we *should* renounce our pretensions to be in charge of our lives, but mere knowledge *that God exists* wouldn't make such renunciation automatic. My knowing that something is so, here as elsewhere, doesn't entail my yielding my will to another will. So, a perfectly loving God wouldn't aim or settle for *mere* human knowing that God exists. God would seek to have humans know that God exists, on God's terms and at God's time, but this knowledge would be a divinely intended component of a more robust divine end: fellowship in morally perfect love between God and humans. Such fellowship would emerge, if it emerges at all, from perfectly authoritative evidence from God, whereby God authoritatively calls people into divine–human fellowship.

Spectator evidence, as we've noted, omits any authoritative call from God for humans to enter into fellowship with God via human repentance and obedience. We can entertain spectator evidence without considering who *we* as responsible agents would be before a perfectly authoritative and loving God, that is, people under God's redemptive judgment that seeks to reconcile people to God via repentance and obedience. Spectator evidence omits a divine call to us to repent of our selfishness for the sake of submitting to God's perfectly authoritative and loving will. It thus easily allows us to ignore what would be a perfectly loving God's main purpose for us: to be made new by the power of God's will as we die to our selfishness and live in fellowship with God as God's dependent obedient children. Spectator evidence easily allows us to treat God as just another undisturbing object of our casual reflection and speculation. It thus allows us easily to ignore a God of redemptive judgment who seeks reconciliation of humans to God. It replaces such a God with a deadly idol, typically a reflection of ourselves, even if supercharged. Our self-discovered spectator-oriented gods end up looking a lot like us, at least in terms of their demands on us. Since they aren't worthy of worship, given their lack of authoritative and moral perfection, they are unworthy of the title "God."

Exactly *how* would God call humans to repent and obey? This question is dangerous if it assumes that we are in a position to explain *exactly* how God would proceed with divine self-revelation. Clearly, given our serious cognitive limitations, we have no reason to suppose that we are in such a position. A recurring theme of Jewish and Christian monotheism has been that we definitely aren't in such a position (see, for example, Job 38–40, Jn. 3:5–8, 1 Cor. 2:6–16). God's ways of self-revelation, according to such theism, often leave us without an exact explanation of how the self-revelation arose or even why it arose as it did. On reflection, this is not surprising at all, and it's amazing that any duly reflective person would think otherwise.

A perfectly loving God would be committed to *self-revelation* to humans (as long as there's hope for reconciliation of humans to God) but not thereby to revealing to humans an *exact explanation* of how the self-revelation arose. Divine self-revelation doesn't require the latter; receiving such revelation can be innocent of explaining its origin exactly. A perfectly authoritative and loving God could call us to repent and obey, for instance, but leave us in the explanatory dark regarding exactly how God does this. Explanatory how-questions, then, can be misleading regarding God's ways, owing to a false assumption about our explanatory and cognitive resources. This lesson parallels a more familiar lesson about explanatory why-questions regarding God's ways, particularly regarding why God would allow evil. (On the parallel lesson about evil, see Howard-Snyder 1996.)

Even so, we aren't completely in the dark regarding what could be God's ways of making demands on us. We are all familiar, for instance, with moral demands impinging on us in conscience; or, at least we should be, if we have become inclined to suppress our conscience. Some of these demands go against our own preferences, including our selfish preferences. They don't arise uniformly from our individual wills or even from the common will of our peer group. We see a clear example of this in the case of a lone moral reformer who, having had his or her own will morally corrected via con-science, speaks against societal racism or some other widespread injustice. Some of the ancient Jewish prophets, including Jesus, evidently fall into this category. Some of our own peers apparently do too; Mother Teresa of Calcutta readily comes to mind. The moral demands found in conscience can serve as ways for God's will to challenge and to redirect us noncoercively, if we are suitably receptive. One must use discernment, of course, toward the various demands of conscience, since one's conscience can become corrupted and confused. Still, the presence of bad input doesn't preclude the presence of good input. It would be obviously unreasonable, even logically fallacious, to suppose otherwise.

Divine use of perfectly authoritative purposively available evidence, as opposed to spectator evidence, can account for God's appearing at times to be cognitively subtle, elusive, incognito, or hidden. (Chapter 2 will consider the relevance of divine hiddenness to atheism; cf. Moser 2004b.) When we disregard perfectly authoritative evidence of divine reality, perhaps for the sake of more convenient spectator evidence, we close ourselves off from what would be purposively available evidence characteristic of God's reality. We then become *unsuited to receive* the authoritative evidence in question, in much the way that our refusing to focus on visual contours would block much salient visual evidence from reaching us. In excluding perfectly authoritative evidence, we would risk harm to ourselves, because we would exclude any available conclusive evidence of a life-giving reconciling relationship offered to us by God. To the extent that we block perfectly authoritative evidence of divine reality, we would block any salient evidence of God's existence.

Is, then, the key cognitive shortcoming with *religious skeptics* rather than with God? Religious skeptics rarely, if ever, consider this question seriously; nor do philosophers of religion in general. This deficiency typically stems from inadequate *cognitive modesty* regarding the matter of evidence of God's existence. Appropriate cognitive modesty requires that we be open to what would be a perfectly loving God's self-revelation *on God's terms*, even if God's terms take us beyond comfortable spectator evidence to perfectly authoritative evidence. In short, humans should be open to God's having cognitive authority regarding divine self-revelation. We'll turn, with this in mind, to a direct challenge to skeptics about God's reality. This challenge will enable us, in good conscience, to develop the promised cognitive shift in knowledge of God's reality.

5. VOLITIONAL KNOWING

Famously and fittingly, skeptics about God's reality demand *adequate evidence* of God's reality. We have agreed with this general demand, on the ground that, otherwise, commitment to God's reality would be cognitively loose, promiscuous, and even arbitrary, at least from the perspective of the person having the commitment. We have suggested, however, that a human demand for casual, spectator evidence of God's reality conflicts with what would be God's perfectly loving character and purposes, particularly divine love's authoritative call for divine–human fellowship, including redemptive judgment on human selfishness and presumed self-sufficiency, even in the cognitive domain. Instead, we have proposed that a perfectly loving God would present a distinctive kind of purposively available *authoritative evidence* that challenges the selfishness of human wills for the sake of reconciling humans to God in divine–human fellowship. We'll see how such evidence leads to a powerful new challenge to skeptics about God's reality, given that skeptics, like others, would have to face the discomfort of divine redemptive judgment even in the area of human knowledge of divine reality.

Spectator evidence, as suggested, is *volitionally casual* in that it doesn't demand that we yield our wills to the source of such evidence. In this regard, it readily permits volitional looseness and even volitional promiscuity. Spectator evidence of God's reality would thus allow for volitionally casual access to God, with no demand on our wills relative to God's will to call us to repentance and divine–human fellowship. It would thereby neglect God's exalted status as perfectly and thus supremely authoritative for us in terms of the direction of our wills. A God without that exalted status would be no God at all, lacking the needed moral and volitional authority for the preeminent position of being worthy of worship. We do well, then, to refrain from the uncritical assumption that evidence of God's reality would be pretty much the same kind of thing as typical evidence for the reality of either numbers, quarks, or physical objects. This dubious assumption guides many skeptics about God's reality, as we'll see in what follows.

Why would the human will matter at all in our receiving some conclusive evidence of God's reality? Isn't the underlying assumption itself suspect, because God could simply coerce our attention to make us notice divine activities of various sorts, even against our resolute will to the contrary, and thereby give us any needed evidence of divine reality? This would be akin to the way that a noisy fireworks display can coercively grip one's attention for a while, even if one would prefer otherwise. Wouldn't a perfectly loving God similarly coerce our attention with divine fireworks or other interventions in order to remove any reasonable doubt about God's existence, even while leaving our *will* free to disobey God's call? In addition, given the absence of such coerced attention, doesn't this settle the evidential question about divine reality in favor of skepticism or even atheism?

The answers to the previous questions are found in what would be a perfectly authoritative and loving God's character and redemptive purpose, if such a God were (still) to have hope for human redemption. (We shouldn't assume, of course, that God would be morally required to redeem, or even to try forever to redeem, people who resolutely and ultimately oppose being redeemed by God.) God's redemptive purpose, given divine hope for human redemption as reconciliation to God, would include our *volitionally knowing God as perfectly authoritative Lord*: that is, knowing God as Lord in such a way that we submit, if imperfectly, to God as the One whose will is perfectly and thus supremely authoritative. Such volitional knowing wouldn't allow us to approach God as a self-serving idol made in our own image or even as just another controllable object for our convenience or casual reflection. Instead, as volitionally conciliatory knowledge, it would include our submission to God as perfectly authoritative even over our own wills. It would thus launch a profound makeover of anyone who volitionally knows God.

A perfectly loving God, in seeking divine–human reconciliation, wouldn't pursue either human knowledge of God's reality as knowledge of "something we know not what" or, for that matter, any human knowledge of God's reality apart from volitional knowledge of God as authoritative Lord. All such volitional knowledge would include obedience to a divine call to human volitional submission to God as Lord, but in reality human submission could come in varying degrees or not at all. Some people, as the Introduction noted, could receive God's call, even for what it is intended to be, but disobey altogether what it demands; they would refuse to submit to God as Lord, despite their acknowledging the reality of God's call. Even so, a perfectly loving God would noncoercively seek perfectly loving human submission to the degree that God's moral character is perfectly represented in willing humans.

The divine call would avoid coerced human submission, given a divine aim for a freely entered, genuinely interactive relationship whereby humans are willingly transformed, perhaps over time, toward God's perfectly loving character. Coercion as an alternative to this aim would depersonalize the person being coerced, and thereby preclude a genuinely interactive relationship. So, a divine fireworks display that coerced our attention and volitional submission wouldn't accomplish God's redemptive purpose. God would, of course, have the sheer power to coerce human attention and volitional submission, but the pursuit of genuinely interactive love between God and humans wouldn't be achieved by such coercion.

God's coercing human attention in a manner analogous to a dominating fireworks display wouldn't necessarily even *contribute* to God's redemptive purpose. It may actually repulse a person, perhaps in the way that coerced familiarity can easily breed contempt, owing to its felt dominating of one's attention. Divine (noncoercive) eliciting of the free yielding of a human will may begin with a rejectable divine intrusion in human attention, but such "modest coercion" of attention wouldn't either preclude human rejection of the intrusion or yield by itself volitional submission to God. It would be significantly different, then, from a strongly coercive, dominating fireworks display that can't be avoided or turned away. Even so, there could be occasions where a perfectly loving God could contribute to divine redemptive purposes by means of striking manifestations of divine power that grip one's attention without becoming strongly coercive in the sense indicated.

As long as I would refuse to acknowledge God's will as perfectly and supremely authoritative for humans, I would refuse to acknowledge God *as God,* where "God" is the pre-eminent title as characterized above. In addition, as long as I would refuse to submit to God as the One whose will is perfectly and supremely authoritative, I would thereby block myself from volitionally knowing God as perfectly authoritative Lord. This would interfere with any divine redemptive purpose of reconciling people, including me, to God. It would also interfere with my receiving available evidence of divine reality dependent on one's yielding to that purpose. So, what I do with my will can be cognitively as well as redemptively significant. Beliefs obviously matter in what one knows and doesn't know, because knowledge entails belief. One's will matters too, especially in the case of receiving purposively available evidence and knowledge of a perfectly loving God who has a redemptive purpose of reconciling humans volitionally to God.

We find a suitable cognitive (as well as ethical) model in Jesus's reported response to God in the Garden of Gethsemane: "Not what I will, but what You will." This was no casual concession to God. On the contrary, Jesus was conceding to God, for the sake of divine redemptive purposes, his upcoming tortuous death by Roman crucifixion. He was yielding his will, even his very life, wholeheartedly to God as One whose divine will is perfectly and thus supremely authoritative. Such yielding of one's will to God doesn't entail extinguishing one's will altogether, or being left without a will at all. It is rather a matter of conforming one's will to God's will, or at least allowing one's will to be conformed to God's will. The underlying idea is that volitional fellowship, and thus reconciliation, with God requires the yielding of one's will to God's perfectly authoritative will. Agreement of our ideas or beliefs with God's ideas or beliefs would fall short of such fellowship and reconciliation. Accordingly, a perfectly loving God wouldn't be satisfied with agreement of our beliefs with God's. Our *volitional agency* too would need to be brought in line with God's perfectly loving purposes for the sake of genuine divine–human personal reconciliation.

If we construe volitional knowledge of God's reality on the Gethsemane model, we are left with volitional knowledge *sub specie crucis,* that is, human knowledge of God's reality from the volitional perspective of the cross of the obedient Jesus. This is volitionally knowing God as Lord that requires human will-yielding to God of the sort exemplified by Jesus on his way, obediently, to crucifixion for the sake of divine redemptive purposes. (Chapter 3 will return to the role of crucifixion in those purposes.) The divine goal would be that we yield all we are and have, wholeheartedly, to a perfectly loving God for the sake of advancing divine redemptive purposes, in fellowship with God. This volitional cognitive model is hinted at in the remark attributed to Jesus in Jn. 7:17: "If anyone wills to do God's will, she will know whether my teaching comes from God or whether I speak on my own." This remark suggests a kind of knowing that makes a demand on the will of knowers relative to God's will. In particular, the relevant kind of knowing involves one's *willing* to do God's will. Such volitional knowing rarely surfaces in philosophical discussions of knowledge of God's reality, but we'll counter that deficiency in order to give Jewish and Christian monotheism a fair hearing.

Willingness to submit to God's will, even if it's an imperfect willingness, is central to volitionally knowing God as Lord. In seeking to be known volitionally as Lord (rather than as an object of casual speculation or voyeurism), a perfectly loving God would tailor purposively available evidence of divine reality to the volitional yielding of potential knowers. This would advance a redemptive aim to reconcile humans to God by transforming selfish human wills without thereby trivializing or otherwise devaluing evidence of God's perfectly authoritative sacred reality. Even if volitional factors figure in knowing humans *as persons* (and I suspect that they do), we have no basis for yielding to mere humans *as perfectly authoritative*. God alone, given a self-sufficiently perfect character, would merit such submission. Mere humans wouldn't qualify, owing to their lacking self-sufficiently perfect moral characters.

Volitional knowledge of God as perfectly authoritative Lord would call for a cognitive taxonomy beyond the familiar options of rationalism and empiricism. Pure rationalism about knowledge of God's reality, characterized broadly, implies that human reason is *the* source of knowledge of God's reality. Pure empiricism about knowledge of God's reality, also stated generally, implies that human (sensory or perceptual) experience is *the* source of knowledge of God's reality. Both positions have many prominent advocates in philosophy and theology, but popularity, here as elsewhere, doesn't vouchsafe truth. We actually need a third alternative.

Volitionalism about knowledge of God's reality, in contrast to pure rationalism and pure empiricism, implies that the human will is a central human "source" (or, perhaps better, "avenue") of conclusive evidence and knowledge of God's reality. More accurately, it implies that the yielding of the human will to a demand of perfectly authoritative evidence from God is a central source, or avenue, *within humans* of conclusive evidence and knowledge of God's reality. God alone, of course, would be the *superhuman* origin of human evidence and knowledge of divine reality; so, we need to distinguish between a source within humans and a source independent of humans for conclusive evidence and knowledge of divine reality. Volitionalism thus gives a key role to perfectly authoritative evidence that is neglected by pure rationalism and pure empiricism. It excludes the dominance of spectator evidence found in such rationalism and empiricism, and preserves a cognitive role for divine *authority* that makes a demand on human wills. Volitionalism thus identifies the kind of available evidence and knowledge of divine reality we should expect of a perfectly authoritative and loving God with noncoercive redemptive purposes for humans.

6. SKEPTICAL TESTS

Skeptics will doubtless ask how we are to test for the *reliability* of the alleged perfectly authoritative evidence. The question is plausible, so long as it doesn't involve a test at odds *conceptually* with what is now being tested for: the reality of a perfectly loving God who, given hope for human redemption, would challenge us with perfectly authoritative evidence. That is, a proposed test shouldn't rule out *in principle* the reality or the suitable evidence of such a God. In addition, if we aim to make a perfectly loving God jump through cognitive hoops of our own making, we are bound to be disappointed. Such a God wouldn't play our intellectual games, given that they (including the ways we distortingly set our cognitive standards, such as in Humean empiricism, in logical positivism, or in Cartesian rationalism) typically insulate us from being challenged by authoritative evidence from a perfectly loving God. We should avoid prejudice and distortion on this front, of course, for the sake of trustworthy belief about whether a perfectly loving God actually exists. We gain nothing by begging the question, either negatively or affirmatively, with dubious cognitive standards.

A perfectly loving God wouldn't owe any human the preeminent role of a supposedly neutral judge over God, including in the cognitive domain. One consideration is that God would have no reason to suppose that selfish humans are indeed neutral. Another consideration is that humans, with their very limited cognitive and moral resources, would be in no position to serve as reliable judges over a perfectly loving God. In addition, God wouldn't owe humans any spectator evidence of divine reality, including any such evidence *before* God makes authoritative demands on them.

Humans do indeed need salient evidence of divine reality, including evidence of who God is, but a perfectly loving God could, and would, supply all needed evidence with purposively available perfectly authoritative evidence. This would be in keeping not only with a perfectly authoritative and loving divine character but also with a divine redemptive aim to transform human wills rather than to treat humans as innocent spectators. A perfectly loving God wouldn't pretend that humans are but spectators. Otherwise, God would be playing fast and loose with the truth about humans regarding their standing relative to a perfectly loving divine will. That would do humans no good at all; nor would it reflect well on God.

Agreeing with proponents of natural theology, some skeptics will demand that we begin with "mere-existence arguments" concerning God. Their demand would be to set aside any consideration of perfectly authoritative evidence for the sake of considering spectator evidence alone. The underlying aim of such a demand is typically to provide for "neutrality" or "impartiality" in the consideration of evidence. This demand is misguided, however, because in the case of a perfectly authoritative and loving God, the crucial *cognitive* role of a perfectly authoritative and loving character and purpose, including any redemptive purpose, must not be ignored or minimized by a demand for mere-existence arguments that exclude an authoritative call to fellowship with God. This book's epistemological approach upholds this important cognitive role, and thus avoids any biased demand for a "mere-existence argument." It aims thereby to highlight the explanatory, psychological, and existential richness in purposively available authoritative evidence that would be supplied by a perfectly loving God who offers volitional fellowship, including, in the case of wayward humans, redemption as reconciliation to God.

The purposively available evidence in question doesn't omit the perfectly authoritative and loving character inherent to a God worthy of worship for the sake of something less robust. It doesn't reduce, in particular, to dubious evidence of God as evidence of "something maximally powerful we know not what" independent of a perfectly authoritative and loving character. Firsthand volitional evidence and knowledge of God's reality involve a *directness* in evidence and knowledge of divine reality that entails their being irreducible to mere propositional evidence or knowledge *that* God exists. The directness involves evidence of an "I–You" volitional interaction between humans and God that is absent from traditional arguments for God's existence. God's side of such a volitional interaction can be mediated via a human will, but it isn't reducible to a human will. My talk of (firsthand) evidence and knowledge of "God's reality" (or of "God") should be understood accordingly, as irreducible to mere propositional evidence or knowledge. Typically my talk of (firsthand) evidence or knowledge of God's reality is interchangeable with talk of evidence or knowledge of God.

In seeking *agent-to-agent volitional interaction*, a perfectly loving God wouldn't need to offer *mere* propositional evidence or knowledge that God exists. In particular, a perfectly loving God wouldn't need to offer evidence of God's "reality" apart from evidence of who God is as perfectly authoritative and loving Lord. Indeed, God's reality would essentially be God's being perfectly authoritative and loving Lord worthy of worship. We aim to accommodate this consideration in the epistemology under development.

Existence evidence regarding a perfectly loving God's reality would be purposively available, in keeping with (and only in keeping with) God's authoritative character and purposes. It thus would come not as a needed preliminary to, but instead *through*, perfectly authoritative evidence of God's reality, including evidence of God's authoritative call to divine–human volitional fellowship. So, we shouldn't begin with a demand for mere-existence evidence that omits consideration of a perfectly authoritative call to divine–human fellowship. Instead, we should entertain any evidence of what a perfectly authoritative and loving God would do, has done, or is doing in terms of intervening in the lives of people. (Chapters 2 and 3 revisit this theme in detail.)

The proposed strategy will avoid the risk of being diverted to deism, mere theism, or something else less robust than the reality of a perfectly authoritative and loving God worthy of worship. We will thus highlight what would be God's offer of reconciliation to all people, even philosophically unsophisticated people, at least as long as there's divine hope of reconciliation. A person, in any case, wouldn't have to be able to follow intricate arguments to receive conclusive evidence of a perfectly loving God's reality. On the contrary, intricate arguments may actually get in the way of what really matters to a perfectly loving God: divine–human fellowship via volitional transformation of humans toward God's perfectly loving character.

Firsthand evidence of God's authoritative call to volitional fellowship wouldn't itself be an *argument* for God's existence. Instead, it would be akin to evidence from conscience regarding, for instance, either the duty (or call or conviction) to undertake an act of self-giving kindness or the duty (or call or conviction) not to perform an act of needless torture. Such evidence from conscience, although genuine, doesn't include an argument against skeptics, but this is no defect at all in the evidence from conscience. In addition, we can suppress such evidence, and we will typically dismiss it if we *will* or intend to do something in conflict with it. Still, the evidence from conscience is genuine, and can even be conclusive if it's unaccompanied by defeaters.

Defeaters can arise directly or indirectly. A *direct* defeater of initial evidence for a claim consists of additional evidence (not to be confused with mere beliefs) that significantly challenges *the support* of the initial evidence for the claim in question. Consider, for instance, my initial visual evidence indicating that there's a bent stick submerged halfway in a tub of water before me. The support it initially offers can be defeated by my additional visual evidence indicating, from a broader visual perspective, that my initial visual evidence fails, when conjoined with my broader evidence, to indicate that there's a bent stick before me. In contrast, an *indirect* defeater of initial evidence consists of evidence that significantly challenges *the truth indicated* by that initial evidence. For instance, my visual evidence indicating that there's a cup before me can be defeated by my broader visual and tactile evidence indicating that *only* a holographic image of a cup is before me. Such defeaters indicate that evidence can be defeated (and is thus defeasible) in two ways by additional evidence (but not by mere beliefs, contrary to many philosophers, since beliefs can be altogether lacking in supporting evidence). Fallibilists about evidence, who hold that evidence can be misleading, will welcome this lesson about defeaters. (For elaboration on the role of defeaters in evidence, justification, and knowledge, see Moser 1989.)

Evidence of God's call to fellowship and repentance would be fallible (possibly misleading) and defeasible (possibly defeated), but could nonetheless be accurate and conclusive in the absence of falsifiers and undefeated defeaters. Such evidence would come to wayward humans with a challenge in conscience indicating that we have fallen short of a perfectly loving God's unselfish ways. This wouldn't be strong, or dominating, coercion of our attention or of our will, because we would be free to reject or to ignore such evidence instead of receiving it for what it is intended to be. In addition, if we received such evidence as actually including a challenge from God, we could still choose to disobey or to ignore the challenge. God would thus treat recipients of a divine challenge as responsible persons rather than coerced pawns, as objects of divine love rather than of dominating coercion. Genuine love, we've suggested, must take the risk of rejection, because it refuses to depersonalize any responsible person with dominating coercion of that person's will regarding the reception of love.

Skeptics are notorious for demanding cogent *arguments*, but genuine evidence, as suggested above, doesn't necessarily include an argument. For example, a person may have undefeated experiential evidence (owing to visual attention-attraction by a red patch, which is not an argument) indicating that there's a red patch in her visual field, but she could still lack an argument for the claim that there's a red patch in her visual field. So, our having evidence, even evidence that satisfies the justification-condition for knowledge, doesn't necessarily include our having a non-questionbegging argument, or any argument, against skeptics. Whether an argument is non-questionbegging varies with the questions actually raised in an exchange (cf. Moser 1993, chap. 1). Evidence itself, however, is not exchange-relative in this way. Skeptics, then, shouldn't confuse having evidence with either having or giving an argument.

Our *having* evidence doesn't entail our *giving* an answer or a claim of any kind. Consider, for instance, how our having a particular sensory experience need not include our giving an answer to a question. Evidence can be present for a person (owing to salient attention-attraction by that evidence) without being described by that person in order to answer skeptical questions. Accordingly, we shouldn't consider one to be without evidence simply because one lacks a non-questionbegging argument relative to an extreme skeptic's questions. One's supporting evidence could still be cognitively impeccable, despite one's lacking the kind of argument demanded by a skeptic. An unbridled skeptical demand for "argument" of a preferred sort often blinds skeptics from seeing that "evidence" need not include an argument at all (see this book's Appendix and Moser 2004a for problems facing extreme skepticism and a non-questionbegging reply to such skepticism). We should, in any case, invite skeptics to consider the kind of evidence suitable to a perfectly authoritative and loving God who would seek redemptive transformation on the basis of authoritative evidence rather than spectator evidence.

Acknowledgment of a perfectly authoritative and loving God with redemptive purposes may offer unmatched explanatory value regarding such matters as who we are as morally accountable persons and why we as such persons have come into existence at all. The overall cognitive reasonableness of robust theistic belief could thus be supported, at least in part, by such belief's yielding a best available undefeated explanation on the basis of the whole range of our experience and other evidence. (See Niebuhr 1949, chap. 10, for use of Pascal's *Pensées* to outline such an argument; cf. Banner 1990, chap. 6, Wiebe 2004, chap. 3.) This could be a plausible strategy if, and only if, it steers clear of questionbegging probability assignments and supplies a lucid notion of explanation that is cognitively relevant. (See Moser 1989 for a detailed effort to meet such challenges in connection with empirical justification and knowledge.)

Regardless of the details about explanation, the foundational evidence of God's reality would be irreducibly a matter of one's *experiencing*, via attention-attraction in conscience, what is evidently God's perfectly authoritative personal call to one to live in divine–human fellowship. As suggested, because God is inherently personal (if real), we should expect the foundational evidence of God's existence to be likewise personal, and not itself a premise or a conclusion in an argument, whether deductive, inductive, or abductive, even though one could, of course, formulate premises and draw conclusions on the basis of the relevant foundational evidence. (Chapter 2 returns to the topic of theism and best available explanation.)

One's firsthand experience of what is evidently God's authoritative call, as suggested, wouldn't be an argument of any kind; nor would it be a propositional answer to skeptical questions. Instead, it would be experiential acquaintance, involving attention-attraction, with what is evidently God's authoritative call on a person's life, via that person's conscience. Consider a situation where the best available undefeated explanation of such an experience is that a perfectly authoritative and loving God has actually intervened in one's life with a call to volitional fellowship with God. Many relatively normal people would suggest that their own experience exemplifies just such a situation, and they aren't in an asylum or otherwise irrational. In that situation, as Chapter 2 will explain, one would have the evidential resources for a plausible argument for the cognitive reasonableness and even the truth of robust theism. Still, the perfect authority one thereby identified would rest in God's authoritative character, and the foundational evidence would reside in one's experience of what is evidently God's personal intervention, not in an argument involving best available explanation. The foundational evidence in experiential acquaintance with what is evidently a personal God wouldn't reduce to a premise, a conclusion, or an argument of any kind, and this is in keeping with experiential foundational evidence in general (on which see Moser 1989).

Of course, not just any challenging call to us in conscience would qualify as divine. Our use of "God" as a morally preeminent title has definite hard edges, and that's a good thing. If a call promotes hate toward people, it isn't from a perfectly loving God, although it may be from a bad imposter. False gods could oppose the true God, and they would be known for what they are relative to the benchmark of perfectly unselfish love as a corrective to selfish ways. This standard will leave us with very few candidates, and perhaps only one candidate, if any. Many familiar candidates will fail at the start, but we won't digress to naming names. A perfectly loving God could thus be put to the test, even by us, as long as the test is fitting and fair in light of the properly demanding standard of *worthiness of worship*.

If God could be put to the test for authenticity, we humans could be put to the test too. Some immediate test questions for us humans, including skeptics, are: (1) Are we *willing* to receive a perfectly loving God's authoritative call to us for what it is intended to be, including a challenging call for enemy-love and enemy-forgiveness? (2) Are we *willing* to engage in the attentive discernment integral to receiving with due care and respect a perfectly loving God's authoritative call? (3) Having received God's authoritative call for what it is intended to be, are we *willing* to be correctively judged and then remade by the power of a perfectly loving God's unselfish love? (4) Are we *willing* to let a perfectly loving God be God even in our own lives, that is, the Lord whose will is perfectly authoritative and supreme for us regarding our own attitudes, actions, and lives? If we honestly answer yes to these questions, we can fruitfully begin to "test for" God's reality. If we can't honestly answer yes, we have to ask if we ourselves obstruct available evidence of God's reality. The cognitive problem may not be with God, after all; instead, a simple hand mirror held at face level, in that case, may reveal where (or, better, *who*) the real problem is.

A suitable test for God's reality would ask, among other things, if any of us has undefeated evidence of the intervention of a perfectly authoritative and loving being worthy of worship. In this connection, we should ask whether there is a potentially sacred place deep within us, beneath the noise and the clutter of this dying world, for receiving divine self-revelation. This would be a place deep in conscience, beyond the superficialities of our lives, where we could receive, and even interact with, the authoritative voice of a perfectly loving God who calls us to turn from selfishness and selfish fear to be remade wholeheartedly after God's morally perfect character. This voice would be the perfectly authoritative but "still, small voice" that reportedly challenged the ancient Hebrew prophet Elijah, among many others, and visited Jesus on various occasions.

Perhaps relatively few people have actually listened for a divine voice with an inclination to take it seriously, because it could change one's life dramatically and put worldly success and social acceptance at risk. Its challenge would be morally serious and thoroughgoing, and thus likely to be rejected or ignored by many people who find it inconvenient or troublesome given their selfish purposes, including perhaps an aim to be ultimately indifferent regarding divine reality. Here we would have a definite clash between a typical human will and the distinctive will of a perfectly loving God.

The perfect authority of God's call would be palpable and transforming when one's conscience is suitably receptive. The divine call wouldn't be a dominating, depersonalizing sledgehammer, but would treat people instead as morally responsible persons. People could thus ignore, suppress, or even reject a divine call to reconciliation via human repentance and divine–human fellowship. Ultimately, however, God's own perfectly authoritative and loving character would yield the correct foundational answers to our suitable test questions, for God to pass the test for divine reality. Otherwise, God would depend ultimately on something other than God's own character to answer our test questions correctly, and thus would lack inherent supreme cognitive authority. In that case, God wouldn't be perfectly authoritative, given ultimate dependence for authority on something other than God's own character. God wouldn't then be inherently worthy of worship, and thus wouldn't satisfy the preeminent title "God."

One's having perfect cognitive authority doesn't entail that one is beyond suitable test questions. It entails rather that one perfectly satisfies what it is to be cognitively authoritative, even if one *could* fail the test. If God would be praiseworthy for being perfectly authoritative, as seems plausible, then we should allow that God *could* fail the test, even if God doesn't actually fail it. So, we shouldn't infer that a perfectly authoritative God would have absolutely free cognitive reign, as if *whatever God happened to will* would be cognitively acceptable. The point instead is that God's cognitive authority would proceed, in keeping with the preeminent divine title, by the perfect authority of God's own perfectly loving character. Evidence of God's reality would fit with this perfect authority, the authority of God's own perfectly loving character.

An authoritatively and morally perfect divine character would anchor and guide divine willing, thus avoiding arbitrariness in divine willing. So, we have no cognitive analogue to Plato's Euthyphro problem, where mere divine willing of whatever sort would create merit. God's perfectly loving character, rather than an arbitrary will, would have ultimate perfect authority. In addition, a being who lacked a perfectly loving character would also lack worthiness of worship, and thus be disqualified to hold the title "God." God, then, would have to meet the preeminent standard of divinity, namely, inherent worthiness of worship, but wouldn't, and couldn't, rely ultimately on an independent authority to meet this standard. (The next section returns to this point.)

Skeptics will rightly note that even if God's character *would* be perfectly authoritative, we need good reason to suppose that the divine character is *actually instantiated* in the real world and thus is no *merely imaginary* construct. Is there really a divine agent who calls one to repentance and fellowship, or, alternatively, is the call in question illusory? This issue can't plausibly be dismissed, if shallow dogmatism is to be avoided. At a minimum, then, we must consider that "...an experience, strongly religious in tone, seeming *sui generis*, ... can come to be seen by the person concerned in altogether a new light, as an encounter not with the transcendent but with some buried element of his own early life, transposed, as it were, into a strange unfamiliar key: but if unfamiliar, then still recognized as his own by an insight equally compelling and authoritative as the original judgement about its self-evident transcendent origin" (Hepburn 1958, p. 47; cf. Hepburn 1963, p. 48). This is certainly the case, and it would be foolish to suggest otherwise.

From a cognitive point of view, we should let the actual evidence, or truth-indicators, in a case (rather than mere possibilities, beliefs, or interpretations) determine what is cognitively grounded and what isn't. For instance, if I have no indication whatever that "some buried element of [my] own early life" is now generating my religious experience, I'll lack evidence that the experience is illusory *on that basis* regarding divine reality, even if the experience is illusory. My experience *might* have yielded a defeating indicator that I'm undergoing a hallucination, for instance, but it actually doesn't, and this is cognitively important regarding what my experience indicates. In the absence of any indication of an illusory experience, I can't justifiably infer that my experience is illusory. In this regard, at least, religious experience parallels sensory and perceptual experience, including the kind of experience underlying knowledge in the natural and social sciences. We do well, of course, to avoid any cavalier rejection of all knowledge in the natural and social sciences.

Skeptics may still have this worry: "Neither felt uniqueness, degree of intensity, nor any other factor I can isolate in [religious] experience guarantees that it is a veridical cognitive experience, that the experience is being correctly interpreted [as an experience of divine reality].... The situation looks ambivalent in respect of theistic or naturalistic interpretations" (Hepburn 1963, p. 49). Of course, an experiential situation *could* be ambivalent between a theistic interpretation and a naturalistic interpretation, but that doesn't entail that all experiential situations will *actually* be thus ambivalent. As always, we do well here to let the relevant evidence, or truth-indicators, determine cognitively rational belief, and this requires attention to the actual truth-indicators in an experiential situation. It is deeply misleading, however, to put all the weight on what a religious experience "guarantees," as if experiential evidence for a truth must *guarantee* that truth. By that standard, sensory and perceptual evidence would very rarely, if ever, justify a belief that a physical object exists or that perceptual objects of the sciences exist, because we can readily imagine massive hallucination that challenges any alleged guarantee based on such evidence. Once again, we are well advised to avoid cavalier skeptical inferences that dismiss experiential knowledge wholesale.

We can entertain cognitively reasonable removal of the ambivalence bothering skeptics if we acknowledge two plausible considerations. First, a claim can acquire cognitive reasonableness for one in virtue of its undefeated superior explanatory value relative to the full range of one's experience and other evidence (on which see Moser 1989; cf. Lycan 2002, Wiebe 2004). Second, one could have, as the Introduction noted, *interactive* diachronic experiential evidence that involves evident interaction, perhaps via one's conscience, between God's will and one's own will. Consider, then, a case where the undefeated best available explanation of my experience is that I have volitional interaction, say via my conscience, between God's will and my own will, whereby God challenges me repeatedly to repent of my selfish tendency to refuse to do what is best for my enemies. I have, let's assume, a hard time loving my enemies, especially those I have to face directly in my life.

In the imagined case, we may suppose, I have no indication either that *I am calling myself* to repent or that *I even want* to repent; nor do I have any indication that the call to repentance is coming either from my own history or from some other merely human or worldly source. I *might* have had such an indication, of course, but I actually don't. In addition, I evidently am in a volitional interaction, an experienced give-and-take of wills, where my will is being challenged repeatedly by a morally superior will that calls for perfect love even for one's (including *my*) enemies. This volitionally interactive "wrestling in conscience" fits perfectly with what would be an intervention by a perfectly loving God, and nothing in my experience or my evidence in general counts significantly against either the reality or my evidence of this intervention.

My experiential evidence in favor of divine intervention is, we may suppose, undefeated for me, even after my careful and extensive reflection on many alleged defeaters offered by rather shrewd skeptics over many centuries. In such a case, the aforementioned ambivalence bothering skeptics could be reasonably removed for a person, relative to that person's overall evidence. I have offered a sufficient condition for its removal, but I don't offer it as a necessary condition, because we shouldn't require extensive consideration of skeptical objections by all people. (Chapter 2 will develop a related line of undefeated theistic evidence, and offer a straightforward argument to answer skeptics.)

The plot thickens, as it typically does in cognitive matters about a perfectly loving God. Humans on their own may be largely (but not completely) blind and deaf, metaphorically speaking, relative to purposively available evidence of a perfectly loving God. This is undeniably a live option, echoed throughout the New Testament, even if it is neglected among skeptics in particular and philosophers of religion in general. So, humans may be in need of *God* to open their "eyes and ears" (again, metaphorically speaking) to receive aright the purposively available authoritative evidence of God's reality. We may see vague glimmers and hear muted echoes of God's reality intruding in our awareness, but we may need God to give us new eyes to see and ears to hear (that is, a new cognitive perspective to receive aright) evidence of God's reality with some transparency.

We may need noncoercive cognitive help *from God* in our coming to know God's reality, and we may need *freely to ask* God for such help in light of initial vague glimmers of divine reality. We do well, here and elsewhere, to avoid commitment to total bondage of the human will (of the kind suggested by Augustine, Luther, and Calvin), in order to leave room for some genuine human responsibility. Perhaps, nonetheless, we need to be empowered by God, at our free request, to value unselfish love aright as cognitively and morally crucial regarding volitional knowledge of divine reality. God would thus be indispensable as our helper even regarding our receiving evidence of God's reality with some clarity, but human free will would also have a critical role. It wouldn't follow that we risk a circular argument, since we're concerned now with purposively available evidence more basic than an argument. Skeptics have consistently avoided consideration of this live option, perhaps because they suffer from a serious cognitive blind spot in this area. The blind spot may arise from an uncritical assumption characteristic of skeptics regarding the propriety only of spectator evidence regarding divine reality. In any case, we do well to overcome cognitive blind spots in this connection.

God may be Lord over what we need in order to receive evidence of God's reality with some transparency, and skeptics should give careful attention to this viable cognitive option. We would, on this option, be in a position of genuine *cognitive* need and dependence relative to God, even if we think otherwise. This would fit with the aim of a perfectly loving God to affirm our proper status as *cognitively* dependent creatures of God and to challenge our prideful assumptions of self-reliance in the cognitive domain.

Pretensions of self-reliance and self-approval emerge with a vengeance in cognitive areas of life, where we readily take self-credit and easily overlook that a perfectly loving God would operate by grace, or unmerited gift, rather than by any human earning that obligates God to reward humans. This is difficult but needed news for those of us accustomed to the ways of self-crediting human achievement. The tyranny of human earning dies hard indeed in cognitive and other areas of human life, because we pridefully tend to think that we have outgrown significant dependence on anyone else, particularly in the assessment of available evidence regarding ultimate matters. We gladly suppose that we have become mature and even "independent," especially in matters of evidence regarding God's existence. Perhaps we need to rethink carefully here, because we may actually be indebted to, and dependent on, a perfectly authoritative and loving God.

7. TRUST AND DISTRUST

A perfectly loving God who seeks human redemption as divine–human reconciliation would aim to build human trust in (that is, reliance on) God *on God's terms*, and not necessarily on humans' preferred terms. Could, however, the God in question *be reliably trusted*? If so, trusted with *what*? With satisfying our desires and delivering us from all evil now? Clearly not. Our desires aren't fully satisfied, and we all suffer from evil and its effects, each and every day. In addition, we shall all undergo physical death some day, perhaps sooner than we think. What, then, could God be trusted *for*? Skeptics about God might answer: for *nothing at all*. In any case, they doubt that the God in question actually exists, on the ground that they find no compelling cognitive reason to acknowledge divine reality.

The best answer to our question is this: God, if real, could be trusted for what God has *actually promised*, in keeping, of course, with God's perfectly loving character. One reported promise from the Jewish and Christian God stands out: the redemptive promise to remain forever in fellowship with God's human children who are willing to be in such fellowship as God frees them from deadly idols by bringing them into volitional conformity with God's self-giving crucified and resurrected human Son, Jesus. Contrary to much popular religion, this does *not* include a promise to save God's human children from temporary pain, suffering, frustration, tragedy, poverty, illness, deformity, or even physical death. It is rather a promise of God's abiding and transforming redemptive presence with God's willing people, *come what may*.

Many people desire something contrary to the divine promise in question (for example, a paradise of pleasure on earth now, perhaps with God as their cooperative vending machine), and thus, by their own admission, have no interest whatever in the divine promise. The desire for something contrary to the divine promise could easily yield a serious cognitive disconnect between these people and a perfectly loving God. Misguided human expectations regarding God can blind people from seeing (evidence of) God's reality even when it's right at hand. So, we should be careful of what we expect, since it may rob us of needed sight and thus of needed apprehension of evidence regarding divine reality.

Skeptics will promptly ask: why should we accept any such answer regarding God's reliability? Such a reason-seeking why-question comes easy and often for them, and that's not itself a defect at all. In fact, it may be a cognitive virtue. We should try to answer all such sober questions, because they helpfully test a proposed position for its reason-based support or its lack thereof. Skeptics themselves will recommend that we simply withhold judgment on the issue of divine reliability. This recommendation, however, is too quick. Whether skeptical or not, we need to pause to assess the will-oriented cognitive position under development.

Part of the needed answer to skeptics has already emerged. As suggested above, we can't give *spectator* evidence of divine reality (free of a volitional challenge) to skeptics or to any other humans; nor should we expect or want to be able to do so. The opposing view makes a category mistake about the relevant evidence of divine reality. Instead, taking a judicious approach, we should consider whether perfectly *authoritative* evidence regarding divine reality is actually available to us humans under certain circumstances. Such evidence would call people to trust, and thereby to be volitionally conformed to, a perfectly loving God, even in the face of temporary pain, suffering, frustration, tragedy, poverty, illness, deformity, or physical death (perhaps even all of these combined in one massively frustrating challenge). The evidence in question would call people to trust God with regard to *God's perfectly authoritative and loving promises* rather than our own (often confused and fleeting) desires.

The perfectly authoritative evidence would come, if at all, from God's call via God's intervening Spirit, the same call and Spirit that reportedly led Jesus into his notorious trials in the wilderness, in Gethsemane, and on Calvary. (See any of the New Testament Gospels for an outline of his trials.) Few people would seem capable to predict with any exactness on their own the ways of God's perfectly loving call to divine–human volitional fellowship. Our selfish natural expectation, and that of many avowedly Christian churches, is that God's beloved children should always triumph and reign on royal, comfortable thrones of worldly success, with plenty of money, food, and clout. Washing the feet of our enemies with an unearned offer of forgiveness, in any case, isn't on our agenda, even as a remote backup plan. Too often people want a predictable God like us, and this want corrodes and corrupts human expectations of evidence of divine reality.

The question now facing skeptics is this: are they *willing* to receive an authoritative divine call for what it is intended to be, and, in that case, to come to trust God as authoritative Lord over their lives? Or, alternatively, is their *un*willingness to do so interfering somehow with their receiving some purposively available authoritative evidence of God's reality (say, in virtue of distorting how they attend to or interpret some available evidence)? Have they put themselves in a cognitive position unfavorable to receiving some of the distinctive evidence in question? At a minimum, skeptics must honestly face such questions, however unfamiliar the questions are to ordinary skeptical ways of thinking.

Skeptics suffer from a cognitive blind spot in neglecting that a perfectly loving God would offer purposively available authoritative evidence of divine reality that aims to transform our wills in the direction of God's perfectly loving will. The clash between humans and a perfectly loving God would be mainly a matter of conflicting wills (human selfish wills in conflict with God's perfectly loving will) rather than merely intellectual ideas. Merely intellectual human obstacles would be comparatively superficial and easily handled by God. Selfish human wills, in contrast, may be cognitively intractable in interfering with receiving some purposively available evidence of God's reality. Skeptics, among others, owe this live option serious consideration.

Opposing destructive human ways, a perfectly loving God would promote a grand divide between two matters: (a) what God aims to do for us without our earning or meriting (and is to be received as a gift via suitably grounded trust in God) and (b) what we have accomplished on our own relative to our supposedly earning or meriting security with God in a way that obligates God to honor or benefit us. This is a divide between *divine grace* (or, unmerited gift) and *human earning*. It allows that God can work noncoercively toward human redemption through our wills and intellects, but it disallows that we "earn" our cognitive or moral standing before God by our obligating God to credit us with what we aim to achieve. The common approach to religion as requiring human earning toward God, rampant among followers of all theistic religions, runs afoul of the conception of God as perfectly loving. It fosters a conception of God as grudging and close-fisted, with human earning as the key to open God's otherwise closed hand. God thus ends up looking a lot like us ungenerous humans, and religion becomes a reflection of us rather than of a perfectly loving God. Much religion in circulation is just that, of course, and thus merits its dubious reputation and even rejection.

In the cognitive domain, a perfectly loving God would be revealed by grace rather than by human earning for a straightforward redemptive reason. A God who seeks human redemption via conciliatory volitional knowledge of divine reality would seek to deflate human pride, boasting, and self-credit, and to promote instead ultimate humble trust in the only One who can sustain humans in life. This would be part of God's redemptive purpose toward humans, if God had any hope left for human redemption. There could come a time when such divine hope runs out, and a perfectly loving

God would be no fool or fraud about the prospects for redemption of humans. Evidence of a perfectly loving God's reality, we've noted, would be suited to a divine redemptive purpose, as long as divine hope for redemption lasted. It would thus be perfectly authoritative evidence initiated by God without human earning, and it would thereby call for human volitional knowledge of God as perfectly authoritative Lord. This important consideration is rarely, if ever, considered by skeptics or by philosophers generally. We are undoing this deficiency now, and thereby providing a fair hearing where it is long overdue.

The kind of ultimate trust promoted by a perfectly loving God would be doubly ultimate: *purposively* ultimate and *cognitively* ultimate. *Purposively ultimate trust* in God would be trust in God, but wouldn't be *merely* a means to another end. One might trust God as a means to various other ends (including health, wealth, social standing, or physical survival, as is selfishly emphasized in many avowedly Christian churches), but purposively ultimate trust in God wouldn't depend on such instrumental trust. It would be trust in God as an *end in itself*, for its own sacred value owing to God's sacred value. Such trust would exclude trusting in God *solely* as a means to another end, and accordingly would give God the honor worthy of God inherently in the area of human trust. It thus wouldn't use God *just* as a means to some independent end. The Gift-*Giver* would be the inherent sacred gift in such trust.

Cognitively ultimate, or foundational, trust in God (which entails belief that God exists) could get its undefeated foundational cognitive support, or evidence, for a person from that person's salient *experience*, via attention-attraction, of what is evidently God's perfectly authoritative, trust-inviting call revealed in conscience to that person. This well-founded basic trust would require the absence of undefeated evidential defeaters, such as equally authoritative or illuminating competing calls, but such absence of defeaters wouldn't be an evidential addition to the (positive) foundational cognitive support for trust in God. The mere absence of undefeated defeaters doesn't amount to or entail positive cognitive support. God, on the present scenario, would have ultimate cognitive authority, owing to a perfectly authoritative and loving divine character, and thus would be well-positioned to invite and to support cognitively ultimate human trust in God.

A feature (such as undefeated maximal explanatory power) in virtue of which a claim has positive cognitive status need not itself be part of *the evidence* for that claim. The evidence for the claim would be its undefeated truth-indicator (a truth-indicator that is, for instance, best explained by that claim). We shouldn't confuse *how* something has its truth indicated (say, in virtue of its explanatory power or its being entailed by a well-grounded proposition) with *what*, in particular, indicates its truth (say, a particular experience explained or a particular entailing proposition). One's evidence, E, for a proposition, P, is evidence in virtue of a particular truth-indicating feature, but one's having E for P doesn't entail one's knowing what makes E evidence for P or even what E is evidence in virtue of. In short, one's having evidence doesn't require one's understanding what evidence is. So, a person could have conclusive evidence for believing that God exists without being able to explain what the relevant evidence consists in.

Perhaps Dietrich Bonhoeffer has cognitively ultimate trust in mind when he writes as follows:

> Faith is when the search for certainty out of *visible* evidence is given up. Then it is faith in God and not in the world. The only assurance which faith accepts is the Word [of God] itself, which comes to me through Christ (1978, p. 110, italics mine).

One's moving beyond *visible* evidence or even beyond spectator evidence in general doesn't entail, of course, one's moving beyond *all* evidence. A move beyond all evidence would be a move into cognitive arbitrariness and thus cognitive irrationality. We won't, and shouldn't, go there, as cognitively responsible truth-seekers. In contrast with imperfect humans, a perfectly loving God whose character exemplified worthiness of worship wouldn't need *another* voice, word, or authority to authenticate God's own perfectly authoritative call to humans for the sake of redemption as reconciliation. God's own perfectly authoritative character could supply the needed authoritative authentication. An unlimited regress of needed authoritative voices, words, or standards thus fails to threaten. Skeptics will find no skeptical foothold here; nor should they want one. One's *wanting* to dislodge evidence of a perfectly loving God would signal not truth-seeking but rather a troubling cognitive bias *against* divine reality. Skeptics would thus do well to reconsider their motives, and the rest of us would too.

Cognitively ultimate trust in God is cognitively *foundational* trust in God. We can ask the following question to illuminate such trust. *Whose* voice has, and should have, primary cognitive authority for me: my voice or God's? We can put a similar question in different terms. *Which* personal relationship has, and should have, primary cognitive authority for me: my relationship *with myself* or my relationship *with God*? Philosophers, including skeptics, rarely take up this question, even though the question is vitally important in revealing cognitive priorities. Clearly, if I don't even acknowledge the reality of God's authoritative voice, God's voice won't have primary cognitive

authority *for me*, at least in terms of what I *acknowledge*. The natural skeptical
response is to infer that there is (at least in all likelihood) no voice of God to
be heard at all. That quick response is, however, much too quick, as we'll see
in detail. We need to let the relevant evidence have its way, even apart from
any of our opposing wants and hopes.

The cognitively careful response would ask: am *I* somehow blocking
myself, intentionally or unintentionally, from suitably receiving God's perfectly authoritative and loving call to fellowship? Perhaps I have set myself
against trusting God above all else, owing to a preference to trust *myself*
instead above all else. In that case, I'll be disinclined to welcome and perhaps
even to acknowledge God's authoritative call to fellowship. I may then prefer
to ignore it, given the exalted status I've assigned to myself and my own basic
preferences. Skeptics about God's reality should examine whether they are in
just such a cognitive position relative to God. They must ask, in particular,
whether they suffer a *cognitive* deficiency owing to an implicit bias against,
if not outright resistance to, God's perfect authority in the cognitive domain
and elsewhere. Here, then, is an unfinished but urgent project for skeptics
about divine reality.

Can we reasonably trust skeptics about God's reality to be sincerely open
with regard to receiving evidence of God's authoritative call to humans?
Many people will hesitate to say yes, given an initially plausible suspicion of
bias in skeptics about God's reality. This doesn't settle anything, of course,
but it suggests a problem worthy of attention. Suppose that I in particular
have saliently experienced undefeated evidence of God's authoritative call to
fellowship in a life-enhancing way similarly reported by many morally and
cognitively responsible people. (We could name names, but we won't digress.)
Why, then, should I give cognitive priority to the (now questionable) doubts
about God's reality from skeptics about divine reality? Why should I trust
that skeptics are better evaluators of evidence regarding the reality of God's
call to fellowship, especially given that cognitive modesty seems rare among
skeptics about God's reality? The latter is evidenced by the typically uncritical
ways they wield their own skeptical cognitive standards and demands. Hume
(1780) and Russell (1953) are familiar textbook examples of philosophers
who wield an implausible empiricist spectator standard regarding the issue
of God's existence and who have a substantial heritage among philosophers.
It would seem cognitively unreasonable for me, given my aforementioned
undefeated evidence, to yield relative cognitive authority to skeptics about
divine reality. I would need some special reason to do so, but I have none.
In particular, I have no undefeated defeater of my experiential evidence of
God's call and reality.

At a minimum, if skeptics about God's reality want people reasonably to agree with them, they must identify the needed cognitive support for their skepticism. In particular, they should identify an undefeated defeater of the perfectly authoritative evidence mentioned above, and a mere *opposing belief* won't serve (because a belief can be altogether lacking in supporting evidence). They would also do well to give us a good cognitive reason to believe that their evaluating evidence for the reality of God's authoritative call to fellowship is at least as reliable as that of careful nonskeptics. Even prior to that, they would do well to give us a good cognitive reason to believe that they are genuinely *willing* to listen attentively for God's authoritative call, despite their skeptical tendencies. I, for one, remain doubtful on these fronts with regard to skeptics, at least until the needed evidence is in. Skeptical doubts themselves remain distinctly questionable, and subject to skepticism, regarding their bearing on purposively available authoritative evidence of divine reality. If we're going to give skepticism a worthwhile hearing, as we definitely should, then we will have to raise skeptical questions even about skeptical doubts. Hence the present challenge to skeptics about God's reality. We can now fairly shift the explanatory burden to them. They now have their explanatory cognitive work cut out.

8. VOICE LESSONS

The authoritative call of a perfectly loving God to divine–human fellowship would manifest the power of perfect self-giving love. This would be a call to people to turn from (that is, repent of) their selfish ways through obedient fellowship with an unselfish, perfectly loving God. Apprehending the power of God's call accurately would be to apprehend it *as the perfectly authoritative call from a God worthy of worship*. This would require apprehending it as authoritative over other voices and wills, including over my own voice and will. So, apprehending God's call accurately would require my apprehending that I *should* (be willing to) yield to God's call. I thus couldn't consistently deem my own voice and will as ultimately authoritative, given the supreme authority of God. This could be difficult and humbling for me, if I have an unduly exalted, prideful view of myself or if I'm wedded to prideful despair.

Suppose that I would be unwilling to yield to God's call to fellowship after having apprehended God's call accurately. I may not *want* to yield on this front, because giving ground here would seem to challenge my very self-definition and everything else I have supposedly self-achieved and credited to myself. I would then be left with a serious cognitive-volitional disconnect, because I would then *apprehend* correctly that I *should* yield to God's authoritative call but still remain *unwilling* to yield to God's call. My will would then be out of line with what I have apprehended correctly regarding God's authoritative will, namely, that it is authoritative for myself and other humans. In that case, I may very well try to sidestep the disconnect by denying that I have actually apprehended God's call. I would then purchase cognitive-volitional coherence at the price of denying what I have actually apprehended. A skeptic in such a position wouldn't be a reliable guide to cognitive matters concerning (evidence of) the reality of God's call. Many skeptics may be in such a compromised position, owing to an unwillingness to yield to any divine call.

Someone might propose that *acknowledging* God's call as authoritative is itself an act of yielding one's will to God. The problem, however, is that yielding one's will to God in the manner required by a perfectly loving God is *not* entailed by one's merely acknowledging God (or, God's call) as authoritative. *Acknowledging* something regarding God doesn't entail, and so isn't the same as, *yielding one's will to God with an attitude of obedience* toward God's will. An authoritative perfectly loving God would rightly avoid trivializing or otherwise devaluing divine revelation in the presence of people unwilling to yield to God's will. This would fit with the sharp injunction of the Sermon on the Mount not to "cast pearls before swine," that is, not to treat divine revelation as if it were dispensable without loss rather than sacred. It would be in the best interest of everyone, including any person not morally ready to obey God's perfectly loving will, for God not to devalue God's character or self-revelation as if it were a disposable commodity.

Nobody would gain, not even skeptics, if evidence of divine reality were readily at our disposal, to be used on *our* preferred terms, as if God should pander to us cognitively. A perfectly loving God wouldn't be cognitively promiscuous in this way, and that would be a good divine trait, even for skeptics. Given a divine commitment to redeem humans, God would have and pursue the redemptive aim to transform our selfish wills into wills genuinely loving toward all persons, even enemies. This aim would inform the character of divine revelation for our own good in such a way that cognitive promiscuity of any kind would be excluded from divine revelation. In this regard, God would differ from many humans in the way they superficially reveal themselves, and this feature of God would be praiseworthy and good for all concerned. Divine evidence would be designed not for mere spectators but for humans in need of an authoritative divine challenge toward repentance and divine–human volitional fellowship.

A perfectly loving God, given a redemptive aim toward humans, would try to supply noncoercively what we truly *need*, however much we resist it or don't want it. Indeed, this effort would seek to break down our selfish willfulness and fear even in the cognitive domain, where we set up cognitive standards to serve our own imperfect purposes and thereby block divine purposes. For our own good, as suggested, divine self-revelation would come through perfectly authoritative evidence for the sake of volitional knowledge of God as perfectly authoritative Lord. The stretching of our cognitive comfort zone would thus be mandatory, and good too. Perhaps, then, we would even find true gain in the temporary pain of cognitive discomfort.

Proper, obedient reception of perfectly authoritative evidence from God would avoid the aforementioned cognitive-volitional disconnect. God's will (promoting unselfish love in place of our selfishness) would thus become mine too as I yield my will to God's will in volitional knowledge of God as perfectly authoritative Lord. Until skeptics about God's reality have dealt carefully and honestly with the option of perfectly authoritative evidence beyond spectator evidence, we should be altogether skeptical about their skepticism. We should doubt meanwhile that they are in a suitable position to report on the reality of God or on purposively available evidence of the reality of God. They would do well, accordingly, to supply evidence that they aren't in a position akin to that of the willful child who refuses to receive the challenging available parental evidence regarding his troubled situation.

Clearly, "out of mind" doesn't entail "out of reality." "Out of mind and evidence" may stem just from a volitional shortcoming on the part of a person reluctant to receive purposively available evidence for what it is intended to be: in the present case, an evident divine challenge toward human redemption as divine–human reconciliation. It's time that this option get a fair hearing among skeptics and philosophers generally. Otherwise, a cognitive blind spot will continue to threaten suitable reception of available evidence.

Skeptics about God's reality typically fail to acknowledge the kind of cognitive difference we should expect between a perfectly loving God (if God exists) and ourselves (if we exist). In particular, they typically assume, if implicitly, that since we humans are content with spectator evidence as a basis for ordinary knowledge, God would be too, *even regarding knowledge of God's reality*. Skeptics thereby neglect cognitively important features of a perfectly authoritative and loving divine character, such as the fact that a redemptive God would seek, with perfect authority, to transform selfish human wills into unselfish, perfectly loving wills, without pretending that humans are just innocent spectators. To the extent that skeptics neglect this, they neglect a central place for purposively available authoritative evidence and volitional knowledge regarding divine reality. Traditional philosophy, including traditional skepticism about God's reality, is marked and crippled by this serious neglect. In identifying this cognitive blind spot, we may hope that it soon gets the attention it deserves. Meanwhile, we may also plausibly remain skeptical about skepticism about God's reality.

Skeptics will likely object as follows. If I, for instance, am willing to submit to God's will, as volitional knowledge of God's reality requires, then I may very well be *biased in favor* of theism in a way that taints me cognitively. I can't then be trusted as a reliable evaluator of God's call to fellowship, because I am listening for God's call in a way that makes me readily *creative* rather than just receptive. This line of objection seems natural, but it's too quick to succeed or even to threaten. Willingness to submit to God's will doesn't entail willingness, or any other tendency, to *fabricate evidence* of God's reality in the absence of such evidence. We have no basis for merging, or even correlating, these two separate phenomena.

Consider a salient analogy. I may like the taste of bitter dark chocolate (say, with 85% cocoa), and willingly seek it in a candy bar. This, however, wouldn't lead me to fabricate (evidence of) the taste if instead I tasted something else that I didn't like, such as sweet milk chocolate (say, with just 30% cocoa). Returning to evidence of God's reality, we can see that the skeptics in question would need to argue that willingness to submit to God's will yields a tendency to fabricate evidence of divine reality in the absence of such evidence. This is a tall order indeed, and I see no reason to think that skeptics will discharge it. In addition, the suggestion of fabrication has no real cogency. Religious frauds are typically *unwilling* to submit to a perfectly loving God's will. They characteristically put themselves first, and their god (of health, wealth, fame, or worldly power, for instance) becomes just a means to their own selfish ends. It doesn't take much discernment to identify a religious fraud, and we have plenty of opportunities.

Some skeptics about God's reality share Thomas Nagel's worry that the existence of God would pose a serious "cosmic authority problem" for us. They, like Nagel, thus hope that God doesn't exist. As Nagel claims: "I want atheism to be true. . . . I hope there is no God! I don't want there to be a God; I don't want the universe to be like that" (1997, p. 130). This strikingly bold attitude misses the tragedy of the desired situation, the tragedy of a missed opportunity of a *lastingly* good life supported by a perfectly loving God. Something has gone wrong here, and some people don't even notice this tragedy. We face yet another blind spot in this connection. Perhaps wayward volitional leanings have blocked good cognitive judgment. I submit that they have, in fact.

It would be a pathetic, demonstrably false God who *didn't* pose a cosmic authority problem for us humans. Part of the status of being *God*, after all, would be that God has unique, perfect authority over the created world, including humans. If God aimed to redeem humans via reconciliation, God would need to try to correct our selfish ways. So, God would need to exercise noncoercive corrective authority for our own good. Fear of God's existence seems widespread among humans, and seems to arise from our human fear of losing our own supposed authority over our lives. A philosopher might think of this as fear of losing "autonomy," whatever that slippery term connotes. Such fear, by way of antidote, could use a perfectly authoritative, corrective word from God. Still, the person embracing such fear may rebuff any corrective word, choosing death instead. Tragically, one can consistently choose death here, including whatever "autonomy" goes with it. The opposing evidence or arguments against choosing death may get no real foothold in a person's life, given human willfulness. Some philosophers may wish otherwise, but evidence and arguments won't always save the day or even the person at the end of the day.

God must ultimately provide the purposively available authoritative evidence of God's reality, and that's a good thing. The big question now is this: are skeptics willing to receive such purposively available evidence? In any case, we have found no easily generalizable support for skepticism about the reality of God. Even *if* a person were to lack conclusive evidence for God's reality, this person would have no ready way to generalize to the truth of skepticism about God *for people in general.* Salient undefeated evidence of God's reality possessed by nonskeptics wouldn't be challenged at all by there being an individual (or even a group) lacking such evidence (as long as the evidence is purposively available to the latter). More specifically, the fact that one person lacks a religious experience doesn't challenge (the veracity of) the religious experience *had by others.* It seems just desperate or cognitively confused to suggest otherwise, and this would signal cognitive weakness that hinders good judgment.

We should always ask *why* a skeptical person lacks evidence of God's reality, in a manner that allows for a cognitive shortcoming in the skeptic. Specifically, we should ask whether that person is genuinely open to receiving purposively available authoritative evidence and volitional knowledge regarding divine reality. If the person isn't genuinely open, we should question whether the person is in a good cognitive position to recommend skepticism about God's reality. If the person is open to receiving perfectly authoritative evidence, we should wait to see if his days as a skeptic are numbered. In either case, skepticism about God's reality poses no general or immediate threat for all concerned.

Proponents of skepticism now owe us an undefeated defeater of purposively available authoritative evidence of divine reality. We are, in any case, no longer playing a spectator sport, since we are ourselves candidates for divine judgment, and this bears directly on the divine evidence we should expect. Skeptics will doubtless look for a defeater in the fact of the elusiveness of evidence of divine reality, and thus the topic of divine hiddenness emerges now. In connection with this topic, then, we turn to cognitive idolatry and its needed antidote: knowledge of divine reality as *volitional attunement* to divine reality. We'll find in this antidote a new conclusive argument for divine reality, at least for those with eyes to see and ears to hear.

2

Knowing as Attunement

We have seen in Chapter 1 that volitional knowledge of a perfectly loving God's reality would be significantly different from our knowing, for instance, that pomegranates exist. Pomegranates are wonderful in many ways, but a God worthy of worship would be even more wonderful in even more ways. Questions about knowledge of *God's* reality always invite questions about what *kind* of God we have in mind.

Are we talking about the tenuous absentee God of deism or minimal theism? Or, alternatively, are we talking about the authoritatively convicting and transformingly loving God of Abraham, Isaac, Jacob, and Jesus? The latter God claims to be the gracious but elusive *personal* God who is a consuming fire against selfishness and all other evil. As a result, this God, even if incognito, claims to love humans in a way that requires divine suffering for us, even in the crucifixion of God's Son, in order to remake us noncoercively in the divine image of self-giving love toward all persons, including enemies.

This chapter identifies major obstacles, so-called "idols," that block recognition of a perfectly loving God's reality. Skeptics may desire to invoke such obstacles as defeaters of evidence of divine reality, but we'll see that such a desire would be misguided. This chapter also elucidates some reasonable divine purposes that would motivate divine elusiveness. In doing so, it clarifies the kind of purposively available evidence of divine reality introduced in the Introduction and Chapter 1, and paves the way for the promised cognitive revolution in matters of knowing God's reality.

1. RATIONALITY AND EXPLANATION

In shying away from a robust conception of God, for the sake of a notion of God from deism or mere theism, philosophers have neglected the distinctive cognitive resources of Jewish and Christian theism in its commitment to a perfectly authoritative and loving God. They have thus overlooked what would be a central divine purpose in human knowledge of God's reality: reconciliation of humans to God in divine corrective love and fellowship. They have also overlooked an epistemology of robust theism that challenges human knowers in the way most needed, in connection with human idolatry, including self-idolatry, that fosters selfishness and blocks reconciliation of humans to God.

The pervasive philosophical retreat from a robust conception of God as perfectly authoritative and loving, ongoing at least since the time of Descartes and the Enlightenment, has contributed much to the demise of Jewish and Christian theism in the western academy. We won't digress, however, to that widely neglected historical topic (on which see Buckley 1987, 2004). We now have more urgent goals than historical assessment, since we ourselves are at stake, living dangerously and fleetingly in the teeth of destructive selfishness and impending death. The epistemology of robust theism, we'll see, has urgent significance beyond the casual speculation typical of professional philosophy.

Our topic is, by any careful count, the world's oldest and largest profession and hobby: idolatry. It's older than even what most people think is the oldest profession. We are, one might argue, leading experts at idolatry; indeed, we excel at it, and (adding insult to injury) we apparently enjoy it. Although seemingly ancient and esoteric, like Sodom and Gomorrah, idolatry seems nonetheless current and popular. Ever a threat, idolatry may be easily overlooked and conveniently ignored, but we'll bring it to center stage in an area where it's seldom, if ever, mentioned: epistemology, particularly regarding knowledge of God's reality. For a very rough start, we may regard idolatry as reliance on an inadequate substitute for God.

Sooner or later, with more or less seriousness, philosophers face the question whether God exists. In doing so, they join the rest of humanity in considering an issue of first importance. Always beware, however, of philosophers bearing theological gifts, as such gifts often come with a high price. The price influences one's mindset, in particular one's *expectations*, regarding divine reality in ways that may be unexamined, unsustainable, or unreasonable. It's thus important to ask this question: What *are* our expectations regarding God? These expectations heavily influence our commitments regarding God, and they may say more about *us*, including our own values and other commitments, than about *God*. In addition, these expectations may prevent us from having suitable "eyes to see and ears to hear" genuine self-revelation from a perfectly authoritative and loving God.

Do we expect certain things of God (*if* God exists) such that those things evidently fail to obtain, thereby calling God's existence or authority into question? Do we, for instance, expect God to entertain us cognitively, with superficial signs and wonders or with dreams and ecstatic experiences? At any rate, what, if anything, *cognitively or rationally grounds* our expectations regarding God? Perhaps our expectations clash with a perfectly loving God's own aim to bring us freely to acknowledge and gratefully to trust God (rather than false gods) as the ultimate source of our flourishing. We'll see how the distinctive nature of the Jewish and Christian God has special implications for familiar questions about God's elusive existence and for cognitive idolatry.

For philosophers, among others, the innocent-looking question whether God *exists* moves quickly to the thorny epistemological question whether it is (cognitively) *rational* for us to believe that God exists. The latter question, although common and engaging, demands immediate attention to its slippery terms "rational" and "God." Otherwise, it's an ill-formed question unworthy of our limited time. Much philosophical and popular discussion of it flounders, however, with inadequately defined terms.

The world-weary term "rational" encompasses, at least, *prudential* rationality (concerning what is prudent in belief, intention, or action), *moral* rationality (concerning what is morally good, right, or praiseworthy in belief, intention, or action), and *epistemic,* or *cognitive,* rationality (concerning the kind of evidence appropriate to *knowledge* that a belief is true). Still other species of rationality compete for our attention, but we'll attend to epistemic rationality, the kind suitable for the justification condition for knowledge (on which see Moser 1989, chap. 5, Moser 1993, chap. 4). Epistemic rationality, as suggested in Chapter 1, doesn't require the kind of deductively valid proof characteristic of logic and mathematics. Otherwise, there wouldn't be much rationality or knowledge at all in the sciences or in ordinary empirical belief-formation (such as our widely tested and well-founded belief that pomegranate juice is red). An exclusively deductivist approach to evidence would exclude much of our evidence that has remarkable undefeated explanatory power, including in the sciences.

Epistemic rationality, as Chapter 1 noted, can depend on an *inference to a best available undefeated explanation* of our whole range of evidence found in our experience and other evidence. Much epistemically rational belief found in the natural and social sciences and in ordinary perceptual commitments depends on such explanatory value. Likewise, epistemically rational belief that God exists can benefit from the fact that this belief plays an indispensable role in a best available undefeated explanation of our whole range of experience and other evidence. More specifically, for such benefit, theistic belief must (a) answer in a fitting (or, congruent) manner, relative to the features of what one evidently experiences, certain crucial why-questions about what one evidently experiences (particularly, why one's evident experience is as it is, in terms of its evident experienced features) and (b) do so in an undefeated way superior to, or at least as good as, any competing available explanation. (See Moser 1989 for the details of this approach and its bearing on experience-based justification and knowledge; cf. Wiebe 2004 for an application of explanatory considerations to theistic belief.)

Aiming for the cognitively best in inquiry, we rightly pursue true beliefs contributing to a best available undefeated explanation of the world, including the whole range of our experience and other evidence. In doing so, we respect holistic features of justification, owing to possible defeaters from any area of our experience and other evidence. Still, we'll see that propositional inference and argument by themselves can't adequately underwrite epistemically reasonable belief that a personal perfectly loving God exists. The cognitive foundation lies elsewhere.

The term "God" has been used to signify everyone from the mythical Zeus of Greece to the ravenous Thor of Scandinavia to the wretched Jim Jones of Guyana to the righteously gracious Yahweh of Israel. So, Chapter 1 introduced some needed refinement of this otherwise unrefined term. In keeping with a longstanding tradition within monotheism, we have introduced the term "God" as a *preeminent, maximally honorific title* that requires of its holder (a) inherent worthiness of worship and of full life commitment and thus (b) self-sufficient authoritative and moral perfection and (c) a perfectly loving character toward all persons, even toward enemies. This semantical approach to "God," as Chapter 1 noted, doesn't settle the ontological issue whether God actually exists, since the title might be conceptually coherent but satisfied by no one at all. That is, the title might connote while failing to denote. In that case, theism would be but fiction, and cognitively worthy of rejection, even though intelligible fiction.

Since God must be inherently worthy of worship and full trust, God must be altogether morally good, a God of unflagging righteousness and perfect love. A morally corrupt all-powerful being might merit our self-protective *fear*, but would not be worthy of our worship and full trust. So, not just any unstoppable bully can satisfy the job description for "God." Even an all-powerful being who is altogether just, or fair, but nonetheless unloving toward enemies wouldn't fit the bill. Many aspiring candidates thus fall by the wayside, with no hope of recovery. People often set the standard for God much too low, but the ideal standard remains perfectionistic and thus truly demanding and strongly exclusive toward candidates. Initially viable candidates are at best few and far between, even though history is littered with imposters.

A being worthy of worship and full trust must be perfectly compassionate toward all people, even enemies; otherwise, a serious moral failing would interfere. So, God must have *all-inclusive* compassion toward other people, and thus must be willing to suffer for the moral good of all those needing help, at least as long as people are genuinely open to such help. This holds true regardless of whether all or even most people will actually accept God's help. Do we have any evidence of such strange universal compassion-in-action, past or present? (On the Jewish and Christian theme of God's suffering and its relation to divine love, see Fiddes 1988 and Fretheim 1984, chap. 9.)

Scanning world history with due care and openness, we find that an initially plausible candidate for the role of perfectly authoritative and compassionate God is Yahweh, the God of Jewish and Christian theism and the avowed Father of that disturbing Galilean Jewish outcast, Jesus of Nazareth. The God of Jesus allegedly possesses, exhibits, and promotes love of enemies as well as friends and mere acquaintances. We can acknowledge, nonetheless, that some seriously confused followers of Yahweh have attributed vicious attitudes, commands, and actions, including hate of others, to Yahweh for their own self-serving ends. (For ample evidence for the latter, see Paul Hanson 1982, 1986; cf. Psalms 5:5, 11:5.) Indeed, we must acknowledge that the history of Judaism and Christianity, including the teaching of various biblical writers, fails to portray Yahweh uniformly as perfectly compassionate toward all others, even though Jesus himself did portray God in that way, as represented in the Sermon on the Mount/Plain and elsewhere (thus correcting the harmful mindset of Psalms 5:5, 11:5, for example; cf. Matt. 5:43–48). Bad counterfeits, in any case, don't destroy the genuine article. If they did, we would have no valuables at all.

Let's consider *evidence*, or *epistemic justification*, for acknowledging the reality of the perfectly authoritative and loving Jewish and Christian God as represented by Jesus. We should consider that acknowledgment of this God's existence may play a crucial role in a best available undefeated explanation of the world, including our own emergence and ongoing status as morally accountable persons in the world. Acknowledgment of God's existence may remove or at least temper what Bertrand Russell (1903) has plausibly called "the inexhaustible mystery of existence" of the world.

One unavoidable explanation-seeking question is: why is there a material world *rather than no such world at all?* Another such question is: why is there the present law-governed material world, hospitable to some extent to the emergence of such moral agents as human persons, *rather than a world markedly different?* There might have been a world of just chaotic short-lived events, like disorganized fireworks, and nothing else. We humans wouldn't be here to talk about it, of course, but that wouldn't preclude such a chaotic world. Evidently, the material world need not have been hospitable at all to the emergence of human persons.

The existence of goal-directed intentions in a perfectly loving God can underwrite plausible answers to some relevant explanation-seeking questions. More specifically, acknowledgment of the existence of divine intentions regarding the world can thus temper Russell's supposedly unexplainable mystery of the world's existence. Acknowledgment of the existence of God as creator and sustainer of the material world could figure crucially in a best available undefeated explanation of (a) why there is a material world rather than no such world at all and (b) why there is the present law-governed material world, hospitable to some extent to the emergence of human persons, rather than a significantly different world. (For helpful discussion relevant to (b) and Darwinian biology, see Miller 1999, chaps. 7–8.)

As an all-powerful creative agent, God would have *goal-directed causal powers* that can underwrite the needed explanation and thereby temper Russell's mystery. Whatever its overall cognitive status, then, theism may have noteworthy explanatory power regarding the world and its personal inhabitants. Even so, an inference to a best available explanation, as commonly understood, will yield at most *theoretical* support for theistic belief, with no authoritative volitional challenge to humans. Faith in the Jewish and Christian God, however, reportedly enjoys support beyond mere theoretical support, in virtue of an authoritative volitional challenge from God. At least, such faith is rarely offered as just an explanatory hypothesis based on theoretical considerations (cf. Cottingham 2005, pp. 21–6). We'll see that there is in fact more to offer in this connection, in terms of firsthand authoritative evidence that delivers a crucial volitional challenge to humans.

Even though acknowledgment of God's existence may temper the mystery of the material world's existence, it will *not* remove all explanatory mystery about existence. Doggedly, mystery chases theism all the way up the gnarly tree of explanation. If, for example, we can coherently imagine that God doesn't exist (and it seems that we can, without too much cerebral effort), then if God actually exists, we are left with the mystery of God's existence, and *God* evidently is too. If God exists, we could then ask why reality is such that God exists rather than being such that God doesn't exist. If God's existence doesn't underwrite the explanation of this feature of reality, then explanatory mystery ensues, perhaps even for God. (A principle of sufficient reason may thereby be threatened, but God's omniscience wouldn't be threatened, because it doesn't follow that there would be truths not known by God. Furthermore, the question at hand doesn't presume that God had a beginning.)

On this approach, theists exchange the mystery of the world's existence for the mystery of God's existence (not to be confused with an ill-formed issue about the *origin* of God's existence). In addition, the lesson doesn't depend on any technical notion of possibility or conceivability.

One might wonder what theists really gain here. Even if theological mystery seems more palatable than cosmological mystery to some people, it is mystery still, and it trims the explanatory sails of theism. A similar lesson follows from the influential view that God exists *necessarily*. On that view, too, we reach a point where explanation runs out, where ontology outstrips available explanation. Even necessitarians about God's existence, in the tradition of Anselm, must grant that some parts of theistic ontology don't enjoy explanation. Mystery does indeed dog theism, and perhaps God, too. Still, not all explanation is lost, and mystery need not be a cause for lament in the end. *Ultimate* existence may reside where explanation runs out and mystery flourishes. At least our ability to imagine nonexistence (coherently, of course) suggests as much.

Some relevant explanation-seeking questions focus on us as *morally responsible agents*. For example, why are there such self-determining (to some extent) beings as human persons with the remarkable feature of conscious free agency (to some extent)? We sometimes act, for better or worse, on *intentions* to achieve our ends, and thereby distinguish ourselves, decisively, from the unconscious material world. The difference is not just that we can *think*; it also includes our being able to *act* intentionally, with an end in view (see Mele and Moser 1994).

We are *purposive* agents who often act in a goal-directed manner. Witness your undertaking the reading of this page, which is no fluke of nature, I hope. (My writing this, in any case, certainly seems intentional, and I have no reason whatever to think otherwise.) Our lives thus manifest self-determining *actions*, and not just *happenings*. This is an astonishing fact about us, a fact that calls for careful explanation. Some philosophers, as expected, intend to deny this fact, but in so doing they exemplify it. It's always dangerous business to intend or undertake to deny the reality of intending or undertaking. The result reflects badly on the enterprise itself, as is common when self-referential woes threaten. (For relevant discussion, see Moser 1993, chap. 5.)

Why are there such remarkable beings as free, self-determining (to some extent) human agents at all? This question concerns why such beings arrived on the scene *in the first place*, not why they have persisted. In addition, it primarily concerns the psychological rather than biological make-up of such beings. *Perhaps* their arrival on the scene was ultimately just an astonishing surprise of nature, without any intelligent guidance at all. Many people, including Russell, find this suggested by a combination of materialism and Darwinian biology. Acknowledgment of the Jewish and Christian God's existence, in contrast, enables us to answer to some extent our otherwise mysterious question in a way that is at least coherent and avoids appeal to an ultimate surprise of unintelligent nature. According to Jewish and Christian theism, God brought about (perhaps very indirectly and even *partly* by means of random mutation and natural destruction) human beings in God's own image of conscious free agency, in order to enable those beings to sustain loving relationships with God and with each other. Such theism affirms that we are thus under-creators made somehow in the image of the original creator.

Of course, we *might* be just a surprise of unintelligent, uncaring nature, but then again we *might* be dreaming all of our lives, too. Seeking refuge in physical variation unguided by intelligence, such nontheists as Russell show their willingness to make a significantly risky commitment (some might say a "faith" commitment) to the world-making efficacy of such physical variation, thereby avoiding acknowledgment of God's existence. So, popular opinion about theism notwithstanding, the risky leap of "faith" may actually be on the *other* foot, on the foot of theorists invoking physical variation unguided by intelligence as world-making. This point doesn't settle any controversy, but it does indicate that an appeal to physical variation unguided by intelligence here may be highly risky indeed, perhaps even more risky than theism or at least as risky as theism. All global theorizing may carry some risk of error in the end, and the same holds for any fallible theorizing. We shouldn't uncritically assume, in any case, that any risk in theorizing is inherently bad.

A perfectly loving God, being morally impeccable, would seek what is morally perfect for us as long as there's divine hope for us, thereby giving us an opportunity to receive, without coercion, God's kind of moral goodness. God, in other words, would seek to be a *redeemer* of humans as long as humans are genuinely open to redemption as reconciliation to God. God's redemption would enable us, through volitional knowledge of God as authoritative Lord, to be rescued without coercion from our moral deficiencies and thereby to become morally like God in fellowship with God. In this regard, we would be able to share in God's perfect moral nature.

The opportunity in question, being inherently moral, would be *volitional* and not just intellectual. It would enable us to have our *wills* transformed, not just our intellects (that is, our thoughts and beliefs). So, the kind of knowledge of God's reality valued by a perfectly loving God would be volitionally transformative rather than merely intellectual. It would seek a change of human will, of volitional orientation, that exceeds belief formation, contemplation, insight, enlightenment, and sensory experience. It would involve us individually as *agents*, not just as thinkers, in personal and moral relation to God. Such agent-to-agent knowledge would suitably relate those being transformed, morally as well as personally, to their noncoercive personal and divine source of transformation.

Moral perfection in relationships among human agents requires self-giving compassion and interpersonal trust for the sake of the moral goodness of all involved. So, any being worthy of the preeminent title "God" must consistently promote such compassion and trust among humans. A perfectly loving God, accordingly, would aim to transform such typically selfish agents as humans into morally new people remade after the unselfish character of God, at least as long as humans are open to such transformation. In keeping with this aim, we humans would be required to become agents of God's purportedly all-inclusive kingdom of unselfish love rather than agents of our own exclusive clans, gangs, and families. "Family" values, of course, can be evil indeed when wealthy families ignore poor outsiders and hoard resources just for their own protection and pleasure. Cruel poverty is an inevitable result. God's way would be strikingly different.

As morally impeccable, the true God would work in human history to encourage human agents to seek God's kind of moral perfection via volitionally knowing God's reality, including divine goodness. More specifically, a perfectly loving God would seek an all-inclusive community of people guided by volitionally knowing divine reality. Our volitionally knowing God's reality (at God's desired time) would be central to God's moral project, because such knowing would enable the kind of personal guidance, fellowship, and transformation crucial to human renewal toward God's moral character. God could be morally *just* in judging and even destroying human agents who have intentionally and ultimately rejected God's unselfish life of goodness, but God wouldn't be gracious in withholding merciful, forgiving compassion toward wayward humans ultimately open to divine redemption as reconciliation. Tragically, not all humans seem to be genuinely open to such divine redemption. Still, we may hope that this is only apparent.

Some parts of the prophetic tradition of ancient Israel (on which see Heschel 1962 and von Rad 1965) exhibit patterns of behavior, instruction, and prophetic promise that are morally extraordinary in promoting unselfish love and justice and in offering redemption to all nations and people, even enemies. These patterns, one might argue, are best explained by the Hebraic view (suggested, for example, in Genesis 12:3, 22:15–18, 28:13–14) that a morally serious perfectly loving God has indeed chosen a certain unlikely group of people in order to transform, morally and spiritually, all the nations and people of the world. The prophetic promise of divine redemption offered to all nations is distinctive and even striking among ancient religious movements. Ancient Israel thus offers some historical evidence, however fallible and mixed, of a redeeming God who seeks to liberate a lowly tribal community from its self-destructive ways and to encourage this community to lead outsiders to God for redemption (on which see Herberg 1951, chaps. 17–19, and Paul Hanson 1986). This, of course, doesn't settle the question of God's existence by any means, but it is noteworthy for our deliberations on the question.

2. ROBUST THEISM

Perhaps Jewish and Christian theism plays a crucial role in a best available undefeated explanation of the world's existence, including our existence as responsible agents, and thereby gains notable epistemic support. Even so, that view would yield at most *volitionally thin theism*: the view that it is epistemically rational, for people with suitable undefeated evidence, to believe *that* God exists. Such theism is volitionally thin indeed, as even avowed enemies of God can rationally believe that God exists and endorse volitionally thin theism. One can believe that God exists but hate God. Even the demons believe and shudder, according to the Epistle of James. Indeed, it would be odd to hate God but not believe that God exists, because we shouldn't waste time on hating a being whom we don't consider real. In any case, volitionally thin theism lacks a volitional challenge and volitional redirection for humans; it thus lacks redemptive value on its own.

A chief deficiency of ours as selfish humans in relation to a perfectly loving God would be in our *volitional moral orientation* regarding divine authority, or lordship, over our lives. So, desiring genuine reconciliation of humans to God, a perfectly loving God wouldn't settle for volitionally thin theism but would promote *volitionally robust theism*: the view that, given suitable undefeated evidence of God's reality, we epistemically should lovingly *believe in*, or trust, God *as the authoritative Lord of our lives*. Volitionally robust theism entails volitionally thin theism but, unlike the latter, it epistemically requires, given a person's having suitable evidence, a *life commitment* to a personal Lord, beyond rational *belief that* God exists. This Lord wouldn't be the conclusion of an argument (since a personal God wouldn't be a proposition or a claim of any kind), but instead would be the personal creator and sustainer of any person offering an argument or even making a claim.

Chapter 1 introduced a widely neglected notion of *volitional* knowing of divine reality. Our volitionally knowing God as our personal Lord would figure in our being reconciled to God by requiring us willingly to trust in God, and thereby to yield our wills to God, as the supreme authority for our lives. In such knowing, we would acknowledge, at least implicitly, our moral accountability to God and even *rely* on God as our ultimate moral authority and guide. Such knowing isn't a matter of mere justified assent to a true proposition, because it entails knowing God as authoritative Lord *in the second-person*, as morally supreme "You," rather than as a nonpersonal propositional object of human knowledge.

Divine lordship entails supreme moral leadership, and moral leadership entails an authoritative call to moral accountability and moral direction. This would be an authoritative call to moral *redirection* and *transformation* in the case of selfish human recipients. Our volitionally knowing God as Lord would require our sincerely committing *ourselves* to God as follows: "Not my will be done, but Your will be done," "Not my kingdom come, but Your kingdom come." Such knowing would thus follow a path through Gethsemane to the obedient, self-giving cross of Jesus, because it depends on our volitional sensitivity and submission to the will of God and hence on our dying to our selfishness and everything else contrary to God. We would thus come to know God not in our own cognitive strength but rather in our weakness relative to the priority of God's perfectly loving will. (On the important theme of human volitional weakness in Jewish and Christian theism, see Savage 1996 and Dales 1994; cf. Johnson 1999.)

Volitionally robust theism acknowledges that a perfectly loving God would call us to moral transformation, away from our selfishness and toward the perfectly unselfish, loving character of God. This authoritative call would come ultimately through personal conscience, and perhaps it would rely on a message brought by other people. However it comes, we would reveal our response, whether positive, negative, or indifferent, by our subsequent actions (on which see Farmer 1946). Do we, however, have a moral or cognitive *right* to know God's reality? In particular, are we morally or cognitively *entitled* to know that God exists without volitionally knowing God *as Lord*, as the perfectly authoritative agent over our lives, including our intellectual and moral lives? Some people uncritically assume so, but this is at best questionable.

Who is entitled to decide how we humans may know God's reality: humans or God? If humans get the nod, *which* humans? Given that we are completely inferior to God, if God exists, could *we* reasonably make demands on God in favor of *our* preferred ways of knowing God's reality? The question seems merely rhetorical, as the answer is obvious. Still, many people proceed as if we have a right to know God's reality on our own preferred terms. This is, however, nothing more than a self-serving assumption. Nothing beyond misguided human demands would require that God supply knowledge of God's reality on our preferred terms. God would evidently owe us no such thing at all, despite brash human expectations to the contrary. We do well to explore this fact.

God would owe us *nothing* beyond fidelity to a perfectly loving character and to the divine promises stemming from such a character, and such fidelity wouldn't result from anything we have earned. On sincere reflection we see that we are in no position, morally or cognitively, to make evidential demands of God beyond such fidelity. Nothing requires that God allow us to have *propositional* knowledge that God exists apart from our *volitional* knowledge of God as the authoritative Lord of our lives. The two ideally emerge together, although philosophers and others have a bad habit of neglecting the key redemptive role of purposively available evidence and volitional knowledge of God's reality.

God could be perfectly loving in supplying purposively available evidence of God's existence that challenges recipients to yield to volitional knowledge of divine reality. A perfectly loving God, as noted previously, would have no need to offer mere propositional evidence or knowledge that God exists. We have no right, furthermore, to demand evidence of God's reality that fails to challenge us to undergo volitional transformation toward God's perfectly loving character. So, God's purportedly corrective hiding from a committed volitionally *casual*, or *indifferent*, inquirer wouldn't count at all against the reality of God's existence. Somehow philosophers have overlooked this important consideration.

God's ways of self-manifestation and of imparting vital knowledge of divine reality wouldn't necessarily meet our natural expectations. For example, we might not naturally expect a divine offer of human redemption by God's *grace*, or free gift, rather than by human *earning* intended to obligate God to aid us. Divine grace has loomed large in Jewish and Christian accounts of redemption, but it has rarely emerged as significant in treatments of *knowledge* of God's reality. This is a strange asymmetry, and it needs correction, sooner rather than later. (Chapter 3 will add further elaboration to what follows here, in this connection.) A perfectly loving God's offering vital knowledge of God's reality to humans would be truly gracious, a genuine *gift* calling for grateful reception. Genuine love is inherently a matter of self-giving by gift rather than a demand for earning that obligates one to give a gift, although divine love may call for grateful obedience that is not to be confused with earning something from God.

How we may know God's reality would depend on what God lovingly wants *for* us and *from* us; likewise for our receiving purposively available evidence of divine reality, that is, evidence offered in accordance with the purposes of a perfectly loving God. We should begin cognitive questions and claims about

God's existence with this fact about evidence and knowledge of divine reality, even though it's widely neglected among philosophers and others. Primarily a perfectly loving God would want us to become, in fellowship with God, genuinely loving as God is, because this would enable volitional reconciliation of humans to God as Lord. As a result, we wayward humans would come to know God as authoritative Lord only if we acknowledged our unworthiness of knowing God's reality, given our selfish failure to love as God loves.

It is illuminating to ask about the relevant motivational attitudes of people inquiring about God's reality. Certainly, a perfectly loving God would attend to such attitudes, and would, as authoritative, turn the tables on human inquirers with some profound challenges for humans. A probing question such as "Who do you think I am?" would be fitting from a God seeking to redeem humans (on which see Farmer 1946). We might expect such an interrogative reversal, because in the presence of a perfectly authoritative and loving God, *we* (rather than God) would properly be under question and even judgment. This figures directly in the cognitive shift under development. It also highlights the importance of "you–I" (from God's perspective) and "I–You" (from a human perspective) personal interaction in firsthand human volitional knowledge of God's reality.

The question becomes this: *who* exactly is inquiring about God's reality? More specifically, what are our *intentions* in seeking to obtain knowledge of God's reality? What do we aim to do with such vital knowledge? Do we aim to use it for our own honor and self-promotion, treating it as self-credit rather than as an unearned redemptive gift? Do we have indifference toward, or even a bias against, volitionally robust theism, in particular against volitional knowledge of God as an authoritative personal Lord who lovingly holds us morally accountable and expects faithful obedience and fellowship from us? I suspect that, in the grips of selfishness, we often do have such indifference. I also suspect that this could obstruct our receiving purposively available evidence of divine reality. At least this consideration merits our careful attention.

3. FILIAL KNOWLEDGE

A tenable epistemology of Jewish and Christian theism will disallow God's being trivialized or otherwise devalued as an undemanding object of our convenient speculation. It will promote instead a distinctive species of volitional knowledge of God's reality: that is, *filial* knowledge of God as one's perfectly authoritative and loving *Father* to whom one yields as God's child in response to a perfectly authoritative and loving call to repentance and fellowship.

On this conception, God is the lovingly commanding personal agent to whom we are ultimately responsible, even as knowers. Filial knowledge of God would give us volitional knowledge of a supreme *personal* subject, or agent, worthy of worship and obedience, not of a nonpersonal object for casual reflection. (On some important cognitive and moral implications of God as personal agent, see Oman 1917, Farmer 1935, 1942, and Brunner 1938; cf. Partridge 1998.)

Filial knowledge of God wouldn't be theoretical knowledge of a mere "first cause," "ultimate power," "ground of being," or "best explanation." It would instead be *morally challenging* firsthand knowledge of a personal and authoritative divine Father who expects and commands faithful love and fellowship by way of our appropriating redemption as reconciliation to God. Such knowledge would include our being correctively convicted, or judged, and found unworthy by the standard of God's perfectly authoritative love, including love of enemies. God's perfectly loving will would thus aim to meet, convict, and noncoercively redirect our selfish wills toward volitional fellowship with the unselfish God who can teach us, and empower us with, genuine unselfish love. Both sides of this cognitive divine–human relationship, then, would be inherently person-oriented and volitional.

Filial knowledge of God would be *reconciling* personal knowledge whereby we enter, if imperfectly, into a (volitional) *child–parent* relationship involving volitional fellowship with God as our perfectly loving Father. Such knowledge would be personally and morally transforming, not impersonally abstract or morally impotent. It would be communicated, via self-revelation, by a personal God who demands wholehearted life commitment from humans, even if such commitment is beyond our own human powers and needs empowerment from God. This firsthand knowledge of a robustly personal God would require inherently *personal* evidence, such as evidence of a personal will, rather than mere nonpersonal reasons. Filial knowledge of God, then, wouldn't be just a true conclusion endorsed on the basis of a good inference. It includes irreducibly personal agent-to-agent reconciliation through volitional fellowship.

Sound arguments, however truth-preserving their inferences, don't supply the kind of personal *power* that would be available in filial knowledge of God. This would be *God's* personal power of authoritative self-giving love as our creator, liberator, motivator, sustainer, and volitional/spiritual Father. Filial knowledge of God would require our commitment to participate as faithful children in God's power and purposes, ideally wholeheartedly, with all that we are and have. It would thus be purposive knowledge as suitably grounded commitment to loving and obedient discipleship toward an authoritative personal agent with definite expectations of us for the sake of divine–human reconciliation. It thus wouldn't be mere well-grounded intellectual assent to true propositions, but would rather be inherently *person*-relational and *will*-changing. We are thus introducing a notion of knowledge foreign to much philosophy and science, on the basis of what would be God's distinctive character and redemptive purpose (at least so long as God has hope for redeeming humans). Genuine divine love, like a surgeon's sharp healing knife, would cut deep into receptive human wills, and the corresponding volitional knowledge of this love's personal source would be equally transformative. The open issue, now cognitively relevant, is whether we are willing to undergo divine love's healing surgery. Philosophers rarely ask, perhaps because the potential fallout is too unsettling and it precludes doing the epistemology of theism with God kept at arm's length.

Moving further away from abstractions about God, let's briefly consider filial knowledge in connection with Jesus, with regard to his controversial suggestion of being God's beloved Son (on which see Fitzmyer 1985). This was no matter of mere intellectual assent to a proposition. Instead, it evidently involved a profound experiential relationship calling for talk of God as *Father* (or, in Aramaic, *Abba*), in keeping with some of the Jewish scriptures (for example, Isa. 63:16). Jesus's avowed experience of being God's Son is clearly expressed in his prayers, including the Lord's Prayer and the (initially) conflicted prayer in Gethsemane (see Matt. 6:9, Mk. 14:36; cf. Jeremias 1967, 2002). Indeed, Jesus seems to have regarded *filial prayer* toward God, in submissive response to God's intervening perfect love, as an ideal avenue to filial knowledge of God's reality. Such prayer is primarily a matter of asking and hearing what *God* as our loving Father would want *from us* rather than what we would want from God. This kind of volitionally humble prayer figures importantly in the issue of what kind of purposively available evidence of God's reality we should expect and pursue. It's worth recalling that *we* wouldn't have the authority to set the cognitive terms here, although a perfectly loving God would.

Filial knowledge of a perfectly loving God's reality, as suggested, would be irreducibly *person-relational* in virtue of being *will-relational*. We come to know another human person's reality firsthand (not just the reality of a human body) by actively relating to that person in *personal volitional interaction*. Likewise, we would come to know God's reality firsthand through personal volitional interaction. In filial knowledge of God's reality, we would become morally (and thus volitionally) accountable to God as our loving Father. Through conscience, in particular, we could be personally convicted on moral grounds of our waywardness (from the standard of divine love) by the intervening personal will of God. Such conviction wouldn't be coercively incapable of rejection, however, as we could ignore, suppress, or disregard it.

Given that a perfectly loving God would be inherently loving toward all people, we would have filial knowledge of this God's reality firsthand only through our apprehending firsthand the reality of this God's love. Filial knowledge of God's reality, like volitional knowledge of God's reality, involves a *directness* of knowledge of divine reality that makes it irreducible to knowledge that a divine being exists. It would also be irreducible to knowledge that the premises and conclusion of a valid theological argument are true. The relevant directness, as Chapter 1 suggested, involves an "I–You" volitional interaction between humans and God that is absent from traditional arguments for God's existence, including those of mainline natural theology. Although God's volitional role in such an interaction can be mediated through a human will, it wouldn't be reducible to a human will.

A personal God who loves, commands, and seeks to reconcile even enemies wouldn't be the silent God of deism or of much natural theology. As a result, the Jewish and Christian scriptures don't rely on what philosophers and theologians call "arguments of natural theology." The Jewish and Christian God appears instead as actively, if elusively, *self-revealing* in a way that makes the traditional arguments of natural theology unnecessary and even irrelevant. A God who is a perfectly authoritative and loving Lord would seek to lead humans, and thus would authoritatively *call* us in certain directions at the appropriate time (at least as long as there's hope for redemption). In particular, God would *command* wayward humans to repent of selfishness, as no argument of natural theology could, and this would result in our being judged at least for our failure to be suitably loving or otherwise obedient toward God. Judgment from divine love would seek to be corrective rather than condemning (that is, merely destructive) of us, but it would be judgment nonetheless. It would call us up short, for our own good, and seek to redirect us, again for our own good. In omitting this consideration, natural theology tends to domesticate and even to trivialize God.

We couldn't have filial knowledge of God if we were seriously dishonest about our *moral* standing relative to a perfectly loving God. The genuine reconciliation between ourselves and God required by filial knowledge would call for honest awareness of *our* need for such reconciliation. So, a perfectly loving God would try to convict us of this need by prompting our awareness of our having fallen short, in selfishness, of the kind of unselfish love central to a filial relationship of volitional fellowship with God. For the sake of our own good, God as reconciler would seek to function at the motivational core of our lives, and not just at the intellectual or emotional periphery. So, God would seek to be found by us, *and to find us,* at a level of considerable moral and personal depth in our lives, rather than at the surface. Indeed, the self-reflective honesty and unselfish love that would be sought and fostered in us by God work at the motivational core of a life *or not at all.*

We can readily acknowledge that "signs and wonders," dreams and ecstatic experiences, and abstract philosophical arguments are motivationally inadequate avenues to God's reality, given what would be God's redemptive purposes. A perfectly loving God would lead us deeper than such morally superficial phenomena, to a level of moral motivational depth in God's presence, perhaps through our facing serious frustration of our will or even impending death. God would lead us to such depth by convicting us of our casual ingratitude, moral dullness, selfish indifference, unwarranted pride, and self-indulgent fear, among other moral deficiencies. Promoting filial knowledge, God as reconciler would offer to change us by convicting us of the stark contrast between these two options: what we are on our own (selfish and then dead) and what we could be (unselfish and lastingly alive) as willing participants in God's redemptive program of filial reconciliation and fellowship.

Left to our own devices, of course, we are all soon dead and buried, however we may try to obscure this by directing attention elsewhere. (Pascal's *Pensées* identifies some of our typical diversionary tactics on this front; our own lives do too.) Our self-supplied resources, cognitive and otherwise, bring us finally to nought, leaving us with no genuine hope for our own lasting future. In this respect, time would only be on God's side, and our impending death could serve as God's firm wake-up call to us regarding our obvious self-insufficiency. In particular, our forthcoming death prompts this urgent question: what, at bottom, are we living *for* in our temporally finite lives, and is it worthwhile, even on our own considered values? Given the dismal long-term fate of our own devices, we evidently need a redemptive *word,* or call, from God, and not the kind of alleged spectator evidence of God's existence associated with thin theism, deism, or traditional natural theology. (For Jewish and Christian endorsement of this need, see, for instance, Deut. 30:11–15 and Rom. 10:6–8.) As a result, we must be willing to be *receptive* toward the evident reality of the needed call and to obey it when it comes to us. Such a response would put us in a filial, child-to-parent mode of fellowship relative to God.

We naturally resist going to self-reflective moral depth in our lives, relative to a standard of perfect love, because doing so is painful, self-effacing, and humbling, given the convictions of conscience. It rarely brings a professional promotion, a salary increase, or even a civic award, and it sometimes brings the exact opposite. It may entail exclusion by our peers when the results are socially challenging or awkward. (Which competitive "professional," for instance, would actually trust a colleague committed to a strange invisible and uncontrollable being called "God" who loves even enemies, including competitors? That would seem just unprofessional and naive, and perhaps bad for competition, too.) In addition, we typically want to be accountable ultimately only to ourselves and to our own preferred moral and cognitive standards. We may say that we *would* be accountable to God *if only* the proper evidence were at hand. Even so, *we* then conveniently set the terms (such as extreme empiricist, deductivist, or rationalist terms) for proper evidence, thereby controlling the overall outcome to a considerable degree. This ploy only obscures any intended intervention by a perfectly authoritative and loving God.

God as reconciler, we have noted, would need to be a benevolent reconstructive surgeon toward wayward humans. This would include divine use of a humanly uncomfortable procedure of deep and sincere conviction, via conscience, of moral shortcoming on our part, in order to begin a desired process of filial reconciliation and fellowship. We must be brought low indeed, even in our own self-evaluation, if a perfectly loving God is to raise us up from our selfishness and pridefulness. A person dominated by selfishness and pridefulness couldn't have genuine volitional fellowship with a perfectly loving, unselfish God. Analogously, on just the human level, Adolf Hitler couldn't have had genuine volitional fellowship with Mother Teresa of Calcutta, because the two were moving in diametrically opposed moral directions, and Hitler wouldn't yield at all to the unselfish love represented by Mother Teresa. Love of enemies wasn't an option by his dangerously dim moral lights, even though he had evil delusions of doing "God's" will. A "God" of our own selfish and prideful making is, of course, no God at all, owing to unworthiness of worship.

A perfectly authoritative and loving God would aim to work as an internal, convicting authority and assurer who makes willing people morally new with a default inclination toward unselfish love and with an assurance that makes Cartesian certainty as logical indubitability seem beside the point. (On the role of God as convicting authority and assurer, see Forsyth 1913 and Camfield 1934.) Advancing filial knowledge, God would invite us to become children of God, whereby God becomes our authoritative Father and Lord whose unselfish love is shared by us as our default motivator. As assuring reconciler, God would offer a unique kind of personal evidential assurance as a gift and not as a tool for abusive or prideful human control. God, after all, would have no need of a cognitive sledgehammer. (We sometimes only think *we* do.) A perfectly loving God would ultimately seek divine–human reconciliation and fellowship, not intimidation, coercion, or condemnation. Otherwise, "God" wouldn't be God, but would be at most a powerful thug. The "God" of many people is just such a thug, but we won't name names (see Juergensmeyer 2003). A particular kind of idolatry, we'll see, is especially inimical to filial and volitional knowledge of God's reality.

4. COGNITIVE IDOLATRY

Volitionally thin theism, focusing on theoretical knowledge that God exists, can obscure the importance of volitionally knowing God as the authoritative personal Lord who calls us to a change of lordship, mindset, and moral direction. Oversimplifications of God (for example, as merely sentimental, friendly, harsh, or distant) can be similarly obscuring, and can even make a self-controllable idol of "God" (where "God," of course, wouldn't be the true God). So, even devout theism can be idolatrous, if the ultimate devotion is toward something other than the true, perfectly authoritative and loving God (such as a moral *law* or a morally distorted *interpretation* of God's purposes, such as one that portrays divine sovereignty as limiting divine love to "the elect").

For our own good, we would be unable to master God either as just another undemanding object of human knowledge, as a manipulatable possession, or as a meritorious reward. As we should expect, God wouldn't be ours to control; similarly for purposively available knowledge and conclusive evidence of God's reality. God as volitionally known would reveal God's knowledge *of us* (including our will), and thereby seek to transform us (including our will) in authoritative love toward God's unselfish character, with due respect for our freedom. Our knowledge *about* God and our quest for it threaten to become idols if divorced from volitional, filial knowledge of God as authoritative Lord over God's obedient children. Volitionally robust theism, in contrast with thin theism, offers a safeguard against this threat.

Idolatry is, at bottom, our not letting the true, perfectly authoritative and loving God be Lord in our lives. It is commitment to something other than the true God in a way that devalues the true God, particularly God's rightful preeminence and authority. It is inherently a rejection, in attitude or in deed, of God's supreme authority and a quest for self-definition, self-importance, and self-fulfillment *on our own terms*. Idolatry flouts the serious challenge we would have from the true God to be free of self-indulgent fear, self-exaltation, self-authority, and selfishness in general. It exchanges, implicitly or explicitly, the supremacy of God over one's life for something inferior to God. Of course, if God doesn't actually exist, idolatry is no longer a real threat; so, my unqualified remarks about idolatry call for the qualifier, "if God actually exists," to be supplied by readers. (See Johnson 1990, chap. 4, Mackay 1969, Halbertal and Margalit 1992, and especially Meadors 2006 on the devious and destructive ways of idolatry.)

In idolatry we seek, if implicitly, a kind of independence of God's perfect authority over us. We thus deny, if implicitly, our status as *dependent* creatures of the true God. In idolatry, we aren't satisfied with being secondary, dependent co-creators who honor God as the only self-sufficient preeminent authority. We devalue God's perfect authority with something other than God. Typically we reassign, in effect, God's supreme authority to *ourselves*, thereby seeking to be ultimately *self*-governing and *self*-defining. This involves a kind of *self*-assertion that disregards the supreme authority of God. Such self-assertion is, of course, as tenuous and ephemeral as the human self behind the assertion. It will soon perish along with that self while the true God would endure lastingly. The ways of human self-assertion are short-lived indeed, and they can obscure purposively available evidence of God's reality, including God's supreme authority.

In *cognitive* idolatry, we deny, if implicitly, God's supreme authority in commending ways of knowing God's reality. Just as God would properly be supremely authoritative in commending ways of human *acting*, so also God would merit supremacy in commending ways of *knowing* God's reality. The latter commending wouldn't be arbitrary, but instead would be anchored in the inherent nature of the One to be known, including God's perfectly authoritative and loving nature. In cognitive idolatry, we rely on a standard for knowledge that disregards the primacy of volitional knowledge of God as authoritative Lord. Such idolatry rests on a cognitive standard, whether empiricist, deductivist, rationalist, or some hybrid, that doesn't let God be authoritative Lord over our knowing God's reality.

Cognitive idolatry typically aims to protect one's lifestyle from serious challenge by the God who would authoritatively and lovingly call, judge, and seek to reconcile humans. In disallowing the primacy of volitional knowledge of God as authoritative Lord, such idolatry favors *at most* theoretical knowledge of God as an undemanding object of human knowledge. Cognitive idolatry exploits epistemological standards, if implicitly, to refuse to let God be supremely authoritative in a person's life, initially in the cognitive area of life. A cosmic authority problem regarding a perfectly authoritative and loving God lies behind much cognitive idolatry and, for that matter, idolatry in general. In cognitive idolatry, we seek to control the terms for knowing God's reality in a way that devalues God's preeminent authority. The resulting potential for human harm is serious indeed, because such idolatry obscures the needed divine solution to the human predicament of destructive selfishness and impending death.

A prominent kind of cognitive idolatry is *the idolatry of volitionally neutral support*. Such idolatry includes our demanding conclusive evidence of God's existence regardless of the direction of our own will relative to God's will. We thereby place ourselves in the position of a supposedly neutral judge over God's reality without requiring ourselves even to be open to commit sincerely to God as Lord of our lives, given suitable volition-sensitive, purposively available evidence. A similar kind of idolatry is opposed in Isaiah 58, where Yahweh reportedly complains as follows about his people in Israel: "... they seek me daily, and delight to know my ways, as if they were a nation that did righteousness and did not forsake the ordinance of their God." Note the reported shared desire to *know* God's ways without willingness to submit to God's morally perfect will. This is a recipe for blocking volitional and filial knowledge of a perfectly loving God who seeks redemption as divine–human volitional reconciliation and fellowship.

As an antidote to the idolatry of volitionally neutral support, Jewish and Christian theism calls for an epistemology that acknowledges the propriety of purposively available *authoritative* evidence of divine reality. (See Chapter 1 on authoritative vs. spectator evidence and on volitional knowing of divine reality.) Conclusive firsthand evidence of divine reality for us would be purposively available authoritative evidence that comes with a personal call to trust and to obey a perfectly authoritative God. This would be, after all, a *personal* God who authoritatively calls humans to repentance, fidelity, obedience, and fellowship in unselfish love. This would be a God who commands people, for their own good, to become humbly loving as God is loving, in fellowship with God. The result would be a divine call away from human selfishness and toward unselfish love toward other people, even enemies. The ultimate divine aim would be the reconciliation of everyone under the supreme authority of God's perfectly loving character.

Questions about the *supreme* cognitive authority for a person concern (a) what (or who) is worthy to be trusted as one's supreme source of evidence and knowledge and (b) what (or whom) one actually trusts as one's supreme source of evidence and knowledge. Jewish and Christian theism identifies a critical human choice between idolatry and trust in God as one's supreme authority, including a choice between cognitive idolatry and trust in God as one's supreme cognitive authority. One's trust in God as authoritative Lord who *will* fulfill divine promises extends in its content beyond the present to the future, and is never fully *causally determined* by past or present evidence, even when conclusively *cognitively grounded* in past and present evidence. Such trust accommodates both the genuine agency of humans to withhold judgment in the face of divine evidence and the genuine agency of God to call people in ways that (causally) go beyond historical precedent. (Witness the novel, reportedly divine call to Jesus to die as God's beloved Son on a criminal's Roman cross.)

Trust in God, according to Jewish and Christian theism, should esteem God as the only ultimate source of power for breaking human bondage to self-destructive idols, whatever they happen to be. Whether cognitive or noncognitive, our idols would encroach on God's rightful supreme authority over us. Even so, God would seek to exercise idol-breaking power noncoercively, and such power would stem from God's authoritative self-giving love toward us that invites us, via trust in God, to be free from our selfish and self-destructive fears, in volitional fellowship with God.

We typically favor idols over a perfectly authoritative and loving God given our penchant for maintaining authority, or lordship, over our lives. Our typical attitude is thus: I will live my life *my* way, to get *what* I want, *when* I want it. We thereby exalt ourselves even over a perfectly loving God. We then risk losing our self-control to our being controlled by idols, from which we seek success, happiness, comfort, health, wealth, honor, and self-approval. We exchange any acknowledgment of God's supreme authority for an inadequate substitute. Accordingly, we naturally give primary, if not exclusive, value to *controllable* knowledge rather than to volitional or filial knowledge of divine reality dependent on the gracious redemptive offer of an *uncontrollable* God. Indeed, the human obsession with self-control over one's circumstances runs afoul of God's calling us to moral transformation through trusting *God* as authoritative Lord of our lives. Since the desired self-control of one's circumstances is rarely, if ever, available, selfish fear of loss emerges and dominates. We then founder and lose in fear, however much we struggle to appear in control.

Despite our typical quest for control, we tend to trivialize, devalue, or otherwise take for granted, at least eventually, what we can control or what is conveniently available to us. Our controlling available evidence for God's reality would be, in effect, to control God in virtue of controlling God's self-manifestation. For our own good, however, a perfectly loving God wouldn't be controlled, trivialized, devalued, or taken for granted by us in terms of humanly controlled evidence of divine reality. Since we don't have control of available evidence of God's reality, we can't preclude God's hiding from us at times. Indeed, such hiding should be expected, given our self-destructive tendencies and our resulting need of God's corrective love. We need to consider, then, the elusive love of a God who would hide as well as seek in order to reconcile humans to God via volitional transformation of humans.

We shall see that divine elusive love would call for a widely neglected kind of human *attunement* to God for the sake of our knowing God's reality.

Cognitive idolatry, as suggested, can obscure available evidence of the reality of a perfectly loving God. We need to refine our understanding of suitable evidence and knowledge of God's reality in the context of divine elusiveness as an antidote to human cognitive idolatry. We'll see that a perfectly loving God who comes and goes incognito would supply a special kind of evidence in light of divine redemptive purposes. In particular, this evidence would call for human *attunement* to God's character and purposes. We'll see how this works.

Ideally, evidence and assurance regarding God's reality would come to us firsthand, from God's direct self-revelation to us rather than from just our own reasoning. A perfectly authoritative and loving God would supply conclusive evidence of divine reality in an inherently personal authoritative manner, because the divine aim would be to indicate the reality of an inherently personal, perfectly authoritative and loving divine agent to whom we should wholeheartedly submit. God's inherently personal conclusive evidence wouldn't be transferable, reproducible, or manipulatable by us for selfish, self-crediting ends in the way that the traditional arguments of natural theology are. Otherwise, this uniquely important evidence would easily be devalued by selfish humans who aren't volitionally ready for it.

As noted previously, God's authoritatively calling people to volitional and filial knowledge of divine reality and love would be respectful of human agency and thus rejectable and not coercive. Recipients of God's call would need, then, to be sincerely volitionally open to God's call to redemptive transforming love in order to receive volitional and filial knowledge of divine reality. They would need to be volitionally receptive of a significant change away from selfishness and toward unselfish love, the kind of love inherent to God's character. Still, if God aimed to call us to a new life of fellowship in divine love, why would God hide from us at all? We need some clarification, since many philosophers take the elusiveness of evidence of divine reality to yield an undefeated defeater of such evidence.

5. DIVINE HIDING

Here's a helpful statement of a common concern regarding divine elusiveness and hiding.

> One might be tempted to see in ... ambivalence [of the universe, between naturalism and theism] a vindication of atheism. For how could such an ambiguous universe be the work of perfect love and perfect power? Could this be a way to love and express love, to leave the loved one in bewildering

uncertainty over the very existence of the allegedly loving God? Would we not have here a refined weapon of psychological torture? That is: if the situation is ambivalent, it is *not* ambivalent, since its ambivalence is a conclusive argument against the existence of the Christian God (Hepburn 1963, p. 50).

We need some explanation, then, of divine elusiveness and the resulting ambiguity of the universe, given the claim that God is perfectly loving. Otherwise, we have a potential defeater of the evidence for God's existence.

Bringing the Hebrew prophetic tradition to a revolutionary climax, Jesus remarked that the pure in heart will see God. He also suggested, in keeping with the Hebrew prophetic tradition, that God "hides" divine ways from ungrateful holdouts and reveals God's reality and ways to those humbly open to God's program of redemptive love even for enemies (see Lk. 10:21–22; cf. Matt. 11:25–27). The upshot is that God hides from those who insist on being in charge even over God and God's ways. (On the recurring theme of divine hiding in the Hebrew scriptures, see Balentine 1983 and Terrien 1978.)

How could a perfectly loving God, who reportedly aims to communicate with people, *fail* to be manifested in such a way that removes all reasonable human doubt about God's reality? Many people, including many philosophers, deny that this is possible. Various writers of the Hebrew scriptures and the New Testament, however, present a perfectly loving God who sometimes hides from people. God's reality, according to these writers, is sometimes less than transparent to people and even open to sincere doubt. We might have thought, at least initially, that a perfectly loving God's existence, if real, would be beyond reasonable doubt for all cognitively normal adult humans. God's existence, however, is not beyond reasonable doubt according to many cognitively normal adult humans. So, according to these people, we may reasonably deny that God exists or at least reasonably refrain from believing that God exists. Some cognitively normal humans, of course, don't believe that God exists, and they claim not to have adequate evidence (for epistemically reasonable belief) that God exists. Would a perfectly loving God permit such doubt about God's existence, especially if such doubt is harmful to people?

We should ask whether the people in question are *able* to acquire evidence of God's reality. If they are, then divine hiddenness isn't a basis for atheism or even agnosticism (contrary to Hepburn 1963 and Schellenberg 1993, 2007, among many others). If the God who on occasion hides has left adequate *purposively available* evidence of God's reality, including indicators of such evidence, for all people, then theism will be cognitively unscathed by divine hiding. People often look in the wrong places for such evidence, as we'll see later in this chapter. The important point now, however, is that God's hiding from some people, at least on occasion, wouldn't automatically recommend atheism or agnosticism. At a minimum, the available evidence, including purposively available evidence, in favor of God's existence merits equal consideration. God's hiding from some people, in any case, wouldn't entail either (i) God's hiding from *all* people always or (ii) *everyone's* lacking adequate evidence for God's existence or even (iii) anyone's lacking *available* evidence for God's existence. (We saw an analogue of this point at the end of Chapter 1.)

Conceivably, God hides on occasion from some people for various perfectly loving divine purposes. At least the following arise: (a) to teach people to yearn for, and thus eventually to value wholeheartedly and above all else, personal volitional fellowship with God, (b) to strengthen grateful trust in God even when times look altogether bleak, (c) to remove human complacency toward God and God's redemptive purposes, (d) to shatter destructively prideful human self-reliance, and (e) to prevent people who aren't ready for fellowship with God from explicitly rejecting God. This list is by no means exhaustive; nor should we assume that an exhaustive list is available to humans. Even so, we can readily imagine that in some cases of divine hiding, some people would apprehend the ultimate emptiness of life without God's presence, and thus heighten their attentiveness to matters regarding God. A perfectly loving God could use this consideration for the good of at least some humans.

A particularly troubling instance of God's hiding underlies the distressing plea of Jesus on the cross: "My God, my God, why have you forsaken me?" (Mk. 15:34; cf. Matt. 27:46). Reportedly, God hid from Jesus at the height of his excruciating suffering from Roman crucifixion. As a result of his suffering and God's hiding, Jesus perhaps learned deeper trust in his often unpredictable but nonetheless perfectly loving Father. Not all of God's hiding, at any rate, would aim to judge human rebellion. Divine hiding would seek, however, to advance God's redemptive purpose of divine–human reconciliation, including divine–human volitional fellowship. That purpose wouldn't be satisfied by human knowledge that God exists; its satisfaction extends beyond such propositional knowledge to volitional knowledge of divine reality.

God's hiding on occasion from people could be constructively challenging for them from a moral point of view. One's taking the presence of God for granted, as if it were automatically at one's personal disposal, would entail a kind of presumed self-reliance or self-importance incompatible with sincerely entrusting oneself to God. Unlike a doting parent, a perfectly authoritative and loving God wouldn't be servile toward us or always at our beck and call. Similarly, divine perfect love, unlike so-called romantic love, wouldn't be obsequious or fawning, but would seek to be morally transforming for human good, even if gradually and painstakingly. In taking God for granted, people would neglect the supreme and indispensable value of filial, reconciling knowledge of God's reality. As a result, a perfectly loving God would sometimes hide in ways that allow people to have serious doubts about God, even at times when they apparently need God's felt presence (see, for example, Psalm 30:7). In doing so, God would offer a distinctive wake-up call, via divine silence, to unduly complacent people.

Part of God's redemptive plan would be to remove, without coercion, human moral indifference of any degree toward God, which often stems from a misguided presumption of self-reliance. God's hiding for this purpose, of course, shouldn't be confused with God's nonexistence, cognitively doubtful existence, or total abandonment of humans. Temporary divine hiding can instill in humans proper recognition of the moral gravity of indifference toward God and God's expectations of humans. God's temporary hiding can also cultivate humility and faithful patience in humans, yielding rare human virtue in fulfilling the recurring Jewish and Christian injunction, "Wait for the Lord!" (Psalm 27:14; cf. Isa. 30:18). God's perfect love, as noted, aims to be morally transforming and edifying, not servile or entertaining. A perfectly loving God would seek humble, perfectly loving servants, not self-confident elitists or know-it-alls. In doing so, God would seek wholehearted commitment from humans, since anything less would fail to honor God aright.

God's hiding at times would prevent human profaning of what is sacred, particularly, the self-manifestation of God. Such hiding would agree with the blunt command of Jesus, in the Sermon on the Mount, not to throw pearls before swine. Still, God's restraint in self-revelation and in manifestation of power would leave room for people freely to mock and to reject God. God's redemptive love, in other words, would allow people the freedom to make mistakes, even horribly cruel mistakes. Witness the torturous Roman crucifixion of Jesus.

Sometimes God's hiding would be a serious judgment against human rebellion (see Deut. 31:16–19, 32:19–20, Isa. 59:2), a judgment typically designed to prompt corrective repentance. Even so, it could sometimes fail to prompt genuine repentance, and this lack of success could result from recalcitrant exercise of human free will. God, in that case, wouldn't get God's own way, as the divine will would be frustrated by wayward humans. In other words, a perfectly loving God's redemptive purpose would allow for God's will (that *all* people be redeemed) to be frustrated by human misuse of free will. This is evidently the price of genuine love as opposed to volitional coercion in any purported divine redemption of humans. In addition, the denial of such human free will would implicate God causally in all manner of evil, thus robbing God of worthiness of worship. (In this connection, my approach to divine hiding contrasts sharply with the predestinarian Calvinist approach of Jonathan Edwards, on which see Wainwright 2002, 1995, chap. 1.)

We should steer clear of some influential approaches to divine hiding, including the following Freedom and Proper-Motivation Responses. Proponents of the Freedom Response contend that God would hide in order to enable people *freely* to love, trust, and obey God. In other words: "... if God were incontrovertibly revealed, then our belief would be constrained, our allegiance forced, and no place would be left for free and responsible decision whether to walk in God's ways and to entrust oneself to him in faith" (Hepburn, 1963, p. 50; cf. Murray 1993). In the interest of forming truly loving relationships with people, God wouldn't force people to respond in a certain way. In fact, the coercion of genuine unselfish *love* seems impossible, since it would rob the one loved of genuine agency in the needed response. Love that can't be rejected is evidently not genuine love at all. So, God, as genuinely loving, would hide in order to avoid coercion of humans.

The Freedom Response invites a simple question: couldn't God supply clear, or at least (somewhat) less obscure, self-revelation without abolishing human freedom in responding to that revelation? God could, it seems, be significantly less elusive while keeping our freedom intact, even our freedom to deny that God exists. *Some* striking revelations of God's power would indeed overwhelm us in ways that stifle our freedom (and perhaps even our very existence), but the removal of divine hiddenness seems not to require any such stifling revelation. So, we should question this exclusive disjunction: either God would be hidden or human freedom in responding to God would be lost. Proponents of the Freedom Response owe us a convincing case for that disjunction; otherwise, the Freedom Response doesn't offer an adequate account of divine hiddenness. It's doubtful that the needed case is forthcoming. In addition, even if God were incontrovertibly revealed, people could still freely reject *allegiance* to God. Acknowledgment of God's existence doesn't entail, of course, a commitment to obey, to trust, or to love God.

Supporters of the Proper-Motivation Response hold that God would hide in order to discourage a human response based on improper motives. For instance, God wouldn't want people to respond to divine self-revelation out of selfish fear or arrogance. God would want people to develop fellowship with God out of sound motives, including genuine unselfish love. God's self-revelation without hiding, however, would prompt us to have selfish fear or arrogance in our response. In the interest of discouraging such fear and arrogance, God would hide. (For relevant discussion, see Pascal's *Pensées* and Swinburne 1981, p. 156, 1992, p. 95.)

The Proper-Motivation Response is troubled by this issue: couldn't God supply a (somewhat) less obscure self-revelation without eliciting improper motives, such as selfish fear and arrogance, in human response to that revelation? It seems that God could be noticeably less elusive while not increasing the danger of our responding out of bad motives. *Some* astonishing revelations of God's power would perhaps prompt many people to respond out of selfish fear rather than love, but the removal of divine hiddenness seems not to require any such fear-creating divine revelation. So, we should refrain from endorsing this exclusive disjunction: either God would be hidden or humans would be (more) likely to respond to God out of improper motives. Supporters of the Proper-Motivation Response need a reasonable case for that disjunction; otherwise, their response won't adequately explain divine hiddenness. It isn't clear, however, that the needed case is forthcoming.

Perhaps the Proper-Motivation Response would fare better if we considered some positive motivational virtues that would be cultivated by divine hiddenness. For instance, one might propose that God would hide in order to prompt sincerity in us about the wretchedness of life on our own, in the absence of God. Such sincerity may lead us to search for God contritely, humbly, and even passionately. If God's self-revelation were very clear, however, then both our sense of our wretchedness without God and our sense of the genuine challenges of a truly passionate faith would be objectionably reduced. God would hide, then, to elicit positive motivational virtues of the kind noted.

Trouble emerges once again for the Proper-Motivation Response. Consider a world where God's existence is less obscure. *Must* that world be less susceptible to human pursuit of God that is contrite, humble, and passionate? It seems not. The mere fact of less obscurity in God's self-revelation wouldn't seem to challenge contrite, humble, and passionate seeking after God. God could readily promote such seeking, with no added difficulty, in an environment of less obscure divine revelation. At least, supporters of the Proper-Motivation Response must find an explanation of why this isn't so, if they are to account adequately for divine hiddenness. Meanwhile, we need to look elsewhere to illuminate divine hiddenness.

A sound approach to the problem of divine hiding includes the *Divine Purposes Reply*: God would restrain divine manifestations, at least for a time, to at least some humans in order to enhance satisfaction of God's own diverse perfectly authoritative and loving purposes regarding humans. The Divine Purposes Reply allows that the amount and kind of God's self-revelation can

vary among people, even *if* there is a common minimal self-revelation purposively available on God's terms to all people. The variation in divine self-
manifestation would result from God's purposes, or intentions, regarding
recipients of divine revelation. If these purposes are perfectly morally righteous and loving, then God can be perfectly morally righteous and loving in
giving varied self-revelation, even elusive varied self-revelation, to humans.
The myth of a cognitively promiscuous, bland, uniform, predictable, or convenient God regarding divine self-manifestation should thus die easily.

God could hide for *various* specific purposes, not just one purpose, just
as God could allow evil for various purposes. Still, the exact details of God's
purposes could sometimes be unclear to us, as we should expect given God's
transcendent cognitive superiority relative to our meager cognitive position.
(The book of Job famously suggests that one may learn this the hard way,
with much self-supported resistance; cf. Ford 2007, chaps. 3–4.) When we
are unclear on such details of divine purpose, we could nonetheless know
and reasonably trust the God who hides for a time, if this God has lovingly
intervened elsewhere in our experience with conclusive evidence. Our having
conclusive evidence of God's existence doesn't require our being able to
explain all of God's intentions and actions, including God's specific purposes
in hiding at times or in allowing evil at times.

The Divine Purposes Reply acknowledges that God could hide on occasion
for reasons other than to judge human rebellion. As long as there's hope for
us, a perfectly loving God would aim to motivate us, via divine love rather
than via extraneous factors or coercion, to welcome our becoming loving as
God is loving, in fellowship with God. So, we should avoid assuming that
God's main aim would be to have us come to believe that God exists regardless
of our volitional discord with God. We should acknowledge that we may not
be ready to handle divine self-revelation aright, and that this may call for
elusiveness in divine self-manifestation.

Some of God's hiding may result from our own (culpable) failure to be
properly receptive to God. Consider this transliterated non-English sentence:

Tov vayashar adonai; tov layisrael elohim; tov vayashar hadavar.

Perhaps most readers don't apprehend the semantic significance of this sentence. In fact, most readers may not even be confident that this sentence
actually has such significance, while some readers may have a vague and ten-
tative glimpse of some of its semantic significance. The problem, however,
lies not in the sentence itself but rather in the overall perspective of beliefs,
intentions, desires, and other attitudes a person brings to this sentence. Call
this perspective a *psychological attitude-set.*

The problem of perceiving meaning in the sentence lies in one's lack of appropriate sensitivity to ancient Hebrew, particularly to the Sephardic rendition of ancient Hebrew. The problem could also include one's *unwillingness* or at least lack of willingness to learn to understand ancient Hebrew. So, the reception of some significant evidence depends on the psychological attitude-set of people who are potential recipients. More specifically, failure to receive some evidence comes from psychological facts, including volitional facts, about the intended *recipients* of the evidence, rather than from flaws in the available evidence itself. The transliterated sentence is fully meaningful and thus altogether above semantic reproach. We can't plausibly blame its message or messenger for its not being received as semantically significant.

An analogous lesson emerges. Some people have a psychological attitude-set closed or even opposed to a divine redemptive program of all-inclusive reconciliation by a gift of divine–human fellowship in unselfish love. Their attitude-set, in guiding what they attend to and how they interpret what they attend to, obscures or even blocks for them purposively available evidence of the reality of God. The volitionally sensitive evidence of God's reality is, I contend, actually available, just as our transliterated Hebrew sentence is semantically significant. People need, however, appropriate, God-sensitive "ears to hear and eyes to see" the available evidence aright, and this requires their willingness to receive the evidence for what it is intended to be: an evident authoritative divine call, via conscience, to repentance and divine–human fellowship.

Additional authoritative evidence of divine reality, beyond the initial call, can emerge as people become willing to be changed by that evidence toward God's moral character. This willingness to be changed will yield a change of psychological attitude-set that guides what one attends to in available evidence and how one interprets what is thus attended to. The correct interpretation of purposively available evidence of divine reality will identify, among other things, the actual divine purpose(s) intended to be served by that evidence. In yielding to those purposes, we acquire evidence of their being realized in us in a way that testifies to the real transformative power of the divine agent behind the purposively available authoritative evidence.

The needed human change for redemptive purposes involves the motivational direction of our overall lives, including our life-priorities, not just our intellectual assent. In particular, on the basis of purposively available authoritative evidence, it involves our committing in intention, and not just thought, to receive the evidence in question for what it is intended to be and then to become loving toward all people, even our enemies, in fellowship with a God of perfect love. This certainly won't win any popularity contest for us, since many vengeful people hate others who love their enemies, that is, the enemies of those vengeful people. The tragic principle seems to be this: I'll hate you as long as you don't hate those whom I hate.

We must become attuned to purposively available evidence of a perfectly loving God's unique self-revelation if we are to receive such evidence in its fullness. Becoming thus attuned need not happen all at once, but it would begin, in response to an authoritative divine call, with a volitional commitment to receive that call for what it is intended to be and then to undergo change toward God's perfectly loving character in fellowship with God. We need to clarify this neglected theme of attunement, in order to understand the core of volitional and filial knowledge of divine reality.

6. ATTUNEMENT

Let's develop an analogy to illustrate purposively available evidence of divine reality. I'm the owner and occasional user of a Uniden Police-Band and Aircraft Scanner. This scanning radio searches for active frequencies between 29 and 956 MHZ, a range that includes communications by many police and fire departments, airlines, national weather services, ambulances, railroads, buses, taxis, some TV stations, and even ham radio operators. My scanner thus enables me to listen in on many important radio communications in my part of the world. Of course, we can't see, touch, taste, hear, or smell the various radio frequencies, but they are nonetheless real and valuable. Indeed, many of the frequencies are crucial to the communication system underlying a stable complex society. Without police radio communication, for instance, we would be in big trouble indeed. Even my scanner would be at risk.

My radio scanner has a telescoping antenna that can be pointed in different directions for improved reception. If I adjust the antenna in a certain way, I can *block* the reception of some frequencies. My scanner also enables me to *skip* undesired frequencies: for instance, those with the seemingly endless banter of ham radio operators. What's more, my scanner comes with "Search Delay," whereby I can *delay* at will the search for new frequencies. So, I have remarkable control over the frequencies received by my scanner; in fact, I am, we might say, the lord of my scanner. I alone am in charge at the controls, and the control can be exciting and even addictive.

The most excitement by far occurs on the police frequencies, which offer striking car chases, foot chases, and other police cases that are the stuff of TV detective shows. I can select which Chicago police district to monitor (some are, as expected, much more active than others), and I can switch between districts with ease. Moreover, with the turn of a dial or the push of a button, I can *silence* the police department dispatcher. I am indeed the lord of my scanner's reception, as I am able and willing to tune in or to tune out the frequencies I choose.

The *reality* of the frequencies activating my scanner doesn't depend, of course, on my tuning in to them. The frequencies are real and actually available to people even if I'm fast asleep at my scanner, or worse, dead. We are, in fact, bombarded with radio waves at all hours, even if we are unaware of them. Similarly, the *available evidence* of the reality of the radio waves is independent of my tuning in to them. (My not actually *having* evidence doesn't entail, of course, that it isn't *available* to me.) My failure to turn on my scanner or to adjust its antenna properly may leave me with no evidence of the reality of, say, the ham radio transmissions in my neighborhood or elsewhere. Even so, the distinctive available evidence of ham radio activity *can* be acquired by all who seek it aright. That evidence is definitely *available* to me, among others.

To acquire evidence of ham radios and their transmissions, one need only turn on a suitable scanner, raise its antenna, and then adjust the scanner to receive the appropriate frequency. In other words, one must *tune in* to the desired frequency, and this requires some careful decision-making, focusing, and maneuvering. People who don't tune in will lack a certain kind of evidence that is nonetheless readily *available* to them and actually possessed by some other people who are attuned. Radio waves can carry good news, such as news of a rescue operation, but if we aren't attuned (tuned in), we'll miss out on such news. The good news can be available to us but, nonetheless, not actually received by us. In that case, the good news can appear to be hidden, and even be hidden, from us, and the source of the good news can seem incognito at best and nonexistent at worst.

Let's extend the analogy a bit. We humans are all on a sinking desert island (say, the one in Defoe's *Robinson Crusoe*), alone with each other and our personal radio scanners. Our food and water supplies are dangerously low, with little hope of being replenished. Our relationships with one another are frayed, and have resulted in selfish factions, fights, and fences, including large forbidding fences. We're even willing to sacrifice the well-being of others for our own selfish ends. Accordingly, genuine community has broken down, and, in the absence of a rescuer, we'll all soon perish. Our island continues to sink, and we do too, as our lives, including our means of entertainment, clearly show. Evidently, successful radio scanning for a rescuer is our only hope. Will we connect with a rescuer? Will we survive? Some of us give up hope, and turn to convenient diversions, including reading, writing, and listening to National Public Radio. Others lack the energy for diversions, and end up as the despairing outsiders among us.

Considering now our actual, real-life shared predicament, we are all on a planetary island (fortunately, not Pluto) facing moral breakdown and physical death. Any daily newspaper will confirm this human predicament, with extensive war stories, unhappy cases of personal and corporate greed, revelations of political and religious corruption, and very sad obituaries. Our conclusive access to the reality of a perfectly loving God would be analogous to our access to rescue frequencies on my radio scanner. We would need somehow to "tune in" to the reality and the purposively available evidence of God. God, after all, would be an invisible Spirit with definite character traits and purposes that are perfectly authoritative and loving and thus morally far superior to ours. We would need, accordingly, to point our scanner's antenna in the right direction. The "right" direction, relative to a perfectly loving God, wouldn't automatically match the self-preferred direction of our own lives. Being perfectly loving, God would have a character and purposes significantly different from our own, given our selfish ways. God's "direction" would thus differ notably from our own, even if we suffer from delusions of being acceptable to God on our own terms.

The desert islanders, just like us, shouldn't expect themselves to have control or authority over which frequency a potential rescuer uses. If they stubbornly insist on such authority, they may very well overlook the frequency actually occupied by a potential rescuer. They should at least ask some simple questions. *Who* is entitled to choose the potential rescuer's frequency for communication? The islanders or the potential rescuer? Once we ask such questions, we should see that the islanders have no authority of their own to demand exactly how the potential rescuer is revealed. Their expectations of the potential rescuer should be conformed to the character and purposes of the potential rescuer, and not vice versa. Likewise, we shouldn't expect a perfectly loving God to appear on our convenient terms (say, on the evening TV news or even a Sunday talk show) if this would be at odds with God's perfectly loving character and purposes. For good reason, including for our own good, God might not want to be heard in the national news media, even on National Public Radio. A media-controlled, domesticated God would be an imposter at best, given the supreme demands of worthiness of worship.

Our initial question becomes not so much whether God exists as what the character and purposes of a perfectly authoritative and loving God would be, if God exists. In addition, we should explicitly ask the following, in keeping with our previous discussion: what *kind* of human knowledge of God's reality would a perfectly loving God seek? The most direct answer is that

God would seek the kind of knowledge that represents and advances God's kind of unselfish love among human knowers and between humans and God. In particular, as suggested above, a perfectly loving God would seek volitional *filial knowledge of God* whereby humans become loving children of God and thus know God, in sacred volitional fellowship, as their loving Father. This is a key lesson of the Jewish and Christian scriptures (see, for example, Isa. 63:16, 64:8–9, Jer. 31:9, Rom. 8:15–16, Jn. 1:12), although the Christian New Testament, under the decisive influence of Jesus, stresses this lesson with a unique emphasis (see Thompson 2000). Did the relevant ancient Jewish and Christian writers just make up their claims about filial knowledge? Or, alternatively, are *we* just out of the loop, owing to our wayward radio scanners?

Suppose that I tune in to just self-indulgent frequencies, and devote my life exclusively to what advances my own selfish purposes (say, a lucrative, comfortable, or even "humanitarian" career where I put myself first whenever possible). I might be the kind of islander who cares only, or at least primarily, about my own rescue, on my own selfish terms, even at the expense of other islanders. In that case, I would be ill-positioned to receive extensive purposively available evidence of the reality of a perfectly loving God, even if I "fit in" with many other islanders and seem to be as smart as the next islander. I would then have my antenna pointed in the wrong direction for purposes of receiving extensive available evidence of God's reality. God, of course, wouldn't be a friend of my twisted self-indulgence, and that's a good thing for all concerned, even for me. God, as perfectly loving, would need to challenge my destructive ways for my own good, but I may intentionally and even intently rebuff the needed challenge. I may also dismiss any intruding evidence of divine reality, in order to minimize challenges facing me.

A perfectly loving God would communicate on a frequency available to *all* people who are open to divine rescue *on God's terms*. God's frequency wouldn't be the exclusive possession of the educated, the "morally good," the physically strong, the wealthy, the "religious," or any group that selfishly excludes other people. A perfectly loving God would seek *all-inclusive* community under the umbrella of divine unselfish love. Such a God would desire that *everyone* be rescued from selfishness and destruction, on God's terms, even the most pathetic and repulsive among us and even all of our enemies, including God's enemies. This isn't, of course, a typical human desire, but it would be integral to the aim of a perfectly loving God. God's ways and purposes would thus differ strikingly from our selfish ways and purposes. We do well, then, not to form expectations of God, including cognitive expectations, on the basis of our own self-images.

An omniscient God wouldn't need to "shoot in the dark" to offer the kind of evidence that prompts a decisive human response, one way or the other, to God. God could make effective use of divine knowledge of a person's tendencies without coercing that person's will (as proponents of divine "middle" knowledge have explained). Even so, human failure to apprehend available evidence of God's reality can result, as suggested above, from one's inquiring about divine reality under a misguided conception of God. I might portray God as grudging, vindictive, excessively restrictive, or harmful to my identity. In that case, my scanning for God's reality might find a frequency reflecting *me*, but I wouldn't find a perfectly loving God worthy of worship. Alternatively, I might conceive of God as offering only pampering, pandering love that doesn't challenge humans to be morally good as God is, in fellowship with God. In that case, my scanning for God would yield mere noise, and not an intelligible frequency. I would then fail to tune in to the purposively available evidence of a God worthy of worship. I would then be looking in the wrong direction, because my attention would be directed toward a convenient idol of my own making. This is all too common regarding pursuit of "God" and of questions about "God's" existence. Indeed, much of institutional religion and much of philosophy of religion move in this direction. (Readers can name names here on their own.)

Some people try to exclude all candidates for divine reality out of self-protective fear, as the end of Chapter 1 suggested, because they fear that God will rob us of something good for us or at least something we rightfully want. As a result, some people might refuse to take seriously the available evidence of God's reality. They might even completely shut down some frequency ranges on their scanner, thereby trying to suppress the very issue whether there is available evidence of God's reality. Many people do just this. Like the prodigal son in the parable from Jesus, they simply run off to a distant place, away from anything having to do with issues regarding a perfectly loving God.

Supposedly self-protective human fear sometimes yields outright antipathy toward God, even to the extent that some people say that if after death they met God directly, they would immediately kill themselves. (I, for one, have met some of these resolute people, and some are highly educated philosophers who have reflected carefully on the matter.) People with such fear would prefer to banish (acknowledgment of) God altogether from human life, on the ground that God would threaten human well-being in some way. Perhaps all wayward humans suffer from a problem of selfish fear of God to some degree at least at some time.

Selfish fear of God reveals, at bottom, the problem of ultimate authority for our lives. We typically want to be, or at least to appoint, the ultimate authority for our lives, as if we had a right to this. We thereby risk deceiving ourselves and blocking ourselves from some evidence of the supreme authority over our lives. We end up looking in the wrong direction, toward a place where God isn't allowed to be a God worthy of worship. Sometimes the fear and the mistake in question stem just from a distorted conception of God wherein God is, from a moral standpoint, little better than a neighborhood bully. In other cases, the obstacle runs deeper, and resists easy correction.

The needed attunement of humans with God's authoritative self-revelation would require more than a good thought or even a good system of beliefs. Assent to creeds and confessions thus won't do the job, contrary to the suggestion of some intellectually earnest theists. Divine self-revelation, comprising God's unique "frequency" for self-communication, would manifest God's perfect authoritative love even for enemies of God. The needed attunement, then, would be *the willing reception of God's perfect authoritative and forgiving love* rather than just a new belief or system of beliefs. Evidence of divine reality would be purposively available to us, in keeping with God's loving purposes, and the latter purposes would seek to transform our wills (and purposes) toward perfect unselfish love in fellowship with God. Because this divine perfect love would announce our need of forgiveness at least by God, it would also pronounce corrective judgment on us as wayward creatures of God.

Our being regarded as needing forgiveness by God would presume that we are, or have been, in the wrong morally. This would imply that my will is, or has been, in the wrong morally and in need of correction by God's will. My willing reception of God's forgiving love would require that I subject my defective, selfish will to God's perfect, loving will; otherwise, I would willingly receive at most a counterfeit. My reception of the genuine article, as opposed to a counterfeit, could be an ongoing struggle, and wouldn't be, in any case, just an intellectual commitment. It would cut to the core of my intentions and desires, the psychological attitudes that motivate me to act in various ways. It would involve, in effect, a motivational power struggle between God and me, and if I "win" in my selfishness, I actually lose out on lasting life. In willingly receiving divine forgiveness and losing my selfishness, in contrast, I would gain lasting life in fellowship with a God who can sustain life, even good life. (Chapter 3 will return to the significance of divine forgiveness.)

We now arrive at the heart of the cognitive revolution under development. A perfectly loving God would seek to reveal to us who we really are, in terms of our selfish tendencies that underlie our need of forgiveness and correction by God. In short, God would seek to know us in a way that reveals to us the reality of our dire moral situation if we're left to ourselves, apart from fellowship with God. In being thus known, we would need to welcome divine forgiveness, correction, and transformation. So, the urgent question is not so much:

(a) Do we know that a perfectly loving God exists?

as:

(b) *Are we humans known by God* in virtue of our *freely and agreeably being willing* (i) to be known by God and thereby (ii) to be transformed toward God's moral character of perfect love as we are willingly led by God in volitional fellowship with God, thereby obediently yielding our wills to God's authoritative will?

Cognitive issues regarding divine reality change dramatically with the shift of focus from (a) to (b), as we are beginning to see.

The usual focus on question (a) suggests that the complete burden is on *God* for supplying the desired knowledge to humans, as if humans were just innocent spectators in the situation. In contrast, our focus on question (b) leads us to ask whether *we* are well-positioned to receive the purposively available divine evidence and knowledge in question. If we aren't thus well-positioned, we do well to consider whether our wills have gone awry and need attunement to reality, particularly to divine reality. The matter of knowing God's reality, then, becomes as much about *us*, as potential recipients, as about a perfectly loving God's contribution by way of noncoercive self-revelation. We thus need to consider, with due resolve and honesty, whether we are genuinely willing to be known, and thereby transformed away from selfishness, by a perfectly loving God. If we aren't, we ourselves could be a sizeable obstacle to our acquiring some purposively available evidence of divine reality.

Our obediently, or conformingly, receiving God's authoritative self-revelation of unselfish love would yield a revolution in our wills relative to God's will. It would lead to a new life direction involving repentance from selfishness and turning toward unselfish love, motivated by the kind of obedient volitional resolve shown by Jesus in Gethsemane toward his Father: "Not what I will, but what You will." This obedient life direction would begin with acknowledgment of our own inadequacy before God relative to God's perfectly loving character. In this respect, we would come under divine love's judgment, owing to our failure to meet the expectations and commands of a perfectly authoritative and loving God, particularly regarding enemy-love. We would need, in the grips of selfishness and selfish fear, to struggle to welcome this purportedly corrective judgment of love and to submit our wills to the perfectly loving will of God. We would need, in particular, to repent of our selfish ways for the sake of needed volitional attunement with God's perfect will, in fellowship with God.

We now can understand why humans (*not* just atheists and agnostics) would have difficulty in knowing, and being known by, an authoritative God of perfect love. The difficulty would come from our resisting God's perfectly loving authority over us in virtue of our resisting God's desired volitional *transformation* of us toward a perfectly loving character in fellowship with God. We thus contradict Gethsemane, in saying, or at least in acting as if we are saying: "Not what You will, God, but what *I* will." We thereby supplant God's authoritative will, and devalue the perfectly loving authority of God over us. We do this, in effect, whenever we yield to selfishness, because we then refuse to participate in any divine redemptive program of unselfish love toward all people, even toward enemies.

The needed *Gethsemane struggle* opposes our own selfishness that conflicts with unselfish divine love and thus with a God worthy of worship. This is a fight against a poisonous enemy within, namely, the selfishness that opposes self-giving love toward all people, enemies included. Given our resistances and failures concerning love toward others, we wouldn't readily line up with God's perfectly loving character and redemptive purposes. Our habitual selfishness shows this beyond any doubt, especially in the ways we hoard wealth and resources needed by others. We would thus be in no position to presume either our acceptability before God on our own terms or our being fit for fellowship with God. We would do well, instead, to welcome God's corrective judgment upon us for the sake of needed transformation. Our folding before God in this manner would be our only plausible option.

In representing and promoting divine love, God would care mainly about what and how we *love*, and not just about what we *believe*. For our own good, God would seek (a) that we love God above all else (by our receiving God's love and thereby subjecting our wills to God's perfectly loving will), and (b) that we thereby live out God's unselfish love toward all people, even enemies. We would thus need to receive God's love toward us, and then yield to it and participate in it, sincerely and consistently, in order to be empowered by it instead of by our selfishness. This would be our ongoing Gethsemane struggle, a struggle won by Jesus on his obedient path to self-giving death and now shared by his followers. His followers too would need to die to selfishness and to live to God's unselfish love toward all people, even enemies. In doing so, they would become disciples of Jesus, and not just his admirers or intellectual proponents.

Our attunement with God's unselfish love would be noncoercive but still difficult for all concerned, owing to frequent obstruction from our selfish wills. The required process of attunement would need to be *shown* to us by God in action and in volitional fellowship rather than simply *stated* to us in sentences or arguments, because God would be after *truth in will and action*, and not just truth believed. We would learn the lessons of attunement in obediently *living* them rather than merely *thinking* them, because the lessons concern *who we are* and *how we exist and act*, not just *what we think*. This bears directly on the needed role of God as the authoritative loving source of our personal transformation in attunement. God would motivate the needed human transformation by offering, manifesting, and promoting authoritative love, even toward enemies. (We'll return to this theme in an approach to divine–human atonement in Chapter 3.)

The divine offer of loving fellowship to humans must be received freely by humans or not at all. Such an offer of love thus has no guarantee of full success in being received by humans, even though God is its perfect source. Not even the true authoritative God, having supreme power, knowledge, and love, could force or otherwise guarantee genuinely loving divine–human reconciliation. The free will of the person loved by God plays an indispensable role, and some people evidently (even by their own testimony) wouldn't willingly receive God's love under any conditions. Divine love, then, would carry the inherent risk of human rejection. Otherwise, it would be coercion, and not genuine love.

The needed human change of attunement would call for acknowledgment that on our own we have failed dismally at exemplifying God's perfectly loving character. This failure would occur in the presence of serious challenges to our existence (namely, death), to our well-being (for example, physical and mental decline), and to our moral standing (for example, our tendency to selfishness). We have no self-made or self-discovered solution to this universal human predicament. This humbling acknowledgment is significant relative to our knowing God's reality, because it requires that we change how we think of ourselves and of our relation to God. It also recommends a change in our intentions regarding our existence and conduct, and such a change would be volitional, a matter of the will, and not just intellectual. As a result, we would be displaced from the prideful center of importance in our supposed universe. We would then become able to appreciate firsthand the explanatory profundity of Jewish and Christian theism regarding the human condition. So, volitional transformation can contribute to our firsthand appreciation of explanatory and thus cognitive value, in giving us a new, cognitively improved firsthand perspective on our human predicament. Our appreciation of some evidence can thus be sensitive to our volitional stance.

Cognitive idolatry, as characterized above, can block us from attunement to God's unselfish love. It often rests on a principle of this form:

Unless God (if God exists) supplies evidence of kind *K*, God's existence is too obscure to justify reasonable acknowledgment.

The problem isn't with a principle of this form but is rather with the specification of kind K. Some philosophers specify K in a way that disregards what would be the distinctive personal character and redemptive intentions of a perfectly authoritative and loving God. They thereby isolate themselves from any divine challenge of volitional attunement, and risk cognitive idolatry too. Such idolatry arises from a cognitive commitment designed, if implicitly, to exclude God as Lord in our lives. It stems from the human desire to be, or at least to appoint, the ultimate authority for our lives, as if we humans were entitled to this. Such idolatry would obscure for us important purposively available evidence of God's reality, by obscuring or distorting what we attend to, and would thus obscure for us the truth about God's reality.

It would be altogether presumptuous for us humans to approach the question whether God exists as if we were automatically in an appropriate moral and cognitive position to handle it reliably. Analogously, it would be implausible to assume that my radio scanner, tuned to fit my own self-indulgent desires, would pick up the frequency of a perfectly loving God. Careful reflection on the distinctive character and purposes inherent to a perfectly authoritative and loving God recommends an approach less cavalier than that typical of humans, including philosophers. We are, after all, inquiring about a very special kind of personal agent with distinctive, perfectly loving purposes, and not an ordinary household appliance or laboratory specimen. Perhaps we humans can't easily abide a perfectly loving God who, for our own good, evades our sophisticated and self-approving cognitive nets.

A perfectly loving God, as suggested, wouldn't be after mere justified true belief among humans that God exists. God would care about *how* we handle purposively available evidence of God's existence, in particular, whether we become more genuinely loving in handling it, in fellowship with God. Contrary to a typical philosophical attitude, then, knowledge of God's reality wouldn't be a recreational sport for casual spectators. It rather would be part of a process of God's extreme, even thoroughgoing makeover of a person as a moral agent in relation to God. From our side of the process, it would be an active commitment to a morally transforming *personal relationship of volitional fellowship*. We would come to know God's reality more profoundly as God increasingly becomes *our God*, the Lord of our lives, rather than just an object of our contemplation or speculation. A perfectly authoritative and loving God would refuse, for our own good, to become a mere object of our cognition, imagination, or entertainment. We exhibit self-destructive arrogance in assuming that we can have knowledge of God's reality without facing God's authoritative call to undergo deep, even painful, moral transformation toward God's perfectly loving character, in fellowship with God.

Purposively available evidence and knowledge of a perfectly loving God's reality would be inherently volitional and ethical rather than simply reflective, because divine love would be inherently volitional and ethical, and God would manifest and command such love. Tragically, supposed mere spectators complaining from remote regions may in fact remain out in those regions by their own self-isolating choices. Knowing a perfectly loving God's reality firsthand would require one's receiving, whether agreeably or disagreeably, a genuine personal call to come in from the remote regions and gratefully join God's all-inclusive plan of redemption as reconciliation, in fellowship with God.

The divine redemptive plan would be no mere intellectual puzzle for philosophers. A perfectly loving God would be more serious than our mental strivings, for our own good. We do, after all, have *lives* to form and to live, not just thoughts to think or intellectual puzzles to solve. After the following section, we shall confront a new argument for divine reality in keeping with divine hiding and purposively available evidence of divine reality.

7. LOVE'S EVIDENCE

According to John's Gospel, Jesus faced a problem of hiding, or elusiveness, raised by his own brothers, who didn't trust in him. The resulting lesson fits well with the previous section on volitional attunement. Jesus's brothers tell him that nobody works in hiding while seeking to be known "openly." Their challenge is straightforward: "Manifest yourself to the world" (Jn. 7:4; cf. Jn. 10:24). Part of Jesus's reply is that the world hates him because he testifies that its works are evil. He thus suggests that the world has the wrong *moral attitude* toward him as God's representative. Being known "openly" isn't his goal; something more subtle is. John portrays Jesus as teaching in the temple that if anyone *wills* to do the will of God, that person will know whether Jesus's teaching is from God (7:17). John thus acknowledges the *cognitive* importance of one's willing to do the will of God.

One of Jesus's disciples asks why he won't manifest himself to the world (Jn. 14:22). The disciple's thinking is familiar: why hide from the world if you have miraculous powers? Jesus offers, as before, a reply that highlights the importance of human moral attitudes. "If a person loves me, that person will keep my word, and my Father will love him, and we will come to him and make our home with him" (Jn. 14:23; cf. Jn. 14:21). The reply assumes that the world doesn't love the purposes of God, and that therefore God's self-manifestation wouldn't have a result desired by God. The desired result includes divine–human volitional agreement.

In another epistemological context, Jesus remarks that "an evil and adulterous generation seeks a sign" (Matt. 12:39). He assumes that God's purposes seek not mere acknowledgment or intellectual assent regarding divine reality, but primarily volitional attitudes of trust, obedience, and love toward God. Purposively available evidence and knowledge of God's reality would conform to this assumption, and divine hiding would too, as an intended means to eliciting the volitional attitudes in question. If a person isn't volitionally ready for divine self-manifestation, divine hiding may be a fitting response, at least more fitting than the casting of divine revelatory pearls before those eager to destroy them. Such hiding, then, may actually be good for people resistant to God's perfectly loving will.

A perfectly loving God, as suggested, would be anything but cognitively controllable by humans. We wouldn't be able to control either God, God's self-manifestation, or God's hiding on occasion, and thus we wouldn't be able to remove divine hiding with our self-made recipes. A perfectly loving God would leave us empty-handed, for our own good, when we insist on seeking with our self-made recipes that intend to earn God's self-manifestation or our acceptance by God. We therefore can't "solve" the problem of divine hiding if a solution requires either a human self-made recipe to remove such hiding or a comprehensive human explanation of God's specific intentions in hiding. We are, after all, neither God nor God's equals nor even God's advisers; at best, we are God's obedient children. So, we shouldn't be surprised at all that we lack our own means to remove, or even to explain fully, divine hiding.

Our inability to explain divine hiding fully doesn't preclude our having conclusive evidence or knowledge of God's reality, including the reality of God's self-giving love for us. Our having such evidence or knowledge doesn't require our having a theodicy (or any kind of full explanation) for divine hiding, just as it doesn't require our having a theodicy for natural and moral evil. In general, one's having conclusive evidence or knowledge of the reality of a person doesn't require one's having a comprehensive explanation of the intentions of that person. We have no reason to deny this truth in the case of divine reality. (The last section of this chapter returns to this lesson.) Humanly unexplained divine hiding, then, doesn't yield a decisive defeater to all evidence of divine reality.

A perfectly loving God would be the supremely authoritative giver of life who, given hope for redemption of humans, seeks us prior to our seeking God. This is what Hebraic covenant love *(chesed)* and Christian grace *(charis)* are all about. If we love God, it's because God *first* loved us and offered God's love and fellowship to us (as is rightly emphasized by Brunner 1949, chap. 15, and Nygren 1953, Pt. II, chap. 6). The divine-to-human order of priority here is crucial, cognitively and morally. For our own good, a perfectly loving God would call for our faithful surrender to God as the compassionate giver of life rather than for our anxiously casting about with our own self-crediting recipes for finding God. So, a perfectly loving God wouldn't be the God of our own schemes, however well-intentioned they may be. Our self-crediting terms would thus be beside the point, at best.

Some widely favored cognitive conditions for human access to God include displays of miracles, dominating powers, and sophisticated wisdom. Such conditions often involve a triumphalist epistemology that readily advances prideful human self-exaltation instead of humble self-giving divine love. We tend to prefer to *earn* our knowledge of God, on our own terms, rather than to settle for grateful acceptance of God's gift of (a) filial knowledge of God and (b) God's personal assurance of God's abiding presence. We would prefer to have cognitive control here as elsewhere in our lives. A perfectly loving God, in contrast, would favor an epistemology of authoritatively self-revealed self-giving love, where God serves as the eager but humble cognitive gift-giver and we serve as grateful recipients. We thus would need to let God be God, that is, perfectly and transformingly gracious, even in the domain of human knowledge of God's reality. Otherwise, frustration and confusion would await us.

A perfectly loving God would inherently value knowing through loving others, rather than knowing as merely contemplating or theorizing in a truth-conducive manner. Such knowing through loving would be altogether fitting for children of a perfectly loving God, and it would have obvious moral consequences. We would thus grow in knowing God and God's reality by sharing increasingly in God's authoritative compassionate love, and thereby become genuinely loving as God is, in fellowship with God. In other words, God's children would need to be conformed, willingly and faithfully, to the moral character of their volitional and spiritual parent and thereby increase in knowledge of the parent, including the parent's sacred reality.

The relevant compassionate love wouldn't be a humanly self-made or independent precondition for knowing God's reality. Rather, it would be God's gift, and its proper reception by humans would depend on sincere human volitional openness to conformity to God's moral character, in fellowship with God. God's transforming love would be infused in willingly receptive people in a way that is cognitively as well as morally important for knowing God's reality. In the absence of such love, we are ever prey to a kind of selfish fear incompatible with genuine love and thus with our welcoming filial knowledge of God's reality.

Our refusal to love unselfishly as God loves would hinder our clearly attending to the subtle moral and cognitive ways of a perfectly loving God. Human ingratitude would be particularly self-blinding with regard to God's distinctive perfectly loving ways. Indeed, ingratitude is a corrosive attitude that could drive a perfectly loving God into hiding, for our own good. Via gratitude for good gifts received, in contrast, we could come to trust and even to love God, thereby growing in knowledge of God and God's reality. (On the central role of gratitude toward God in the Jewish and Christian scriptures, see Baillie 1962, chap. 12, Guthrie 1981, and Hardy and Ford 1985.) More specifically, we would need to welcome the gift of God's presence sincerely for it to benefit us as intended by transforming us noncoercively toward God's moral character, in fellowship with God. Proper seeking of God, accordingly, would involve sincerely inviting and welcoming God with gratitude, on the basis of purposively available authoritative evidence of divine reality.

8. REVELATION FOR CHANGE

We have distinguished two kinds of knowledge: (i) *propositional* knowledge that God exists, and (ii) *reconciling, filial* knowledge of God's reality as one's humbly standing in a childlike, volitionally submissive relationship to God as perfectly authoritative and loving Lord and Father. (We do well, of course, not to confuse our being child*like* and our being child*ish*.) Filial knowledge of God's reality requires propositional knowledge that God exists, but it obviously exceeds such propositional knowledge. One could know that God exists, on the basis of conclusive evidence, but fail altogether to submit volitionally to God as Lord. Filial knowledge of God's reality, in contrast, includes our being reconciled to God (at least to some degree) through volitional submission to God as Lord and Father, on the basis of conclusive purposively available authoritative evidence. It requires our entrusting ourselves as obedient children to God in grateful love, on the basis of undefeated evidence, thereby becoming transformed in *who we are* and in *how we exist and act*, not just in what we believe. We may think of this as *filial* attunement to God.

As perfectly loving, we've noted, God wouldn't be satisfied by our merely knowing that God exists. Such mere propositional knowledge falls far short of what God would value by way of redemption: namely, that all people, in response to purposively available authoritative evidence of divine reality, freely yield to God's call to receive transformation by God from selfishness to unselfish love toward all people, even enemies. (For Jewish and Christian suggestions of this ideal, see, for example, Deut. 6:5, 10:12–13, Lev. 19:18,

Mk. 12:28–31.) As perfectly loving, God would aim that all people freely come, in fellowship with God, to be morally perfect as God is morally perfect. Given this aim, God would have no reason to offer *undeniable*, or *insuppressible*, evidence that would produce *mere* propositional knowledge that God exists. Even so, seeking redemption as divine–human reconciliation, God would offer *conclusive purposively available* evidence of divine reality as integral to the authoritative evidence intended to ground filial knowledge of God's reality.

Regarding its ultimate source, filial knowledge of God's reality gives primacy to *self-revelation from God*, and thus offers a top-down rather than a bottom-up approach (cf. 2 Cor. 4:6). This explains the absence of philosophical reasoning from supposedly neutral premises to God's reality in the Jewish and Christian scriptures. Even if filial knowledge of God's reality is available to all honest seekers, its realization in us would come via – and not in advance of – our attitude of sincere volitional openness to loving God with the kind of love characteristic of God. This fits with the theme that God *is* love, that is, inherently loving (see 1 Jn. 4:8,16; cf. 2 Cor. 13:11). In light of this, our resisting God's characteristic kind of love, in selfish practice as well as mindset, would be, in effect, to resist *God*.

In the context of a divine redemptive aim to transform all persons morally via filial knowledge of God's reality, each person would individually need to seek and welcome such knowledge, even if with some help from other people. You couldn't give me your filial knowledge of God's reality; nor could anyone else. In fact, only God through self-revelation could show me God's reality as perfectly loving in a way that would yield, *with (and only with) my volitional compliance*, reconciling, morally transforming filial knowledge of God's reality that is firsthand for me. Other people couldn't accomplish the acquisition of such knowledge for me. They could help only with some of the preconditions for my knowing God's reality in such a filial manner.

The needed turning away from selfishness, selfish fear, self-righteousness, pridefulness, and ingratitude – the multifaceted core of resisting a perfectly loving God – demands a kind of repentance, or turning of mindset and will, that is necessarily personal and firsthand. It couldn't be done without a will or by proxy. Personal repentance need not, however, be evidentially arbitrary. Mature human persons can have conclusive evidence via their conscience that their selfishness, self-righteousness, and pridefulness toward others lack adequate support from the moral quality of their actual moral character. Our frequently presumed status of superior moral importance is but presumption and presumptuousness, and we can readily know this on due moral reflection. Our recurring moral pridefulness is indeed a thin veneer that fails to cover up the moral reality of our troubled situation, particularly regarding our selfishness.

Some philosophers, as suggested, have objected that God's alleged self-revelation is too unclear, at best, to merit reasonable acknowledgment. Surely, their objection goes, God would owe us more miraculous signs and wonders, whatever God's redemptive aims. Why doesn't God entertain us, once and for all, with a *decisive* revelation of God's awesome power? After all, it wouldn't cost God anything, and it may vanquish nagging doubts about God's reality. As a result, we're told, a truly loving God would surely use strikingly miraculous self-revelation to free us from our doubts. This, however, hasn't happened. God's redemptive purposes, many people will thus object, wouldn't exonerate God from the charge of excess restraint in self-revelation.

The charge is that God, if real, is altogether blameworthy for inadequate self-revelation. N. R. Hanson, for instance, comments on the absence of observable happenings that would establish God's existence: "There is no single natural happening, nor any constellation of such happenings, which establishes God's existence.... If the heavens cracked open and [a] Zeus-like figure ... made his presence and nature known to the world, *that* would establish such a happening" (1971, p. 322). Hanson claims that nothing like the Zeus-event has ever occurred in a way that recommends theism to all reasonable people. He concludes, therefore, that theism lacks adequate justification for universal acceptance. If God exists, God is blameworthy for cognitively inadequate self-revelation.

Many people, including Hanson, have misguided expectations about what exactly miraculous signs will accomplish in a person. Miracles, like ordinary events, are interpretively flexible in that they logically admit of various coherent interpretations (not to be confused with *correct* interpretations), including naturalistic, nonmiraculous interpretations. Miraculous events, at any rate, don't impose their interpretations on us. For better or worse, we interpreters must decide on our interpretations of events, and variable background beliefs and motives typically influence our interpretive decisions. We thus shouldn't regard miraculous signs as *inescapable proofs for all inquirers.* A miraculous sign could prompt and build trust toward God in people agreeably open to God's intervention, but not in all people. If such a sign included undefeated authoritative (rather than spectator) evidence, it could supply the kind of evidence suited to an authoritative God, but it doesn't follow that all psychologically capable people would acknowledge it as a universal justification for acknowledgment of divine reality.

The best available explanation of a striking event may be, at least in principle, that it is miraculous in virtue of being supernatural. Even so, if our background assumptions and explanatory standards were thoroughly materialistic, in terms of what they allow, such an explanation wouldn't prevail for us by our assumptions and standards. We would then find an alternative treatment of the striking event, perhaps even withholding judgment on its interpretation. We could freely and consistently reject even the best available explanation of such an event given certain revisions in our system of beliefs. Accordingly, the conclusion of Jesus's story of the rich man and Lazarus is this: "If [people] do not listen to Moses and the prophets, neither will they be convinced even if someone rises from the dead" (Lk. 16:31). John's Gospel concurs regarding the ineffectiveness of miraculous signs in producing suitable faith as grounded trust: "After Jesus had said this, he departed and hid from them. Although he had performed so many signs in their presence, they did not trust in him" (Jn. 12:36–37).

What about people agreeably open to God's intervention but not yet believing in God? Wouldn't they benefit from miraculous signs by thereby coming to believe in God's reality? Perhaps, but perhaps not, too. Let's distinguish between people *passively* open to belief in God's reality and people *actively* open to belief in God's reality. People passively open to such belief don't put any serious effort into examining carefully whether God has actually intervened, for example, in the life, death, and resurrection of Jesus. Such people are "open" to God's reality with striking indifference. This indifference manifests itself in failure to act in ways that take seriously the purposive availability of evidence for God's reality. Passive openness is, accordingly, mere lip service to taking an interest in the availability of evidence for divine reality. We don't appropriately value evidence for God's reality, however, if we don't take a morally and volitionally serious interest in the availability of such evidence. Passive openness is thus an improper, insufficiently serious attitude toward available evidence of divine reality. It trivializes a matter of the utmost importance for all humans. A perfectly loving God would rightly try to challenge such passive openness, even if noncoercively.

People actively open to belief in God take a *morally and volitionally serious* interest in the availability of evidence for God's reality, and such an interest has potential morally and volitionally transforming effects on people who have the interest. These people aren't morally or volitionally indifferent about whether God has actually been revealed to us, for example, in the life, death, and resurrection of Jesus Christ. Instead, they have a morally and volitionally significant interest in any evidence for God's self-revelation available to them. (For elaboration on the relation between God and moral seriousness, see Thielicke 1972, pp. 104–13.)

Filial knowledge of God's reality, in keeping with volitional knowledge, requires that people be *actively willing* to be morally transformed toward the perfectly loving moral character of God, in fellowship with God. An important question regarding such people is whether their coming to believe in God's reality – at least for some of them – either requires or crucially stems from their being directly presented with a miraculous sign from God. Are there, in other words, morally and volitionally serious seekers after God who would believe in God if and only if they had firsthand a miraculous sign from God? Perhaps, but the question is vague owing to vagueness in the familiar phrase "a miraculous sign from God."

Miraculous signs could come in two forms: *agape impotent* and *agape potent* miraculous signs. *Agape impotent* miraculous signs can astonish people, but they aren't intended to transform a person to become less selfish and more loving, in fellowship with God. In contrast, *agape potent* signs are intended to reveal divine love and to elicit love of God from people by way of response; in particular, they are intended to move a person toward God's moral character of perfect unselfish love, or *agape*, in fellowship with God. The miracles of Jesus are *agape* potent, intended to elicit *agape* transformation of humans via volitional fellowship with his divine Father. People often seek excitement and entertainment from striking visible phenomena, such as a holiday fireworks display. In contrast, a perfectly authoritative and loving God would seek our personal transformation toward divine love, in fellowship with God, at the deepest motivational level of our being. In addition, we could frustrate this divine aim, even in the face of amazing miraculous signs, including signs intended to transform us toward God's moral character.

As perfectly loving, God wouldn't be in the trivial entertainment business regarding our coming to know God's reality, because the matter is critically important for all concerned. Our supposedly "seeking after" God without our being willing to obey God's loving demands at all would be pointless from God's redemptive perspective. Hanson's aforementioned example falls short of being *agape* potent. In addition, contrary to Hanson's suggestion, his example wouldn't actually "establish God's existence." The realization of his Zeus example is perfectly compatible with the nonexistence of a perfectly loving God and even with the *improbability* of the reality of such a God. Hanson's Zeus-like figure could very well be a moral tyrant, bent on hate and destruction toward all humans. Hanson seems to have confused supernatural power with divinity, and such a confusion trivializes the character of a God worthy of worship.

A perfectly loving God would give personally transforming evidence of divine reality (at God's appointed time) to every person actively open to change toward God's moral character of perfect love. The needed evidence would be a salient truth-indicator of the reality of a God of morally perfect love toward every person, even toward enemies of God. So, we should expect this evidence to manifest the moral character of God: namely, God's perfect authoritative love toward all people. Some New Testament writers confirm this expectation in no uncertain terms, and we now do well to give some attention to their position.

The apostle Paul observes: "Hope [in God] does not disappoint, because God's love has been poured out in our hearts via the holy Spirit given to us" (Rom. 5:5). This "pouring out" of God's love, according to Paul, is inherently *personal*, owing to the indispensable role of God's personal intervening Spirit. It involves a new *filial* relationship, on Paul's understanding: "When we cry, 'Abba! Father!' it is the Spirit [of God] himself bearing witness with our spirit that we are children of God" (Rom. 8:15–16, RSV). (See 1 Cor. 2:4–16 on the role of God's intervening Spirit in Paul's epistemology; cf. Hays 1997, pp. 26–47.) As we respond to God's self-revelation of perfect love with filial acceptance and fellowship, we become transformed into obedient children of God. God's evident self-revealed love would then emerge not just as conclusive evidence of God's reality, but also as the central motivation of our lives. It would beget divine love in us, in filial relationship as fellowship with God, the personal source of genuine unselfish love.

God's evident self-revelation of transforming love is, I submit, the key *cognitive* foundation for filial knowledge of God's reality. This experienced love, in other words, is a foundational, noninferential (because nonpropositional) ground of knowledge of God's reality. (See Col. 2:2, 1 Cor. 8:2–3, and Eph. 3:16–19 for some important Pauline thinking on this theme.) Such evident love, when willingly received by humans for what it is, is salient and even (when undefeated) conclusive *evidence* of God's reality and presence. It is a matter of an evident personal, self-revealing intervention by God and thus the cognitive basis of a filial relationship as fellowship with, and knowledge of, a personal God worthy of worship. So, filial knowledge of God's reality rests on an evident divine self-revelation of love that produces a loving character (at least to some extent) in willing children of God, even if at times they obstruct God's desired transformation of humans toward divine love. This *agape* transformation would *happen to a willing person*, in part, and thus would be neither altogether self-made nor simply the byproduct of a self-help strategy. We need the phrase "in part" owing to the crucial role of human free will in responding, and tuning in, to God's authoritative self-revelation in volitional fellowship.

The supernatural evidence of divine love in God's self-revelation would be available at God's appointed time to anyone who calls on God with due moral and volitional seriousness. The clause "at God's appointed time" respects the fact that God has a cognitively privileged position in identifying *when* one is duly serious and ready to respond appropriately to God's self-revelation. We are, after all, considering a God who has distinctive purposes in offering evidence and knowledge of divine reality. One's obediently receiving the evident self-revelation of God's love at the opportune time would transform one's will in such a way that empowers gratitude, trust, and love toward God and unselfish love toward other humans, even enemies. One New Testament writer thus reports: "We *know* that we have passed from death to life because we love one another ... Whoever does not love does not know God, for God is love" (1 Jn. 3:14, 4:8, NRSV, italics added). We can now begin to appreciate the suggested connection between experienced love and knowledge of divine reality.

Under the authority of a perfectly loving God, we need to learn how to apprehend, and to be apprehended by, God's evident self-revelation of love for all people. This takes us beyond apprehending *truths about* God's love, and given our deep-seated selfish ways, it could be a slow, difficult process of *agape* transformation. Neither God nor God's evident self-revelation of love, as irreducibly personal, is a proposition or an argument. In particular, God's evident self-revelation of perfect love is a power that exceeds any power of an accepted proposition or argument, and it can underwrite durable hope and ultimate rescue for us as persons facing the dire human predicament of destructive selfishness and impending death. We shall see below how it also yields a distinctive argument for divine reality.

The available evidence of God's reality offered by profound *agape* transformation in a human cuts much deeper in a willing recipient than the comparatively superficial evidence found in spectacular signs, wonders, visions, ecstatic experiences, and philosophical arguments. We can readily and consistently dismiss any such sign, wonder, vision, ecstatic experience, or argument as illusory or indecisive, given certain alterations in our beliefs. In contrast, profound human transformation toward God's unselfish love doesn't admit of easy dismissal by a transformed recipient. It bears directly on *who one really is*, specifically, the kind of person one actually is now. As filial, it also identifies *whose* one is, as one enters in a childlike (but not childish) way into belonging to God as one's perfectly authoritative and loving Father and Lord. Such rare transformation goes too deeply against our natural tendencies toward selfishness to qualify as a self-help or even a peer-help human construct. It constitutes genuine, purposively available evidence of God's reality that resists casual dismissal by its changed and changing willing recipients who testify to volitional fellowship with God.

God's evident self-revelation need not either exceed the presence of God's authoritative morally perfect love for a person or be available to humans as conclusive evidence of divine reality apart from morally and volitionally serious human openness toward God's preeminent authority. Specifically, God's self-revelation need not include miracles irrelevant to human transformation toward God's moral character of unselfish love, even though God could use such miracles on occasion to get our wayward attention. A perfectly loving God who aims at human redemption could, and would, seek human knowledge of divine reality that arises simultaneously with filial knowledge of God's reality. Accordingly, God will be impervious to the charge of negligent restraint in performing spectacular miracles, so long as God conclusively reveals divine reality, in self-manifestation of perfect love, to anyone suitably receptive.

Hanson's aforementioned use of the Zeus-example overlooks the considerations at hand, and thus trivializes a perfectly loving God's redemptive aim to reconcile humans to God in keeping with God's morally perfect character. As perfectly loving, God would aim noncoercively to lead naturally selfish people to love God and others unselfishly, even others who are avowed enemies, in fellowship with God. No aim would be more difficult or more important for God and humans. Given the difficulty of this aim, we shouldn't be surprised that communities of unselfish people are few and far between. In fact, one has to wonder if any such community has existed for any length of time. The relevant empirical evidence is mixed at best and less than encouraging.

God's self-revelation of transforming love would take its willing recipients beyond an assessment of historical and scientific probabilities to a cognitive foundation of evident *personal acquaintance* with God. As we noted from the apostle Paul, in our sincerely crying out "Abba, Father" to God (note the Jesus-inspired filial gist of this cry), God's evident intervening Spirit would confirm to our spirits that we are indeed children of God. We would thereby receive God's evident personal assurance of our filial relationship with God. This assurance would be more robustly personal than any kind of theoretical evidence offered by the traditional theistic arguments of philosophers and theologians, and it would save a person from dependence on speculation, tenuous inference, or guesswork about God. The evident personal assurance of God's Spirit would yield a distinctive kind of grounded confidence in God's reality unavailable elsewhere. God would thus merit credit even for grounded human confidence in God's reality. Humans who boast of their own intellectual skills in knowing divine reality, therefore, would have misplaced boasting. Such prideful boasting would erect a cognitive and moral barrier between humans and a perfectly loving God and between the boasting humans and other humans.

This chapter's Divine Purposes Reply to the problem of divine hiding enables Jewish and Christian theism to assume the burden of cognitive support for commitment to a God of perfect authoritative love who is at times incognito. The reality of the true God worthy of worship is testable now in a morally serious manner, and, given our dire human predicament, God's reality *should* be tested now by every capable person. Each person must test by willingly and attentively considering, with due sincerity, humility, and moral seriousness, the reality of authoritative evidence from God in conscience. Pride and indifference will automatically obstruct our seeing not only God's evident reality but also our genuine need of a God worthy of worship.

The appropriate test requires one's being willing, given suitable evidence of divine reality, to forsake all diversions for the sake of a needed filial relationship with God. This relationship includes personal transformation, in fellowship with God, toward God's moral character of unselfish love for all people, even repulsive enemies. Filial knowledge of God, as noted, would be by grace (as a divine gift) rather than by human earning, and the needed cognitive grace would be available at God's appointed time to all who are volitionally open to fellowship with God in sincere humility and due moral seriousness. A perfectly loving God would want to give all humans lasting good gifts, but we often cling, selfishly and self-destructively, to lesser goods and thereby block out what we truly need. Even our own lives and our knowledge, including philosophical and theological knowledge, can become idols blocking reception of fellowship with a perfectly loving God.

Divine perfect love, as suggested, is perfectly authoritative merciful love, and such merciful love is forgiving love that, in its forgiveness, doesn't condone evil at all. (As promised, we'll return to the nature of divine forgiveness in Chapter 3.) So, the reality of a perfectly loving God could be known firsthand by a wayward person via the willingly experienced power of perfectly merciful, forgiving love for that person. If I'm not volitionally open to receiving the offered power of such merciful love, I'll risk obscuring and perhaps even blocking for myself available evidence of God's reality. The direction of my will could get in the way of my attending to available evidence of divine reality.

Let's consider a definition and an argument that elucidate the cognitive significance of divine merciful love. We begin with a definition of "the transformative gift":

The transformative gift = *df.* via conscience, a person's (a) being authoritatively convicted and forgiven by X of all that person's wrongdoing and (b) thereby being authoritatively called and led by X both into noncoerced volitional fellowship with *X* in perfect love and into rightful worship toward *X* as worthy of worship and, on that basis, transformed by *X* from (i) that person's previous tendencies to selfishness and despair to (ii) a new volitional center with a default position of unselfish love and forgiveness toward all people and of hope in the ultimate triumph of good over evil by *X*.

Given this definition, we have the following concise argument for the reality of an authoritative perfectly loving God:

1. Necessarily, if a human person is offered, and unselfishly receives, the transformative gift, then this is the result of the authoritative leading and sustaining power of a divine *X* of thoroughgoing forgiveness, fellowship in perfect love, worthiness of worship, and triumphant hope (namely, God).
2. I have been offered, and have willingly unselfishly received, the transformative gift.
3. Therefore, God exists.

Clearly, the divine transformative gift in question can be offered to a person but rejected, ignored, or selfishly "received" by that person. So, its being offered doesn't guarantee its being properly, unselfishly received for what it is intended to be: a redemptive gift that seeks to trump human selfishness with divine love for the sake of human transformation by God. It's definitely not coercive of humans or irresistible by humans, just as divine gracious love in general isn't. Only a harmful and ultimately self-defeating misunderstanding of divine sovereignty, such as that found in extreme Calvinism, would suggest otherwise.

If God is inherently perfectly loving, then God is inherently personal as an intentional agent with definite purposes. In that case, purposively available conclusive evidence and knowledge of God's reality *as God* would include evidence and knowledge of God *as personal and perfectly loving* as an intentional agent. We thus can't separate God's existence, or reality, from God's perfectly loving personal character that defines God's reality. Correspondingly, we can't separate conclusive evidence and knowledge of God's reality from conclusive evidence and knowledge of God's perfectly loving personal character.

Knowledge of God's reality and character that is directly firsthand for me would include my being acquainted with *God's personal and perfectly loving will*, which would seek to lead me noncoercively toward fellowship with God in unselfish love while convicting me of any wrongful obstacle to such leading. In other words, my personal will would be challenged via my acquaintance with a perfect personal will that seeks to lead me from selfishness to unselfish love in divine–human fellowship. My conscience, whatever else it is, would be a focal place for this person-to-person volitional challenge whereby I could come to "know together" with God my actual situation before God. It would include intended conviction of my waywardness and noncoercive nudging of my will toward divine–human fellowship in perfect love. Even if one chooses to speak of divine evidence in terms of causal "traces" (cf. Cottingham 2005, pp. 133–8), those traces will have to be understood as inherently agent-oriented if they are to indicate a God worthy of worship.

When we are acquainted with perfect unselfish love, we are acquainted with God's inherent personal character and thus with the reality of God, even if we don't know *that* we are acquainted with divine reality. In knowing perfect unselfish love, we know God's reality, even if our understanding of *what* (or, better, *whom*) we then know is inadequate or misguided. When acquainted with such love, we face a person-defining and life-guiding choice: either to be welcoming and promoting or to turn away, directly or indirectly, in opposition or indifference. Faced with such a choice, we have a sacred cognitive opportunity, and we may be accountable for how we handle it.

Insofar as we have been acquainted with perfect unselfish love, we have been shown what's being offered by God in the transformative gift. We thus aren't left in the dark about God's transformative gift on offer. Perhaps we have experienced only vague glimmers of the gift, but these are enough to invite us to welcome and to promote the gift rather than to turn away in either indifference or outright rejection. The unselfish love intruding in our troubled lives is God's noncoercive attempt to find us and to lead us from despair to hope, from death to life. So, a person could be offered an invitation from God and not even know it, given obstructing confusions and corrupted motivational attitudes in that person. It's a separate issue whether the person *should* know what's being offered. In any case, some cognitive and volitional pollution control may be called for among humans faced with divine intervention.

Three significant obstructions deserve comment. First, we often look for God's reality in the wrong places, if we dare to look at all. Philosophers typically look in areas involving abstruse, esoteric arguments that have nothing directly at all to do with God's inherent character of perfect authoritative love. For instance, endless disputes about probabilities involving apparent design in biology or cosmology or about the need for an inaugural cause behind any parade of contingent causes and effects illustrate the point abundantly and decisively. One's antecedent commitments about God tend to color one's understanding of how the relevant probabilities or causal requirements go.

So, it's unclear what, if anything, one is typically gaining from those wearisome disputes, beyond digging in deeper with one's antecedent commitments. Fortunately, we need not go there to get to God's reality. Instead, a perfectly loving God would come to us in God's unique irreducibly authoritative and personal way. Perhaps this will take the wind out of many philosophers' sails, but that may not be a bad thing after all.

Second, many people think of perfect unselfish love as just another *natural* human capacity, akin to vision, speech, and mobility. In doing so, they uncritically think that we humans have the power of perfect unselfish love on our own. This is presumptuous at best, and also implausible on careful reflection that attends to actual human tendencies. We are hard put indeed to come up with a human community that exemplifies perfect love on its own, and this is very telling of the actual human condition. Left to ourselves, we are too conflicted motivationally and too selfishly fearful of personal loss to generate and sustain perfect unselfish love; we thus need power beyond ourselves. We shouldn't take self-credit, then, where self-credit isn't due, in the case of perfect unselfish love. If the love in question were under our own power, via exercise of self-help or peer-help among humans, we humans would be much more effective at conflict-resolution, peace-making, and community-building. Our general record, however, leaves a lot to be desired (to put the matter charitably), and suggests that perfect unselfish love isn't ours to deliver.

The genuine divine offer and unselfish human reception of the transformative gift, according to premise 1 above, requires a divine source that has the power of thoroughgoing forgiveness, fellowship in perfect love, and transformation of willing humans to a new volitional center of *default unselfish love and forgiveness toward all people*. Indeed, it's part of the concept of the transformative gift, as characterized, that the source of this gift (when this gift is real) is a powerful divine authority of thoroughgoing forgiveness, fellowship in perfect transformative love, and worthiness of worship. The transformation integral to this gift is, on the concept at hand, the change of a person's motivational center to a default position of unselfish love and forgiveness for all people. This change involves a reported experienced reality prominent in the Jewish and Christian tradition: the impartation of God's Spirit to humans whereby divine power is made available to humans at their motivational center. So, the change isn't represented at all as just a product of human self-help or peer-help.

The volitional change in question may now be seen as crucial to filial knowledge of divine reality: one comes to know God as one's authoritative loving Father in virtue of the willingly received impartation of God's Spirit to one at one's motivational center. The relevant *filial* relation is thus a *spiritual* filial relation. The following chapter will elaborate on this position. It will allow for an understanding of the new volitional center and the impartation of God's Spirit to a person in terms of the immediate, directly firsthand reception and continuing, or ongoing, availability of the morally perfect power of God's Spirit by a willingly receptive person, in fellowship with God. This approach sidesteps metaphysical intricacies that aren't essential to present explanatory purposes. It also enables us to avoid both a moralistic approach that characterizes a new motivational center just in terms of actual moral actions or episodes and a mystical approach that proposes that God's Spirit literally inhabits a human spirit. (For relevant discussion, see Brondos 2006, chap. 6.)

Third, many people think that conclusive evidence and knowledge of God's reality, if they are available at all, could be acquired by us without our receiving an authoritative challenge to participate in the kind of perfect love definitive of God. We naturally prefer to keep God's authoritative perfectly loving reality at arm's length, lest it overturn our self-serving tables in our self-made temples. A perfectly loving God, however, would offer us selfish humans an authoritative challenge to have divine unselfish love pervade our lives, including our interactions with enemies and morally perverse people. We would do well, then, to shake off the idea that we could have conclusive evidence and knowledge of God's reality without being authoritatively challenged by God.

In keeping with perfectly authoritative firsthand evidence of divine reality, as opposed to spectator evidence, premise 2 above is irreducibly first-person, self-implicating, and self-involving. It rests on undefeated authoritative evidence of divine reality that is inherently and directly firsthand and purposively available in the manner characterized earlier. In particular, the evidence involves my evident willing reception of an authoritative call in conscience to volitional fellowship with One worthy of worship. It also includes an evident new volitional center with a default position of unselfish love and forgiveness for all people. For reasons already presented, we shouldn't confuse the firsthand evidence in question with an argument of any kind. Arguments, as noted, don't have (and can't have, given a threat of endless inferential regress) a monopoly on evidence.

In the face of skeptical challenge, I could argue for the cognitive well-foundedness of premise 2 on the basis of its central role in an undefeated best available explanation of the whole range of my experience and my other evidence. (See Moser 1989 for details on such explanation.) This kind of well-foundedness is rightly more demanding than a mere "consistency relation" with evidence (as proposed, for example, by Cottingham 2005, p. 24). It also avoids worries about a cognitively naive realism that face a less demanding principle of credulity (as proposed, for example, by Swinburne 1979 and Davis 1989; see Wiebe 2007, pp. 142–4, for some of those worries). As a result, skeptics couldn't plausibly accuse me of just preaching to the choir, although even the choir could use some good preaching on occasion.

Cognitive support for premise 2 could be *diachronic* rather than just synchronic, because God could manifest God's worship-worthy reality over time via the transformative gift as a person willingly receives that gift ever more deeply. To the extent that we are unwilling to undergo such reception of the transformative gift, we would block from ourselves significant evidence of divine reality, including the distinctive kind of divine evidence that underwrites premise 2. Philosophers often look just for synchronic evidence of divine reality, and thus miss out on the significant evidence of divine reality involved in *ongoing* human reception of the transformative gift. We have, of course, no good reason to disregard such diachronic evidence; on the contrary, we should look for it, given the purposes of redemptive human transformation that a perfectly loving God would have.

Someone might object that not all people share my evident experience underlying premise 2. That claim seems undeniably true, but it's no objection at all to premise 2, because that premise doesn't entail that all people have the experience in question. In addition, cognitive support for a claim, including for premise 2, can vary among people, owing to variation in experiences and corresponding evidence among people. As a result, some people know some things that aren't known by others. This isn't mysterious or objectionable at all; it's rather a commonplace about evidence and knowledge. Of course, one might add that the explanation offered by premise 2 for my experience is not only false but ultimately ungrounded. In that case, the critic will owe us a falsifier of premise 2 and an undefeated defeater of my evidence for premise 2.

Clearly, I *could* have a defeater supplied by my experience (such as an indication of hallucination), but the fact that I actually *don't* have one is cognitively significant indeed and thus shouldn't be taken lightly. This chapter and the previous chapter contend that the needed falsifier and defeater aren't as readily available as many skeptics have supposed (see Wiebe 2004 for additional support). In addition, given my appeal, for anti-skeptical purposes, to an undefeated best available explanation of the whole range of my experience and other evidence, the scope for potential defeaters is broad indeed and isn't implausibly restricted to what fits with naive realism. So, we aren't narrowly stacking the evidential deck against skeptics. Even so, we can't plausibly excuse skeptics from their considerable evidential burden now.

We shouldn't offer the conclusion of the previous argument 1–3, that God exists, as a conceptually necessary truth, that is, as a truth whose denial isn't coherently imaginable. We can coherently imagine that God doesn't exist, although, as argued above, it's true that God exists and there is purposively available conclusive evidence that God exists. Clearly, the power of our imagination (in terms of what it can coherently present) outstrips what is real and what is conclusively supportable for us. So, one would risk implausible special pleading in suggesting that divine existence is conceptually necessary, unless, of course, one introduced a merely technical notion of conceptual necessity independent of what we can coherently imagine. At any rate, it's enough for purposes of sound argument that the steps of argument 1–3 are true and its inference is valid.

Human reception of the divine transformative gift, like volitional and filial knowledge of God's reality, can come over time, and can come in varying levels, degrees, or extents, owing to varying depths of being led into noncoercive volitional fellowship with God. Even so, one's undergoing the required transformation to a new volitional center with a default position of unselfish love and forgiveness for all people is a matter of an *absolute* change: either the new volitional center is in place for a person or it isn't. In this respect, the transformative gift in question fits well with the striking cognitive lesson of Jn. 3:3–8, which gives God credit for an absolute human transformation that is cognitively relevant. Still, the absolute change can be accompanied over time with ever deepening reception of the transformative gift.

One can receive the transformative gift in any circumstance that allows for volitional compliance with the demands of the gift, including any circumstance of extreme personal suffering, frustration, and perplexity. As a result, humans have an opportunity to receive purposively available evidence of divine reality in *any* circumstance where they are sincerely volitionally open to receive the transformative gift, including any circumstance of suffering, frustration, and perplexity. The God of perfect love, then, doesn't need to offer evidence of divine reality in the dubious explanatory gaps of human theorizing, as some proponents of natural theology assume, particularly regarding arguments from design in biology or cosmology. Every occasion in the life of a willing person serves as an opportunity to receive ever deepening evidence of divine reality in keeping with ever deepening willing reception of the divine transformative gift.

Many people will object that, even given the experiential evidence in question, the world's unexplained evil provides an undefeated defeater of any such evidence. Careful reflection, however, suggests that the matter is actually more complicated. One's *having conclusive (undefeated) purposively available evidence of God's reality*, as suggested, isn't the same as one's *having a comprehensive explanation of God's ways and purposes*. We thus need to distinguish between:

(a) When you seek God with due volitional openness to authoritative divine reality, you will find God's self-revelation on the basis of conclusive purposively available evidence,

and

(b) When you seek God with due volitional openness to authoritative divine reality, you will find a comprehensive explanation of why God acts as God does.

The promise of (a) regarding God's self-revelation doesn't depend for its correctness or justification on our understanding all of God's purposes, and thus doesn't underwrite a theodicy that fully explains and justifies God's purposes in allowing evil. So, (a) doesn't entail (b). The promise of (a) regarding God's self-revelation, if satisfied, entails one's acquiring conclusive evidence of God's reality, *not* one's acquiring a comprehensive explanation of God's purposes, including God's purposes in allowing evil. It would be invalid, however, to infer that, according to the kind of robust theism at hand, "... we simply are *in the dark* about the goods that God will know, and the conditions of their realization" (Rowe 2006, p. 90; cf. Schellenberg 2007, pp. 300–2). Given the clear ingredients of perfect divine love, our (limited) explanatory darkness regarding some divine purposes in allowing evil can't plausibly be generalized in that skeptical manner. On that dubious kind of generalization, one could never know that an agent is truly morally good when one lacked a comprehensive understanding of the agent's purposes, including the purposes in allowing evil. That implication is obviously excessive.

In demanding human seeking toward God, God upholds the supreme value and authority of divine self-revelation, thereby saving it from devaluation by naturally selfish humans. God thus aims to have humans *supremely and wholeheartedly value* divine love, and to be *personally transformed* by it, in fellowship with God, not just to think about it or formulate arguments about it. Still, human seeking, even when accompanied by one's finding God, wouldn't yield a theodicy, because it wouldn't produce a comprehensive explanation and justification of God's purposes in allowing evil.

Even when one's seeking God results in one's having conclusive evidence of God's reality, the person who has thereby experienced God can lack understanding of the specific intentions motivating God's actions at times. This should be no surprise, given the notable differences, cognitive and otherwise, that exist between God and humans. Our lacking a comprehensive explanation and justification of God's purposes, however, doesn't challenge anyone's *having conclusive evidence* of God's perfectly loving reality. (The closing chapters of the book of Job famously agree with this; cf. Ford 2007, chaps. 3–4, Schneider 2004.) We shouldn't be cognitively timid, then, about our lacking a theodicy regarding evil. In addition, people who hope to find God shouldn't delay their search on the ground that they lack a theodicy that fully explains and justifies God's intentions in allowing evil. As suggested, finding *God*, with conclusive evidence of divine reality, isn't necessarily finding a *theodicy*; nor is it necessarily finding a full explanation and justification of the purposes in occasional divine hiding.

It would be question begging to portray divine hiding as falsifying widespread religious experience of God's perfectly authoritative and loving reality. Divine hiding facing some people at some times, or even some people at all past and present times, doesn't entail divine hiding relative to *all* people at *all* times. So, there is no clear defensible way to generalize on actual cases of divine hiding to encompass *all* people with regard to evidence of divine reality. A generalized argument for atheism or agnosticism, then, doesn't emerge from divine hiding, and this fits with a central lesson of Chapter 1. Any such argument would require specific premises independent of divine hiding, but it's unclear what such premises would be in a cogent argument. Their absence suggests a special problem of *evidential* hiding that confronts a generalized case for atheism or agnosticism from divine hiding. That is, the needed evidence for such a case seems hidden at best and perhaps nonexistent after all.

The world actually looks, at least at times, as if it's the kind of place where we humans are to learn humbly to love as God loves. It certainly isn't the kind of place where we are to receive either maximal pleasure, maximal pain, or maximal understanding. If, however, we ourselves become properly attuned to purposively available evidence of God's reality, including God's authoritative self-giving love, God's reality will emerge as adequately indicated by undefeated authoritative evidence. We would do well, then, to seek and to appropriate the purposively available authoritative evidence of God's reality, however morally challenging the process is. Our cognitive and moral adventure of learning to love as God loves, in volitional fellowship with God, will then be underway, even through personal suffering, frustration, perplexity, and physical death.

The next chapter specifies how a perfectly authoritative and loving God would intervene in human experience for the sake of human renewal at our motivational center. We'll see that a perfectly loving God must be as much a killer as a life-giver. The story is anything but easy for us in our tragic human predicament. Still, it's a story well worth telling and even living, despite our obviously falling short of omniscience and perfect love.

3

Dying to Know

The previous chapters introduced some topics unfamiliar to ordinary philosophical discourse: for instance, God's authoritative *call*, God's intervening *Spirit*, and human *transformation by noncoercive divine power*. We need to fill out these topics in connection with both the proposed cognitive shift in knowledge of divine reality and the dire human predicament of destructive selfishness and impending death. This chapter undertakes that task. We shall see that the ways of a perfectly loving God are unsettling indeed, and call for the killing of certain wayward human attitudes and deeds, for the sake of needed human transformation by divine power. Firsthand knowledge of divine reality follows suit, as this chapter shows in its moving further from abstraction to specific features of knowing the reality of the perfectly loving Jewish and Christian God. Hence, we may talk of "dying to know" God's reality.

1. SPIRIT

Given the evidence and argument of the previous chapters, we may say that a perfectly loving God goes beyond revelation as the imparting of information and nonpersonal experience to revelation as purposively available divine self-revelation. This God, being perfectly loving, offers a distinctive kind of purposively available evidence widely overlooked in philosophical and theological discussions of divine reality. Given our root problem of selfishness, the evidence includes divine self-revelation in the intended *imparting of God's Spirit* to humans as the irreducibly personal power behind volitional transformation of humans toward God's moral character.

If humans lacked access to divine power, they would have an authoritative call from God to undergo change, but lack the needed power for the change. God, of course, could rightfully make a moral demand on us that we are unable to meet by our own power and need divine power to meet. So, contrary to many philosophers, "ought" doesn't imply "can" if "can" means "can solely by our own power." Even so, a perfectly loving God who seeks human redemption would make available to humans, in keeping with divine purposes, the power needed for human redemption. Because the needed power is personal, given a need for human redemption as divine–human personal fellowship, the relevant power and basic evidence thereof are deemed personal in Jewish and Christian theism. The Spirit-oriented power and evidence in question are reported widely in the Jewish and Christian tradition, and receive special acknowledgment in the undisputed letters of the apostle Paul. His distinctive cognitive perspective calls for attention to the human conditions for receiving the Spirit of a perfectly authoritative and loving God. Philosophers of religion seldom attend to this vital topic, despite its prominence in the Jewish and Christian tradition. We'll counter that neglect here.

Paul writes: "...hope [in God] does not disappoint, because the love of God has been poured out in our hearts through the holy Spirit given to us" (Rom. 5:5). Through God's Spirit given to us as we willingly yield to God's authoritative call in conscience to volitional fellowship, our innermost personal center (that is, our "heart," on which see Meadors 2006) would willingly welcome God's powerful self-revelation of perfect love and thereby begin to be changed from being selfish to manifesting God's imparted unselfish love. This would be an agent-to-agent power transaction that moves us noncoercively from human selfish fear to shared divine unselfish love, and from death to life. It would occur at the innermost personal center of a human life, where the problem of selfishness emerges and persists, but it wouldn't automatically remove all human selfishness, all at once. The power transaction would yield nonetheless a new default motivational center in a manner that no merely intellectual or similarly surface work could. (Here and throughout I use selected biblical passages *not* as inherent authorities, but instead for the explanatory illumination they provide, in keeping with the epistemology developed in this book.)

Paul's Spirit-focused theme bears directly on our purposively available *evidence* of divine reality. Human hope in God (to fulfill divine promises) can find a conclusive *cognitive* anchor in our evident experience of willingly receiving God's Spirit, whereby God's love begins to change our hearts toward the distinctive character of divine unselfish love. Paul expresses a related theme in referring to the God who "has put his seal upon us and given us his Spirit in our hearts as a guarantee" (2 Cor. 1:22, RSV; see also 2 Cor. 5:5; cf. Eph. 1:13). According to Paul, the Spirit given to receptive human hearts guarantees, as an evidential, cognitive down payment, that God will complete the work of transformation begun in those hearts. Such human volitional transformation toward divine love is salient evidence of God's reality and intervention in a receptive human life, as the concluding argument of Chapter 2 illustrated. We can benefit now from attention to that distinctive evidence in human transformation.

James Dunn has helpfully characterized the powerful role of God's willingly experienced Spirit acknowledged by Paul:

> The Spirit is that power which operates on the *heart* of man – the "heart" being the centre of thought, feeling, and willing, the centre of personal consciousness.... The Spirit is that power which transforms a man [or a woman] from the inside out, so that metaphors of cleansing and consecration become matters of actual experience in daily living (1 Cor. 6:9–11). The Spirit is the source of that wave of love and upsurge of joy which overwhelms the forces that oppose from without (Rom. 5:5; 1 Thess. 1:5f.) (1975, p. 201).

The Spirit of God, according to Paul, brings new noncoercive *power* to a receptive person, in keeping with divine perfect love, and this power is felt volitionally by its recipient and is observable by others. In particular, this divine power can even move one's will as one willingly consents to this (cf. Phil. 2:13). In addition, it could be observed by someone looking for the rare power of unselfish love in a human life. Still, an observer must have "eyes to see" the power of divine love at work in a life, and this requires attending to an elusive divine power that stands in sharp contrast with worldly powers.

God's Spirit, as characterized by Paul, empowers willingly receptive people to love as God loves, in the self-giving way and power exemplified by Jesus in his life, death, and resurrection. As a result, Paul portrays life in the power of God's Spirit as "dying and rising with Christ" (on which see the final two sections of this chapter; cf. Tannehill 1967, Gorman 2001, Byrnes 2003). First-hand evidence of God's reality can arise from the power of divine self-giving love revealed and put into practice in a willingly receptive human life. Our obediently appropriating such evidence firsthand calls for our welcoming and willingly being moved by the power of self-giving love toward conformity to God's perfectly loving moral character. Eduard Schweizer has thus characterized the Spirit of God, in Paul's thought, as "... the power which involves [a person] in the saving act of God in Christ, ... makes impossible for him all confidence in his own 'flesh' *(sarx)*, and lays him open to a life of love *(agape)*" (1961, p. 80). God's Spirit is portrayed, accordingly, as an agent of divine transforming love in willingly receptive humans, where this powerful love participates in God's process of redemptive transformation exemplified by Jesus.

We would easily overlook the power of God's intervening Spirit if we were looking for power that coerces or subdues people or otherwise advances one person at the expense of others. Indeed, the power of God's Spirit could even seem to be foolish pseudo-power to people out of attunement with, and thus negligent of, divine self-giving love. To know God's reality aright, according to Paul's Spirit-oriented epistemology, is to be volitionally united with God in the power of God's transforming Spirit, and this is to be united in the power of the divine self-giving love that motivated the obedience of God's crucified Son, Jesus. Schweizer thus remarks:

> At the very place where Paul writes about the demonstration of the Spirit and of power, he states he has nothing to preach but the Crucified [Jesus], which is a stumbling-block to the Jews and folly to the Greeks (1 Cor. 1:23, 2:2). Thus the power of the Spirit is demonstrated precisely where normally nothing is to be seen but failure and disintegration. What no eye has seen nor ear heard God has revealed to his own through the Spirit which "searches everything, even the depths of God": salvation in the Crucified [Jesus]. . . . Thus it is above all the Spirit that reveals . . . that the "power of God" is to be found in the Crucified [Jesus] (2 Cor. 13:4; cf. 12:10) (1989, p. 411).

Firsthand evidence of the divine Spirit's presence, then, involves a kind of manifested *power* foreign to natural expectations. This foreign power is divine self-giving love, as manifested paradigmatically in the crucified Jesus fully obedient to his divine Father and, derivatively, in his obedient followers who follow suit. Accordingly, J. Louis Martyn notes: ". . . knowing by the Spirit can occur only in the form of knowing by the power of the cross [of Jesus]. . . . [T]he cross is and remains the epistemological crisis, and thus the norm by which one knows that the Spirit is none other than the Spirit of the crucified Christ" (1997a, p. 108). The fundamental cognitive norm here is the power of divine self-giving love, which is perfectly manifested in Jesus as God's fully obedient Son.

The Spirit of God, according to Paul, is also the Spirit of Jesus, who gave his life as God's obedient Son in order to manifest his Father's powerful servant love for humans in need of that love and thereby to offer divine–human reconciliation, in fellowship with God. Accordingly, the Spirit of God is the Spirit of *adoption* of humans into God's family of obedient children, who thereby acknowledge God as "Abba, Father" (see Rom. 8:9, 15), and this adoption entails one's being led by (the power of) God's Spirit (Rom. 8:14). This approach to God's Spirit thus fits well with the previous chapter's emphasis on the importance of *filial* knowledge of divine reality. Worldly powers of coercion, oppression, and selfishness go in the opposite direction of (one's being led by) the self-giving power of a perfectly loving God's Spirit.

In expecting evidence of God's reality to fit with worldly powers, including worldly religious powers incompatible with self-giving love, people blind themselves from apprehending God's reality.

God's intervening Spirit, according to Paul, reveals God's reality and our relationship with God: " . . . we have received . . . the Spirit from God, *in order that* we may know the things freely given to us by God" (1 Cor. 2:12, italics added; cf. 1 Cor. 12:7–8, where Paul speaks of the "manifestation" of God's Spirit). The Spirit of God, as God's own internal divine agent of intervention and communication, would automatically know the things of God, including divine intentions and other attitudes; so, ultimately, the Spirit of God could authoritatively reveal God's reality and God's ways to humans. Paul thus concludes that we are given the Spirit of God *in order that* we may know God's reality and God's ways of self-giving love. He evidently has volitional and filial knowledge in mind, since human reception of God's Spirit requires human willingness to be adopted into God's family of obedient children, in fellowship with God. By giving God's own Spirit to willingly receptive humans, as a resident default but noncoercive guide and motivator, God extends volitional and filial knowledge of God's reality to humans. Indeed, God's intervening Spirit confirms to a willingly receptive individual's spirit (or, constitutive agent), via conscience, that he or she is a child of God, called into filial relationship and fellowship with God as perfectly authoritative and loving Father (see Rom. 8:15–16, Gal. 4:6–7, 1 Cor. 1:9; cf. 1 Jn. 4:13).

A filial relationship with God involves noncoercive perfectly authoritative and loving *ownership* of a child on God's part and willingly *being owned* by God on the child's part. Paul thus remarks that followers of Jesus under God as Father are not their own but "have been bought with a price" and thus belong to God (1 Cor. 6:19–20; cf. Rom. 14:7–9). He would say, accordingly, that the urgent question for a human is not so much "Who am I?" as "*Whose* am I?" John's Gospel follows suit: "The one who is of [that is, belongs to] God hears the words of God; on account of this, you do not hear them, because you are not of [that is, do not belong to] God" (8:47). A fundamental motivational question thus arises: *by whose power* am I living? By the lasting power of God's Spirit of authoritative unselfish love, or by my own short-lived, largely selfish power? The presence of one's selfishness, particularly in regard to outsiders and enemies, is a litmus test for one's being motivated by dying human power antithetical to the lasting unselfish power of a perfectly loving God.

By "individual's spirit," I mean just what constitutes an individual person's being an *intentional, morally responsible agent*. If a person were to survive bodily death (a possibility that seems coherently imaginable to many psychologically competent people), the person's spirit would be what survives.

For present explanatory purposes we can make do with this general approach, without digressing to metaphysical intricacies about the fundamental constitution of a human spirit. It seems clear, however, that one could, at least in principle, be an intentional agent without being physically embodied. Otherwise, we could rule out God from the start as a candidate for being an actual intentional agent. Of course, we can't thus rule out God's existence from the start, and that's no loss at all. So, we'll proceed with our general understanding of a spirit, and bracket metaphysical disputes that aren't directly relevant to the explanatory purposes at hand. (See Wiebe 2004, chap. 3, for relevant discussion of spirits; cf. Moser 1999.)

A perfectly loving God worthy of worship must be inherently and perfectly *personal* in virtue of being a perfect moral *agent* with supreme authority. So, the intervening personal Spirit of God would be the best source, including the most direct source, to confirm God's authoritative reality and our subordinate standing before God. Indeed, given God's being inherently personal, God's intervening personal Spirit would be the only *directly self-authenticating* source of firsthand veridical evidence of God's reality, since *the genuinely experienced presence* of God's intervening personal Spirit, via conscience, would constitute the firsthand veridical evidence in question, and only God's Spirit could provide this evidence.

By analogy, I myself am the only directly self-authenticating source of firsthand veridical evidence of my own reality, because I myself and only I myself could supply the needed firsthand veridical evidence. It doesn't follow at all, however, that there are self-authenticating religious *experiences*, subjectively considered. Religious experiences subjectively considered neither are nor entail *personal sources* of what is experienced in such experiences. We can coherently imagine, perhaps with help from an imagined far-reaching hallucination, that a person's religious experiences of God (subjectively characterized) exist, however intense and prolonged, but God doesn't exist. So, serious trouble will face any suggestion that a person's religious experiences of God (subjectively characterized) are self-authenticating in virtue of guaranteeing true belief that God as their evident object actually exists (cf. Yandell 1993, pp. 166–82, Hepburn 1958, 1963).

If God's own intervening personal Spirit couldn't authenticate firsthand veridical evidence of God's reality for humans (say, by actually intervening in human conscience with God's evident presence), then nothing else could either. Certainly, in that case, nothing *other than God* could. As an agent, I myself can be self-authenticating of firsthand veridical evidence of *my being a genuine agent*, because I can act in ways that *create* and *sustain* firsthand veridical evidence of my being an agent for a person by actually intervening as an agent, even as the agent who I am uniquely, in that person's experience. God's Spirit would have, of course, the same capability with regard to firsthand veridical evidence of God's reality.

Propositions, or truth-*bearers*, themselves aren't self-authenticating sources of firsthand veridical evidence, because they aren't intentional veridical evidence-*makers* in the way agents can be. Agents, unlike propositions, have causal powers that can bring about specific states of affairs, including veridical evidential states of affairs, and thus make certain propositions true, including evidential propositions. Although widely overlooked in philosophical discussions of evidence and knowledge of divine reality, this lesson figures centrally in a distinctly *pneumatic* epistemology for Jewish and Christian theism that focuses on salient, personally transforming power available as evidence to humans. We shall characterize this power below.

In picking something other than God's intervening Spirit as the direct source for veridically confirming God's reality, we could always plausibly ask this: what is the cognitively reliable connection between *that other thing* and *God's reality*? This question will leave a vast opening to doubt, even in a cognitively serious manner, the authenticity of the supposed veridical witness to God's reality. So, with unsurpassable authority and in agreement with God's character of perfect love, God's intervening Spirit directly witnesses to, and thus confirms, God's reality *directly* for willingly receptive people at God's chosen time. In thus witnessing with personal intervention in human conscience, the personal source of divine veridical personal evidence becomes the veridical evidence itself. This kind of *cognitive inspiration* yields firsthand foundational (that is, noninferential) evidence and knowledge of God's reality. It's doubtful, furthermore, that God could supply any other kind of direct confirmation of divine reality, given God's inherently personal and authoritative character.

Of course, if we want to engage skeptics on their own ground, without begging their key questions, we'll need to begin with *evident* experience that admittedly may be nonveridical, and then invoke the explanatory considerations presented in Chapter 2 (particularly in connection with its concluding argument from volitional transformation). Those considerations, however, are perfectly compatible with the more specific pneumatic epistemological considerations at hand. Indeed, the latter considerations can themselves be recommended on the kind of non-questionbegging explanatory basis offered in Chapter 2. Even so, having already challenged skeptics on their own evidential turf, we now can move on to a more fine-grained explanation of human knowledge of divine reality. The needed epistemology of such human knowledge isn't *just* a reply to skeptical doubts about divine reality.

It includes broader explanatory concerns, and we'll attend to those concerns below.

What else could God supply as firsthand veridical evidence of inherently personal and authoritative divine reality, besides God's evident intervening personal and authoritative Spirit? This was the personal and authoritative Spirit who reportedly called and empowered God's unique Son, Jesus, to demonstrate in life and in death God's authoritative and self-giving redemptive love for all people, in ways that surprise our natural expectations of God (on authority, see, for instance, Mk. 10:35–45; cf. Jn. 13:14). God's evident intervening personal Spirit provides the best firsthand evidence imaginable and the only firsthand evidence worthy of *full* commitment to God. Other kinds of alleged evidence, including those invoked in natural theology, suffer from a questionable inferential and cognitive *distance* from the perfectly authoritative and loving personal character and will of the God in question.

The second-best kind of veridical evidence, after firsthand acquaintance with God's intervening personal Spirit, comes from firsthand acquaintance with people transparently in volitional fellowship with, and thus led by, God's intervening Spirit. They can personally, saliently, and veridically manifest the reality of God's loving character to others, even if somewhat indirectly. Thus Paul writes: "...thanks be to God, who in Christ always leads us in triumph, and through us spreads the fragrance of the *knowledge of him* everywhere" (2 Cor. 2:14, RSV, italics added). God, according to Paul, leads obedient followers of Jesus in the triumph of divine self-giving love exemplified by Jesus, thereby making available volitional *knowledge* of Jesus and of his Father.

Paul regarded the Corinthian Christians themselves, in virtue of their volitionally transformed lives, as a "letter of recommendation" confirming the veracity of Paul's message of the reality of God's powerful redemptive love in Jesus. He writes to the Corinthian Christians: "You yourselves are our letter of recommendation, written on your hearts, to be known and read by all men; and you show that you are a letter from Christ delivered by us, written not with ink but with the Spirit of the living God, not on tablets of stone but on tablets of human hearts" (2 Cor. 3:2–3, RSV; cf. Jer. 31:31–34). God's intervening personal Spirit, according to Paul's pneumatic epistemology, changes a willingly receptive person's heart (or, volitional center) to make that person a living sign, even breathing and speaking evidence, of the reality of God's powerful transforming love. Even so, *my* fully appropriating the purposively available evidence of God's reality requires that I *myself* be acquainted directly, firsthand, and willingly with God's intervening Spirit, in fellowship with God.

Our willingly experiencing God's intervening personal Spirit, as a foundation of firsthand knowledge of God's reality, figures centrally in an ongoing
struggle between our destructively selfish wills and the life-giving will of a
perfectly loving God. The key question becomes this: what ultimately *empowers me* in my life? Is it my own, often selfish will, or is it the unselfish will of
God's intervening Spirit welcomed by me? A perfectly loving God, according to Jewish and Christian theism, eagerly offers God's Spirit to willingly
receptive humans to empower them to obey God wholeheartedly and thus
to love as God loves, in fellowship with God. Otherwise, apart from such
empowerment, we would lapse into unloving, selfish ways and thereby violate any command to love unselfishly as God loves. As human history and
our own lives show, if they show anything, we lack the power on our own to
love unselfishly as God loves. A little reflection on our own lives, particularly
on our meager aid to others in real need (such as the poor, the elderly, the
imprisoned, and the mentally or physically disabled) and to our enemies
(especially foreign enemies, on which see Via 2007), confirms this without a
doubt. We hoard resources while others suffer and die, and, when pressed,
we also promptly change the subject or invoke self-serving principles.

If we are to be divinely empowered, we need to be sincerely *willing* (on
the basis of purposively available evidence of God's reality) to have God's
intervening Spirit empower us to love unselfishly, because a perfectly loving
God won't coerce or otherwise depersonalize us in this regard. God doesn't
opt for coercion over genuine love, because coercion can't gain what God
seeks: namely, freely given volitional fellowship in divine unselfish love. (For
some horrifying 20th-century effects of neglecting this theological lesson, see
Forstman 1992.)

The actual power for us to love unselfishly would come from God's intervening Spirit, not from ourselves, because we have an obvious power deficiency in this area. There's no paradox here. God's intervening Spirit is what
actually empowers a willing person in unselfish love, even though one must
exercise one's will in yielding to, and thereby appropriating, the available
motivational power of God's Spirit. In being willing to have God's intervening
Spirit empower us, we put ourselves in a position to acquire both (a) otherwise
unavailable power to love unselfishly and thereby (b) otherwise unavailable
conclusive evidence and even knowledge of God's powerful reality. In yielding
to such power and evidence, we would yield to God's authority via perfectly
authoritative evidence from God's intervening Spirit (on such evidence, in
contrast with spectator evidence, see Chapter 1). In addition, as we see more
of the power of divine unselfish love in our own lives, courtesy of God's intervening Spirit, we thereby acquire more firsthand evidence of divine reality,

including God's character and Spirit working in our lives. Yielding to a divine call to unselfish love is thus cognitively as well as morally significant.

2. ACQUAINTANCE WITH POWER

One's willingness to befriend a person can, of course, put one in a position to acquire significant evidence of that person's reality. Still, I can have evidence *that* a person (say, the President of the United States) is real even though I am unwilling to befriend that person. What about *firsthand* evidence and knowledge of a person's reality? Do such evidence and knowledge depend on one's willingness to befriend the person in question? Let's approach this question regarding God, who has distinctive, perfectly loving purposes, including purposes regarding human purposes, such as the divine purpose to bring human purposes noncoercively in line with divine purposes.

As perfectly loving, the Jewish and Christian God seeks to promote firsthand evidence and knowledge of God, including the reality of God, in order to advance loving relationships among all persons on the basis of divine–human volitional fellowship. God seeks to promote such relationships by means of people being directly and willingly acquainted with God's intervening and empowering Spirit. In coming to know firsthand the reality of a person, I become acquainted with some of the personal, or agent, traits of that person. I must be willing not only to apprehend those traits but also to treat them as traits *of a person,* or an agent. I must be willing to attend to the personal traits in question as traits of a person rather than traits of a mere object. Knowing a person's reality firsthand thus goes beyond mere knowing *that* a person is real.

My mere knowledge that a person is real is compatible with my having no direct acquaintance with that person at all. Such factual knowledge that God is real wouldn't by itself please a perfectly loving God. The writer of the Epistle of James has in mind something analogous to mere factual knowledge when he says, with biting sarcasm: "You believe that God is one? You do well: even the demons believe [that this is so] and shudder" (Jas. 2:19). This is *not* to say or imply that factual knowledge that God is real has no importance. It's rather to say that, for the sake of pleasing a perfectly loving God, such knowledge must go together, and should arise together, with firsthand volitional, filial knowledge of God as authoritative Lord and Father. Given divine redemptive purposes, the two shouldn't be separated in actual knowers of God's reality, even though a conceptual distinction between them exists.

Firsthand filial knowledge of God includes love toward God as our supremely authoritative and loving Father, and thus engages our wills at the deepest level, that is, at the level of what (or better, whom) we love most. Paul thus puts mere factual knowledge in its proper place, given the reality of a perfectly loving God: " ... if I understand all mysteries and all knowledge ... but have not love, I am nothing" (1 Cor. 13:2). Paul's assumption behind this striking remark is that "love ... is the evidence (and, by implication, the test) of the presence of Christ by his Spirit in a person or community" (Gorman 2001, p. 157). So, Paul holds, without having an experience of love a person will lack evidence for what a person truly needs for lasting significance: namely, God's loving presence in that person's life. The evidential need for love from and then toward God thus entails that human factual knowledge of divine reality falls short of God's cognitive purposes. Filial knowledge of God offers the needed improvement.

The reality of God inherently includes a personal perfectly loving Spirit who isn't necessarily embodied but who, for redemptive purposes, would actively seek from humans their filial knowledge of divine reality. Given God's preeminent moral character, we should expect the knowledge in question to be distinctive. A perfectly loving God, we've noted, is inherently worthy of worship, and one's properly coming to know the reality of such a God entails one's coming volitionally to know firsthand the reality of God *as perfectly authoritative Lord.* ("Properly" here means "in a manner that satisfies the divine redemptive purpose of divine–human volitional fellowship in human knowledge of divine reality.") In addition, one's coming volitionally (and filially) to know firsthand the reality of *God as perfectly authoritative Lord* requires one's willingness to attend obediently to God's presented traits (including God's expressed love and mercy) as traits of a worship-worthy *personal agent* rather than a mere object. In excluding full volitional opposition to God, such knowing exceeds mere knowing that God exists.

Our obediently attending to God's presented traits, in keeping with God's authoritative call to divine–human volitional fellowship, requires our willingness to interact with them as traits of a personal agent worthy of worship and thus of wholehearted obedience and love. To satisfy divine cognitive purposes, then, we must be willing to receive God's self-revelation in a manner suited to worship, obedience, and love. This volitional response is no matter of mere reflection, but rather engages our wills in terms of the direction of our lives, and includes a response to some pressing, life-defining questions. Will we value as preeminent God's manifested will of perfect authoritative love toward all persons, even enemies and us, or will we cling to our own selfish wills and resulting projects? Will we respond in obedience to the authoritative call, via conscience, of God's love toward all persons, or will we languish in our own selfish willfulness? Life-defining answers to such questions rest on volitional commitment, not mere reflection, as they determine the ultimate direction of our lives. They define who we are and how we exist as moral and cognitive agents.

Volitionally (and filially) knowing God's reality firsthand, as noted, is *direct* in a way that mere factual knowledge that God is real isn't direct. It involves the willing reception of (the power of) God's intervening Spirit, and includes receiving a kind of *volitionally direct divine self-revelation* different from the alleged evidence of traditional natural theology. Volitionally knowing God's reality firsthand is knowing *God* firsthand, owing to willing acquaintance with God's intervening Spirit. Unlike the propositional knowledge alleged by natural theology, it isn't merely knowledge of propositional conclusions on the basis of propositional premises. It is *direct person-to-person* knowing, not just propositional knowing. It would thus be misleading to suggest (as does Scott 2006) that Paul's pneumatic epistemology follows a "coherentist," rather than a foundationalist, structure, given its role for nonpropositional experiential evidence.

As Chapter 2 suggested, human knowledge of God's reality comes as a divine gift out of genuine divine love, and not as a human earning of any kind that obligates God. This fits well with Paul's remark: "In the wisdom of God, the world did not come to know God through its wisdom...." (1 Cor. 1:21; cf. Isa. 29:14). Divine cognitive grace isn't part of the world's wisdom, owing to the latter's neglect of divine perfectly authoritative love as the foundation of human knowledge of God's reality. This neglect results in disregard of the key role of volitional fellowship in human knowledge of divine reality.

Volitionally knowing God's reality firsthand is underwritten, as suggested, by the superhuman *power* of God's intervening personal Spirit. Hermann Gunkel has characterized the kind of power in question:

> The Christian possesses a force more mighty than the natural man. What the latter could not do, the former is able to do. The natural man languished under the reign of sin; the Christian has become free from it. It was impossible for the Jew to keep the Law; Christian love is the fulfillment of the Law. The demons with dark impulse led the heathen astray to dumb idols; the Christian is able to cry, "Jesus is Lord." Thus a person cannot by himself create that mode of life which seizes the Christian; he cannot attain to the power over which the Christian disposes. This power is absolutely suprahuman. Therefore, in whomever this power dwells, he "receives" it (1 Cor. 2:12, Gal. 3:2, 14, 2 Cor. 11:4, Rom. 8:15). It is "given" to him (2 Cor. 1:22, 5:5, Rom. 5:5, 1 Thess. 4:8), "supplied" (Gal. 3:5), and "sent" (Gal. 4:6). This

power is "experienced" (endured: *pathein*), as are its activities (Gal. 3:4)....
The Christian is "led" by it (Gal. 5:18, Rom. 8:14).... The Christian life therefore rests upon a power that would be an impenetrable mystery if it were
explained in terms of human capabilities (1979 [1888], pp. 93–4).

The evident power in question is explained fittingly and best, if not explained
only, by the Good News that God's Spirit has truly intervened as a gracious
and powerful redemptive gift in human lives, under the lordship of Jesus,
the authoritative human dispenser of God's Spirit. Such evident power, as
Chapter 2 argued, yields salient and conclusive, if elusive, evidence of the
reality of a perfectly loving God. Even so, our recognition of such evidence
for what it is intended to be depends on our willingness to acknowledge that
it is not of our own making. For divine redemptive purposes, it must be
received as a gift or not at all. This is a central feature of divine cognitive
grace.

Although experiential, the obedient human reception of God's intervening
Spirit isn't a merely subjective matter. It yields one's becoming unselfishly
loving (at least to some discernible degree) as God is unselfishly loving, even
toward troublesome enemies. It bears distinctive and discernible fruits of the
intervening Spirit of a perfectly loving God, such as love, joy, peace, patience,
kindness, goodness, faithfulness, humility, and self-control (cf. Gal. 5:22–23).
These fruits aren't merely subjective phenomena; on the contrary, they are
discernible by anyone suitably attentive to them. As the powerful overflow of
divine love in a willingly receptive human life, they emerge in human lives in
ways that are readily identifiable and testable, even if one needs willing "eyes
to see and ears to hear" them.

The fruits of God's Spirit arise and function in a larger context of a willing
life under transformation by this Spirit as a gift from God to be received via
experientially grounded trust (Gal. 3:2, 14). David Brondos has identified the
central features of the power found in such a life:

> The Spirit enables believers to fulfill the just requirement of the law (Rom.
> 8:4), guides them and gives them wisdom and new life (Rom. 7:6, 8:14, Gal.
> 5:18), pours God's love into their hearts (Rom. 5:5), transforms them (2 Cor.
> 3:18), and produces good fruits in them (Gal. 5:22). Above all, the Holy Spirit
> is associated with power, since that Spirit empowers believers to live a new
> life according to God's will (Rom. 1:4, 15:13, 19, 1 Cor. 2:4, 12, 1 Thess. 1:5). At
> the same time, because they are "led by the Spirit," they are "not under the
> law" (Gal. 5:18), since they fulfill the just requirement of the law by living
> according to its spirit, ... and the Spirit gives them the power and wisdom
> necessary to live according to God's will, which the law alone cannot give
> (2006, pp. 86–7).

Attention to such distinctive power in a human life can yield an otherwise neglected source of evidence of divine reality. This purposively available evidence is inherently personal in that it reflects the personal moral character of a perfectly loving God who offers such evidence to be received via fellowship.

Some people will plausibly object that any number of contrary religious positions, including those of vile religious cults, can claim to derive support from a divine intervening spirit. In fact, they do claim this, and there should be no doubt about their doing so. As a result, firmly opposing fideism, one New Testament writer wisely advised people to "test the spirits to see whether they are [actually] of God" rather than to believe every spirit (1 Jn. 4:1). Otherwise, people would readily be led away from truth into serious error by any number of false teachers with immoral motives. Such teachers seriously hindered Paul's preaching and teaching of the Good News in the earliest Christian community in Corinth and Galatia. See, for instance, his corrective letters to the Corinthians and the Galatians (cf. Brown 1995, Martyn 1997b, and Martyn 1997c, pp. 117–26).

Jesus offered clear warnings about the need to test competing people and their positions: "Beware of false prophets, who come to you in sheep's clothing but inwardly are ravenous wolves. You will know them by their fruits. . . . Every sound tree bears good fruit, but the bad tree bears evil fruit. A sound tree cannot bear evil fruit, nor can a bad tree bear good fruit" (Matt. 7:15–18). Likewise, one can know the authenticity of God's intervening Spirit by means of the fruits demanded and yielded by the Spirit in one's own life. This Spirit noncoercively demands and empowers one, in fellowship with God, to become loving (at least to some degree) as God is unselfishly loving, even toward enemies. This is, in keeping with God's perfectly loving character, the primary fruit of God's intervening Spirit in a willingly receptive person (1 Cor. 13:1–13; cf. Eph. 3:17–19, Col. 2:2, 3:14), and it is identifiable and testable in a willing person's life. God's intervening Spirit thus comes with salient evidence observable by any suitably attentive person, and such evidence enables one to exclude imposters.

According to various New Testament writers, the intervening Spirit of God empowered Jesus in his perfect obedience to God, and thus is manifested uniquely in his life, death, and resurrection. (Both Paul and Luke, for instance, highlight this theme.) We will properly apprehend this Spirit's reality, in accordance with God's redemptive purposes, only if we are *willing* to have "eyes to see and ears to hear" this Spirit in keeping with God's redemptive purposes. That is, we ourselves must be open to become volitionally attuned to God's transforming Spirit. (Chapter 2 emphasized the cognitive significance of the needed volitional attunement.)

In connection with human knowing of divine reality, a perfectly loving God would seek noncoercively to move our wills to have us learn to love as God loves, in fellowship with God. How exactly would God's Spirit "intervene" to lead us toward God's character in this way? More specifically, what would be involved in "acquaintance" with the "power" of God's intervening Spirit? In addition, how, if at all, would the intervention of God's personal Spirit be related to the death and resurrection of Jesus as God's authoritative Son? We need to face such questions head on, but, as is usual in philosophy and theology, a bit of methodological stage-setting must come first.

3. JERUSALEM AND ATHENS

We have been going back and forth between philosophy and theology for our explanatory purposes as if the two areas are actually importantly related, especially regarding human knowledge of divine reality. Contemporary philosophers seldom follow suit, perhaps owing to fear of things theological, but that fear may be a reason to proceed as we have, after all. In any case, we won't, and shouldn't, hesitate to cross disciplinary boundaries when explanation, knowledge, and truth are served. It's time to comment briefly on the two areas for the sake of setting a methodological context. Chapter 4 will extend this treatment in ways foreign but challenging to contemporary philosophy and theology. It will thus move us beyond business as usual in philosophy, in light of the dire human predicament of destructive selfishness and impending death.

What, if anything, does Jerusalem, the center of the earliest (Jewish-) Christian movement of Jesus's disciples, have to do with Athens, the center of western philosophy in its inception? Do they share *intellectual purposes*? Do they share *means* to achieving their intellectual purposes? Do they share *anything* significant at all? The latter three questions demand *yes* answers, if only because Jerusalem and Athens both aim to achieve *truth* (at least of a certain kind), and they aim to achieve truth (at least of the kind in question) via *knowledge* of truth. These two factors are significant in terms of what defines Jerusalem and Athens. So, Jerusalem and Athens do share something significant, however much they differ and fear each other.

The fact that Jerusalem and Athens aim for truth via knowledge of truth doesn't set them apart from many other movements. The later natural and social sciences, properly understood, aim for truth via knowledge, but they aren't native citizens of either Jerusalem or Athens. The earliest western philosophy definitive of Athens aims for a kind of truth whose discovery didn't wait upon the later investigations of the natural and social sciences.

Accordingly, Socrates and Plato proceeded with their philosophical work even though the natural and social sciences were at best immature, if they existed at all, strictly speaking. Likewise, the theology characteristic of the earliest Christian movement in Jerusalem didn't wait for the empirical work of the later natural and social sciences. Its theology of the Good News of God's redemptive intervention in Jesus as God's Son and authoritative dispenser of God's Spirit went out to the wider world in a manner independent of the natural and social sciences. So, the original philosophers and theologians from Athens and Jerusalem didn't need to consult the natural or social sciences to launch their respective enterprises of seeking truth via knowledge.

An illuminating question is: what *distinguishes* Jerusalem from Athens? Speaking generally and roughly, we may say that Socrates and Plato launched a *wisdom movement* whereby they aimed to characterize, via explanatory knowledge, humans as cognitive and moral agents in pursuit of the good life. The wisdom movement of Socrates and Plato assumed that "... those who really apply themselves in the right way to philosophy are directly and of their own accord preparing themselves for dying and death" (*Phaedo* 64A). Death, they held, is the release of the soul from the body, whereby the soul can, without bodily distraction, attain finally to unadulterated truth and clear thinking. The person of wisdom (that is, the philosopher, of course) thus welcomes death as an opportunity for intellectual purification from the physical, sensory, and emotional toxins of the present transitory world. Plato's *Phaedo* is the founding manifesto for this intellectual-enlightenment philosophy characteristic of ancient Athens as the birthplace of western philosophy (although the sophists and other interlocutors offered much annoying resistance).

Jesus and his devout follower Paul of Tarsus, in contrast to the philosophers of Athens, promoted a *Good News power movement* that offered people the power of bodily, moral, and spiritual redemption by God as gracious reconciliation to God in divine–human fellowship (see, for example, Lk. 15:11–24, 24:1–35, Matt. 20:1–16, 1 Cor. 1:9, 15:12–32, 2 Cor. 5:16–21). They proceeded in the light of such ancient Hebrew prophets as Isaiah, Jeremiah, Ezekiel, Daniel, and Hosea, even drawing a general idea of divine Good News, whether in noun or verbal form, from the book of Isaiah (see Isa. 52:7, 61:1; cf. Fitzmyer 1979, Wenham 1995, chap. 2, Watts 1997, chap. 4, and Stanton 2004). The promise of divine redemption preached by Jesus and Paul included a promise of *bodily* resurrection that isn't to be confused with resuscitation of a dead person or with immortality.

Socrates and Plato hoped for immortality for humans but had no place for bodily resurrection, because the human body, by their lights, would only obstruct purification as intellectual enlightenment. Jesus and Paul, however, taught in the tradition of Genesis 1–2 that God's creation of the physical world was initially good, and not a mere impediment to our intellectual purification. They embraced and extended the divine promise to some of the ancient Hebrew prophets that the people of God would be raised from the dead, even bodily (see Isa. 26:19, Dan. 12:2, Job 19:25–27, Mk. 12:18–27, Lk. 20:27–40, 1 Cor. 15:12–57). Without such resurrection, they assumed, divine redemption of humans would be gravely incomplete and thus imperfect, because God intended humans to be embodied. Full resurrection, in their eyes, thus included embodiment; accordingly, Paul and various other earliest followers of Jesus preached the actual bodily resurrection of Jesus and, for the future, his followers (see Bockmuehl 2001; cf. Filson 1956, Williams 1982, 2000a). Jerusalem thus contradicts Athens, and the two won't be reconciled in their attitudes toward the value of the physical world and what humans ultimately need. (On the status and role of human spirits according to Jesus and Paul, see Moser 1999.)

The Good News of God's redemptive self-revelation in the life, death, and resurrection of Jesus is, according to Paul, "the power of God for salvation for everyone who trusts [God] . . . " (Rom. 1:16; cf. 1 Cor. 1:18, 2 Cor. 5:19, and Snodgrass 1994). Paul thought of the obedient death-by-crucifixion undergone by Jesus and the resurrection of Jesus by God from the dead as two decisively related moments in a single life-giving, redemptive power movement by the one true God of authoritative perfect love. Indeed, the resurrection of Jesus was so central to Paul's understanding of salvation as divine redemption from evil and death that he held: ". . . if Christ has not been raised [from the dead], your faith is futile and you are still in your sins" (1 Cor. 15:17). We need to consider why this is. Paul speaks of the kind of "knowing Christ" that is essential to human redemption, or salvation, as involving our knowing "the power of his resurrection" via our being conformed to Christ's death (Phil. 3:10). Paul, in short, was a proclaimer of the cross of Jesus *because* he was also a proclaimer of the resurrection of Jesus by God for divine redemptive purposes regarding humans. His considered view is that the two must be portrayed together to capture God's redemptive Good News accurately (see, for example, Rom. 3–6).

The personal divine power central to the Good News movement of Jerusalem is not only morally significant but also cognitively important. Somehow philosophers of religion have missed this, and hence the needed epistemology of Jewish and Christian theism hasn't been developed adequately. As a result, we aim now to correct this deficiency. Paul holds that he knows the risen Jesus on the basis of his knowing firsthand the power of Jesus's resurrection (cf. Phil. 3:8–11). Redemption, according to Paul, consists in one's knowing firsthand the divine power of Jesus's resurrection in such a way that one is transformed by it to conform to Jesus's self-giving death, in fellowship with the God who raised Jesus from the dead.

Joseph Fitzmyer comments:

> This "power" [of Jesus's resurrection] is not limited to the influence of the risen Jesus on the Christian, but includes a reference to the origin of that influence in the Father himself. The knowledge, then, that Paul seeks to attain, the knowledge that he regards as transforming the life of a Christian and his/her sufferings, must be understood as encompassing the full ambit of that power. It emanates from the Father, raises Jesus from the dead at his resurrection, endows him with a new vitality, and finally proceeds from him as the life-giving, vitalizing force of the "new creation" [cf. 2 Cor. 5:17] and of the new life that Christians in union with Christ experience and live.... [T]he knowledge of [this power], emanating from Christian faith, is the transforming force that vitalizes Christian life and molds the suffering of the Christian to the pattern which is Christ (1970, pp. 208–9).

This portrayal of resurrection power fits well with Paul's aforementioned view that the Good News of what God has done through Jesus is "the power of *God*" for human salvation (Rom. 1:16; cf. Eph. 1:19–20). As a result, the Good News movement advanced by Paul is no narrow Jesus or Christ cult. Instead, Paul announces it as a power movement of the one true God of the whole world, including Jews and Gentiles (Rom. 3:29, 15:15–17; cf. Dunn 1993).

God's intervening personal Spirit supplies both the needed *power* of resurrection (Rom. 1:4) and the needed firsthand authoritative *evidence* and *knowledge* of this power (cf. Rom. 5:5, 8:15–16) to willing recipients. Such a pneumatic approach to evidence and knowledge of divine reality is altogether foreign to modern ways of thinking about knowledge that neglect purposively available authoritative evidence offered in accordance with divine redemptive purposes. As a result, this approach is widely neglected in contemporary philosophy of religion and theology.

Regarding evidence of divine reality, philosophers of religion and theologians often leave inquirers without an authoritative volitional challenge, and at the level of merely theoretical assessment of propositional evidence, including historical propositional evidence. At this level, we can't make good sense of the revolutionary Good News movement launched by Jerusalem, particularly by Jesus and, in his wake, Paul. Such a life-transforming revolution needs an authoritative volitional anchor deeper than merely theoretical assessment of propositional evidence, including historical propositional evidence (see Williams 1982, 2000a, and Allison 2005 on this point, in connection with theoretical historical evidence for the resurrection of Jesus). We are redirecting religious epistemology, accordingly, to the authoritative personal evidence that offers the needed volitional challenge and thus moves beyond merely theoretical assessment.

What, then, does Jerusalem have to do with Athens? Athens yields an intellectual-enlightenment wisdom movement that holds out no hope or even desire of lasting life via bodily resurrection. Contemporary western philosophy, for the most part, follows suit, particularly given its widespread abandonment of any kind of robust theism. Jerusalem, following Jesus, offers a Good News power movement of human redemption as fellowship with God and eventual deliverance by God from both evil and death into lasting life, including bodily resurrection. The resurrection of Jesus, the otherwise obscure Galilean troublemaker, is thereby proclaimed as the first fruits of this revolutionary movement of God's intervening Spirit. The movement, as represented by Jesus, focuses on the gracious redemptive intervention of a divine personal Spirit that empowers lasting life in divine–human fellowship, including freedom to love and to forgive all people, even enemies, in the face of impending physical death. Life, according to this Good News movement, can offer, via divine empowerment, progressive moral and spiritual renewal toward God's character of unselfish love and, in the future, bodily resurrection.

The pressing question from Athens to Jerusalem is cognitive, if typically skeptical: how can one *know* that the seemingly farfetched redemptive promise of the Good News movement is actually reliable rather than just wishful thinking? The answer from Jerusalem is straightforward but widely neglected: by volitionally knowing firsthand the promise-*Giver*, via one's willing participation in the available power of God's life-giving and life-transforming Spirit. The last two sections of this chapter will clarify such participation. The question from Jerusalem to Athens is thus, as always, volitional: are we truly *willing* to participate in the powerful life of a perfectly loving God, thereby giving up our selfish lives for the sake of lasting lives in God's unselfish love and forgiveness, even toward our enemies? We await an answer from Athens, conveniently focused as it is on various other, less urgent matters. Meanwhile, let's move deeper into the power of the Good News, the heart of the Jerusalem movement stemming from Jesus himself.

4. GOOD NEWS

The Good News movement in Jerusalem underwent a dramatic shift between the time of the earthly Jesus and the time after his crucifixion that resulted in the preaching, by Paul and many others, of the bodily resurrection of Jesus by God. Somehow Jesus as the preacher of the Good News about *God's* arriving kingdom, under formative influence from the book of Isaiah (cf. Mk. 1:1–15), became *an object of focus* in the preaching of the Good News by his earliest, Jewish disciples. In short, the *preacher* became part of the *preached*; the *proclaimer* became part of the *proclaimed*, as many New Testament scholars have noted (see Filson 1956, Kümmel 1973, Beasley-Murray 1986, Snodgrass 2005, and Lemcio 2006).

Taking a lead from C. H. Dodd (1936), Eugene Lemcio (1991) has identified a common kerygmatic core regarding the Good News in nineteen of the twenty-seven books of the New Testament. This core, according to Lemcio (1991, p. 118), has the following six common ingredients:

(1) God
(2) sent (in Gospels) or raised
(3) Jesus.
(4) A response (receiving, repentance, faith)
(5) toward God (regarding God's sending or raising Jesus)
(6) brings benefits (variously described).

Lemcio has isolated this kerygmatic core in all of the main representatives and traditions of the New Testament. He sums up the unifying kerygma thus: "It declares the Good News of God's sending [Jesus] or raising Jesus from the dead. By responding obediently to God, one receives the benefits stemming from this salvific event" (1991, p. 127; cf. Lemcio 2006). Lemcio's landmark work on the New Testament message enables us to speak of *the* Good News kerygma, beyond any multiplicity of kerygmata. (For one of the earliest statements of such an approach, see Forsyth 1907, 1913; cf. Dillistone 1977, p. 134, on Forsyth's influence on Dodd.)

In one of the earliest statements of the Good News in the New Testament, Paul writes:

> For I delivered to you of first importance what I have received: that Christ died for our sins according to the Scriptures, that he was buried, that he was raised on the third day according to the Scriptures, and that he appeared to Peter, and then to the twelve. After that, he appeared to more than five hundred brothers at the same time, most of whom remain until now, but some have fallen asleep. Then he appeared to James, then to all the apostles, and last of all he appeared also to me, as to one untimely born. . . . If Christ has not been raised, our preaching is futile and your faith is futile too. We are also then found to be false witnesses about God, because we have testified about God that he raised Christ from the dead. . . . If Christ has not been

raised, your faith is futile; you are still in your sins.... If we have hope in Christ only for this life, we are to be pitied more than all men. But Christ has been raised from the dead, the firstfruits of those who have fallen asleep (1 Cor. 15:3–8, 14–15, 17, 19–20).

After Jesus, Paul had unsurpassed influence in clarifying the Good News; so, we do well now to attend to his thought. The Goods News, according to Paul, includes that "Christ died for our sins" and was raised from the dead. Paul regards the Good News as "useless," "false," and "futile" in the absence of the resurrection of Jesus. In particular, he links the resurrection of Jesus to the forgiveness of human sins in such a way that if there is no resurrection of Jesus, "you are still in your sins." As suggested above, this needs clarification.

According to various New Testament writers, a central theme of the Good News is that human sins are forgiven by God, and humans are thereby offered reconciliation with God, in connection with the life, death, and resurrection of Jesus. What specifically this connection involves has been and remains a topic of controversy among philosophers of religion and theologians. If we understand *atonement* as divine–human reconciliation that properly deals with human sin as resistance to divine unselfish love, we may understand the heart of the controversy about the life, death, and resurrection of Jesus as a debate about atonement. How, specifically, do the life, death, and resurrection of Jesus figure in (intended) divine–human atonement? In addition, how is such atonement to be appropriated by humans? Furthermore, is such atonement really needed by humans? If so, why? These are just a few of the many pressing questions that emerge regarding the person and mission of Jesus. Such questions have prompted seemingly endless controversy, and they bear directly on the human predicament of selfishness and death.

At the Last Supper, according to Matthew's Gospel (26:28), Jesus announced that he will die "for the forgiveness of sins." The atoning sacrifice of Jesus as God's sinless offering for sinful humans is, at least according to Matthew's Jesus, at the center of God's redemptive work. Among other New Testament writings, John's Gospel (cf. Jn. 1:36) and Paul's undisputed letters (cf. 1 Cor. 5:7, 2 Cor. 5:21, Rom. 3:24–26) concur on this lesson about atonement. This unique role assigned to Jesus in divine–human atonement sets him apart from Abraham, Moses, Paul, Peter, Confucius, Krishna, Gautama the Buddha, Muhammad, the Dalai Lama, and every other known religious leader. Only Jesus, as portrayed at least by Matthew, John, and Paul, offered himself as God's atoning sacrifice to God for sinful humans. Only

Jesus, therefore, emerged at the center of the Good News of God's intended redemption of wayward humans.

Many people share the apostle Peter's initial denial that the death of Jesus is central to the divine plan of reconciliation of humans to God (see Mk. 8:31–32). In fact, they doubt that the crucifixion of the Son of God would even be compatible with God's merciful love. Paul evidently faced similar doubts about the cross of Jesus among the earliest Christians in Corinth. His response: "... I resolved to know nothing while I was with you except Jesus Christ *and him crucified*" (1 Cor. 2:2, italics added). The obedient death of Jesus is, in Paul's portrayal of the Good News, no less important than his resurrection for divine–human reconciliation. We do well to consider why, for the sake of better understanding of human knowledge of God's reality in connection with the Good News reconciliation movement.

The crucifixion of Jesus seems to brand him as a dismal failure, even as one "cursed" before God (see Gal. 3:13, Deut. 21:23; cf. Brondos 2001). Nonetheless, the cross of Jesus is proclaimed by Paul, Matthew, and John, among other New Testament writers, as a central place of God's incognito atoning sacrifice and turnaround victory. Out of the fatal apparent defeat of Jesus, according to the Good News, God brought a unique demonstration of divine love and forgiveness toward humans, even toward God's enemies. The crucifixion of Jesus is offered as a central part of God's intended grand reversal of the dark human tragedy of alienation from God.

The divine reversal aims at divine–human reconciliation, or atonement, by means of a stark but powerful manifestation of God's character as exemplified in Jesus, the God-sent innocent victim who offers forgiveness and fellowship instead of condemnation to wayward humans (on which see Williams 1982, 2000b). As a result, we may call this *the divine manifest-offering* approach to atonement. What is being made *manifest* is God's character of righteous and forgiving love, and what is being *offered*, in keeping with that character, is lasting divine–human fellowship as a gracious divine gift on the basis of both (a) the forgiveness offered and demonstrated via God's atoning sacrifice in Jesus, the innocent victim of humans, and (b) God's resurrection of Jesus as Lord and as Giver of God's Spirit. The manifestation of God's self-giving character in Jesus reveals the kind of God who is thereby offering forgiveness and lasting fellowship to humans. Although the death of Jesus doesn't bring about divine–human reconciliation by itself, it supplies God's distinctive means of intended implementation via divine manifestation and offering. For the sake of actual divine–human reconciliation, humans must still *receive* the manifest-offering of forgiveness and fellowship via grounded trust, or faith.

Paul acknowledges that on its surface his message of the cross of Jesus as central to divine–human atonement appears to some people to be sheer nonsense:

> ... the message of the cross is foolishness to those perishing, but to us being saved it is the power of God. ... Jews request signs and Greeks look for wisdom, but we preach Christ crucified, a stumbling block to Jews and foolishness to Gentiles, but to those called [by God], both Jews and Greeks, Christ the power of God and the wisdom of God. For the foolishness of God is wiser than human wisdom, and the weakness of God is stronger than human strength (1 Cor. 1:18, 22–25).

The power and wisdom of God's self-giving, forgiving character are manifested, according to Paul, in the crucified Jesus, whom God approvingly raised as Lord from death on the cross. Such divine power and wisdom, Paul contends, overcome even death, thereby surpassing any human power or wisdom, including the human power of evil, and even human hate toward other people.

According to the Pauline Good News, God sent God's own beloved Son, Jesus, to live and to die and to be resurrected by God for a twofold divine purpose: to manifest God's righteous and forgiving love for all people, even God's enemies (Rom. 5:6–8), and thereby to offer people forgiveness and lasting divine–human fellowship under Jesus as Lord and as Giver of God's Spirit (1 Thess. 5:10). Jesus, on this portrayal of divine–human reconciliation, came from God to identify with us humans in our weakness and trouble, while he represented his Father in righteous and merciful self-giving love. He thus aims as divinely appointed mediator to represent, and to serve as a personal bridge between, God *and* humans by seeking to reconcile humans to his Father with the divine gift of fellowship anchored in merciful, forgiving love and (the power of) God's own intervening Spirit.

Jesus's obedient death on the cross, commanded of him by God (Rom. 3:25, 1 Cor. 5:7, Phil. 2:8; cf. Mk. 14:23–24, Jn. 18:11), aims to manifest how far he and his Father will go, even to gruesome death, to offer divine forgiveness and fellowship to wayward humans. By divine assignment, Jesus gives humans all he has, avowedly from his Father's self-giving love, to manifest that God mercifully and righteously loves humans to the fullest extent and offers humans the gracious threefold gift of unearned forgiveness, fellowship, and membership in God's everlasting family via reception of God's own intervening Spirit (cf. Rom. 5:8, Jn. 3:16–17). Here is the very core of the Pauline Good News that emerges from Jerusalem and goes far beyond anything in the wisdom movement from Athens.

God, as proclaimed in the Good News, uses the cross of the obedient Jesus as the place where our selfish rebellion against God is mercifully judged and forgiven by God. This does *not* mean that God punished Jesus, a reportedly innocent man. No New Testament writer teaches otherwise, contrary to some subsequent, less careful theologians. (Someone might counter with Mk. 14:27 or Gal. 3:13, but neither passage states or implies that God punished Jesus.) According to the Good News, God sent Jesus into our troubled, rebellious world to undergo, willingly and obediently, gruesome suffering and death at human hands that God would deem adequate for dealing justly, under divine righteousness, with our selfish rebellion against God and God's unselfish love. Jesus thus pays the price on our behalf for righteous divine reconciliation of sinners, and thereby, in manifesting and offering divine forgiveness, removes any need for selfish fear, condemnation, anxiety, shame, guilt, and punishment among us in relation to God (Rom. 8:1).

The Good News implies that Jesus, in dying "for our sins," aimed to manifest God's perfect forgiving love for us and thereby to offer reconciliation of us to his righteous Father as Jesus becomes our trusted Lord and Redeemer. This message of atonement as a divine manifest-offering of reconciliation through Jesus is central to the Good News, according to which the cross of Jesus is a crucial focal point of divine–human reconciliation. In the writings of Paul and John, among other New Testament writers, the self-giving, crucified Jesus is the manifest power and mirror-image of a perfectly loving and forgiving God. The divine resurrection of Jesus, according to the Good News, confirmed this unique redemptive role for Jesus.

According to Paul, the ultimate motive for the crucifixion of Jesus is his Father's *righteous love* for humans:

> ...Now apart from law, a righteousness of God has been manifested, to which the Law and the Prophets bear witness. This righteousness of God comes through trust in Jesus Christ to all who trust [in him]. There is no difference, for all have sinned and fall short of the glory of God, and are justified freely by his grace through the redemption in Christ Jesus, whom God put forth as an atoning sacrifice, through trust, in his blood. He did this to manifest his righteousness, because in his forbearance he had passed over the sins previously committed. He did this to manifest his righteousness in the current time, in order to be righteous and the one who justifies those who trust in Jesus (Rom. 3:21–26).

Three times Paul here identifies the *manifestation* of God's righteousness as central to God's redemptive plan involving Jesus, including his death. In addition, Paul twice suggests that this divine manifestation is aimed at God's graciously justifying, or reconciling, humans before God via trust in Jesus. The previous passage thus repeatedly endorses the proposed divine manifest-offering approach to atonement in Jesus. God's graciously forgiving offer of divine–human reconciliation, according to Paul, comes with a manifestation of God's righteousness in the crucified Jesus; so, divine grace is anything but cheap grace.

Unlike many later theologians, Paul decisively links God's aforementioned righteousness, or justice, with God's love: "God manifests his own love *(agape)* for us in that while we were yet sinners, Christ died for us.... Since we have now been justified by his blood, how much more shall we be saved by him from the wrath [of God].... [W]hile we were enemies [of God], we were reconciled to God through the death of his Son...." (Rom. 5:8–10). God, according to Paul, thus takes the initiative and the crucial means through Jesus in offering a gracious gift of divine–human reconciliation. This offer manifests God's forgiving love as well as God's righteousness. Indeed, Paul takes the sacrificial death of Jesus to manifest divine forgiving love and righteousness. He seems, accordingly, to have thought of divine gracious love as *righteous love.*

Given purposively available evidence of an authoritative offer from God's intervening Spirit, humans are to receive the gracious gift via trust, or faith, in God and Jesus. The Pauline call to faith in Jesus (cf. Gal. 2:16) stems from his being God's perfect human atoning representative (Rom. 5:8–11, 15–19). The offered gift can't be earned by human "works" that obligate God to redeem us (Rom. 4:4), because humans have fallen short of the divine standard of perfect unselfish love (Rom. 3:10–12, 23). Even so, obedience as internal volitional submission to God's authoritative call to human repentance and divine–human fellowship is central to appropriating the offered gift (cf. Rom. 1:5, 6:16, 16:26, 2 Thess. 1:8). Such appropriating, of course, must not be confused with earning a reward. The divine gift of righteousness to humans comes not by human earning but rather by divine gracious reckoning via human trust, which includes volitional yielding, toward the Gift-Giver (see Rom. 4:5–11, 10:8–10). As a result, human prideful boasting, or taking of self-credit for personal achievement, is altogether misplaced before God (Rom. 3:27, 1 Cor. 1:28–31).

According to the Good News, the God of perfect love, the Father of Jesus, is also a God of *righteous wrath and judgment* (Rom. 1:18, 2:2–8; cf. Reiser 1997, Meadors 2006). This idea has been distorted by many people to serve as a license for cruelty, and often it's simply ignored altogether. Both extremes are harmful in neglecting an important lesson about God's righteous character. The sound idea is twofold: (a) *because* God is inherently loving toward all other persons, God loves all sinners, including God's enemies, and (b) *because* God loves all sinners, God has wrath and judgment toward sin, given that sin leads to death (as separation from God) rather than life (as obedient fellowship with God). God as perfectly loving seeks to reconcile humans to God, even via judgment, in a way that exceeds mere divine forgiveness and satisfies God's standard of morally perfect love in divine–human reconciliation and fellowship (see Rom. 11:15, 30–32, 1 Cor. 1:9).

Mere forgiveness of humans by God wouldn't adequately deal with the basis of the wrongdoing that called for divine forgiveness, namely, human neglect of divine gracious authority (on which see Rom. 1:21, 28). (We'll return to the topic of forgiveness in the next section.) In exposing and judging the basis of human wrongdoing, God upholds perfect moral integrity in divine redemption of humans, and avoids the condoning of human evil. Through the loving self-sacrifice of Jesus, according to the Pauline Good News, *God* meets the standard of morally perfect love *for us*, when we couldn't, wouldn't, and didn't, and then God offers this gracious gift of divinely provided righteousness to us, as God's Passover lamb for us (1 Cor. 5:7), to be received by trust in Jesus and God as redeeming Gift-Givers. Otherwise, our prospects for meeting the standard of divine perfect love would be bleak indeed. (On gift-righteousness from God, in contrast to human righteousness via the law, as central to Paul's thought, see Phil. 3:9, Rom. 3:21–26, 10:3–4, Gal. 3:11–12; cf. Westerholm 2004, chap. 15, Stuhlmacher 1986, chap. 5.)

Paul reports that "God was in Christ reconciling the world to Himself," not counting our sins against us (2 Cor. 5:19; cf. Fee 2007, pp. 197–98). This theme of divine reconciling forgiveness is at the heart of the Good News of Jesus Christ. We typically hold a less demanding standard of righteous love than the divine standard, and we thereby domesticate God and the Good News, if we retain either at all. The image of a perfectly righteous but reconciling and forgiving God, as represented by Jesus, is scandalously offensive to selfishly prideful humans. God's righteous but self-giving forgiving love in Jesus, as an alternative to coercive selfish power, makes no sense to us in the competitive terms we ordinarily use to understand ourselves and the world. Accordingly, the Good News as represented by Paul can seem to us to be foolish at best.

The heart of the cross *for Jesus* was his perfectly loving obedience to his Father on our behalf for the sake of divine–human reconciliation via divine forgiveness, and not his physical suffering. Jesus expressed the central place of obedience to his Father in Gethsemane: "Not what I will, but what You will" (Mk. 14:35–36; cf. Mk. 14:22–25). Likewise, Paul vividly identified the crucial role of Jesus's obedience: "Christ Jesus, who, being in the form of God, did not consider equality with God something to be grasped, but he emptied himself, taking the form of a servant, being made in human likeness. Being found in appearance as a man, he humbled himself and became *obedient* to death, even death on a cross" (Phil. 2:6–8, italics added; cf. Rom. 5:18–19 and Fee 2007, chap. 9). The acknowledged obedience of Jesus in his death is, of course, obedience to the redemptive mission of his Father, who gave Jesus his salvific cup of suffering and death for the sake of reconciling humans to God (Rom. 8:3–4; cf. Jn. 18:11). Jesus, accordingly, obeyed in Gethsemane in order to be able to manifest and offer divine merciful reconciliation to humans.

Jesus can be and is presented as God's Passover lamb on our behalf (1 Cor. 5:7; cf. Jn. 1:29), that is, God's atoning sacrifice to God for us (Rom. 3:25), because he was perfectly obedient, fully righteous, in the eyes of his perfectly righteous Father. Jesus's perfectly obedient life toward God, according to at least Paul, Matthew, and John, is an acceptable sacrifice to God for us and is offered on our behalf by Jesus and God. Gethsemane and the Last Supper manifest these central lessons about Jesus's obedience toward God. Gethsemane shows Jesus passionately resolving to put his Father's will first, even in the face of death. The Last Supper shows Jesus portraying, with the bread and the wine as emblematic of his body and his blood, the ultimate self-sacrifice pleasing to his Father on our behalf. The notion of a Passover sacrifice has roots in ancient Judaism (see Ex. 12:1–27), but it continued to figure in the Good News preached, at least by Paul, among the earliest Christians in Corinth and Rome, including non-Jewish Christians. These considerations suggests that an idea of sacrifice offered by God and Jesus is central to the kind of redemption offered in the Good News, at least as understood by Jesus and Paul (see Stuhlmacher 1986, chaps. 3, 6; cf. Daly 1978, 2003).

Given God's perfect righteousness and human sin, according to the Good News proclaimed by Paul and others, God graciously took the initiative to supply a perfect atoning sacrifice on our behalf. The perfectly obedient Jesus provided the divine sacrifice for us, at the command of his Father. Whereas we ourselves have fallen short of the divine standard of perfectly righteous love, such righteous love is manifested in Jesus's life of obedient submission to God, even on the cross, on our behalf. Jesus, as proclaimed in the Good News, voluntarily and uniquely pays the price of our selfish rebellion against God by obediently meeting for us God's standard of perfectly righteous love. Going beyond dying for us, he is thus uniquely qualified to dispatch God's own Spirit to empower willing people to enter into genuine fellowship with God and obedience toward God. Jesus, then, is announced as the Lord and Savior who takes away the sin of the world (Rom. 5:17–19, 7:24–25, Jn. 1:29; cf. 1 Jn. 2:2). This message about Jesus is central to the Good News preached by Paul and others, and there is no comparable message on offer elsewhere.

This message depends on God's perfectly righteous character and redemptive plan for the world (as identified in Isaiah, for instance) rather than on abstract principles of justice or love that typically misrepresent the actual motivation for what Paul calls God's "redemption in Christ Jesus" (Rom. 3:24; cf. Rom. 5:10–11).

The Good News redemptive mission of Jesus, as proclaimed by Jesus, Paul, and many other first-century Jews, included not only his death but also his resurrection by God. The divine manifest-offering approach to atonement captures this fact by acknowledging the divine gracious offering of *lasting* divine–human fellowship under Jesus as Lord. Such divinely offered fellowship requires, of course, that Jesus be alive to be Lord lastingly on behalf of humans. This illuminates Paul's otherwise puzzling remarks that Jesus "was raised for our justification" and that "we shall be saved by his life" (Rom. 4:25, 5:10; cf. Brondos 2006, pp. 74–7), once we acknowledge that justification and salvation from death are, like forgiveness, for the sake of lasting divine–human fellowship under Jesus as Lord (cf. 1 Thess. 5:10).

The resurrection of Jesus, as proclaimed by Paul, is part of God's indelible signature of approval on, and even exaltation of, God's obedient, crucified Son, the atoning sacrifice from God for humans (Phil. 2:9–11). The resurrection of Jesus thus gets some of its crucial significance from the cross, where Jesus gave full obedience to his Father in order to supply a manifest-offering of divine–human reconciliation, including divine forgiveness, to humans via trust in God. In his full, life-surrendering obedience, Jesus manifested his authoritative Father's worthiness of complete trust and obedience, even when death ensues. More generally, Jesus confirmed through his perfect obedience the preeminent authority of his Father for the sake of forgiving and redeeming humans, and his Father, in turn, approvingly vindicated and exalted Jesus, likewise for the sake of forgiving and redeeming humans. Both Jesus and his Father, then, play a crucial role in the divine manifest-offering aimed at the atoning redemption of humans. We shall clarify the key idea of divine forgiveness of humans before returning to the significance of resurrection in the Good News.

5. FORGIVENESS UNTO RECONCILIATION

The forgiveness involved in the Good News, as the previous section indicated, is a *means* to divine–human reconciliation and fellowship, and not an end in itself. We need to clarify this important lesson in light of some common misunderstandings of forgiveness. Morally perfect divine love is perfectly merciful, that is, perfectly forgiving. Forgiving of whom? Morally perfect love entails love toward *all* persons, even toward enemies, including God's enemies. Specifically, morally perfect love, being perfectly merciful, entails forgiveness toward *all* persons, even toward enemies. Indeed, enemy-forgiveness is a litmus test, as a necessary condition, for a God worthy of worship. Various philosophers and theologians have overlooked or rejected this requirement, but we'll see that it merits acceptance. At any rate, in requiring enemy-love and enemy-forgiveness, divine love is starkly different from much familiar human "love" and is thus inherently offensive to humans. Such divine love is a real stumbling-block, if not an outright scandal, for people who want to continue with selfishly competitive business as usual.

What, however, is forgiveness? Various concepts of forgiveness populate the philosophical and theological terrain. For instance, a familiar legal concept portrays forgiveness as release from a punishment or a debt owed as a result of violation of a law. In addition, a familiar social concept represents forgiveness as overlooking wrongdoing for the sake of saving a person from social exclusion. Neither of these adequately captures the perfect forgiveness appropriate to a perfectly loving God.

Perfect forgiveness characteristically seeks perfect *reconciliation* with a person under the demands of morally perfect love, despite that person's having violated those demands. Without condoning wrongdoing, the one offering perfect forgiveness sets aside condemnation of a person for that person's moral violations, and demonstrates instead unselfish love, including an offer of pardon, for that person. The aim is to invite, with full pardon, the violator of love's moral demands into a new relationship of fellowship in accordance with morally perfect love. Such forgiveness thus typically aims to be conciliatory in terms of fellowship, and thereby goes beyond familiar legal and social concepts of forgiveness. This kind of *conciliatory forgiveness* is suggested in the apostle Paul's report that "God was in Christ *reconciling the world to Himself, not counting humans' sins against them....* God has assigned to us this message of reconciliation.... He made him who knew no sin to be sin for us, in order that we might become the righteousness of God in him" (2 Cor. 5:19–21, italics added; see Fitzmyer 1975 and Martin 1981 for the broader context of Paul on reconciliation). Such divine forgiveness is central to the manifest-offering approach to divine–human atonement outlined in the previous section.

Conciliatory forgiveness is *not* offered only to those who have already "merited" forgiveness owing, say, to regret, remorse, repentance, or reform. On the contrary, the offer of such forgiveness typically aims *to lead a person to repentance*, that is, to that person's turning away from whatever violates perfect love (cf. Rom. 2:4, 5:8). In this respect, the divine offer of conciliatory forgiveness is *unconditionally gracious* (as an unearned gift) toward a violator, even if this offer is loaded with expectations and even demands of moral transformation, perhaps because God seeks to make people "worthy of His call" (2 Thess. 1:11; cf. Gal. 1:6). Repentance, as turning away from idols and related evils, may be a necessary condition of *receiving* divine forgiveness, but the conditions for receiving such forgiveness don't determine the conditions for the divine *offering* of forgiveness. Henceforth, my talk of forgiveness concerns morally perfect conciliatory forgiveness, unless otherwise noted.

Incidentally, perfect forgiveness only *typically* or *characteristically* seeks repentance and reconciliation, because God can know that a particular person who needs forgiveness will never yield to repentance and reconciliation. Still, God would offer forgiveness to reveal, if only to that person, the person's wayward intentions and actions for which the person is morally responsible. In all cases, the offer would be intended for the moral and spiritual good of the person to whom the offer is extended, even if the person is resolutely set against the primary good on offer: namely, divine–human fellowship.

A divine offer of forgiveness carries a word of *judgment*, but this judgment isn't *condemnation* of a person. If I condemn *a person*, I intend to bring genuine harm to that person. If, however, I judge a person's *attitudes* or *actions* as wrong, I don't thereby condemn that person. In saying that I forgive a person, I say that the person has done something wrong, something that needs pardon, and this is a word of judgment. Even so, in conciliatory forgiveness, this is judgment intended for the moral and spiritual good of the person offered forgiveness. It typically aims to pardon the person, and to bring the person into fellowship under genuine love, while refusing to condone wrongdoing. It characteristically seeks to free the person from lasting pain of moral failure, and even to replace a threat of alienation with fellowship. Such are the ways of conciliatory forgiveness: they aim to turn evil into good without condoning evil.

Some people think that they have no serious need of forgiveness, and thus are puzzled when they consider how Jesus related to people who expressed their desires to him. For instance, some men carried a paralyzed man to him for healing, and he responded first by announcing that the man's sins are forgiven by God (Mk. 2:2–7). He thus identified forgiveness as a primary human need. Why? The best answer is that Jesus regarded the primary human need to be the reconciliation of humans to God as their perfectly loving Father. Humans, he assumed, weren't naturally in fellowship with God, but needed to *enter into* the fellowship of God's kingdom, via turning to God in repentance, trust, love, and obedience (see Mk. 1:15, Matt. 7:21–23; cf. 1 Cor. 1:9). God's forgiveness of human wrongdoing, according to Jesus, was the gracious doorway to reconciliation with God as life free both from bondage to alienating sin rooted in selfishness and from final death.

Adding offense to forgiveness, Jesus regarded his own death, the death of an uneducated outcast Galilean, as God's watershed manifestation and offering of forgiveness for human wrongdoing. He used his last Passover meal, the so-called "last supper," as an enacted parable to reveal his role as God's Passover lamb offered up to manifest God's righteousness and to offer conciliatory forgiveness to humans. (This is the heart of the divine manifest-offering approach to atonement sketched in the previous section.) Only Matthew's Gospel attributes explicit talk of "the forgiveness of sins" to Jesus at that final meal (Matt. 26:28), but the notion is suggested by Mark's language of "the blood of the covenant poured out for many" (Mk. 14:24), especially when read with the language of Mark's Jesus "giving his life as a *ransom* for many" (Mk. 10:45). This talk of "ransom" suggests release from bondage, in this case, the bondage of sin, rooted in selfishness, that alienates humans from God. (For Paul's influential development of this theme, see Rom. 3:21–26, 4:24–5:2; cf. 1 Cor. 11:25. On the authenticity and background of Mk. 10:45, see Gundry 1993, pp. 587–93.)

Unfortunately, as suggested above, some of the Christian tradition has offered a twisted reading of Jesus's role in divine forgiveness. The misguided reading implies that God's forgiveness of humans required that *God* punish and kill the sinless Jesus as the "just payment" for human sins. The source of this morally distorted claim is, as noted, not in the New Testament but rather in later theology that suffers from a serious misunderstanding of divine righteousness and a wooden misreading of Isa. 53:10. (For correction of the misunderstanding, see Brondos 2006, pp. 112–18, on this and related passages.)

As Paul and John portray divine forgiveness, it demanded of Jesus a life-giving gracious manifestation and offering to humans of his divine Father's perfectly righteous and forgiving love *(agape)* that characteristically seeks to reconcile humans to God (see Rom. 5:8, 10, Jn. 15:9–15). God, they suggest, sent Jesus as a Passover lamb who receives not *God's* punishment but rather God's unique approval as the perfect human manifestation and offering of God's perfectly merciful righteous love for the sake of divine–human reconciliation. In this manifest-offering sense, Jesus died "for our sins" (1 Cor. 15:3; cf. Rom. 4:25), and in an extended sense, one can say that Jesus "was made to be sin for us" (2 Cor. 5:21), and that his self-giving death represents God's condemnation of sin (Rom. 8:3) in virtue of God's reckoning it as such. We may call the latter extended sense a "divine-reckoning" sense, because it's directly analogous to the sense of Paul's seminal view that "... [human] trust is reckoned [by God] as righteousness" (Rom 4:5; cf. Gal. 3:6). This approach can fully accommodate the following observation by Vincent Taylor: "Jesus was conscious of feeling the weight of [the] wrath of God which rests upon human sin; not as a penalty transferred from the guilty to the guiltless, but as the destiny of a love which makes itself one with sinners and shares their plight" (1948, p. 46). The divine reckoning, in both cases, is no fiction, but is instead a redemptive gift to humans that manifests divine righteousness (cf. Rom. 4:4).

Human trust, or faith, is the means by which God supplies and we receive the divine gift of righteousness, and thus God reckons such trust as righteousness. Analogously, the cross of Jesus is central to the means of God's manifest-offering of divine–human reconciliation, and thus God reckons it as the place of God's dealing with sin in a manner that removes God's condemnation and curse (cf. Gal. 3:13). None of these ideas requires that divine forgiveness involve divine punishment of Jesus. In addition, we should expect God, in keeping with divine perfect love for all persons (rather than with independent abstract principles of justice), to have the prerogative in the mode of manifesting and offering divine forgiveness to humans.

The reconciliation typically *sought* by an offer of forgiveness isn't necessarily *achieved* by the offer of forgiveness. We can offer forgiveness and reconciliation only to have these decisively rejected by another person. That, of course, is no surprise, given the socially destructive and isolating ways of people. The reconciliation in question would be a new relationship of fellowship between God and humans (and thereby among humans) in accordance with the authoritative demands of morally perfect divine love. A common fact of human life is that the offer of morally needed reconciliation is often roundly rejected on the basis of selfish fear. Peacemakers, for instance, are often complete failures, *if* success requires realization of their peaceable intentions in this world.

Some theologians and philosophers seek an easy success story by portraying divine forgiveness and reconciliation as humanly *irresistible*. God is absolutely "sovereign," so the dangerously bold story goes, and therefore God irresistibly reconciles the elect to God and, by implication, chooses not to reconcile the non-elect to God. This may sound godlike, but such a god, to put the point with blunt honesty, wouldn't be worthy of worship and thus of being God, given a failure to love people universally and noncoercively. Such a god would coerce human wills selectively in a way that robs humans of their moral agency and thus their personhood, at least in a definitive area of life. This would be to preclude genuinely personal interaction and thus genuinely loving interaction. It would also make Jesus a hypocrite or a deceiver in proclaiming his Father's love for *all* people, even his enemies (Matt. 5:43–48; cf. Lk. 19:41–42, Jn. 3:16). So, this approach is a nonstarter, despite its holding sway in the minds of many writers in the theological tradition of Augustine, Aquinas, Luther, Calvin, and Pascal. As our best evidence indicates, we aren't God's coerced pawns in an ultimately empty, pre-determined chess game. (For further elaboration, see Meadors 2006, chap. 12; and for an otherwise illuminating treatment of Paul that falls prey to this common mistake, see Westerholm 2004.)

Offering forgiveness is one thing; *receiving* it, another. Both, however, are actions that require the intentional exercise of one's will. Neither is a matter of coercion of one's will; as intentional actions, they aren't coerced happenings. In addition, as intentional actions, they are subject to moral assessment. In particular, I might offer or receive forgiveness for morally wrong reasons, say, for purely selfish reasons. That would be to distort the characteristic purpose of divine conciliatory forgiveness: namely, its goal of all-inclusive reconciliation under perfectly righteous unselfish love.

Our properly receiving divine forgiveness (that is, receiving it fully) isn't as quick and easy as it might seem at first glance. In Matthew's and Luke's Gospels, Jesus links our being forgiven by God to our forgiving people who sin against us (see Matt. 6:12, 14, Lk. 6:37, 11:4). In particular, the link is that if we don't forgive others, then God won't forgive us. That seems altogether strange at first. Why exactly won't God forgive us in that case? A plausible answer begins by noting that talk of forgiving is ambiguous between *offering* forgiveness (perhaps unsuccessfully) and *receiving* forgiveness offered. It then proposes that God won't forgive us if we don't forgive others, *in the sense that* we won't have properly *received* God's *all-inclusive* forgiveness. In that case, God's offer of forgiveness will be unsuccessful to some extent, because it will fail to some extent in bringing us into the desired *all-inclusive* reconciliation.

If we have been offered God's all-inclusive forgiveness but withhold it from another person, we then aim to make it something contrary to what it's intended by God to be. We then aim to make it *exclusive* to some extent (at least regarding one person), although it's intended and offered by God to be *all-inclusive*. We thus misrepresent and mishandle it in a way that shows that we haven't actually fully received the genuine article, namely, the kind of forgiveness intended (by its original source) to go out to *everyone*, even enemies and the cruelest and the most arrogant among us. We may then have received a poor counterfeit.

In Matthew's and Luke's Gospels, Jesus suggests with regard to divine forgiveness that it's "either use it aright or lose it," in particular, that it isn't the kind of thing that may be used exclusively to any extent. This hard message is rarely repeated among followers of Jesus, perhaps because it makes one's properly receiving divine forgiveness difficult business indeed. In neglecting this message, however, we rob the offer of divine forgiveness of its profound challenge to all humans. One result is that some people who fancy themselves as having received divine forgiveness haven't actually done so. This result has definite explanatory value regarding immoral human behavior in the name of religion, but we can't digress to religious immorality.

We resist receiving all-inclusive conciliatory forgiveness for various reasons, all of which boil down to selfishness, selfish fear, or confusion of some sort or other. Perhaps the most common reason is the complaint that certain enemies or disgusting people just don't *deserve* forgiveness. For instance, we often hear that a God of justice wouldn't forgive devoted Nazis, and so *we* shouldn't either. Whatever the details, the claim is that some people aren't *worthy* of forgiveness. We might go along on the ground that *nobody* is worthy of forgiveness, but this isn't the basis under consideration.

According to Jean Hampton, among many others, we should resist all-inclusive forgiveness on moral grounds. Morality, she proposes, recommends a kind of (rightful) *moral hatred* that "involves believing, by virtue of the insulter's association with the evil cause, that she has 'rotted' or 'gone bad' so that she now lacks some measure of goodness or moral health" (1988, p. 80). She adds: "Some of the more frightening mass murderers of our time have prompted the sober judgment that they are totally without goodness. No matter how protracted or severe their punishments, how could one even *consider* reconciling oneself with people such as Hitler or Stalin or Charles Manson, who really may not have any decency left in them – nor even any possibility of decency?" (pp. 80–1). The person with (rightful) moral hatred toward a wrongdoer, according to Hampton, seeks the "harm" or "hurt" of the wrongdoer as a way of hindering the evil cause, and even "takes satisfaction in the wrongdoer's suffering" (1988, pp. 146–7).

Hampton looks for support from Jesus's remark in Matt. 10:34–36: "I have not come to bring peace, but a sword. I have come to set a man against his father, and a daughter against her mother, a son's wife against her mother-in-law; and a man will find his enemies under his own roof" (Matt. 10:34–36). She takes this remark to suggest that "Jesus does appear to encourage us to sustain opposition to our moral opponents, and not to reconcile ourselves with them for as long as they remain committed to their bad cause" (p. 149; cf. p. 153). More specifically, she finds that Jesus is not uniformly opposed to moral hatred toward people. The alleged basis here is that "... not to have moral hatred for the immoral cause upon which the wrongdoer acted, and not to feel this same aversion *toward the wrongdoer himself* if he thoroughly identifies himself with that cause, appear to involve giving up one's commitment to the cause of morality" (pp. 148–9, italics added).

The proposed condoning of (rightful) moral hatred toward unrepentant evil people bears directly on forgiveness. "Forgiveness," according to Hampton, "involves seeing the wrongdoer as, despite it all, a person who still possesses decency and one whom we ought to be *for* rather than against" (p. 151). In addition, "... there are occasions when [forgiveness] is not morally appropriate – in particular, when too much of the person is 'morally dead'" (p. 153). The underlying idea is that some unrepentant evil people are morally hopeless as candidates for participation in a morally good relationship, and thus *should* be hated and not forgiven. Love and forgiveness, then, should *not* be extended to all people. In particular, those who are "irredeemably rotten" should be excluded from an offer of forgiveness as they receive our resolute moral hatred. Clearly, given this view, a God of perfect love toward all people would be morally deficient at best. In addition, enemy-love would offer no litmus test as a necessary condition for a candidate for divinity.

By my lights, the aforementioned position itself, along with any other position endorsing hatred of some people, is worthy of moral hatred, but I won't and shouldn't recommend such hatred toward any *person*. It's altogether coherent to recommend hating a *position, attitude,* or *action,* while at the same time recommending love toward *the person* advancing that position, attitude, or action. It's likewise coherent to recommend hating (that is, wanting and even willing the worst for) *a sin,* as an evil action, attitude, or habit, while at the same time loving (that is, wanting and willing the best for) *the sinner*. Moral hatred includes one's wanting, on moral grounds, genuine harm and perhaps even destruction to be brought upon the object of hatred. Typically, such hatred stems from the belief that the object of hatred is irredeemably rotten from a moral point of view.

Two questions arise. First, are we humans ever in a cognitive position to judge conclusively that another human is in fact irredeemably rotten from a moral point of view? Second, even if we could reach such a decisive judgment about a person, why should we, from a moral point of view, refrain from loving (rather than hating) that person? Regarding the first question, I've seen enough moral surprises in my own life and in the lives of many others to doubt reasonably that I could ever judge conclusively that a person is irredeemably rotten. I can't get my moral hopes up about *everyone,* of course, but it doesn't follow that I have conclusive grounds for moral hopelessness regarding some people. Incidentally, I doubt that I'm alone on this matter.

The second question is the real troublemaker for proponents of (rightful) moral hatred toward other persons. There's no reason to suppose that "the cause of morality" itself requires that I hate an irredeemably rotten *person,* even if it requires that I hate the person's evil attitudes, evil actions, and their bad effects. In particular, the cause of morality doesn't require us to harm or to eliminate rotten *persons* as sources of evil *at the expense of loving those people.* (If it did, incidentally, God couldn't be perfectly loving toward all people, including enemies.) Morality, in other words, doesn't require any kind of opposition to irredeemably evil people that conflicts with our willing what is best, even perfectly loving, for them as persons.

It's altogether puzzling why anyone would think that morality requires hatred toward an unrepentant evil *person* rather than toward only that person's evil attitudes, evil actions, and their bad effects. It's never the case that one must hate an unrepentant evil person to challenge that person's evil attitudes and conduct. So, we should resist any recommendation that our moral hatred extend beyond evil attitudes, evil actions, and their bad effects to the evil persons responsible for those attitudes, actions, and effects. Otherwise, we risk doing a kind of moral harm, if only to ourselves *as haters* of persons, that is akin to the harm done by evil people who hate others.

Perfectly merciful love includes an offer of morally perfect forgiveness even to irredeemably evil people. An offer of morally perfect forgiveness need not succeed or even be likely to succeed as a means of reconciliation. There's no reason, in addition, to suppose otherwise. What is actually morally perfect by way of merciful action doesn't depend on cognitive assessments of likelihood of receiving forgiveness. Otherwise, a dubious kind of consequentialism based on *likely success in reconciliation* creeps into morality, and morality becomes a morass. *How likely* must the success be? Is there a percentage threshold? If so, what's the basis for that threshold? In addition, what's the reference class for the relevant likelihood? And so on. Morality becomes lost in a thicket, and then we're no longer talking about morality as we know it.

Contrary to Hampton's suggestion, my offer of morally perfect forgiveness *doesn't* require that I see a potential recipient as decent at his or her core. It's altogether misleading for Hampton to ask, as noted, in this connection: " ... how could one even *consider* reconciling oneself with people such as Hitler or Stalin or Charles Manson, who really may not have any decency left in them?" An offer of morally perfect forgiveness definitely isn't an offer by the bearer of forgiveness to reconcile herself to the person needing forgiveness by condoning the relevant evil. Instead, the offer is to have the evil person reconciled to the one offering forgiveness on the basis of perfect love. Accordingly, God didn't reconcile God *to the evil world* through Jesus; instead, God sought that the evil world would be reconciled *to God* through Jesus in his self-giving manifestation and offering of divine forgiving love. The direction of reconciliation is morally crucial. Once we get this direction right, we can uphold divine perfect love as perfectly forgiving toward all persons without condoning evil.

We can now acknowledge perfect enemy-love, including enemy-forgiveness, as a litmus test, in terms of a necessary condition, for divinity and as a central component of the Good News movement from Jerusalem. Such love and forgiveness seem to be unique to that movement, even going beyond the Hebrew scriptures (cf. Snodgrass 2005), and, according to Chapter 2, they offer powerful evidence of divine reality. The cognitive import of divine conciliatory forgiveness is clear: as one receives and participates in such forgiveness, even toward enemies, the evidential power of divine reality becomes increasingly clear in one's own life. The next section pursues how such evidence emerges in a human life. In doing so, it illuminates the distinctive cognitive basis of the Good News movement.

6. DYING AND RISING

At the heart of the Good News of God's redemption of humans, we find a recurring but neglected theme that goes beyond divine forgiveness for human sin. It involves, on the basis of prophecies from Jeremiah, Ezekiel, and Joel, *one's being made new in spirit by God's Spirit* as one dies to one's selfish life and participates in God's Jesus-manifested life of self-giving love. God's Spirit, we're told, intervenes in a person's spirit (or, motivational center) to empower that person to love as God loves, in fellowship with God. Accordingly, one must die to selfish ways, including selfish autonomy, in order to live to God. In Paul's thinking, we must be "crucified with Christ" (Gal. 2:19–20; cf. Col. 3:1–4), in dying to the anti-God ways of the world and of ourselves. Only then can we be free to love as God loves, unselfishly and with forgiveness toward enemies. Only God's Spirit within us can motivate the sea change from selfishness to unselfish love, even toward enemies. This change is akin to a heart transplant, but at the level of one's spirit, or motivational center. It alters the core of our nagging problem of selfishness, even if some residue persists, and it offers an opportunity for a lasting life of fellowship in place of death.

We can sidestep puzzling metaphysical intricacies about how a divine Spirit can be "in" a human spirit if we avoid a literal use of "in" and opt instead for an understanding in terms of the *immediate, directly firsthand reception and ongoing availability* of divine personal power by a willingly receptive human agent. A similar understanding can remove needless mystery from the Pauline talk of "Christ in you" (Col. 1:27) and of one's being "in Christ" or "in the Spirit" (Rom. 8:1, 9). Indeed, Paul himself seems to understand the crucial idea as that of "being led" by the Spirit of God (Rom. 8:14). We can plausibly understand the relevant kind of "being led" in terms of the immediate, directly firsthand reception and ongoing availability of divine personal power by a willing human agent, including the power to love unselfishly, and thereby we can avoid a range of metaphysical perplexities. Still, we need to characterize the human appropriation of the leading power in question, and Paul's idea of dying and rising with Christ can help.

Our dying to selfish autonomy is no loss of enduring value at all. It only seems so, superficially. Autonomy of that kind isn't genuine freedom at all, but is, rather, slavery to fearful insecurity and anxiety, to self-seeking ambition, and to an illusion of ultimate self-control. We are too fearful and weak on our own to love unselfishly as a perfectly loving God loves. Even facing the prospect of our being guided by self-giving love, we typically fear a significant loss to us without corresponding gain. God's intervening Spirit, however, aims to bring liberation from human bondage to such selfish fear (cf. Rom. 6:15–23, Jn. 8:34–36). Through God's Spirit dispatched by Jesus, according to the Pauline Good News, we are to be empowered to be free from selfish fear as we become fully loving toward all people in the self-giving manner of a perfectly loving God. The unselfish love empowered by God's intervening Spirit in willing people is the inclusive glue needed to unite members of any lasting community in genuine fellowship. Such a community, under God's authority, is the goal of divine–human redemption that includes resurrection (1 Cor. 15:23–28).

Our being Spirit-led citizens of God's new, liberated community requires the death of our old, selfish life and its destructive tendencies. The authoritative call from God's Spirit, according to the Good News, is thus a call to suffer and to die with the crucified Jesus to anti-God ways, as we noted in Paul's thought (cf. Phil. 3:7–11, Gal. 2:19–21, Rom. 6:3–14, Col. 2:11–12). Jesus himself puts the idea starkly, in his typically disturbing fashion: whoever doesn't follow him by carrying the cross of suffering, self-giving love *cannot* be his disciple (Matt. 10:38–39; cf. Mk. 8:34–35). After Jesus made such remarks, according to John's Gospel (6:53–66), many of his disciples complained that this teaching was too difficult and then stopped following him. The perceived cost was too high. They feared significant personal loss without corresponding gain.

A person's adopting God's way of unselfish love is unsettling and even divisive, owing to selfish resistance in any sizeable human audience (cf. Matt. 10:34–36, Mk. 3:31–35, 1 Cor. 11:18–19). According to the Good News, the authoritative call from God's Spirit is nonetheless inherently cross-shaped, after the pattern of Jesus in faithfully obeying his Father at any expense, even to the point of death. If we aren't dead serious about this call, we shouldn't answer it at all, according to Jesus (Lk. 14:28–33). Jesus, accordingly, didn't offer his death as a replacement for human suffering, but instead called humans to be full-time *imitators* of, and even *participants* in, the divine power involved in his self-giving life and death. More specifically, according to Paul, humans are called by God to be conformed, in mind and in will, to the obedient death and life of Jesus by the same divine Spirit that empowered Jesus (Phil. 2:5–13). This divine call is as central to the Good News of Jesus as is the message of God's gracious manifest-offering of forgiveness of sins for the sake of divine–human reconciliation, because this call specifies how the Good News is to be received by humans in the obedience of (grounded) faith, or trust.

According to the Good News, God works redemption, or reconciliation, in willing humans through the weakness of human suffering and death, in order to demonstrate that genuine saving power is altogether *God's*, and not ours (see 1 Cor. 1:17–25, 2 Cor. 4:7–11, 12:8–10). God demonstrates through divine power in our weakness that no human has a right to boast in God's presence (cf. 1 Cor. 1:28–29, Gal. 6:14). Our own strengths, real or apparent, don't amount to the saving power belonging to God alone. For instance, we can't overcome death by our own resources, however much we try, and we can't counter selfish fear on our own with a suitably powerful antidote. Trust and hope based on the power of humans, rather than on the power of God, are as redemptively impotent as humans themselves. Indeed, God's redemptive love (that is, grace) supplemented by human self-credit undermines such love. Here we can only *receive*, and not earn. The claim to earn the love of a perfectly loving God (whereby *we* obligate God to love us) involves a category mistake, because it twists genuine divine love given as a gracious gift, including the power to love unselfishly, into a counterfeit incompatible with such a gift.

All spiritual power from God's Spirit, according to the Good News, comes to us on God's Jesus-shaped terms of human volitional weakness, in being subsidiary to God, rather than on our self-crediting terms. So, our boast and hope should be in God alone, and not in our self-crediting accomplishments (see 1 Cor. 1:31; cf. 2 Cor. 13:4). God's redemptive power, including the evidence it generates, is set in sharp relief against a background of human volitional weakness relative to God's perfectly authoritative will. Anyone contradicting this lesson with a triumphalist self-exalting attitude, including in the area of human knowledge of God's existence, betrays the Good News by offering a counterfeit corrupted by anti-God human power (see 2 Cor. 11:1–12, 12:1–10). Any such person would be, by Paul's lights, an "enemy of the cross of Christ" (Phil. 3:18). Here we have a divine direct reversal of natural human expectations and boasting tendencies, including in philosophy and epistemology.

Paul identifies the goal of "suffering the loss of all [nondivine] things for Christ" as mandatory for properly responding to the authoritative call of God's Spirit, including for "knowing Christ" (Phil. 3:7–11). Paul suggests, in Phil. 2:7–8, that Jesus himself set the perfect model for responding to his Father by suffering the loss of all nondivine things in wholehearted self-yielding obedience to God. According to Phil. 3:10–11, humans should pursue a similar goal: "to *know* Christ and the power of his resurrection and the fellowship of his sufferings, by being conformed to his death, if somehow I may arrive at the resurrection of the dead." This kind of "knowing Christ" is, of course, no mere intellectual matter. Instead, it requires wholehearted volitional self-commitment, on the basis of purposively available evidence, to an authoritative personal agent with a demanding will, not just to ideas, principles, practices, or virtues.

In identifying the model established by the obedience of Jesus, Paul commands: "Be wisely disposed among yourselves in the way found in Christ Jesus, who ... humbled himself, becoming obedient unto death" (Phil. 2:5, 8). It's misleading, then, to say: "In Paul's thought, Jesus did not die for the purpose of setting an example for others to follow...." (Brondos 2006, p. x). Paul clearly regards the obedient death of Jesus as an example for people to follow in response to God's Good News challenge; indeed, he regards such obedience as central to trust (or, faith) in God and as the perfect way to appropriate the Good News from God. This lesson is cognitively important, as we'll see, because it highlights a distinctive kind of evidence of divine reality.

Why does Paul link "knowing Christ" with suffering the loss of all nondivine things? This may seem extremist at best. The answer involves, however, Paul's talk of the necessity of regarding all nondivine things as trash, or excrement, in order to "gain [needed knowledge of] Christ." We must genuinely deem all nondivine things as worthless "on account of the surpassing value of (personal) knowledge of Christ Jesus (as) my Lord" (Phil. 3:8). Personal volitional knowledge of Christ as one's Lord is, according to Paul, of incomparably supreme value relative to all things that could get in the way of such knowledge. We thus must treasure such knowledge, such well-founded relationship of fellowship, above all else, if we are to give it its due sacred preeminence. So, we shall be in a position to receive the gift of such knowledge properly only if we put all potentially competing things in relative perspective: they are at best "garbage" in comparison. (Paul used the Greek equivalent of a four-letter English word beginning with "s"; no soft-pedaling there.)

In keeping with Jesus's aforementioned demanding portrayal of our receiving him as Lord, Paul's theme is difficult indeed. Even so, we aren't dealing with ordinary propositional knowledge, but are rather considering personal volitional knowledge of God and God's unique Son. Such knowledge requires human volitional submission, including due honor and gratitude, toward its supremely exalted personal object (see Rom. 1:21). We are thus called to know God and his unique Son respectively *as worship-worthy God and as incomparably supreme Lord of all things.* Otherwise, suitable volitional knowledge of God's reality would be unavailable to us. A perfectly loving God, as noted above, wouldn't trivialize or otherwise devalue the unsurpassed value of one's knowing God as the God worthy of worship. In particular, God wouldn't confuse such knowing with spectator entertainment or casual speculation.

Paul suggests that obediently following Jesus yields grounded hope that doesn't disappoint us, as an antidote to despair (Rom. 5:3–5). More specifically, suffering with Christ (that is, in the obedient mode in which he suffered) produces a special kind of hope for God's deliverance, and this hope is grounded by God's intervening personal Spirit. This leads Paul to recommend that we should boast, even rejoice, in our sufferings, because God is redeeming them for good (2 Cor. 7:4, 12:9–10; cf. Rom. 8:22–28, Col. 1:24). Sufferings can reveal God's distinctively powerful presence in one's perseverance and thereby further God's work of self-revelation toward redemption as divine–human reconciliation. By means of God's convicting Spirit, our sufferings can empty us of our selfish and self-exalting tendencies and our supposed self-sufficiency, and they can rid us of any false hope in things of this dying world. They thus can enable us, by means of God's Spirit, to be filled with, and motivated by, God's self-giving love via deeper trust, and more clearly perceived need of trust, in God rather than in things of this dying world (see Rom. 8:14–17). Our sufferings can thereby become a basis for our rejoicing in God's peculiar redemptive work. This sounds just strange enough to merit our attention.

We now confront a widely neglected lesson, even among Jewish and Christian writers: a perfectly loving God would have to be a *killer.* God would hate not bad *people* (contrary to Psalms 5:5, 11:5, explicitly corrected by Jesus in Matt. 5:43–48) but rather the evil *deeds* and *attitudes* that preclude life in fellowship with the perfectly loving God worthy of worship. God would thereby resolutely want the demise of such deeds and attitudes. Without such hate, God would lack genuine love toward people. In addition, God would seek to kill such evil deeds and attitudes in a specific manner. Paul puts the lesson as follows: "... if by the Spirit you put to death the [anti-God] deeds of the body, you will live" (Rom. 8:13, RSV). He suggests that such killing of deeds by the power of God's Spirit is essential to being "led by God" and thus to being a child of God and a disciple of Jesus; indeed, this seems to be central to trust, or faith, in God for Paul. God thus leads willing people by empowering them to kill their own evil deeds and attitudes that hinder a life of fellowship with God and others.

The lesson of divine killing applies to the cognitive domain as well as the moral domain. Indeed, our refusal to kill, via divine power, our anti-God, selfish deeds and attitudes obstructs our volitional knowledge of God. This leads one New Testament writer to state bluntly: "He who does not love does not know God" (1 Jn. 4:8). We can now make sense of this otherwise puzzling remark. The obverse lesson is that as I kill, via divine power, my anti-God deeds and attitudes, and thereby die with Christ to sinful, disobedient options, I acquire more firsthand evidence of powerful divine reality, because I become acquainted further with God's intervening and transforming Spirit powerfully at work in me. This divine power that kills (what brings death) in order to bring genuine lasting life isn't continuous with, but goes directly against, our own selfish powers. So, in looking for divine power, and evidence thereof, we need to look for power antithetical to our own typical powers. We thus need to be humbled by a power foreign to our natural ways.

According to the Good News, we should think of Jesus, who died to sinful, disobedient options and was raised to life by God, as an *empowering life-model*, including cognitive model, for us, and not a mere *substitute* for us. Clearly, Jesus offered himself as a life-model (see, for example, Lk. 9:23–24, 14:27–33), and Paul likewise offered Jesus as a life-model, even for our ongoing suffering and dying (see Phil. 2:5–13, 3:7–11, Rom. 8:17; cf. 1 Pet. 2:20–25). In obediently humbling himself, even to the point of suffering and death, Jesus aimed to manifest what a perfectly forgiving, self-giving God is really like and what *we* too should be like as children of such a God. Jesus, accordingly, aimed to manifest and offer what it is to be truly a human person, a person fully in the image of God under the power of God's Spirit, serving in the kingdom family of God as perfectly loving Father. To the extent that Jesus is actually our empowering life-model, we can be persons empowered to receive filial knowledge of God as perfectly loving Father.

A perfectly loving God would naturally expect receptive humans, in the wake of Jesus's self-giving exemplary life, to manifest, and thereby to witness to, this God's powerful unselfish love (cf. 2 Cor. 3:18). Human lives are to *manifest* that God is powerfully real, in ways that add needed *power* to our otherwise empty words. God thus calls willing people to look backward and forward: backward to what God has uniquely and lovingly done in Jesus as a perfect divine manifest-offering for the sake of divine–human forgiveness and reconciliation, and forward to what God will analogously do through willing imperfect people, after the authoritative life-pattern of Jesus in his dying to sin and living to God. We need to ask how *resurrection*, so foreign to Athens but so common to Jerusalem, fits with this uniquely challenging portrait of power-based evidence and knowledge of divine reality.

7. DANCING ON GRAVES

According to the Good News, as outlined above, our receiving as a gift God's life of fellowship via volitional, filial knowledge of God calls for our dying to our selfish lives, after the obedient pattern of the crucified Jesus. We have seen that Paul deemed such dying as central to "knowing Christ" and thereby to receiving as a gracious gift the resurrection power of self-giving love in fellowship with God. The dying in question, according to Jesus and Paul, is integral to human resurrection by God. We need to clarify the unfamiliar idea of human resurrection by God for the sake of bringing together some of our lessons about the human predicament and proper knowledge of God, that is, knowledge of God in keeping with God's gracious character and purposes.

An immediate question is whether divine perfect love would yield everlasting life as a definite consequence, at least for willing recipients of such love. Timothy Jackson has raised some doubts, on the ground that "to have love is not to have all good things [for example, everlasting life], but it is to have the *best* thing" (1999, p. 170). This line of reasoning may seem initially plausible, but serious doubt emerges on reflection. The main problem is that the "best thing" would be for us to have divine love *endlessly*, not just for the short term. If God is perfectly loving, and thus wants the best for us, God would therefore give us the opportunity to have divine love endlessly. Failing to give this view due consideration, Jackson claims that "love can endure even without faith in one's own resurrection" (p. 168), but that claim isn't to the point now. The pressing issue is whether a perfectly loving God's wanting "the best" for us would include God's giving us the opportunity to have a life of divine love endlessly, rather than just for the short term. The answer is clearly yes. Indeed, Jackson himself unwittingly offers the needed support: "Love is concerned with preserving and enhancing *all* good things, to the greatest extent possible. . . ." (p. 218). It follows that God, as perfectly loving, would offer willing humans the opportunity to receive a life of divine love endlessly, in fellowship with God.

Spiritual Resurrection

In Paul's message, the Good News of the gift of divine perfect love manifested in Jesus includes an offer of *dual* resurrection, despite this being overlooked by many commentators and theologians. The duality includes a person's being raised *spiritually* now to new life with God and a person's being raised *bodily* later after the model of Jesus's bodily resurrection. Paul has spiritual, but not bodily, resurrection in mind when he writes: "We were buried therefore with [Christ] by baptism into death, so that as Christ was raised from the dead by the glory of the Father, we too might walk in newness of life. . . . So you also must consider yourselves dead to sin but alive to God in Christ Jesus. . . . [Y]ield yourselves to God as [people] who have been brought from death to life" (Rom. 6:4, 11, 13, RSV). These remarks in an undisputed letter of Paul's undermine the following prominent view among New Testament scholars: "The idea that believers have not only died but also risen with Christ does not appear in the undisputed Pauline letters but is found in both Eph. 2:1–7 and Col. 2:13, 3:1–4" (Brondos 2006, p. 182). As the previous quotation from Romans indicates, Paul supposes that followers of Jesus will "walk in newness of life" *now* to God, "as Christ was raised from the dead" (cf. 2 Cor. 5:17). He assumes that they are already "alive from the dead," as a literal translation of Rom. 6:13 would go. Clearly, Paul holds that *bodily* resurrection for humans awaits a future time (1 Cor. 15:22–24); so, he must have *spiritual* resurrection in mind, in a sense to be specified below.

The Pauline thought in Colossians 2:12 (which may come from Paul himself) echoes Rom. 6:4, 11, 13: ". . . you were buried with [Christ] in baptism, in which you were also raised with him through faith in the [power] of God, who raised him from the dead" (RSV; cf. Col. 3:1, Eph. 2:5–6). In keeping with Romans 6, the Pauline idea here is that followers of Jesus *have already* been "buried with him . . . [and] . . . raised with him." Clearly, this isn't an idea of being raised bodily, which awaits the future in Pauline thought. It is rather an idea of being raised *spiritually* owing to the personal renewal involving faith, or trust, in the God who powerfully raised Jesus to new life. Some New Testament scholars hold that Paul himself is responsible for the ideas in the Epistle to the Colossians, even if he himself didn't pen the whole letter (cf. Col. 4:18), and I find no conclusive reason to dissent in the letter's content, style, or grammar. If, however, Paul isn't directly responsible for this letter, we have an outstanding disciple of Paul who takes Rom. 6:4, 11, 13 at face value in its suggestion of spiritual resurrection *now* for followers of Jesus.

Paul, of course, acknowledged a future bodily resurrection beyond currently available spiritual resurrection: "[I]f we have been united with [Christ] in a death like his, we shall certainly be united with him in a resurrection like his" (Rom. 6:5, RSV). We thus have an unavoidable duality regarding resurrection in Paul's thought: spiritual resurrection and bodily resurrection. Both involve powerful renewal by God, but they involve renewal of different realities: spirits and bodies. In addition, spiritual resurrection is, according to Paul, available now, but bodily resurrection awaits the future. The Good News is thus a hybrid regarding resurrection, according to Paul. (The same is true regarding John's Gospel, but we won't digress to exegetical details; see Wright 2003, pp. 440–8, 662–82.)

Regarding spiritual resurrection, Paul acknowledges the Spirit of the crucified Jesus as the divine Spirit to be sent by God to receptive humans now, "into [their] hearts, crying 'Abba! Father!'" (Gal. 4:6; cf. Rom. 8:9, 1 Cor. 15:45, and Gorman 2001, chap. 3). In addition, in John's Gospel, Jesus as God's atoning sacrifice is identified directly with the one who gives God's Spirit to receptive people now (Jn. 1:29–33, 20:21–23; cf. Mk. 1:8). The divine manifest-offering atonement in Jesus, according to the Pauline and Johannine Good News, thus includes the *empowering means of realizing* this atonement in receptive humans: the sending of God's Spirit through Jesus to empower receptive people, on the basis of filial knowledge of God, to live anew now in fellowship with God and with each other. Paul thus proclaims: "If anyone is in Christ, [that person is a] new creation" (2 Cor 5:17; cf. Gal. 6:15, and see Hubbard 2002, chaps. 10–11).

Paul's Good News "new creation" proclamation echoes the startling prophecy of Ezek. 36:26–27: "A new heart I will give you and a new spirit I will put within you; and I will take out of your flesh the heart of stone and give you a heart of flesh. And I will put my spirit within you and cause you to walk in my statutes and be careful to observe my ordinances" (RSV; cf. Ezek. 37:14, Jer. 32:39–40). In keeping with this heartening promise (no pun intended), the cross and the resurrection of Jesus are proclaimed by Paul as the manifest-offering redemptive avenue for God to impart God's Spirit to all receptive people, including Gentiles as well as Jews (see Rom. 10:11–21; cf. Acts 10 on the novelty of this inclusiveness).

People are called to receive divine redemption as a gracious re-creative gift, because they are unable on their own to please God or to uphold fellowship with God, owing to their inability on their own to love as God loves. God's Spirit is offered as the personal power enabling willing people to enter into the redemption and fellowship provided by God through Jesus. This is an integral, if widely neglected, part of the Good News of Jesus, and it was anticipated at the end of Chapter 2, with talk of a "new volitional center with a default position of unselfish love."

We now can credit the new volitional center, as suggested above, to the immediate, directly firsthand reception and ongoing availability of God's empowering Spirit by a willingly receptive human agent. Such a new volitional center is at the heart of spiritual resurrection as understood by Paul and John (cf. Jn. 3:1–12; see Gaventa 1986 and Moltmann 1992, chap. 7, for relevant discussion.) The cognitive relevance of spiritual resurrection is straightforward: it yields experiential acquaintance with powerful evidence of God's intervening Spirit at work in one's motivational center, leading one away from selfishness and toward self-giving love, in fellowship with God. Such evidence indicates what Paul calls a "new creation" in a person and what John calls "a person's being born from above."

Bodily Resurrection

Bodily resurrection of humans seems preposterous in the absence of a purposive God with a redemptive plan. Given the reality of a perfectly loving God, however, we shouldn't find it incredible at all. In Acts, accordingly, Paul is portrayed as asking: "why is it thought incredible by any of you that God raises the dead?" (Acts 26:8, RSV). If God exists, bodily resurrection wouldn't pose an insurmountable problem, cognitive or otherwise, even in the area of personal identity. God would have the power to preserve, even through physical death, what constitutes one's being the agent one inherently is. (See Wiebe 2004, chap. 3, for some relevant discussion.)

Some recent writers, including Swinburne (2003) and Wright (2003), evidently hold that a rationally compelling account of evidence for the bodily resurrection of Jesus can proceed without acknowledgment of the role of *God's intervening Spirit* in testifying to believers regarding the resurrection of Jesus (cf. Moser 2004c, 2006, and Allison 2005, for detailed criticism). They thus omit a crucial cognitive role for God's intervening Spirit in evidentially well-grounded human belief in the resurrection of Jesus. At a minimum, we can agree with Swinburne and Wright that sober historical assessment hasn't excluded the resurrection of Jesus and can't rule it out as a matter of course, without specific historical evidence against the resurrection.

We shall briefly consider Wright's abductive historical approach in order to identify a cognitive shortcoming to be avoided here. Wright contends that two beliefs are historically secure in terms of being widely held by early Christians: the belief that the tomb of Jesus was empty on the first Easter, and the belief that the resurrected Jesus had appeared to some people. He holds that neither belief is individually sufficient for the emergence of the early Christian belief that Jesus was resurrected. He explains: "Nobody in the pagan world would have interpreted an empty tomb as implying resurrection; everyone knew such a thing was out of the question. Nobody in the ancient Jewish world would have interpreted it like that either; 'resurrection' was not something anyone expected to happen to a single individual while the world went on as normal" (pp. 688–9). As a result, evidence that goes beyond an empty tomb was needed to underwrite early Christian belief that Jesus was resurrected. In the absence of such evidence, the dominant belief would have been that Jesus's body was removed from the tomb by some natural process.

Human experiences of meeting with the risen Jesus were also insufficient to give rise to early Christian belief that Jesus was resurrected. Such experiences would have been interpreted in various ways by first-century Christians, according to Wright, including as mere visions or as visitations by angelic beings. Human experiences of meeting with the risen Jesus would thus have to be supplemented with evidence that the experience is of a real body, such as a body that had left an empty tomb. So, Wright contends, belief that the tomb of Jesus was empty and belief that people had met the risen Jesus are, taken individually, "insufficient to generate early Christian belief" that Jesus was resurrected. "Bring them together, however, and they form in combination a sufficient condition" (p. 692).

Wright develops his account with a simple analogy:

> The combination of empty tomb and appearances of Jesus was clearly not sufficient for the rise of Christian belief in everyone who heard about it. ... Granted that those who found the empty tomb and saw the risen Jesus were second-Temple Jews, most of whom had followed Jesus and were hoping he would turn out to be Israel's Messiah, the two pieces of evidence would be sufficient to make most of them conclude that he had been raised from the dead. ... The doubts of some at the time, and the refusal of others later on to believe the witness of Christian preachers, do not substantially affect this point. (The fact that, because of poor weather or ground conditions, or indeed reckless or hostile action by other parties, not all first-rate planes flown by first-rate pilots make it safely to land does not affect the general point.) (p. 693).

Wright's story becomes murky here. We now have the refined claim that the evidence regarding the empty tomb and the appearances of Jesus was sufficient *only for some, and not for all*, first century Jews directly familiar with Jesus to believe that Jesus was resurrected. What exactly is the *relevant evidential difference* between those who believed and those who did not believe? Without an answer, we may plausibly suppose that some unidentified factor plays a crucial role in the emergence of early Christian belief that Jesus was resurrected.

It doesn't explain much, if anything, to say that those who didn't believe in the resurrection faced "poor weather or ground conditions, or indeed reckless or hostile action by other parties." We need to know specifically what constitutes such "poor" conditions and such "hostile" action. Otherwise, we won't understand the relevant difference between the two groups with regard to their receiving and handling available evidence of divine intervention, particularly in the proclaimed resurrection of Jesus.

The known first-century Jews who came to believe, on the basis of their evidence, that Jesus was resurrected held that *God* had raised Jesus from the dead and to an exalted status with God (see, for example, 1 Cor. 15:15, Phil. 2:8–11). Resurrection, then, was inherently *theological* (that is, God-empowered) by their lights. These Christian Jews had an understanding of God according to which this was a *live option* regarding God's action toward Jesus. In contrast, the first-century Jews who refused to believe, on the basis of their evidence, that Jesus was resurrected may have had an understanding of God according to which this wasn't a live option regarding God's action toward Jesus. God, they may have held, wouldn't act in this way toward Jesus, given who God is and what God has planned. Paul of Tarsus was one such first-century Jew, until his understanding of God was significantly reoriented, somewhere and somehow along the road to Damascus. Paul could have written off the appearance of Jesus to him as an illusory experience (owing, say, to Pharisaic missionary exhaustion), but his newly altered understanding of God allowed him to hold that the appearance was truly that of the risen Son of God – the resurrected Jesus. Paul's transformation is indeed mysterious in some ways, but it clearly includes a reorientation of his understanding of *God* relative to Jesus, the crucified Galilean.

We don't have anything like an algorithm for what determines one's understanding of God, even relative to the resurrection of Jesus. Nonetheless, the crucial role of one's understanding of God is undeniable. As long as my understanding of God is inimical to God's raising Jesus to an exalted status, I will be closed to belief that God resurrected Jesus from the dead. Paul himself held that one's response to God's Spirit plays a crucial role in whether one acknowledges Jesus as having been exalted by God: "No one can say [with duly grounded confidence] that [the risen] Jesus is Lord except by the holy Spirit" (1 Cor. 12:3). Wright fails to give adequate attention to the explanatory role, including the evidential role, of the experienced Spirit of God in early Christian belief about Jesus as risen Lord. This is a serious deficiency in his account, and it puts the account at odds with Paul's approach to the resurrection.

Wright extends his position to a claim about a necessary condition: "... the bodily resurrection of Jesus provides a *necessary* condition for these things [namely, the tomb's being empty and the Easter and post-Easter 'meetings' with Jesus taking place]; in other words, ... no other explanation could or would do" (p. 717). Wright's claim about a necessary condition seems to be this: if the tomb of Jesus is empty and the "meetings" with Jesus took place, then Jesus has been resurrected from the dead by God. This claim isn't obvious at all, given the possibility of other causal sources of the phenomena in question.

A key issue concerns what we mean by "meetings with Jesus." If we have in mind *possibly* merely subjective experiences (to avoid begging a key question about the veracity of the appearances), the claim to a necessary condition fails. In that case, we could imagine that the body of Jesus was stolen by thieves and some of the disciples had extensive and shared illusory experiences of Jesus after his death. So, the resurrection of Jesus by God isn't a logically necessary condition for the tomb's being empty and the "meetings" taking place. Wright's language is confused regarding a logically necessary condition for a proposition, *P*, and a necessary condition for a good or best *explanation* of *P*. His main concern seems to be an inference to "the best explanation" of the tomb's being empty and the "meetings" taking place, and he recognizes that such an inference is abductive and probabilistic rather than logically demonstrative (p. 716).

The problem with Wright's abductive approach is twofold. First, even *if* the resurrection of Jesus by God figures in the best available explanation of the tomb's being empty and the "meetings" taking place, how does this consideration cognitively underwrite that Jesus is *now* risen as divinely appointed Lord? What reason do we have to believe that the resurrected Jesus *continues* to live and reign as divinely appointed Lord who *now* brings God's manifest-offering of forgiveness and fellowship? This involves the crucial "question of why the resurrection should be good news *now*" (Williams 1982, p. 119). For all our historical evidence indicates, Jesus could have ceased to exist at some time in the distant past. So, there is a chasm, a distinct chronological chasm, in Wright's abductive historical account.

Second, even if the resurrection of Jesus by God figures in the best available explanation of the tomb's being empty and the "meetings" taking place, how does this consideration yield anything beyond *merely theoretical historical evidence* that Jesus was resurrected by God? The kind of evidence suitable to faith as trust in Jesus as Lord, however, seems not to be just a matter of theoretical abductive historical evidence. At least, the earliest proclamation, by Paul and others, of the Good News of Jesus as risen Lord doesn't proceed timidly or tentatively with merely theoretical historical evidence. (The same two problems challenge the approach to resurrection in Swinburne 2003.)

The dominant grain of New Testament teaching, including Paul's writing, implies that the God who raised Jesus as Lord over death goes beyond merely theoretical evidence by offering purposively available authoritative evidence of divine reality and the lordship of the risen Jesus. Such evidence, as noted, is widely overlooked in contemporary philosophical and theological discussions of God's reality. The reason may be that philosophers and theologians typically want to abide by standards of secular epistemology, including secular historical epistemology, that disregard a purposive superhuman personal object of knowledge (see Buckley 1987). It's arguable that peer pressure in the academic life of western universities tends to have a corrosive effect in this regard, obscuring the vital role of purposively available evidence regarding divine reality. The cognitive idolatry characterized in Chapter 2 comes to mind in this connection. The distinctive evidence for bodily resurrection, in any case, is purposively available in accordance with divine redemptive purposes (of the sort noted in previous chapters), and it involves the *revelation of God's authoritative Spirit* to willingly receptive humans, particularly regarding the reality of the risen Jesus. Such evidence is reported widely in the New Testament (for example, from Paul to Matthew to Luke to John), and it receives special acknowledgment in the primary letters of Paul to the earliest churches.

The church planted by Paul at Corinth (1 Cor. 3:6) was deeply confused about, among other things, the bodily resurrection of Jesus and of followers of Jesus. Paul wrote to clear up some of the confusion prior to his intended lengthy visit. He begins by characterizing his earlier preaching at Corinth of the crucifixion and bodily resurrection of Jesus:

> My message and my preaching were not in persuasive words of wisdom, but in a manifestation of the Spirit and power, so that your faith might be not in the wisdom of humans, but in the power of God.... As it is written: "What no eye has seen, nor ear heard, nor the human heart considered, what God has prepared for those who love him," God has revealed to us *through the Spirit* (1 Cor. 2:4–5, 9–10, italics added).

Paul contrasts human wisdom with God's wisdom. The latter, according to Paul, comes from what "God has revealed to us *through the Spirit.*" Here we find a central feature of Paul's pneumatic epistemology, which is neither fideist nor coherentist but foundationalist in virtue of its acknowledgment of nonpropositional experiential evidence from God's intervening Spirit.

Paul included the divine resurrection of Jesus in God's wisdom, given that the resurrection was a central part of his divinely appointed Good News "message" and "preaching." The resurrection of Jesus by God wasn't offered by Paul as part of human wisdom derived from empirical historical inquiry without revelation from God's intervening Spirit. Accordingly, by Paul's lights, familiar historical assessment will fall short of properly confirming the divine resurrection of Jesus, even if such assessment could confirm the resuscitation of a body. Paul evidently has the same lesson in mind when he says, as quoted above: "No one can say [with duly grounded confidence] that [the divinely raised] Jesus is Lord except by the holy Spirit" (1 Cor. 12:3). Paul's epistemology of resurrection is thus pneumatic, that is, Spirit-oriented and Spirit-grounded. (One could argue the same for the epistemological approaches to resurrection in the Gospels of Matthew, Luke, and John, but we can't digress.)

Human hope and trust in God's promised bodily resurrection of his people after the model of Jesus have a cognitive anchor, according to Paul, in God's giving God's Spirit of perfect unselfish love to willingly receptive people. Their willing hearts (or, motivational centers) are thus moved by God's Spirit of love toward the character of divine unselfish love (Rom. 5:5). The offered Good News resurrection, as suggested, includes bodily as well as spiritual resurrection; the latter is available now, and the former awaits, for humans other than Jesus, a future divine intervention. Paul expresses a similar theme in referring to the God who "has put his seal upon us and given us his Spirit in our hearts as a guarantee" (2 Cor. 1:22, RSV; cf. 2 Cor. 5:5, Eph. 1:14).

God's Spirit given to willing human hearts guarantees, as a cognitive down payment according to Paul, that God will complete the work of transformation begun in willing people, after the model of Jesus. God's willingly experienced intervening Spirit, according to Paul's Good News, supplies the conclusive purposively available *evidence* of God's reality and of God's having raised Jesus from death. Even if Jesus was seen alive after the crucifixion (1 Cor. 15:3–8), *God* would have to show (in God's preferred way, of course) willingly receptive people that *God* (rather than something else, such as a fluke of nature) raised Jesus to lasting life and will raise his disciples likewise. Involving the transforming power of an invisible God, the latter Good News message is no straightforward empirical matter, contrary to the zealous allegations of some Christian apologists. The message is driven by a definite redemptive purpose, that of divine–human reconciliation, and the same purpose underlies the appearances of the risen Jesus. We should treat evidence of those appearances accordingly, in keeping with this book's approach to purposively available divine evidence.

Helmut Thielicke has pointed in the right direction regarding the cognitive basis of belief in the resurrection of Jesus.

> ... [T]hink of an historian investigating the resurrection [of Jesus]. Even if he should come to the scientific conclusion that the historical documentation for the resurrection of Jesus was without loopholes of any kind and

beyond all doubt, would he experience anything more than a great shock or bewildered astonishment in the presence of an historical anomaly? This line of procedure would never bring him to confess, "My Lord and my God." The fact that Thomas [in Jn. 20:24–29] did not simply say "it fits," but rather "my Lord" shows that he recognized the Lord by his love and not by physical characteristics . . . (1968, p. 185).

There's a world of difference between recognizing the resurrection of Jesus as just an actual historical event (perhaps a fluke of nature or some other kind of fortuitous occurrence) and recognizing it as God's resurrection of one's divinely appointed Lord out of the motive of redemptive love for oneself and others. Thielicke rightly suggests that empirical history won't by itself cognitively underwrite the latter kind of recognition. It's the latter kind of God-oriented recognition, however, rather than just empirical history, that underlies New Testament preaching of the Good News of God's offered redemption via the death and resurrection of Jesus.

God's Spirit, according to Paul, seeks noncoercively to "lead" all willing people to the risen Jesus and his Father as, respectively, their Lord and their God. This experience of "being led," or being volitionally prompted, by an authoritative call is cognitively significant, and goes beyond empirical history. It includes the authoritative divine call to relinquish our selfishness for a life of fellowship in God's unselfish love manifested in the crucified and risen Jesus. This call works through human conscience (cf. Rom. 2:15, 9:1, 2 Cor. 4:2, 6, Gal. 1:6), and comes with a serious moral challenge to us, even if we are inclined to ignore or to dismiss it. Human failure to hear this call may be the result of our not wanting to hear it on God's terms of unselfish love. We typically prefer, for instance, not to have to forgive or to love our enemies in the way God does and demands. We ordinarily fear personal loss without corresponding gain, and we need definite power to overcome this fear.

The proposed volitional theological approach to evidence of the resurrection doesn't omit the cognitive significance of the earliest appearances of the risen Jesus; instead, it puts them in proper theological perspective. They involve an authoritative divine call, and thus go beyond merely empirical data. Rowan Williams comments: "The apparitions have no independent [empirical] significance precisely because of what they in fact communicate. They are not simple manifestations of an apotheosized Jesus. . . . To see the risen Jesus is to see one's own past and one's own vocation, to 'see' the [divine] call towards the new humanity" (1982, p. 118; cf. p. 106). Making the resurrection Good News now, the relevant divine call includes a call to receive and to communicate the divine forgiveness manifested and offered by the crucified and risen Jesus, and this points recipients to a community in need of resurrection renewal. Even so, as Williams rightly emphasizes, the divinely raised Jesus is irreducible to his community of followers, given his independent authority over his people (2000a, p. 192).

In the wake of Paul's thought on the Good News, and in keeping with the approach being developed here, Emil Brunner has asked how a person can credibly believe in the message of the resurrection of Jesus. His answer:

> I cannot know for certain whether that is true which the Gospels record; I cannot go back and prove it. . . . [Even so, a] faith whose authority is merely history has no worth. The real Easter faith does not come from the fact that one believes the report of the apostle without doubting; rather, it comes from the fact that one is reconciled to God through Jesus Christ. This reconciliation is not a mere belief but a rebirth, a new life. Through this reconciliation, godlessness and anxiety are rooted out, and one becomes a new [person]. From this reconciliation through Jesus Christ, faith in his resurrection from the dead arises of itself (Brunner 1961, p. 92).

Following Paul, Brunner identifies a way to escape the abyss of merely theoretical historical assessment, even given the resurrection as occurring in time. The escape comes from God's evident authoritative intervention in the lives of willing people with a call to divine–human reconciliation. This intervention isn't just a matter of imparting theoretical information, as if our problem were fundamentally the lack of information. Instead, when willingly received, the divine intervention makes the receptive person volitionally and spiritually new by the unique power of God's intervening Spirit, as suggested by Paul and John (2 Cor. 5:17, Gal. 6:15, Jn. 3:5–8).

The needed newness in life, as Chapter 2 suggested, resides ultimately in one's new volitional center, empowered by God's Spirit, whereby one becomes free to participate in volitional fellowship with God (and God's reconciled people) and in God's self-giving and forgiving love, even toward enemies. In other words, one's willingly receiving spiritual resurrection firsthand from God, on the basis of purposively available evidence of divine reality, gives one a firm basis for extending belief in resurrection, in light of the preached Spirit-grounded Good News and its promises, to the bodily resurrection of Jesus and (in the future) his disciples. A perfectly loving God, as noted, would naturally seek lasting fellowship in community with all willing people, and thus God would eagerly sustain willing people in community life (on God's terms) rather than death, ideally (according to the Good News) even transformed, imperishable bodily life, for the sake of such fellowship in historical community. The resurrection of Jesus serves to fulfill the divine promise to sustain lasting divine–human fellowship in historical community under Jesus as divinely appointed Lord. Spiritual resurrection, then, can contribute to grounded belief in bodily resurrection by God.

Following Paul's Epistle to the Romans, Brunner pulls no punches in characterizing attitudes toward the resurrection of Jesus.

> [Y]ou say you cannot believe [in the resurrection of Jesus].... You cannot believe it because you are not reconciled to God, and you are not reconciled to God because you do not really wish to repent for your godlessness. All unbelief without any exception comes from this unwillingness to obey, from the unwillingness of sin that separates us from God. In the moment when you... sincerely acknowledge your sin, then you can also believe in the reconciliation; no, in this moment you are reconciled to God through Jesus Christ and the truth of the Easter message is clear to you. Then you believe in the resurrection, not because it is reported by the apostles but because the resurrected One himself encounters you in a living way as he who unites you with God, as the living Mediator. Now you yourself know it: he lives, he, the Reconciler and Redeemer (Brunner 1961, p. 93).

Brunner is not referring to unbelief owing just to one's lacking information about God's ways, as in the situation of infants, for example. He has in mind not mere intellectual doubt but rather unbelief as willful resistance to the Good News of God's intended divine–human redemption via the crucified and risen Jesus.

Brunner doesn't have in mind a body-to-body encounter with the risen Jesus. He rather invokes an encounter with the risen Jesus through his Spirit, the Spirit of God (1961, p. 94). This Spirit, according to the Good News, intervenes noncoercively to bring, via conscience, an authoritative offer of forgiveness and reconciliation with God to willing humans. Human reception of this divine intervention yields what Brunner calls "a living certainty" toward the Easter message of the Good News of God's redemption via Jesus. Brunner thus identifies the volitional and pneumatic heart of Paul's understanding of the cognitive basis of the Good News of divine gracious redemption available to humans.

One's volitionally receptive "encounter" with the intervening Spirit of Jesus as God's authoritative representative would bring not only Easter faith as a well-founded response to the Good News, but also well-founded confidence regarding one's lasting life in fellowship with God and God's reconciled people. It would unite one volitionally with the God of lasting life whose experienced Spirit assures one of continued life with God and the historical community of God's people. Indeed, one would actually begin to *participate*, via the power of God's intervening Spirit, in God's lasting life of unselfish love, after the model of the crucified and risen Jesus. One would thus become attuned to God and thereby to God's resurrection people. In having imperfect humans deliver the perfect Good News, in the wake of the risen Jesus, God edifies and extends the forgiven resurrection community called to live in divine–human fellowship, even for the sake of outsiders and enemies.

The "well-foundedness" of a receptive human response to the resurrection Good News is ultimately anchored in willing volitional acquaintance and fellowship with God's authoritative intervening Spirit, not in theoretical hypotheses or arguments. It would be a dangerous category mistake to suggest otherwise. In the Good News thus understood, we find the key to overcoming the twofold human predicament of destructive selfishness and impending death. We also find, in the pneumatic evidence and epistemology presented, the needed alternative to the skepticism introduced in Chapter 1. Each person, however, must himself or herself face the authoritative call of God's Spirit to forgiveness and reconciliation through Jesus. One cannot have the volitional encounter by proxy, and that's a good thing for all concerned. Responsible humans need, and have, direct accountability before the redemptive God worthy of worship.

One might wonder, finally, whether proponents of *every* religion could offer the kind of epistemological account at hand. Having already noted such a concern, we may acknowledge that the matter is now clear: *only if* the religions in question offer a perfectly loving God who has intervened to redeem people by divine grace rather than by human earning. Not all religions, of course, offer this; in fact, many explicitly reject it. (That's a verifiable empirical point, and it undermines any naive thesis of the redemptive unity of religions.) If a religion does offer just the kind of perfectly loving God in question, then we may be talking about the same God under different names. Of course, we would have to look carefully to see if that's actually the case. This would become, at any rate, an empirical sociological matter for another occasion. The theological epistemology of this book clearly excludes (as it should) an "anything goes" approach to theological evidence, but it allows (as it should) for God's intervening in the lives of people from various ethnic, racial, intellectual, and religious traditions. In fact, we would readily expect the latter from a perfectly loving God worthy of worship.

Skeptics will likely object that the alleged evidence from the presence of God's intervening Spirit doesn't include an argument for God's reality. This, however, is no real problem, because, as noted, the reality of evidence doesn't depend on an argument. Much of our conclusive (defeater-free) evidence, including firsthand evidence from sensory and perceptual experience, doesn't rely on any argument, and this applies as well to our firsthand evidence regarding our psychological states. Likewise, God could have God's intervening Spirit call people, via conscience, to turn to God in forgiveness and fellowship without God's providing them with an argument for divine reality. This would be no real problem at all from a cognitive point of view. Even so, the previous chapter offered a simple argument from "the transformative gift" to condense the account of evidence offered here. The argument is not only valid but also, I submit, sound as well. We have gone the extra mile, then, to attend to sincere skeptics.

Paul characterizes God's intervening Spirit further: "... all who are led by the Spirit of God are sons of God. For you did not receive the spirit of slavery to fall back into fear, but you have received the Spirit of sonship. When we cry, 'Abba! Father!' it is the Spirit himself bearing witness with our spirit that we are children of God" (Rom. 8:14–16, RSV; cf. 1 Cor. 2:10–14). Paul thus holds that God's intervening Spirit has cognitive significance, but that no argument need be provided by God's Spirit. In particular, people can receive an evidence-conferring experiential witness directly from God's Spirit that they are God's children. Paul thus comments, in a different context: "Where is the wise man? Where is the scribe? Where is the debater of this age? Has not God made foolish the wisdom of the world? For since, in the wisdom of God, the world did not know God through [its] wisdom, it pleased God through the folly of what we preach to save those who believe" (1 Cor. 1:20–21, RSV). According to the Good News characterized by Paul, God provides God's own distinctive means for humans to know divine reality, including the ratifying experienced witness of God's own intervening Spirit, on the basis of purposively available authoritative evidence. In the absence of undefeated defeaters, such evidence is conclusive and adequate for genuine knowledge of divine reality. God, we might say, is ultimately God's own evidence-source, even regarding divine reality.

An adequate assessment of evidence for the Good News of divine redemption must attend to the cognitive role of God's intervening Spirit, including the significance of corresponding purposively available authoritative evidence. Philosophers of religion, including Christian philosophers, have generally overlooked this important consideration. As a result, the distinctive evidence underlying the Good News has been widely neglected. Once we open the door of epistemology to such evidence, we are left with a simple but life-defining challenge: are we willing to yield to such authoritative evidence, and then be changed profoundly, even from within, by the power of God's perfectly loving Spirit? I, of course, can't answer for anyone else, by proxy. No one can, and thus each of us has an urgent challenge directly at hand.

All of a sudden, what may have looked like just another abstract epistemological pursuit has become life-defining. Epistemology in the bright light of
the Good News is like that, and that's a good thing.

We turn now to the immediate implications of this book's volitional theistic
epistemology for intellectual inquiry in general and philosophy in particular.
The intellectual landscape will never look the same. Our lives won't either.

4

⟡

Philosophy Revamped

We have seen that the existence of a perfectly loving God would challenge everything at odds with God's character, from false expectations to cognitive idols to us. We need to ask how this bears on our favorite intellectual and theoretical projects, including philosophy itself. Few have asked, but we'll do so here, and find that the results are surprising indeed.

One result will be a portrait of intellectual pursuits, including philosophical pursuits, that rarely, if ever, has received public display. The volitional pneumatic epistemology outlined in the previous chapters involves an authoritative divine call to volitional transformation toward God's perfectly loving character. This call includes definite love commands that demand, by implication, the reorienting of philosophy as a discipline. We need to characterize the main results of this demand. We shall see that philosophy becomes, if not itself kerygmatic, at least kerygma-oriented, relative to the redemptive Good News outlined in Chapter 3.

1. BEGINNING AGAIN

Philosophy, according to Plato (*Theaetetus* 155d) and Aristotle (*Metaphysics* 982b12), begins in wonder *(thauma)*. Wonder, as they understood it, involves not just a feeling of astonishment but a *question* about what is real or true. Plato typically asked questions of the form "What is X?" where "X" may stand for "knowledge," "justice," or "courage," for instance. (On such questions and their central role in philosophy, see Moser 1993.) Grammatical form, however, doesn't explain the substance of philosophical questions. It is itself a substantial (and not merely formal) question of philosophy to ask what, specifically, a philosophical question is. Philosophers have offered a wide range of answers to this question, and no consensus is anywhere in sight. The philosophy of philosophy thus resembles much of first-order philosophy: its questions linger and even multiply, apparently without end. So, whatever else it has, the discipline of philosophy has staying power, as virtually any university curriculum will confirm.

The questions of philosophy seem perennial indeed, if only because they generate perennial controversy. Perhaps here, in the kind of controversy generated (if nowhere else), we find a key feature of a philosophical question. Perennial controversy seems to dog most, if not all, areas of philosophy. Still, the reality of philosophical questions seems undeniable even if we are hard put to define or otherwise to analyze their reality. Some realities, for better or worse, stubbornly resist clear analysis, but these realities aren't therefore at risk, in terms of their reality; only our purported analyses are. We could, of course, stipulate an analysis or offer a definition by fiat, but little, if anything, would thereby be gained. Some of what others deem philosophical questions would then be omitted, and controversy would arise over *that* matter.

In the interest of disciplinary congeniality, let's settle now for a broadly lexical approach: the questions populating the writings of self-avowed philosophers are, for our purposes, philosophical questions. See, for example, the writings and questions of Plato, Aristotle, Sextus Empiricus, Plotinus, Augustine, Aquinas, Leibniz, Descartes, Kant, Hume, and so on. If someone prefers a narrower definition, so be it. We can proceed now with a more inclusive approach, and stay above the fray regarding a philosophy of philosophical questions. Otherwise, the metaphilosophical nature of philosophy will have a way of delaying our getting on with pressing concerns. We'll never get beyond the philosophy of philosophy, the philosophy of the philosophy of philosophy, and so on *ad infinitum*. Endless regress will be our common fate, and we won't reach even the starting blocks for guidance in life (assuming there's life beyond metaphilosophy).

Why do we, as philosophers, ask the questions we do rather than either no questions at all or significantly different questions? The easy answer is this: we want *answers*; in particular, we want answers to the questions we raise. This answer is acceptable as far as it goes, but it doesn't go very deep, and is, in fact, superficial. In asking questions in philosophy, we don't simply raise questions; we *pursue* the questions we raise, with considerable time and energy, and sometimes even with other people.

We sometimes become preoccupied, if not obsessed, with the questions we raise. Our questions become projects, so-called research programs. They fill our lives, including our nights as well as our days. They become projects we love, or at least projects about which we deeply care. They define what we do with the bulk of our lives, and given finite time and energy, we find ourselves excluding, or at least ignoring, other available projects and even other people. Our philosophical questions compete for our time and energy and win out, by our own choice, over other options. As a result, Wittgenstein and others have vigorously sought ways to defuse philosophical questions as a group. They have, in this vein, sought freedom from the obsessions of philosophy, although such freedom is indeed hard to come by. Philosophical questions resist easy escape for us, and actually crop up in pretty much every context where we talk or think. They find us if we don't find them.

Why, in the competition for our time and energy, do we allow philosophical questions to win out over the wide range of alternative competitors? What explains this, and is our rationale viable? We'll ask if Jesus, the human focus of the Good News of divine redemption for humans identified in Chapter 3, has anything to say about our tendencies toward philosophical questions, and we'll see that he does indeed. At a minimum, he shows us how to be free of philosophy as an obsession that interferes with life lived freely and fruitfully. We'll see, in addition, that his distinctive commands extend the volitional theistic epistemology developed in previous chapters, and invite us to receive increasing evidence of divine reality and its corresponding benefits.

Self-avowed Christians, at least, should care about the bearing of Jesus's teachings on philosophy, if only because they proclaim him as their author-itative Lord. Others should care too, because much of the wisdom of Jesus about human life is undeniable, even from a reflective secular standpoint. Even if Jesus doesn't comment directly on philosophy as we now know it, his teachings, particularly his love commands, have straightforward implica-tions for philosophy as a pursuit of truth and wisdom. We do well to attend to these implications, given the obvious need to avoid a confusing "anything goes" attitude in philosophical pursuits. It is surprising, therefore, that the relevance of Jesus and his love commands to philosophy is largely ignored by philosophers, including self-avowed Christian philosophers. This chapter takes steps to correct this neglect. In doing so, it draws out some striking implications of the volitional pneumatic epistemology and the Good News movement outlined in previous chapters. We'll see that once a perfectly loving God enters the large wobbly tent of philosophy, its anchors and boundaries are altogether new and firm. They take on a new orientation, a kerygmatic orientation centered on the Good News of divine redemption.

2. PURSUING QUESTIONS

Do some people love philosophical questions more than they love God and other people? There's no doubt that some do, however perverse this may sound. Some people love philosophical questions but don't love God at all, and that's by their own acknowledgment. Some of these people also acknowledge that they love philosophical questions more than they love other people. I, for one, know a number of professional philosophers who love their philosophical questions passionately but, by their own admission and actions, care not at all about most other people. In addition, they aren't ashamed of this, and they lack an inclination to change in this regard. They are, in fact, proud of their *thoroughgoing* philosophical pursuits, since they consider truth-seeking in philosophy to be more important, all things considered, than loving God and other people. In addition, they live their lives accordingly, with apparent consistency in their beliefs and practices as devout philosophers. Still, such consistency doesn't by itself recommend their position, given that any number of positions can boast in consistency of that sort.

Typically, the questions we eagerly pursue manifest what we truly care about. (My talk here and below of what one does *eagerly* concerns what one does willingly and gladly, and not compulsively or grudgingly.) Suppose that I eagerly spend all, or even almost all, of my time and energy pursuing questions about, say, the nature of abstract entities of the kinds treated in advanced philosophy of logic and metaphysics courses: properties, propositions, sets, and the like. I then must care about the nature of abstract entities more than I care about the alternatives to which I give less time and energy: God, other people, and so on. If the reference to concerns about abstract entities seems far-fetched (even though it actually isn't far-fetched among many professional philosophers), we may substitute reference to a more familiar philosophical concern (for example, the nature of knowledge, the nature of minds, or the nature of values). The same lesson will apply.

I might *say* that I care more about God and other people than about my favorite philosophical concerns, but my eager commitments of time and energy toward those concerns can belie this. By identifying my eager time and energy commitments, one can tell what I truly care about, even if I claim otherwise, perhaps owing to embarrassment or an uneasy conscience. What I eagerly (as opposed to compulsively or grudgingly) spend my life on provides a window into my true cares and concerns, into what I truly love. *Talk* about what one loves is cheap indeed, but my life's eager commitments show my priorities, my true loves, and my "heart" as my motivational center.

A person who eagerly chooses to spend virtually all of his time watching entertainment television (say, sports and comedy shows) loves watching television more than he loves serving God and other people, regardless of this person's avowals to the contrary. Likewise, a person who eagerly chooses to spend virtually all of his time pursuing questions about the nature of abstract entities cares more about the nature of abstract entities than about serving

God and other people. God and other people, we may plausibly assume, aren't mere entertainment episodes or abstract entities, even if some philosophical discussions suggest otherwise in their levity or abstractness.

One likely reply is noteworthy: in pursuing questions about the nature of abstract entities, for example, I am pursuing *truth*, and all truth is *God's* truth; so I, as a truth-seeking philosopher, am pursuing the things of God, if under a different heading. Such an appeal to "all truth as God's truth" has loomed large in Reformed Protestantism at least since the time of Ulrich Zwingli and John Calvin, and it has analogues in parts of Roman Catholicism, including the Thomist and Jesuit traditions, and in branches of Judaism. In addition, the reply continues, our having truth is good for all people, and thus my pursuing truth about abstract entities is in the best interest of all people. Some Christians would add that, in keeping with Genesis 1:26–28, we have a "cultural mandate" from God to exercise dominion under God in *all* areas of human life, including intellectual areas of human life. Our pursuit of philosophical questions, according to this reply, is just faithful obedience to a divine cultural mandate, and is thus above reproach.

By way of a counter-reply, let's consider whether truth-seeking, even philosophical truth-seeking, can clash with the love commands from a perfectly loving God. In particular, can my truth-seeking lead me to fail to love God and other humans? We are using the term "God," in keeping with the previous chapters, as a maximally honorific title, to signify (that is, to connote) a supremely authoritative being who is worthy of worship and thus is perfectly loving. We are considering, therefore, the kind of God who advances the love commands central to Jewish and Christian monotheism.

Drawing from the Hebrew scriptures, Jesus summarized the divine love commands in the following way:

> [O]ne of the scribes came up and heard them disputing with one another, and seeing that he [Jesus] answered them well, asked him, "Which commandment is the first of all?" Jesus answered, "The first is, 'Hear, O Israel: The Lord our God, the Lord is one; and you shall love the Lord your God with all your heart, and with all your soul, and with all your mind, and with all your strength.' The second is this: 'You shall love your neighbor as yourself.' There is no other commandment greater than these." (Mk. 12:28–31, RSV; cf. Deut. 6:4, Lev. 19:18).

These commands, found in both the Hebrew scriptures and the Christian New Testament, give a priority ranking to what we should love. They entail that at the top of a ranking of what we love should be, first, God and, second, our neighbor (as well as ourselves). They thus entail that any contrary ranking is morally unacceptable, and that our projects are acceptable only to the extent that they contribute (noncoincidentally, of course) to satisfying the divine love commands, which find their basis in the authoritative moral character of a perfectly loving God. Indeed, Jesus offered the love commands in order to have his followers manifest God's distinctive character and thereby offer divine–human reconciliation to others (see Matt. 5:14–16, 43–48; cf. Jn. 13:34–35).

Whatever else loving God and our neighbor involves, it requires *eagerly serving* God and our neighbor for their best interests. Characterized generally, eagerly serving God and our neighbor requires (a) our eagerly obeying God to the best of our ability and (b) our eagerly contributing, so far as we are able, to the life-sustaining needs of our neighbor. Such eager serving is central to love as *agape*, the New Testament kind of merciful love incompatible with selfishness or harmfulness toward others. Even so, we shouldn't confuse our neighbors' best interests or life-sustaining needs with mere preferences expressed by our neighbors. Otherwise, we would risk making love servile in a manner that benefits no one.

We humans, undeniably, have limited resources; in particular, we have limited time and energy for pursuing our projects. For better or worse, we don't have endless time and energy to pursue all available projects or even all available projects we prefer. We thus must *choose* how to spend our time and energy in ways that pursue some projects and exclude others. If I eagerly choose projects that exclude, for lack of time or energy, my eagerly serving the life-sustaining needs of my neighbor (when I could have undertaken the latter), I thereby fail to love my neighbor. I also thereby fail to obey God's command to give priority to my eagerly serving the life-sustaining needs of my neighbor. To that extent, at least, I fail to love God and my neighbor (cf. 1 Jn. 4:20–21). Given the divine love commands, we aren't allowed to love even God to the exclusion of loving our neighbor. (By "divine love commands," I mean the love commands issued by the perfectly loving God characterized throughout the previous chapters; they are summarized in the aforementioned love commands put forth by Jesus.)

The lesson about failing to love applies directly to the typical pursuit of philosophical questions, although this is seldom noticed. If my typical eager pursuit of philosophical questions blocks my eagerly serving the life-sustaining needs of my neighbor (when I could have undertaken the latter), I thereby fail to love my neighbor. I also fail then to obey the divine love command regarding my neighbor. In this case, my typical eager pursuit of philosophical questions results in my failing to love God and my neighbor as God has commanded. The failing is a deficiency in serving God and my

neighbor, owing to my eager choice to serve other purposes instead, in particular, philosophical purposes independent of loving God and others.

Even if a philosophical purpose is truth-seeking, including seeking after
truths about God (even truths about divine love), it could run afoul of the
divine love commands. It could advance a philosophical concern, even a
truth-seeking philosophical concern, at the expense of eagerly serving God
and one's neighbor. For instance (examples come easily here), I could eagerly
pursue an intriguing metaphysical truth about transfinite cardinals or about
null sets in ways that disregard eager service toward God and my neighbor.
Not all truth-seeking, then, proceeds in agreement with the divine love commands. This lesson applies equally to philosophy, theology, and any other
truth-seeking discipline. We need not digress to the specific conditions for
truth; the lesson holds for any of the familiar conceptions of truth in circulation. (See Moser 1989, chap. 1, on some noteworthy alternatives and a modest
objectivist approach to truth.)

Will a "division of labor" regarding the duty to love salvage philosophical
pursuits without qualification? Some philosophers will propose that they
have a special calling to philosophy (a "vocation") that, in effect, exempts
them from full-time obedience to the divine love commands. The difficult
questions of philosophy demand whole-hearted attention, according to this
reply, and this allows philosophers to delegate the duty to serve neighbors to
others who have a more practical calling. Just as not all people are called to be
teachers or evangelists, this reply suggests, philosophers aren't called to focus
on eagerly serving others in love. Instead, the proposal goes, philosophers are
called to pursue philosophical questions full-time or at least almost full-time,
and this exempts them from focus on eagerly serving others. Allegedly, the
labor of loving others must be divided up in a way that leaves the bulk of the
labor to people outside philosophy. Philosophers, according to this proposal,
have a special right to pursue philosophical questions, even at the cost of
failing to love others.

A division of labor makes perfectly good sense in some areas, of course,
but not in others. The different *ways of loving* others should be divided up
among people with different talents, skills, and gifts. For instance, some
people (including teachers, we hope) are talented in the area of imparting
needed information to others, whereas others (including relief workers, we
hope) are talented in feeding and comforting the poor. These people, in
accordance with their varying talents, express love to their neighbors, but
they do so in different ways. This kind of division of love's labor is effective,
advisable, and morally acceptable. No capable person is here exempted from
the duty to love others as God loves.

The love commands from a perfectly loving God (as summarized above) don't exempt any capable person or group of capable people, not even truth-seeking philosophers. Their purpose is to call *all* capable people to reflect the morally perfect character of God, their perfectly authoritative and loving creator, in volitional fellowship with God. Jesus identifies this purpose in the Sermon on the Mount, after calling his followers to love even their enemies (see Matt. 5:44–45, 48; cf. Lk. 6:35–36, Rom. 12:10–21). Given that all capable people are created by God to be obedient creatures relative to God, all capable people are called to reflect God's moral character of self-giving love. As a result, no capable person is exempt from loving God and neighbors.

A person isn't permitted to exclude himself or herself, even for the sake of philosophy, from a central divine purpose of human existence: to learn to love as God loves, in fellowship with God. In the presence of a perfectly loving God, truth-seeking doesn't trump the requirement to love others, because it doesn't override the requirement to mirror God's perfectly loving character. An assumption of the autonomy of philosophers relative to the love commands conflicts with God's universal purpose for capable humans to become loving as God is loving, in fellowship with God. Accordingly, the divine love commands bear on all capable people, not just on people outside philosophy or other special truth-seeking vocations.

Some philosophers will resist with this question: who are *you* to say that some philosophical questions aren't worthwhile or are at odds with the divine love commands? In other words, by what authority do you bar some philosophical questions from pursuit acceptable to God? These philosophers will use such questions to circle the wagons around philosophical business as usual, given the felt challenge of the divine love commands.

Two replies are noteworthy. First, I haven't commented on whether philosophical questions are "worthwhile," because what is "worthwhile," as typically understood, can vary widely relative to varying *human purposes*. Second, the authority of a perfectly loving God and of Jesus as divinely appointed Lord underwrites the divine love commands. If, as Christians acknowledge, Jesus is divinely appointed Lord, then he is Lord of all of life, including one's intellectual life. So, if Jesus is Lord, he is Lord of the questions one may pursue. In other words, as Lord, Jesus issues commands, including the aforementioned love commands, that bear directly on the questions one may pursue. As a result, I am not myself lord of my questions if Jesus is Lord. The common assumption that I am lord of my questions denies the status of Jesus as divinely appointed Lord. Bracketing talk of Jesus, we could make directly analogous points regarding the authority of a perfectly loving God. In other words, a perfectly loving God has authority over the questions created beings may pursue.

We can put the point about the divinely given authority of Jesus over our *pursuit of questions* in terms of our *use of our time*. If Jesus is divinely appointed Lord of the Sabbath, as he claimed (Mk. 2:23–28), then he has the authority to say what is permissible and what isn't on the Sabbath. He actually did exercise this authority in a way that created serious controversy about God's expectations for humans (cf. Meier 2001, pp. 332–40, 639–45). If, in addition, Jesus is Lord of the Sabbath, then he is the Lord of the other days of the week too. As divinely appointed Lord, he is, in other words, the Lord of *all* of our time, from Sabbath to Sabbath. That is, he has the authority to say what use of our time is permissible and what use isn't. This is his unqualified prerogative in virtue of being divinely appointed Lord over all creation (for Pauline affirmation of this theme, see Col. 1:12–22; cf. Hurtado 2003, chap. 2, Fee 2007, pp. 298–303, 317–25).

When I assume that *I* am Lord of my time, I thereby deny that Jesus is divinely appointed Lord of all creation. In particular, when I pursue philosophical questions in ways that violate the divine love commands issued by Jesus, I deny, at least implicitly, that Jesus is Lord. I then acknowledge and favor someone *other* than Jesus as Lord, perhaps Plato, Aristotle, Plotinus, Kant, Hume, Russell, or (most likely) *myself*. The result is, if implicitly, opposition to Jesus as Lord, and this is the heart of oppositional unbelief. Such unbelief is at least as much volitional (a matter of the will) as it is intellectual, and thus it differs from doubt or confusion that is merely cognitive or intellectual.

The divinely appointed authority of Jesus as Lord is the authority of one moved by divine unselfish love, and thus seeks to give humans the focus they need to flourish (by divine standards) in life and in death. Philosophy, as the supposed love of wisdom, might claim to do this on its own, with respect for full human autonomy. Philosophy would then emerge as the putative guardian of human wisdom and autonomy. Apart from a perfectly loving God, however, it won't deliver what we really need in the dire human predicament of selfishness and impending death: namely, to be loved by a merciful, forgiving God who sustains us in all afflictions, including death, and teaches us to love unselfishly as God loves, in fellowship with God. Given the reality of a perfectly loving God, it truly matters which questions we pursue, because, in light of the divine love commands, it truly matters how we spend our time and thereby relate or fail to relate to God.

Given a divine charge to love God and others, we are morally accountable for the use of our time. If, as responsible agents, we eagerly spend our time on projects, even on truth-seeking philosophical projects, that disregard the priority of loving God and others, we are guilty of misusing our time. If our time is a gracious gift from a perfectly loving God who has life-giving expectations for us, then God is in a position of authority to make demands on our time, particularly demands for our own good. This bears directly on our pursuit of philosophical questions, and any other questions, for that matter. Our lives thus become charged with moral accountability, even regarding our daily use of time.

The understanding regarding use of our time is very different in a secular perspective that omits acknowledgment of a perfectly loving God. My time, according to a widespread variation on such a perspective, is ultimately a result of unintelligent nature and not the gracious gift of a God with loving purposes for me and all others, even my enemies. (It isn't surprising, then, that secular philosophical ethics typically has nothing to say about our use of time.) Nature, being unintelligent, doesn't give me commands to love others, or *any* command for that matter, even if it gives me demonstrable bumps and bruises against my will. Despite setting limits on us and our efforts, nature remains altogether silent on moral injunctions, and on other injunctions, too. In particular, nature doesn't state, or even imply, how I should use my time. So, from a secular perspective, I am under no command (beyond possible merely human commands) to use my time with the priority to love others.

Given certain goals I have, I might find it advisable to use my time in specific ways that advance my goals. Such instrumental advisability, however, doesn't amount to an unconditional command to love others. From a secular perspective omitting God, my use of time would be free of any absolute love command, owing to lack of an absolutely authoritative source that demands perfect love. As a result, from a secular perspective, philosophical questioning isn't constrained in the way it is in a position acknowledging a perfectly loving God. In overlooking this, one can easily be taken in by a secular attitude toward the use of time in general and toward philosophical questioning in particular. In that case, the philosophical pursuits of advocates of Jewish and Christian theism may be indistinguishable from those of agnostics and atheists. Something then has gone wrong, and philosophy, even in the hands of Jewish and Christian theists, proceeds as if God isn't really Lord of all creation after all.

3. GOING FOR BROKE

The love commands issued by Jesus reveal his priority in life: wholeheartedly loving God and thereby others, too. His earthly life's commitment to this priority was passionate and evidently wholehearted. Indeed, his earthly life goes for broke in upholding this priority, as he allows nothing to interfere with his realizing this priority, avowedly at the command of God as his perfectly loving Father (cf. Matt. 5:45–48). He resolutely commits all he is and has to it, and he holds nothing back, not even his own life, as his obedient willingness to undergo crucifixion manifests.

According to the Good News introduced in the previous chapter, the crucifixion of Jesus is primarily about (a) his fully obedient, self-giving love toward his Father on behalf of humans (and not his physical suffering), and (b) God's thereby manifesting divine merciful and righteous love for humans in order to offer divine–human forgiveness and reconciliation (see Phil. 2:4–8, Rom. 3:21–26, 5:8–11, 2 Cor. 5:15–21). The cross of Jesus is thus central to the Good News of God's redemptive love for humans in manifesting divine merciful and righteous love for the sake of offering divine–human reconciliation. The exact details of this manifest-offering approach to atonement can be worked out in different ways, but we need not digress now. The cross of Jesus doesn't *bring about* divine–human reconciliation, as if humans had no role in its reception. Instead, it manifests the kind of divine love motivating an offer of such reconciliation, and the offer is to be received by "the obedience of faith" (Rom. 1:5, 16:26; cf. Matt. 7:21). (We'll return below to the crucial role of faith, or trust, in God.)

Jesus was clear about the priority of eagerly serving God wholeheartedly even when this priority requires that certain treasured things be released. A good illustration of this occurs in the case of the rich man who asked Jesus what he must do to have eternal life (Mk. 10:17–22; cf. Lk. 18:18–30). Jesus mentions obedience to some of the Mosaic ten commandments, but the man responds with a claim to his having obeyed these since his youth. Jesus, however, is not satisfied. He identifies a serious lack, as follows: "Jesus looking upon him loved him, and said to him, 'You lack one thing; go, sell all that you have, and give it to the poor, and you will have treasure in heaven; and come, follow me'" (Mk. 10:21, RSV). The rich man was holding on to earthly treasure (namely, his wealth) that prevented him from sincerely following Jesus as the way to lasting life with God. So, Mark reports: "At that saying his countenance fell and he went away sorrowful; for he had great possessions" (Mk. 10:22, RSV). This is a kind of disobedience that refuses to put Jesus first as divinely appointed Lord and God first as God. It puts wealth, instead of Jesus and his Father, in the place of priority. The rich man evidently found his self-importance and security in his great wealth rather than in Jesus as Lord and his Father as God. He was honest enough, however, to acknowledge that he couldn't follow Jesus as long as wealth was the priority in his life. He was, in the end, unwilling to go for broke with Jesus as divinely appointed Lord. Idols, cognitive or otherwise, typically interfere in that way.

Many philosophers are like the rich man with regard to their philosophical pursuits, in a manner analogous to others with regard to nonphilosophical pursuits. Jesus issues love commands that exalt loving God and others as the priority for humans, but some philosophers go away empty, owing to preoccupation with many self-selected philosophical questions. They may think of themselves as having obeyed many of the ten commandments since their youth, but Jesus issues divine love commands as supreme for human attitudes and conduct. So, philosophers, among other people, must, and in effect do, choose what will have priority: either Jesus and his divine love commands or self-selected pursuits (philosophical or otherwise). We have seen that these alternatives don't always agree, and thus that a choice between them is sometimes needed.

If we put our own philosophical pursuits first, we thereby risk a refusal to go for broke with Jesus and a perfectly loving God. That is, we then risk refusing to trust and to honor a perfectly loving God above all else. In addition, we risk demoting Jesus from the status of Lord and God from the preeminent status of One worthy of worship and full obedience. Our philosophical pursuits, in that case, can acquire for us an importance superior to Jesus and his perfectly loving divine Father. We thus could follow straightaway in the sad anti-God steps of the rich man of Mk. 10:17–22. Philosophy without divine guidance readily leads one in such futile anti-God steps.

Philosophers, among others, do well to ask *what* they are going for broke for: are they seeking the acquisition of philosophical truth rather than the unselfish love and corresponding divine–human fellowship advanced in the divine love commands? This is a person-involving and person-defining existential question that won't easily go away, even if it rarely is allowed to surface in professional philosophy. Jesus asked the following: "What good is it for one to gain the whole world, yet forfeit one's soul? Or what can one give in exchange for one's soul?" (Mk. 8:36–37). Gaining the world of philosophical truth (to whatever extent) doesn't amount to faithful obedience to Jesus as Lord or to a perfectly loving God. In addition, the pursuit of such philosophical gain can take us away from what would give us the life we humans need in volitional fellowship with a perfectly loving God.

In postponing, through philosophy or some other means, a decision to go for broke with a perfectly loving God, on the basis of purposively available evidence, we fail to submit to God as our preeminent authority. In that case, something or someone else would function as our guiding preeminent authority. So, we would be akin to the rich man who departed from Jesus when Jesus presented the divine love commands as authoritative. As a representative philosopher, Socrates *raises questions*, but Jesus *commands* divine love under his Father's authority, and then seeks to manifest such love to humans for the sake of offering divine–human reconciliation (as identified in, for example, Mk. 10:42–45, 14:22–25, and Rom. 5:8–11). We must, and do, choose our lord: either Jesus on his terms of divine redemptive love or philosophy (or something else) on our inferior, nonredemptive terms.

In giving humans divine love commands as supremely authoritative (in virtue of coming from a perfectly authoritative and loving God), Jesus calls humans into not just reflection but primarily an adventurous *mission* to the whole world, in fellowship with God. The divinely appointed mission involves obediently receiving, participating in, and manifesting with our lives (ever increasingly) the Good News of God's perfect self-giving redemptive love and forgiveness, as manifested and offered perfectly by Jesus as divinely appointed Lord and Redeemer. This mission is cognitively grounded in the purposively available authoritative evidence outlined in the previous chapters, and it is empowered ultimately by the divine source of this evidence: God's inter-vening Spirit, the Spirit behind the crucified and risen Jesus. The faithful followers of Jesus, therefore, are *primarily* not scholars, theorists, or philo-sophers, but rather *obedient disciples* set on the mission of receiving, partici-pating in, and manifesting divine perfect love and forgiveness for all people, including enemies. Such faithfully obedient discipleship, represented paradigmatically and perfectly by the life and death of Jesus himself, is nor-mative throughout the New Testament, in the wake of the earthly life of Jesus (cf. Phil. 2:5–13, 1 Cor. 11:1; see also Johnson 1999, Longenecker 1996).

An early Christian statement of the importance of faithfully obedient dis-cipleship reports: "And Jesus came and said to them, 'All authority in heaven and on earth has been given to me. Go therefore and make disciples of all nations, baptizing them in the name of the Father and of the Son and of the Holy Spirit, teaching them to [obey] all that I have commanded you; and . . . I am with you always, to the close of the age'" (Matt. 28:18–20, RSV; cf. Acts 1:8). This mission-defining commission identifies the priority of obedient discipleship toward Jesus as God's authoritative representative over all alter-natives, including over our self-selected philosophical pursuits. The authority of Jesus as Lord is "given" to him by God, whose authority is absolutely self-sufficient in virtue of self-sufficient divine perfect love. Given Jesus as divinely appointed Lord, then, obedient discipleship toward him, the authoritative giver of divine love commands, has priority over our ordinary tendencies in philosophical truth-seeking. Our philosophical quests must then submit to Jesus and his authoritative divine love commands. (This chapter's final section outlines how philosophy in general is to be brought under the divinely appointed lordship of Jesus.)

Why do some philosophers, even philosophers avowing Christian commitment, ignore or even resist the priority of Jesus as Lord and his authoritative divine love commands? The most straightforward answer is this: we humans seek, as much as possible, to be in charge of our lives, perhaps relative to peer-approved standards. In other words, we aim to retain as much authority in our lives as we can, and, as a result, many people share Thomas Nagel's "cosmic authority problem" with acknowledgment of God, as outlined earlier (see Nagel 1997, p. 131). The underlying sentiment is that if I relinquish my authority over my own life, I then will be susceptible to harm by someone who doesn't have my best interests at heart. So, the reasoning goes, it's in my best interest for *me* to maintain authority over my life. This suggests that I am, and should be, in charge regarding how I use my time and my other resources. If, in exercising my authority over my life, I deem it important to pursue philosophical questions above all else, then it is permissible for me to pursue such questions above all else. *I* am, according to this view, the proper authority over my life's pursuits and resources.

The question, then, is this: who *should*, all things considered, be in charge of my life? Clearly, we shouldn't relinquish authority over our lives lightly, because disasters threaten and even occur if we place authority in the wrong hands. Human history demonstrates this without a doubt, given its long lines of religious and political tyrants and terrorists. Supposed authorities who initially seem helpful often turn out to have hidden harmful agendas, and this is true even in longstanding avowedly Christian groups (sadly, even regarding treatment of children). So, caution is definitely in order when anyone considers acknowledging an authority over one's life. *Caution* about authority, however, isn't *resistance* to proper authority. Here as elsewhere, the baby shouldn't be thrown out with the dirty bath water.

Jesus amazed and troubled many in his audience, because, unlike the intellectuals of his day, he taught and acted "with authority" (Mk. 1:22). When challenged about his authority, he gave no direct answer; instead, he put the challengers themselves under a challenge. Contemporary challengers face a similar turned-tables challenge from him. If Jesus is truly divinely appointed Lord over humans, then we shouldn't assume a role of authority over him. Instead, we should then defer to him and obey him as God's representative authority over us. We will go for broke with Jesus only if we acknowledge and trust him as divinely appointed Lord over us, but we shouldn't recommend cognitively ungrounded commitment in this connection. Fideism would be a lost cause here as elsewhere, given the cognitive arbitrariness it allows.

Fortunately, however, we don't need to be authorities over Jesus to have his divinely appointed authority cognitively grounded for us.

How exactly are we to decide whether Jesus is the proper authority over us? What would confirm his divinely appointed authority over us? The authority of Jesus, in keeping with the unique authority of his divine Father, doesn't fit with our ordinary preconceptions of authority. Jesus himself warned of this, as follows:

> You know that those who are supposed to rule over the Gentiles lord it over them, and their great men exercise authority over them. But it shall not be so among you.... [W]hoever would be great among you must be your servant, and whoever would be first among you must be slave of all. For the Son of Man also came not to be served but to serve, and to give his life as a ransom for many (Mk. 10:42–45, RSV).

The distinctive authority of Jesus is anchored and confirmed not in coercive power but rather in the power of his self-giving, merciful, and righteous divine love toward others, even enemies. Jesus attributed the same kind of unselfish perfect love *(agape)* to his divine Father (Matt. 5:43–48; cf. Lk. 6:27–36), the ultimate authoritative source of such unique love. We ourselves, in our selfishness, are inadequate sources for the power of such love, and suggestions to the contrary rank among the most destructive human myths.

Abraham Heschel has noted the strangeness of the character of divine supremacy in this connection, as follows:

> When in response to Moses' request, the Lord appeared to tell him what He is, did He say: I am the all-wise, the perfect, and of infinite beauty? He did say: I am full of love and compassion. Where in the history of religion prior to the age of Moses was the Supreme Being celebrated for His being sensitive to the suffering of men? Have not philosophers agreed, as Nietzsche remarked, in the deprecation of pity? (1955, p.67).

If we disparage or otherwise devalue divine merciful love, we will likewise disparage or devalue the divinely appointed authority of Jesus. Our recognition of the authority of Jesus has as much to do with what we ourselves *value* as what we think. If we refuse to love what Jesus loves (in particular, self-giving obedience to his Father, even for the merciful good of our enemies), we will overlook or set aside his divinely appointed authority over us. Indeed, in that case, there is a sense in which the divinely appointed authority of Jesus will be "hidden" from us, by our own misplaced likes and dislikes (cf. Matt. 11:25–27, Lk. 10:21–22). (See Chapter 2 on the significance of divine hiding for redemptive purposes.)

What we love can influence what we know. Love can thus be *cognitively* important in ways that philosophers and others rarely consider. Helmut Thielicke has observed:

> ...in human matters there are things that are perceptible only to the personal category of love. In them love has [an] epistemological function.... Nobility of soul, or even charm, cannot be known in an objective, unprejudiced, and unloving way. This is surely what Goethe meant when he said one can understand only what one loves (1974, p. 210).

A similar theme evidently underlies 1 Jn. 4:8: "The one who does not love does not know God, because God is love." A person's likes and dislikes, including morally relevant likes and dislikes, can be in conflict with the moral character and commands of Jesus and his perfectly loving Father. In that case, the person in question will be inclined to set aside or at least to minimize the authority of Jesus and his Father and even evidence of such authority. This person's moral character, in terms of its ultimate authority, will then be at odds with the moral character of Jesus and his Father. Jesus will be set aside by this person as an implausible candidate for being the Lord of this person's life under the ultimate authority of his perfectly loving Father. So, it can matter significantly what one likes and dislikes, in terms of what one allows to be real candidates for known authorities in one's life.

Exercising authority as divinely appointed Lord, Jesus calls (that is, commands) people to move away from old, natural likes and dislikes for the sake of new loves. The needed new loves emerge in the divine love commands as central to volitional fellowship with the perfectly authoritative and loving God responsible for those commands. This kind of personally redefining move from old to new threatens to create social and professional turbulence in a person's life as old securities, honors, and alliances are put at risk and even left behind. As divinely appointed representative of God's love commands, Jesus becomes a nuisance and a stumbling-block for the sake of needed new loves, and his disciples follow suit, if stumblingly. Nobody, at any rate, should have thought that this outcast Galilean was an ordinary choir boy. He resists any easy domestication, for our own good, and leaves us wondering, perhaps with fear and trembling, how far he aims to take us into his Father's transforming redemptive mission. It would seem easier if he would just go it alone, and this may explain why some approaches to divine–human atonement mistakenly divorce redemptive faith from human volitional transformation.

Thielicke remarks on the commanded change for humans:

> With [the authoritative] calling [from Jesus,] I and my existence are put under obligation. Not just my ears and my perceptive reason are engaged.

In biblical terms, my heart, the core of my being, is also engaged. I am not just summoned to hear and ponder; I am called to discipleship and fellowship. This means existential participation to the utmost. The goal is not to grasp the truth but to be in it, i.e., to exist in the name of the faithfulness of God which confronts me bodily in Christ. Thus discipleship cuts deep. It means *breaks and partings*. I put my hand to the plow. I cannot look back. I am confronted by the transvaluation of all values. I am called out of the familiar world and its security. I must renounce even what I previously regarded as pious duties (Matt. 8:18–22) (1974, p. 206, italics added).

The demanded "breaks and partings" call for new likes and dislikes, new securities, new alliances, and new ways of thinking and living, under the authority of divine fellowship and its love commands. We must either renounce or reconceive old ways in the light of Jesus as Lord who authoritatively issues divine love commands (cf. Matt. 9:16–17, 2 Cor. 5:17). The life-giving shakeup demanded by Jesus as divinely appointed Lord is palpable and thorough, but to the extent that we insist on our own ways of thinking and living, or on our own likes and dislikes, we will firmly resist the shakeup. We will thus resist Jesus as Lord who seeks to bring the unique life-giving power of his perfectly loving Father to humans, even to enemies. Many philosophers, among others, choose to resist, on the alleged ground that Jesus doesn't truly merit the status of divinely appointed Lord over all humans.

In John's Gospel, as Chapter 1 noted, Jesus offers a straightforward way to discern whether he is God's unique authoritative spokesman rather than an imposter: "Jesus answered them, 'My teaching is not mine, but his who sent me; if [any person's] will is to do his will, [that person] shall know whether the teaching is from God or whether I am speaking on my own authority.'" (Jn. 7:16–17, RSV). One's "will is to do God's will" only if one chooses to obey the divine love commands, because those commands are a central expression of God's perfectly loving will and moral character. In addition, one chooses to obey the divine love commands only if one resolves to undergo "breaks and partings" with unloving, selfish ways of living, including truth-seeking that disregards the vital needs of others.

The needed movement of one's will away from selfishness and toward obeying the divine love commands aids a person in recognizing, and even appreciating, the authority of Jesus as Lord anchored fully in divine perfect love. The direct personal confirmation of Jesus's divinely appointed authority for receptive humans comes from the authoritative witness of the Spirit of God in conscience, in keeping with the pneumatic epistemology developed in the previous chapters. (This, incidentally, fits with the lesson of Matt. 16:15–17; cf. Matt. 11:25, 1 Cor. 2:9–16.) Even so, for salient confirmation, we must be volitionally open to this witness for what it is intended to be, including its being a confirming source of the divine love commands. Being noncoercive, the witness in question can be, and often is, suppressed and ignored by us, and thus has an elusive role in our lives.

Suppose that I, for instance, hear the divine love commands of Jesus for the first time, and I am convicted in conscience for failing to obey both commands. I could either (a) harden my heart (that is, my motivational center) in resistance, (b) try to maintain casual indifference, or (c) begin to yield to the conviction in my conscience. As I begin to yield, God's intervening Spirit would noncoercively bring deeper conviction and new clarity regarding my moral and cognitive situation relative to God and others, and I would have a cognitively improved basis for seeking divine help in overcoming my selfish situation. I would then acknowledge the needed "breaks and partings" with my old selfish ways, and turn with grounded conviction toward God and God's authoritative ways of unselfish love. This is no clean recipe, given the messy backgrounds we bring to our cognitive and moral situation, but it does point to how a perfectly loving God can seek noncoercively to begin to transform a selfish person.

If we find our self-importance primarily in pursuing philosophical questions, we won't find our self-importance supremely in being beloved and forgiven children of the perfectly authoritative and loving Father of Jesus. We will then find our self-importance primarily in something that can't satisfy or sustain us in what we need, given the human predicament of destructive selfishness and impending death. In the end, we will then be left exhausted, joyless, and dead. Since philosophical and theological questions tend, at least in academic settings, to be abstract and disengaged from our actual lives, they tend to divert our attention from our destructive selfishness and impending death. If we thus don't attend to the urgency of our human predicament, we won't be inclined to reflect in a morally serious way on how we use our time and energy. We may then disregard any reported need for human redemption and transformation by a perfectly loving God. Many philosophers, among others, fall prey to this dangerous kind of cognitive blind spot.

Philosophical questions and answers can't give or sustain life, let alone a joyful life of unselfish love; nor can a philosophical system, and few things seem as obvious. In this respect, at least, philosophy resembles the Mosaic Law: it lacks the needed divine power to give humans life sustained and approved by God in fellowship with God (see Gal. 2:16–19, 3:18–22, Rom. 8:2–4; cf. Wenham 1995, pp. 219–36). The human tragedy revolves around our looking for our primary self-importance in all the wrong places, in places that can't give us what we supremely need, regardless of what we happen

to want. In the wake of Socrates, Plato, Aristotle, and their prolific succes-
sors, philosophy in its normal mode, without being receptive toward divine
authority, is one of those wrong places.

When we go for broke with something that can't sustain us, *we* end up
broke, sooner or later. We may try to obscure this with peer approval, badges
of intellectual honor, exalted academic titles, endless theoretical discussions,
and various other diversions, but the truth of our predicament will ultimately
emerge and prevail. We can't hide for long the fate of our chosen sources of
self-importance. Philosophy in its normal mode, without being receptive
toward divine authority, isn't our savior; nor is it a trustworthy avenue to
the divine savior we need, given our tragic predicament of selfishness and
impending death. Accordingly, Jesus doesn't call people into philosophy as
the way to approach him or his perfectly loving divine Father, although
he could in principle have done so, in the footsteps of a Jewish wisdom
tradition. As divinely appointed Lord, he calls us instead directly to himself
and his ultimately authoritative Father, in authoritatively grounded trust
and obedience (see Mk. 4:40, 11:22, Matt. 7:21–28). In that connection, he
calls us into eager obedience to the divine love commands regarding God
and others, for the sake of divine–human fellowship in human community
under his Father's authority.

Our philosophical questions might not be as innocent as they seem on
initial reflection. One harmful use of them turns them into purported delay
tactics whereby we aim to postpone our seriously facing both the divine love
commands and who(se) we are relative to those commands. We sometimes
aim to avoid or at least to delay the judgment of divine love upon us, because
it calls for extensive reorienting changes in our lives, including in our intellectual lives. Such intended delay tactics, however, don't actually delay our
responding to the divine love commands; in effect, they rather set aside, and
even disobey, the love commands as less than supreme. They substitute other
pursuits in place of one's directly facing and obeying the divine love commands. Whatever the actual intention, this is to replace rather than simply
to delay obeying the divine love commands. In this respect, diversions are
rarely, if ever, harmless. As long as they divert us from something we urgently
need, they are actually harmful and thus call for diversion from themselves
for the sake of securing what we urgently need. In diverting our attention
from the love commands, we may obscure our need of divine forgiveness for
failing to meet God's moral standards.

A closely related harmful use of philosophical questions turns them into
idols, that is, things we embrace in ways that detract from the love and
trust we owe to God alone. They become idols whenever they detract from

the supremely authoritative status of God as Lord of our lives, including our intellectual lives and our available time. So, whenever philosophical questions lead us into violation of the divine love commands, they become idols. In that case, *philosophy* itself becomes idolatry and thus a kind of rebellion against God. It then presents a false god that, as an imposter, competes with the perfectly loving true God. An ever-present danger of such philosophy is that it papers over our desperate moral and mortal predicament in the absence of a perfectly loving God.

Some philosophers venture to make a god in our own philosophical image to underwrite the pursuits of philosophy. Consider, for example, Aristotle's tenuous god as "thought thinking thought" (in Book Lambda of the *Metaphysics*), a god that is purely intellectual and altogether devoid of unselfish love in action. The result of such philosophical idolatry is sure death, however honored, sophisticated, and rigorous the pathway. Going for broke with philosophy, and without the God of authoritative perfect love, will leave us broke indeed. We will then have no effective antidote to our destructive selfishness and impending death. The human predicament will then crush us all, even while we are pursuing philosophy wholeheartedly on our preferred terms.

We give philosophy too much power, even dangerous power, when we allow it to demote, in theory or in practice, the love commands of an authoritative perfectly loving God. We do this whenever we let philosophy result in our ignoring or disobeying the divine love commands, because we then give it an authority proper only to a perfectly loving God. In that case, we have to face a choice between two competing authorities and thus two perspectives regarding authority: (a) in the beginning was *the philosophical question*, and (b) in the beginning was *the perfectly loving God*. These are alternatives regarding ultimate authority, and not just regarding a temporal beginning for inquiry.

Suppose that we begin with philosophical questions as ultimately authoritative about reality (at least in virtue of yielding ultimately authoritative answers about reality), and we have no authority independent of philosophy in its normal mode, lacking receptivity toward divine authority. We can then raise metaphilosophical questions *about* those philosophical questions and then meta-metaphilosophical questions about those metaphilosophical questions, and so on *ad infinitum*. So, we invite an endless regress of ever-higher metaphilosophical questions. Philosophical questions at some level or other will then be our beginning and our end, and our middle too, in seeking authoritative answers about reality, even if the metaphilosophical questions themselves have no end in principle. They will, at any rate, have a corner on our lives; in particular, our lives will then never get around to the matter of the ultimate authority of a perfectly loving God who issues divine love commands. We will then dismiss such authority simply by looking elsewhere for ways to spend our time on philosophy in its normal mode. Philosophy has a notorious way of leading one to do just this, often in the name of truth-seeking.

Philosophy in its normal mode might present itself as a trustworthy avenue to eventual acknowledgment of God's authority, but this avenue would be superfluous at best. A God who needs philosophy in its normal mode as the avenue to reach humans will fail to reach most humans (relatively few of us humans are philosophers, after all), and will actually not reach humans where they need to be reached. We humans need to be reached at a level much deeper than our philosophical thinking in its normal mode. We need to be reached at the level of what we *love* and *hate*, at the level of our *will*. Philosophical thinking in its normal mode rarely engages or forms what we love or what we will in any significant way.

We can, of course, raise philosophical questions *about* love, hate, and volition; and many philosophers have done so. Still, philosophy in its normal mode doesn't yield conclusive authoritative evidence of, or volitional fellowship with, the needed Giver of love commands who intervenes powerfully in receptive human lives to redeem them from futile and destructive ways. Such a Giver comes to us only by grace, by a powerful gift unearned by philosophical or other intellectual means. This is integral to the Good News of the Jewish and Christian God of Abraham, Isaac, Jacob, and Jesus, as outlined in the previous chapter.

Philosophy in its normal mode has no authoritative Good News of its own, but it doesn't follow that philosophy must stay in its normal mode, without Good News. Given the evidential role of God's intervening Spirit, the Good News doesn't need philosophy in its normal mode to reach people with a cognitively well-founded message. Jerusalem has no inherent need of Athens to carry out its Good News power movement, contrary to what many philosophers have suggested (cf. 1 Cor. 1:17–25). Still, its Good News is intended to go to the citizens of Athens as well as to the people of the nonphilosophical world (cf. Acts 17:16–33), always on the redemptive terms of Spirit-given divine wisdom rather than on the inferior terms of human wisdom (1 Cor. 2:4–16; cf. Ford 2007, pp. 176–91, Brown 1995, and Fee 2007, pp. 130–31). A twofold desired result is a new focus on divine cognitive grace (or, gift) in genuine wisdom and an elimination of any boasting in human power and achievement that obscures divine power and redemption (cf. 1 Cor. 1:29).

4. TWO MODES

Jesus *commanded* humans, in no uncertain terms, to love God wholeheartedly and thereby to love others too, as the top two priorities demanded by God. Unlike a typical philosopher, Jesus didn't simply *propose* questions, topics, and arguments for philosophical discussion. He issued vital commands, with the God-given authority of self-giving divine love. The contrast between Jesus and Socrates here is striking, and points to two different modes of being human: *an obedience mode* and *a discussion mode*. In an obedience mode, one responds to an authority by *submission of one's will* to the authority's commands, ideally on the basis of conclusive evidence. In a discussion mode, one responds with *talk* about questions, options, claims, and arguments. We undermine the self-avowed God-given authority of Jesus as Lord when we respond to him just in a discussion mode that doesn't include an obedience mode. We then treat him as something less than the divinely appointed Lord who perfectly represents the authority of his divine Father. We reduce him to a philosophical interlocutor, and thus, by our questionable lights, he wouldn't qualify as authoritative Lord.

Kierkegaard, writing as Climacus in *Concluding Unscientific Postscript*, has compared Socrates with Jesus in terms of an allegedly common emphasis on the so-called "inwardness of faith." He suggests that such inwardness "cannot be expressed more definitely than this: it is the absurd, adhered to firmly with the passion of the infinite" (1992 [1846], vol. 1, p. 214). Christian commitment, according to Kierkegaard, is at its heart a faith commitment to mystery that doesn't go away, and that doesn't yield to either explanation, nonparadox-ical description, or philosophical resolution. The speculative philosopher, he claims, is "the naughty child who refuses to stay where existing humans belong, in the children's nursery and the education room of existence where one becomes adult only through inwardness in existing, but who instead wants to enter God's council, continually screaming that, from the point of view of the eternal, . . . there is no paradox" (1992, vol. 1, p 214).

At times Kierkegaard suggests that the "absurd" and the "paradox" are just the divine incarnation in Jesus as a human with historical existence (see 1992, vol. 1, pp. 209–10, 213). *If* this is *all* he means (and we won't digress to potentially endless exegesis of Kierkegaard), his language of "absurdity" and "contradiction" is harmfully overloaded. In addition, he then blocks Socrates and others who existed before the incarnation of Jesus from the "inwardness of faith" as specified above. The proclaimed incarnation of Jesus may be shocking and mysterious, but it isn't, strictly speaking, absurd or contradictory. At a minimum, we should demand a careful demonstration of any alleged contradiction in this area.

Redemptively significant Jewish and Christian faith is most plausibly regarded as a human volitional response of *trust* toward God (and God's promises) on the cognitive basis of human experience of God's intervening in human lives with redemptive actions and thereby calling people to trust and obey God. (This book's previous chapters have characterized the relevant cognitive basis via purposively available authoritative evidence in the context of a volitional pneumatic epistemology.) Such faith isn't an inward embracing of absurdity or contradiction, at least in any ordinary sense of those terms. Kierkegaard has gone astray here, given his loathing of systematic philosophy, if we take his language at face value. (I doubt that his mature considered view, after his transitional experience of 1848, recommends that we take his language here at face value, but that's beside the point now.)

Even if Socrates manifested and recommended a kind of "existential inwardness" (and showing this would be no easy task, given our thin evidence), this wouldn't compare him favorably to Jesus. The difference between them is, in the end, too vast. Jesus, as the self-avowed authoritative Son of his perfectly loving divine Father (cf. Mk. 12:1–12, Matt. 11:25–27, Lk. 10:21–22), commands people to have faith as obedient and loving trust in his Father (cf. Mk. 11:22), on the basis of divine purportedly redemptive intervention in human lives. Such trust moves outward obediently, by divine command, in love toward God and thereby toward others. It transcends a discussion mode for the sake of an obedience mode of existence under perfectly loving divine authority. The apostle Paul, accordingly, speaks of "faith [or trust, toward God and Jesus] working through love *(agape)*" (Gal. 5:6). This is likewise the consistent focus of Jesus as divinely appointed Lord, and it is absent from Socrates (at least as represented by Plato). In this regard, the difference between Jesus and Socrates is more striking and substantial than any similarity.

A misguided understanding of *faith* leaves many people, including many people sympathetic to the Good News as presented by Paul, with uneasiness about the redemptive significance of Jesus's love commands. As suggested, redemptively significant faith in God is best understood as human *trust* in God in response to human experience of God's redemptive intervention in human lives. Such faith as trust in God is a needed motivational anchor for human *faithful actions* toward God. It includes one's general *receptive volitional commitment* to receive manifested and offered divine power of redemptive love as a gracious gift (perfectly found in Jesus Christ) and thereby to obey God in what God commands and promises, even if one occasionally disobeys God and thus violates one's general commitment. Such a volitional commitment, when actually carried out by a person in action, includes that person's submitting his or her will to God's authoritative will in a particular case of action, just as Jesus did in Gethsemane.

Redemptively significant faith includes, at its core, *obediently receiving and volitionally committing to* God and what God graciously offers for the sake of obedient volitional fellowship with God. The redeemed life is inherently the life that obediently receives and volitionally commits to God's authoritative call to divine–human fellowship and thus knows God volitionally (as characterized in Chapters 1–2; cf. Jn. 17:3). It would be a mistake, then, to contrast redemptively significant faith, or trust, and obedience to God's call to divine–human fellowship. Such faith is an obedient response of volitional commitment to receive and follow agreeably a divine authoritative redemptive call that offers lasting forgiveness and fellowship. The receptive feature of this kind of faith, toward a genuine divine call, excludes a characterization in terms of pure imagination or wishful thinking. It also points to a kind of experiential cognitive support that counts against fideism.

The apostle Paul uses talk of *obedience* and talk of *belief/faith* interchangeably in certain contexts (see, for instance, Rom. 10:16–17; cf. Rom. 1:5, 6:16, 16:26, 1 Cor. 7:19, Gal. 5:5–7, 2 Cor. 9:13). Likewise, setting a model for Paul, Jesus acknowledged a crucial role for human obedience to God's will in entering his Father's kingdom family (Matt. 7:21, 16:24–26, 19:16–22, 21:28–32; cf. Matt. 6:24–29). The obedience (of faith) in question isn't just a number of obedient actions on their own. It's rather *attitudinal obedience* that includes obediently receiving, and volitionally committing and thus yielding to, God as perfectly authoritative and worthy of worship, for the sake of agreeably participating in God's powerful redemptive offer to humans of volitional fellowship with God. We might thus call this faith *obedience of the heart*, and acknowledge that such obedience of faith can be, for various reasons, less than perfectly represented in corresponding actions. (A classic case illustrating imperfect corresponding actions can be found in Simon Peter's "hypocritical" behavior toward Gentiles described by Paul in Gal. 2:4–16; cf. Martyn 1997c, pp. 240–45, Bruce 1977, pp. 173–87.)

Many people shy away from the important theme of faith as (a) including a general volitional commitment to receive and follow God and God's authoritative call to fellowship and thus as (b) being itself a distinctive kind of obedience (of the heart) to God's call and will. They fear that faith may then be confused with what some people call human "works" and regard as unnecessary for, if not incompatible with, gracious divine redemption of humans. *Obedience*, however, isn't what Paul dubs "works"; instead, Paul thinks of "works," at least in his Epistle to the Romans, as what one does to *obligate* God or to *earn* something from God (see Rom. 4:4). From the standpoint of ordinary language use of "works," the word is a technical term in Paul's letter to the Romans that contrasts with "gift."

In keeping with the redemptive significance of obedience (of the heart), Paul says the following without hesitation, regarding identity markers for God's forgiven and redeemed people: "For neither circumcision counts for anything nor uncircumcision, but *keeping the commandments* of God" (1 Cor. 7:19, RSV, italics added). In Paul's understanding, God's commandments included not only the aforementioned divine love commands issued by Jesus (cf. Gal. 5:14) but primarily the gospel of Jesus Christ itself, in virtue of its authoritatively calling people to "the obedience of faith" in God and Jesus (see Rom. 16:26; cf. Matt. 28:18–20). Accordingly, after presenting the Good News of divine grace as gift-righteousness, Paul speaks of "obedience which leads to righteousness" (Rom. 6:16, RSV). He identifies this obedience with one's being "obedient from the heart," and suggests that it underlies one's "having been set free from sin" (Rom. 6:17–18, RSV). These remarks fit well with Paul's talk of the "obedience of faith" (Rom. 1:5, 16:26), understood as one's general volitional commitment (of the heart) to God and God's call to fellowship as one obediently receives the powerful redemptive gift of fellowship with God.

Paul doesn't shy away at all from acknowledging a key *human role* in the divine redemption of humans, in connection with human *obedient reception of,* and *volitional commitment to,* of the Good News gift of divine righteousness. Unlike proponents of extreme divine sovereignty who leave no room for a crucial role for human volitional response (for example, Westerholm 2004, among many others in the Augustinian and Reformed traditions), Paul states *why* Abraham and many relevantly similar humans are reckoned with divine righteousness: namely, *their faith*, as their grounded trust in God, is reckoned to them as divine righteousness (see Rom. 4:16–25). Correspondingly, the human rejection of such faith will exclude some humans from fellowship with God (see Rom. 11:20). The divine redemptive gift on offer (without coercion), in the Good News, falls short of its salvific goal in the absence of being received in faith, or trust, by humans.

One might think of faith itself as a divine gift (cf. Eph. 2:8), but in that case there would still be a crucial role for human volitional response in *willingly receiving* this gift. In any case, Paul, following Jesus, thinks of human faith as the means of receiving divine redemptive grace (Rom. 4:16) and as something that humans can willingly relinquish by yielding to resolute distrust in God (*apistia*, Rom. 4:20). Abraham didn't fail in that manner relative to God and God's main redemptive promise (despite his occasional acts of disobedience), and "that is why his faith was 'reckoned to him as righteousness'" (Rom. 4:22; cf. Gal. 3:6–9). Such faith precludes any ground for human boasting, earning, or self-credit, because it is just the human means (for Gentiles and Jews) to receive the gracious powerful gift of redemption promised by God, including the gift of divine–human volitional fellowship via God's empowering Spirit (see Rom. 3:29–30, 4:16, 5:2, Gal. 3:14).

Paul thinks of human faith, in terms of obedience of the heart, as the means of receiving God's empowering Spirit whereby divine love commands can be obeyed by a human in virtue of the power of divine love in one's receptive heart (see Rom. 5:5, Gal. 3:2–5,14, 5:5–7,22). Paul thus thinks of divinely received love, via trust in God, as empowering the human *fulfillment* of (the spirit of) the divine law when such love is lived out toward others (see Rom. 13:8–10, Gal. 5:15; cf. 2 Cor. 3:5–8, Gal. 6:2, Matt. 5:17, 20–22, and Brondos 2006, pp. 77–84). He thus would support the following grace-laden approach to the Good News of divine redemption through Jesus:

> Jesus Christ has a twofold meaning for the religious experience of mankind. He is God's call to the world to take history with absolute [moral] serious-ness, and he is God's sign in history that [this] invocation has His eternal benediction. Those who hear the invocation without the benediction are either fatigued by the prospect of realizing anything ultimate in history or inflamed by the desire to do so on their own terms. The whole Gospel is not at hand, however, until it is known that in Christ God gives what he commands. That knowledge is the ground of repentance for the rebellious and the resigned alike (Michalson 1967, p. 192).

God's giving, as a gracious powerful gift, what the divine love commands demand of humans is central to Paul's Good News of God's inviting humans into the divine kingdom family as "the power of God for salvation to everyone who has faith" (Rom. 1:16, RSV; cf. 1 Cor. 4:20).

The divine love commands demand a kind of power among humans, the power of self-giving love, that God's own Spirit (and only God's Spirit) pro-vides to receptive humans. Faith as attitudinal obedience of the heart is the human means of receiving the needed power of God's Spirit, and such obe-dience should be not cognitively blind but grounded in human experience of purposively available authoritative divine evidence (as outlined in pre-vious chapters). The divine love commands invite divine–human volitional fellowship, and thereby offer increasing purposively available evidence of divine reality as God's power of self-giving love is increasingly manifested and offered in the life of an obediently receptive person. The kind of divine manifest-offering of redemptive love found perfectly in Jesus thus finds an imperfect analogue in obediently receptive humans, who (in Pauline terms) "have been set free" to love by God's power and so can "fill up what is lacking in Christ's afflictions" for the sake of God's people (cf. Rom. 6:22, Col. 1:24).

The history of philosophy in its normal mode, without being receptive toward divine authority, leaves us in the discussion mode, short of the obedience mode under divine authority. As noted, philosophical questions prompt metaphilosophical questions about philosophical questions, and this launches a parade of higher-order questions, with no end to philosophical discussion. Hence, the questions of philosophy are, notoriously, perennial. As divinely appointed Lord, however, Jesus commands humans to move, for their own good, to the obedience mode of existence relative to divine love commands. He thereby points humans to his perfectly loving Father who ultimately underwrites the divine love commands for humans, for the sake of divine–human fellowship.

Humans need to transcend the discussion mode, and thus philosophical discussion itself, to face with sincerity the personal Authority who commands what we need: the obedient reception of divine–human fellowship via our obedient commitment to the perfectly loving Giver of divine love commands. Such obedience of the heart, involving the conforming of a human will to a divine will, is the way we are truly to *receive* the gift of divine redemptive love. We were made, according to Jesus, to live in faithful obedience to the Giver of divine love commands, whereby we enter into volitional fellowship with God and thus properly receive the divine love that intrudes in our lives before we seek it. We languish in selfishness and then die when we do otherwise. Lasting life then escapes us, and the dire human predicament wins out as we lose out.

Many philosophers are very uneasy with Jesus, if not ashamed of him, because he himself transcends their familiar, honorific discussion mode, and even demands that they do the same. Still, there's no suggestion here of being thoughtless, anti-intellectual, or unreasonable on the part of Jesus or his right-minded disciples. Philosophical discussion becomes advisable and permissible, under the divine love commands, if and only if it genuinely honors those commands by sincere compliance with them. Jesus calls us, in any case, to move beyond discussion to faithful obedience to his perfectly loving Father. He commands love from us toward God and others *beyond* discussion and the acquisition of truth, even philosophical truth. He thereby cleanses the temple of philosophy, and turns over our self-crediting tables of mere philosophical discussion. He pronounces judgment on this longstanding self-made temple, in genuine love for its wayward builders. His corrective judgment offers humans what they truly need to flourish in lasting community with God and other humans, including philosophers: namely, a life infused with divine–human fellowship via faithful obedience of the heart to a perfectly loving Giver of love commands.

The divine love commands issued by Jesus aren't ordinary moral rules that concern only actions. As suggested, they call for volitional *fellowship relationships* of unselfish love between oneself and God and between oneself and other humans. Such relationships go beyond mere actions to volitional fellowship, friendship, and communion between and among personal agents, with God at the center as the personal source of power needed for unselfish love. The background, foreground, and center of Jesus's divine love commands are thoroughly and irreducibly *person*-oriented and *person*-focused. They direct us to persons and fellowship relationships with persons, particularly with God and other humans. The love commands can't be reduced, then, to familiar standards of right action. They cut much deeper than any such standards, even cutting into who we are and how we exist in the presence of the authoritative self-giving God who issues the love commands.

The divine love commands correctively judge us by calling us up short by a morally perfect divine standard. In addition, in our failure to meet their standard, they facilitate our being called to obedient reception of divine redefinition of ourselves, even "new creation" of ourselves, by a gracious and powerful divine redemptive gift of volitional fellowship with the perfectly loving God manifested by Jesus. We move beyond the discussion mode, then, to personal transformation in the obedience mode, in a relationship of volitional fellowship with the God who commands unselfish love as supremely life-giving. In such transformation, pride, even intellectual pride, gives way to the humility of obedience to the divine love commands and their personal powerful Source. We turn now to some specific results of this volitional approach for philosophy as a discipline.

5. YIELDING

What exactly is philosophy in the obedience mode, in contrast with its normal mode, and what questions does it pursue in the obedience mode? At its core, it is faithful "obedience of the heart" to a perfectly loving God and to Jesus as divinely appointed Lord, including Lord of our intellectual and philosophical lives. Philosophy under the lordship of Jesus must attend to his divinely appointed mission (rather than our independent intellectual projects, however earnest and fascinating) and even participate eagerly in this redemptive mission. I shall outline what philosophy thus revamped, as kerygma-oriented, looks like in practice. Such a unifying metaphilosophical project is needed and even overdue, given the splintered disarray of contemporary philosophy, even regarding an ultimate goal.

If we know anything about the earthly Jesus at all (and we do know plenty, certainly more than we can handle on our own), we know that (a) he put an absolute priority on faithful obedience of the heart to his Father's perfectly authoritative and loving will and (b) he regarded all good things as gracious, humanly unearned gifts from his Father. Regarding (a) (that is, the primacy of his Father's will), Jesus taught his disciples to pray, "Thy kingdom come, *Thy will be done*, on earth as it is in Heaven" (Matt. 6:10, italics added; cf. Lk. 11:2, Mk. 14:36–37, Jn. 12:27–28). He also set an absolute priority for his disciples: "Seek first the kingdom of God" (Matt. 6:33; cf. Lk. 12:31). In this connection, he warned against letting *anything* encroach upon the unmatched primacy of his Father (Matt. 6:24), and he identified one's *doing his Father's will* as necessary for one's entering the kingdom family of God (Matt. 7:21). Clearly, Jesus meant business, life-or-death business, about doing his Father's will, for his disciples as well as himself.

Regarding (b), that is, gracious gifts from his Father, Jesus taught that his Father freely gives good things to people, including lasting life in divine–human fellowship to volitionally receptive people (Matt. 7:11; cf. Lk. 11:13). He also offered the parable of the talents to illustrate that we are fully responsible to use our God-given gifts faithfully toward God (see Matt. 25:15–30, Lk. 19:12–27). Our God-given gifts, according to Jesus, aren't ours to use as *we* see fit. We owe their Giver our wholeheartedly obedient use of them for the Giver's kingdom. In other words, given the primacy of God's perfectly loving will, Jesus taught and manifested in his life that our gifts from God must be used in full obedience to his Father's authoritative will. More specifically, our use of these gifts must be *wholeheartedly* for God, as the first of the divine love commands implies, in demanding that we love God with *all* of our heart, soul, mind, and strength.

The immediate implications of the aforementioned considerations (a) and (b) for philosophy are straightforward. The intellectual gifts underlying and yielding philosophy as a truth-seeking discipline are gifts from a perfectly loving God and, as such, must be used in eager obedience to God's perfectly loving will. Under the divinely appointed lordship of Jesus, we aren't entitled to use these gifts in just any way we like; they are too valuable for such a casual, potentially self-indulgent approach. Jesus himself said things that bear, if only by implication, on what is involved in using philosophical gifts for his Father's kingdom. We'll consider what is at the heart of his teaching, without getting side-tracked by historically complicated exegetical issues about the actual language he used or the particular social context in which he said something. We'll attend instead to a prominent theme that emerges across a range of his teachings and from different strata of the New Testament Gospels.

Given his divine love commands in the context of his redemptive Good News movement, we should expect Jesus to direct us toward loving others in using our various gifts in faithful commitment to him and his Father, and he does. This lesson emerges clearly from an exchange between Jesus and the apostle Peter in John's Gospel, after Peter had betrayed Jesus.

> When they had finished breakfast, Jesus said to Simon Peter, "Simon, son of John, do you love *(agapas)* me more than these [disciples]?" He said to him, "Yes, Lord; you know that I love you." He [Jesus] said to him, "Feed my lambs."
>
> A second time he said to him, "Simon, son of John, do you love *(agapas)* me?" He said to him, "Yes, Lord; you know that I love you." He [Jesus] said to him, "Tend my sheep."
>
> He said to him the third time, "Simon, son of John, do you love *(phileis)* me?" Peter was grieved because he said to him the third time, "Do you love me?" And he said to him, "Lord, you know everything; you know that I love you." Jesus said to him, "Feed my sheep" (Jn. 21:15–17, RSV).

Peter proclaims love of Jesus, and Jesus straightaway commands him to care for his disciples. Commitment to Jesus as Lord, according to Jesus himself, should lead immediately to caring for his followers. (For the same theme, see Jn. 13:12–17 and Matt. 25:34–45.) Once we acknowledge Jesus as authoritative in virtue of being divinely appointed Lord, we must use our gifts to care for his disciples, and other people as well, of course. This is required by self-giving love and thus by the divine love commands issued by Jesus on behalf of his divine Father. In addition, this requirement serves the manifest–offering Good News approach to divine–human atonement outlined above.

In the shadow of Jesus and his self-giving offering of atonement, the apostle Paul develops an *agape*-oriented approach to gracious gifts from God *(charismata)*. Immediately before identifying wisdom *(sophia)* and knowledge *(gnosis)* as gracious gifts from God's Spirit (1 Cor. 12:8; cf. 1:5), Paul states that God's gifts are for "the common good" of the body, or church, of Christ (1 Cor. 12:7; cf. Rom. 12:4–21). As a result, Paul advises the Corinthian Christians as follows: "Since you are eager to have spiritual gifts [from God], seek to abound in edification of the church [of God]" (1 Cor. 14:12). God-given gifts such as wisdom and knowledge, according to Paul, are graciously given by God to followers of Jesus for the purpose of building up the church of God. Paul thus states that "God has placed" teachers "in the church" as a gift to (and for) the church (1 Cor. 12:28), and Paul would include philosophers committed to Jesus as divinely appointed Lord in this category of teachers. (On the important question of why Paul started churches at all, in connection with the Pauline goal of conformity to, or attunement with, the image of Christ, see Samra 2006; cf. Brunner 1953.)

The theme of thinking and knowing as self-giving ministry underlies Paul's striking remark that "If I ... understand all mysteries and all knowledge ... but have not love *(agape)*, I am nothing" (1 Cor. 13:2, RSV; cf. 1 Cor. 8:1). Wisdom and knowledge, including philosophical wisdom and knowledge, count for "nothing" before God, according to Paul, if they don't contribute to the loving edification of others, including the church of God whose divinely appointed Lord is Jesus. Some members of the Corinthian church had neglected this truth, and the result was serious division in the church, owing to their selfish and prideful misuse of intellectual gifts. They had neglected that, at God's command, Jesus lived and died as a self-giving Lord willing to undergo humiliation for perfectly loving divine redemptive purposes (see 1 Cor. 1:10–2:5).

The neglect in question is not at all unique to the first-century Corinthian church. On the contrary, it flourishes wherever and whenever a quest for truth proceeds with disregard of self-giving love toward others. Given the aforementioned lessons from Jesus and Paul, we should think of philosophy in the obedience mode as philosophy under divine authority and thus in the eager philosophical service of people in need. The latter people include a peculiar imperfect community, called the "church," of people united under the divinely appointed lordship of Jesus as God's representative Good News community on earth. This calls for revamping philosophy to be used as a spiritual gift designed for compassionate philosophical ministry within the community of God's people. This church community, in turn, is to minister the Good News of God's redemptive love in Jesus to a needy, dying world, as is commanded by Jesus in the previously noted discipleship commission of Matt. 28:18–20. (Clearly, we aren't talking about the church as a clout-hungry political entity or as a tax-free American corporation, despite common distortions and abuses in the name of the church.) In serving the church as a community united and motivated by redemptive Good News, philosophy becomes, if not directly kerygmatic, at least kerygma-oriented. It thus seeks to facilitate the Good News kerygma of the church under Jesus as risen Lord.

Philosophers should eagerly serve the church by letting their focus in philosophy, including its questions, be guided by what is needed philosophically to build up the church as a compassionate ministry of the Good News of God's redemptive love in Jesus. (See Chapter 3 on the Good News as anchored in a distinctive power movement guided by God's Spirit.) As a result, there is no place under the divinely appointed lordship of Jesus for lone-ranger philosophers who choose their questions apart from the philosophical needs of the community of God's forgiven and redeemed people. Nor is there any place for an exclusive or a competitive "smarter-than-thou" spirit among philosophers, because they are to be united in a common Good News ministry of unselfish redemptive love in and for the community of God's people and others. This unity of mission is altogether foreign to philosophy in its normal discussion mode (see any segment of ancient or modern philosophy or any national philosophy conference), but defines philosophy in its obedience mode under the divinely appointed lordship of Jesus.

Clearly, if Jesus is divinely appointed Lord and King, then we are not. So, any aspiration to our becoming philosopher Kings or Lords should go by the wayside. Equally clearly, if Jesus is divinely appointed Lord, then our questions and projects must get in line with his life-or-death Good News discipleship mission under God's redemptive love. This means that philosophers should actually participate eagerly in the church community of God's people, as philosophical *servants* rather than self-avowed intellectual superiors, to identify its philosophical needs for the sake of the Good News and then to serve those needs in redemptive love. So, philosophers in the obedience mode aren't permitted to be outside observers, as many actually are by their own choice. This lesson alone, if obeyed by philosophers, would dramatically change the face of philosophy as we know it, enriching it beyond imagination. This lesson merits serious consideration given the growing irrelevance of philosophy in its normal mode as it becomes increasingly specialized, esoteric, and fractured, without the corresponding explanatory or applied benefits of topical specialization in the natural sciences. (The key difference here is, I suspect, that the natural sciences deal directly with natural kinds that are causally specific whereas the *a priori* topics of traditional philosophy don't do this.)

The reorienting of philosophy under the divinely appointed lordship of Jesus doesn't fit with philosophy as typically practiced in secular settings unreceptive to a perfectly loving authoritative God. This is no surprise, of course. The mission of Jesus is, owing to its unrelenting exaltation of the authoritative will of a perfectly loving God, altogether out of place in a secular perspective on reality. Indeed, the mission of Jesus, when adopted, makes *everything* we do sacred, with nothing left as secular, in that everything we then do is assessable, and should be assessed, relative to the authoritative will and love commands of a perfectly loving God. Philosophy is no exception in this case. Philosophy under the divinely appointed lordship of Jesus is sacred throughout, for it is eagerly committed to God's Good News discipleship mission throughout, whether in epistemology, metaphysics, ethics, aesthetics, or any other subdiscipline. Philosophy needs such an overarching, enlivening, and focusing purpose, lest it deteriorate into random truth-seeking, casual speculation, linguistic trivia, or sterile technicality. Secular philosophy, in particular, neglects divine authority and thus offers no room for such an overarching Good News mission. As a result, it offers no lasting hope for people in the dire human predicament of our destructive selfishness and impending death.

Philosophy as compassionate, kerygma-oriented philosophical ministry within the community of God's people is perfectly understandable once we acknowledge the God-given redemptive mission of Jesus. This Good News mission, in keeping with God's outgoing perfect love, is to build a fellowship community for Jesus's divine Father, "called out" from selfishness, despair, and other evils (literally, an *ekklesia*, a "church"). In such a community, fellowship *(koinonia)* under divine authority serves as the enabler and the outgrowth of divine *agape* obediently received by humans. Accordingly, Paul reports that the members of the Corinthian church were "called" by God "into the fellowship" of God's Son, Jesus (1 Cor. 1:9; cf. Gal. 1:6). The unselfish, self-giving love of God for all people, exemplified in Jesus even toward his enemies (including toward us), seeks to build a lasting fellowship community among *all* humans, under God's authority of conciliatory love in Jesus. This unique, supernaturally motivated community is to live out and make known the Good News of God's redemptive love for all people, even using words when necessary (see the summary of this theme in Eph. 1:9–10, 3:10–11; cf. Jn. 13:34–35, and Samra 2006, chap. 7).

God's building of lasting community in divine perfect love requires humans, including philosophers, to minister to people in community, after the example of compassionate servant love established by Jesus. Such ministering requires our being empowered with gifts of God's Spirit designed to build up community members in their discipleship (including fellowship) relationship with Jesus and his divine Father. The mission of the Good News church of God is a discipleship ministry under the perfect authority of Jesus and his Father, without exemption for any disciples, not even philosophers. Philosophical capacities, like other intellectual or spiritual gifts, have their central God-given purpose here, in human discipleship and fellowship under divine authority, and nowhere else. Philosophy under the authority of divine love commands, therefore, must not be the pursuit of casual or idiosyncratic intellectual concerns, however truth seeking and theoretically intriguing. It must, instead, formulate its questions, projects, and theories in light of the needs of the Good News church community founded and commissioned by Jesus himself to make and to nourish disciples for his perfectly loving Father. As indicated, philosophy must become kerygma-centered and thus redemptive.

Philosophy as philosophical discipleship ministry under a perfectly loving God will include a range of ethical issues that serve the church community and other people, but it won't be limited to ethics. It will be open to consider *any* philosophical issue prompted by the actual needs of the church community in its Good News discipleship mission for the sake of divine redemptive love for all people. Even questions about abstract entities *may* merit attention from philosophy under divine authority, if, for instance, questions about the nature of truth bearers merit attention in connection with the Good News of divine redemptive love. The needs of the church community are urgent, given that the redemptive Good News mission of Jesus is urgent and the church community is the divinely appointed bearer of this mission. As a result, philosophical pursuits under Good News discipleship ministry acquire an urgency that philosophy would otherwise lack. Philosophy thus takes on a needed new relevance under Jesus as divinely appointed Lord.

Issues extraneous to the redemptive needs of the church community, however intriguing, will not occupy the attention of philosophy under divine authority. For instance, an issue whose answer contributes nothing whatever to the divinely appointed Good News mission of the church community should be set aside as not compelling, given the church's being defined and governed by that mission. The apostle Paul (if he is behind the pastoral epistles, or if not, then a notable disciple of Paul) gives such instruction to Timothy, just before referring to "the Good News of the glory of the blessed God" (1 Tim. 1:11), as follows:

> ... remain in Ephesus so that you may command certain people not ... to devote themselves to myths and endless genealogies. These people promote speculations rather than God's community *(oikonomian)* in faith. ... The goal of this command is love *(agape)* that comes from a pure heart and a good conscience and sincere faith. Some have wandered away from these, and turned instead to pointless talk *(mataiologian)*. They want to be teachers of the law, but they do not know what they are saying or what they so confidently assert (1 Tim. 1:3–6).

Paul advises Timothy to avoid talk that is "pointless" relative to the church community of God, in order to give primacy to God's unselfish redemptive "love" offered in the Good News of Jesus. This chapter's thesis regarding philosophy as kerygma-oriented philosophical ministry under the divinely appointed lordship of Jesus, including the divine love commands, parallels Paul's advice. Questions that are pointless relative to the actual Good News redemptive mission of God's church community should be set aside by philosophy under the divinely appointed lordship of Jesus.

Philosophy in its normal mode, unreceptive to divine authority, sometimes wanders into the "myths and endless genealogies" proscribed by Paul. For example, some philosophical disputes about the interpretive minutia of the history of philosophy are of a piece with "endless genealogies." Readers may carefully and constructively supply their own examples, because candidates are indeed abundant. Just for the sake of simple illustration, one familiar example concerns whether there is conceptual development in Plato's dialogues regarding the theory of forms and what exactly this development is. Another example concerns whether there are multiple theories of primary substance *(ousia)* in Aristotle's *Metaphysics* and what exactly they are. These are areas of ongoing meticulous philosophical scholarship (and I must confess to having contributed to it many years ago), but no one has suggested that such pursuits contribute, or even will likely contribute, to the actual Good News redemptive mission of the community of God's people. We can allow for the possibility of a surprising contribution here, but actuality, of course, isn't settled by mere possibility and a claim to actuality would need to be substantiated.

Undeniably, conceptual taxonomy in philosophy is often very important to our intellectual and practical lives, and is similarly important in connection with the church's divinely appointed redemptive mission. In contrast, philosophical disputes over interpretive minutia of the history of philosophy are of a different category and aren't typically crucial to our lives or to the church's redemptive mission. Some conceptual taxonomy, however, can become sterile and even counterproductive relative to contributing to the church's ministry of the Good News of divine redemptive love. When we find ourselves drawing conceptual distinctions just for the sake of either drawing distinctions, extending philosophical controversy, or promoting our reputations, we have lost sight of the central purpose of the gift of philosophy under the divinely appointed lordship of Jesus. As always, the church's ministry of the Good News gives philosophy its unifying kerygma-centered purpose under Jesus as divinely appointed Lord. It also gives philosophy some hope of speaking effectively, and even urgently, to our dire human predicament of destructive selfishness and impending death.

A philosophical issue (or any issue) that nobody aims, even after careful reflection, to use to contribute to the Good News redemptive mission should be bracketed as not compelling (at least for now) for philosophy under the divinely appointed lordship of Jesus. If nobody has found a way to relate a philosophical issue to the church's redemptive mission, the issue should be bracketed as extraneous, at least until it does relate. An issue is extraneous if and only if its pursuit doesn't advance the divinely appointed Good News redemptive mission of the church community. Many philosophical issues haven't been related at all, even after careful reflection, to the church's redemptive mission, and nobody is prepared to relate them in any plausible way. For instance (and we could cite many more examples), the medieval philosophical dispute over the metaphysics of angels regarding whether they can inhabit the same place at the same time (see Thomas Aquinas, *Summa Theologiae*, I, q.52, a.3) may safely be set aside as not compelling, at least for now. Given the divinely appointed redemptive mission of the church community, the church's needs are clearly and urgently elsewhere. The urgency of this mission and of the questions it must face, including philosophical questions, recommends that philosophy under the authority of Jesus bracket extraneous philosophical issues, however intriguing or philosophically popular they may be.

The needs of the church community are determined ultimately by the Good News mission and commands of Jesus as divinely appointed Lord relative to the church's audience in need of divine redemption. My talk of *the church*, as suggested above, concerns the divinely redeemed community of God's people *overall*, and not just an individual part or congregation of the overall body of forgiven obedient disciples. So, the fact that an individual congregation hasn't (yet) seen the need to answer a particular philosophical question doesn't entail that the same is true of the church as the overall community of God's people. As always, we need to assess the bearing of a philosophical question on the advancement of the divinely appointed redemptive mission of the overall community of God's people. Some philosophical questions won't be compelling in connection with this divinely appointed mission, and they will properly fall to the side, at least at this time, for the sake of urgently relevant questions, including such philosophical questions.

When the community of God's people is challenged to explain matters it can responsibly explain, the intellectual gifts given to it by God, including philosophical gifts, should be available for eager service, in compassionate love. The use of these gifts shouldn't be distracted or dulled by extraneous matters, whether philosophical or nonphilosophical, lest vital redemptive opportunities be missed by the church. Only people who actually participate in the divinely appointed Good News mission of God's community relative to its audience needing redemption will be well-positioned to assess whether particular questions are urgent or extraneous. This calls for situating philosophy, as a vital ministry, in the actual context of the redemptive discipleship work of the community of God's redeemed people. This calls also for philosophy in the obedience mode, under Jesus as divinely appointed Lord who commands people, philosophers included, to receive and to live out divine redemptive love toward all people, even enemies. In the relevant church context the dire human predicament of destructive selfishness and impending death will receive due attention among obedient philosophers, even if certain medieval questions about location conditions for angels won't.

Philosophy, we have seen, isn't automatically a friend of Jesus as divinely appointed Lord; nor is he automatically a friend of philosophy in its normal mode, unreceptive to divine authority. A friend of Jesus as divinely appointed Lord must acknowledge the supreme lordship of Jesus under authoritative divine love. John's Gospel portrays Jesus as commenting as follows regarding divine love commands:

> As the Father has loved me, so have I loved you; abide in my love. If you keep my commandments, you will abide in my love, just as I have kept my Father's commandments and abide in his love. These things I have spoken to you, [so] that my joy may be in you and that your joy may be full. This is my commandment, that you love one another as I have loved you. Greater love has no [one] than this, that he lay down his life for his friends. You are my friends if you do what I command you (Jn. 15:9–14, RSV).

Jesus as divinely appointed Lord anchors friendship with him in obedience to him, in particular, to his love commands from his perfectly loving Father (cf. Matt. 7: 21). He offers himself as the divinely appointed Lord and Reconciler who can also be one's Friend. Indeed, he offers his Lordship, including his love commands, as the avenue to joy, even complete joy. This isn't the tenuous "happiness" of the world that ebbs and flows with varying circumstances. It is rather the experienced, well-grounded affirmation of being loved, come what may, by the One who can sustain a person in divine–human fellowship in any circumstance, even in a person's suffering, frustration, perplexity, and death. This, only a loving God supplies. This, our own philosophy in its normal mode can't supply. Given his authoritative manifestation and offering of divine redemptive love, for the sake of divine–human reconciliation, Jesus merits attention as divinely appointed Lord not only of the Sabbath but of philosophy as well.

Even philosophers, rumors to the contrary notwithstanding, need lastingly good life and joy, beyond passing worldly happiness, and they need to find these in a source that (or, better, who) can genuinely supply lastingly good life and joy, come what may. When philosophers yield to the Good News of divine redemptive love, on the basis of purposively available authoritative evidence in conscience, they can continue to do philosophy with an urgent Good News message for everyone in the human predicament, even their enemies, and not just for other professional philosophers. The group in need of that redemptive message includes *every* human, and thus philosophy takes on new relevance, reach, and even urgency. Its kerygmatic orientation knows no human limits.

Philosophy in its normal mode, unreceptive to the redemptive mission of a perfectly loving God, won't supply the powerful gift of unselfish divine love we need to begin living in love toward ourselves and others, including our enemies. In particular, it won't supply the kind of powerful merciful forgiveness we need to be freed from our shame, worry, fear, hiding, anxiety, and other obstacles to genuine love in fellowship, including peace, among humans. Divine love's purportedly corrective judgment upon us is unrelenting and ubiquitous apart from our sincerely receiving and living out the powerful merciful forgiveness of the Giver of the love commands. Whatever else it supplies, philosophy in its normal mode, without being receptive to a perfectly loving God, doesn't deliver the merciful forgiveness and power of transformation we desperately need as selfish and dying moral agents. It leaves us in the unforgiving human predicament of destructive selfishness and impending death. Hope naturally wanes, then, and philosophy suffers accordingly. Philosophers follow suit, in the absence of receiving needed Good News.

Given the reality of a perfectly loving God, with the promise and plan of merciful divine redemption of humans, philosophy is no longer business as usual. It can still be the "love of wisdom," but *wisdom* must be understood ultimately, in keeping with the divine Good News and love commands, in terms of obediently receiving and committing to divine grace and thereby loving God and others, in divine–human fellowship (see 2 Cor. 1:12; cf. Ford 2007). Philosophical pursuits under the divinely appointed lordship of Jesus will be commendable only insofar as they contribute (in a noncoincidental manner, of course) to faithful obedience to this divine Good News call to humans. Accordingly, Paul portrays philosophy as "bringing every thought into captivity to the obedience of Christ" as divinely appointed Lord (2 Cor. 10:5). This "obedience of Christ" focuses on the One who brings divine Good News and love commands and thereby on philosophical ministry toward divine redemption of humans in divine–human fellowship.

We now can say what philosophy is *not* to be: philosophical truth-seeking independent of the divine Good News mission and its divine love commands. So, philosophy is no longer to be business as usual in its normal, nonredemptive mode. It can, nonetheless, be rigorously evidentialist and thus cognitively responsible, with no place for fideism. In addition, it can acknowledge that human volitional yielding to God, on the basis of authoritative divine evidence, is distinctively evidence-yielding, owing to the reception of experienced divine power in human agents. Such evidential power can renew and refocus philosophy in virtue of the person-transforming and person-redefining role of this divine power. Philosophy itself will then become kerygmatic in virtue of being integral to the Good News power movement stemming from Jesus and Jerusalem. It will thereby move toward an urgent redemptive ministry, beyond the dying human-wisdom movement stemming from Plato and Athens. (See the previous chapter on the relevant contrast between Jerusalem and Athens.)

Philosophical truth-seeking, given the redemptive mission of a perfectly loving God, shouldn't float free of Good News ministry in obedience to the divine love commands. In particular, it shouldn't become bogged down in the discussion mode, but should aim instead for a genuine contribution to philosophical ministry within the church community of God's people. The fine points of this portrayal will need to be worked out in a specific context of faithful obedience among people working together in the church community of God's people. Even so, philosophy under the divine Good News and love commands has a distinctive redemptive purpose, focus, and ministry within the church community of God's people. This divine purpose takes philosophy clearly and decisively beyond philosophy in its normal mode, including its discussion mode.

Someone might raise a potential self-referential problem: is this book itself bogged down in the discussion mode and thus illicit by its own standards, relative to the divine love commands? The short, best answer: no. This book aims, on the basis of purposively available authoritative evidence, to acknowledge Jesus in his divinely appointed status of Lord even over philosophical pursuits. It thus moves beyond discussion and truth-seeking (after properly accommodating their rightful place) to re-issue the divine Good News and love commands, under the authority of the perfectly loving God who has issued the Good News and its corresponding commands as a redemptive gift. This book thus aims to transcend philosophy as discussion or truth-seeking to point us to *Philosophy*, the love of lasting grace-based wisdom, as faithful fellowship with, and obedience to, the Giver of every good gift, including every good gift of Philosophy.

If willingly receptive and obedient toward divine grace, we can begin to live wisely, even with Philosophy, beyond endless discussion. We can then give our lives, wisely, to something beyond discussion and truth-seeking, something we can take to a dying world in need of divine redemption: the Good News of the authoritative perfect love offered by the human representative of divine wisdom, Jesus himself as divinely appointed Lord even over Philosophy (see 1 Cor. 1:30, Col. 2:2–4, 8–9). The "something" in question is thus inseparable from an authoritative "Someone," and not just another idea, principle, inference, or virtue for potentially endless philosophical discussion. Philosophy, accordingly, can become valuable redemptive philosophical ministry within the kerygmatic church community of God's people. If one seeks a concrete example of Philosophy in the obedience mode, I submit that this book itself can modestly serve, if incompletely and imperfectly.

As philosophers under divine lordship, we do well to receive and to obey divine grace, and not just to discuss or to seek truth. Philosophy will then be in its proper place as consciously and eagerly subservient, within the church community of God's people, under the authority of the perfectly loving Giver of grace, love commands, and philosophical spiritual gifts. We as philosophers will then be in our proper servant place too, humbly and kerygma-centered, for our own good. If we are philosophers under the divine Good News and love commands, we will be obedient disciples of Jesus first and foremost. As a result, our purpose in doing Philosophy will transcend philosophy itself in its normal mode to involve faithful obedience to the Giver of all genuine, grace-based wisdom and every other good gift, including every gift of Philosophy, beyond philosophy in its normal mode. Philosophy can and should still be conceptually rigorous and evidentially hard-nosed, but always for its higher end, for the sake of the divine Good News of gracious redemption via divine–human fellowship.

Under the authority of divine Good News, Philosophy will never languish in discussion, speculation, or even truth-seeking. Throughout it will be person-oriented because *agape*-oriented, under the God-given authority of Jesus himself. Philosophy under divine lordship will thus be intentionally reflective of Jesus himself in moving constantly toward self-giving redemptive ministry that faithfully obeys and honors his perfectly loving divine Father. It will also, as a result, support the cognitive shift developed throughout this book, where the question,

> "Are we willing to be known and thereby transformed by a perfectly loving God?"

takes the first focus away from the familiar and tired question,

> "Do we know that a perfectly loving God exists?"

In this seismic shift, the cognitive focus is as much on *us humans*, as potential knowers of God, as on God's character and reality. In particular, our focus as philosophers and epistemologists will then consider whether our wills have gone astray and are thus in need of attunement with reality, including divine reality. We have supported this needed focus for reorienting philosophy and epistemology in the previous chapters. In addition, we have denied that a perfectly loving God could simply fix everything for us, apart from our own wills, given the noncoercive nature of genuine perfect love and given our deep-seated selfishness.

We can now find a genuine solution to the human predicament of destructive selfishness and impending death, if only we're willing to undergo volitional attunement to divine reality. In that case, we can begin to find relief from the winter of our human discontent and to echo, with our lives as well as our renewed, redemptive Philosophy, the following lines from Christopher Fry's play, "A Sleep of Prisoners" (1961, p. 209):

> The human heart can go to the lengths of God.
> Dark and cold we may be, but this
> Is no winter now. The frozen misery
> Of centuries breaks, cracks, begins to move.
> The thunder is the thunder of the floes,
> The thaw, the flood, the upstart Spring.
> Thank God our time is now when wrong
> Comes up to face us everywhere,
> Never to leave us till we take
> The longest stride of soul men ever took.
> Affairs are now soul size.
> The enterprise
> Is exploration into God.

This book's concluding chapter will identify the immediate benefits for the enterprise of Philosophy as "exploration into God," with special attention to the role of human suffering, dying, and death. In doing so, it will round out the book's volitional theistic epistemology in the face of unavoidable and ongoing human tragedy. The portrait of reality isn't altogether pretty, but it is laced with well-grounded Good News and hope.

5

∾

Aftermath

We have seen that the landscape of philosophy in general and epistemology in particular shifts significantly once we acknowledge the reality of purposively available evidence of God's existence (that is, evidence available only in keeping with God's perfectly loving character and noncoercive redemptive purposes for humans). We then become aware of a kind of elusive noncoercive evidence that philosophers and others have overlooked or ignored. In doing so, we become aware also of our own responsible role, particularly the role of our wills, in receiving purposively available evidence of God's existence. We then recognize that the relevant evidence of divine reality must be not only given to us by God but also *willingly received* by us, on God's terms of redemptive love.

By way of a general conclusion to this book, we'll clarify some of the immediate significance of human responsibility toward available authoritative (as opposed to spectator) evidence of divine reality, particularly in connection with the twofold human predicament of destructive selfishness and impending death – topics rarely considered in epistemology. Attention to this ongoing predicament reveals, among other things, that sincere questions about human knowledge of God's existence are urgently significant, and not just the stuff of casual speculation. Such attention should move us beyond philosophical parlor games to issues that truly matter. Accordingly, an adequate epistemology of human knowledge of a perfectly loving God should acknowledge the epistemological significance of human selfishness and death. A perfectly loving God would use purposively available authoritative evidence and knowledge of divine reality to challenge human selfishness in an effort to transform it into unselfish love, and would use impending death as an opportunity for a divine wake-up call for humans to the vital importance of volitional knowledge of divine reality.

1. EVIDENCE WITHOUT COERCION

Even if some evidence, such as that of a throbbing toothache or a splitting headache, coerces our attention and thus "just won't go away" apart from either altered consciousness, medical intervention, or death, some other evidence is only *non*coercively available. The latter evidence, when it comes from a perfectly loving God, may intrude a bit into our experience, say in conscience, but it can readily be overlooked, ignored, suppressed, or dismissed by us, because it's intended by God not to coerce a will toward or against God but to be willingly received by humans. In particular, it's designed to woo or to invite us rather than to force or to dominate us. The evidence central to a respectful offer of an interpersonal friendship relationship supplies a familiar example of noncoercive evidence, and contrasts sharply with coercive stalking or any other kind of forced interference. In the case of a divine offer of fellowship to humans, we as recipients must be genuine *agents* in the needed willing reception of the purposively available evidence in question. The evidence in that case isn't like the coercive evidence of a splitting headache that just won't go away.

Purposively available evidence is ideally suited to the moral character and redemptive purposes of a perfectly loving God. Such a God must be non-coercive in promoting loving relationships with humans, since coercion of a person toward or away from God would suppress the will, and thus the personhood, of that person, thereby excluding that person as a genuine candidate for a loving relationship. A personal God who seeks to be known by humans on God's terms and to know humans for the sake of loving relationships must, then, rule out coercion of human wills toward or away from God, and seek loving relationships via purposively available noncoercive evidence. For redemptive purposes, this God must seek to be known *as a personal agent* (rather than a nonpersonal object) and to know others *as personal agents*. Direct knowledge of this God's reality must not therefore be confused with knowledge of an axiom, an argument's conclusion, or any other kind of proposition or a system of propositions.

Philosophers have neglected, intentionally or unintentionally, the distinctive consequences of the existence of a perfectly loving personal God for available evidence of God's reality and for the corresponding epistemology of knowing God's reality. A common trend among philosophers and theologians has been to think of evidence of God's existence along the lines of an *argument* for God's existence. This trend has been so strong that some proponents of "reformed epistemology," under the influence of Alvin Plantinga, have inferred that we don't need evidence of God's existence at all for rational belief on the ground that we don't need arguments for God's existence. This inference, as explained earlier, is invalid; truth indicators that constitute evidence need not be arguments. (Plantinga 2000, incidentally, seems to have moved away from this misleading inference; see Moser 2001 and Wiebe 2004, pp. 206–11, for relevant discussion.)

If all the relevant evidence of divine reality is captured by the premises and conclusion of an argument, then the job of a truth-seeker regarding God's existence is just to examine all relevant arguments carefully for the validity of their inferences and the truth of their premises. In that case, one will decide on the soundness of relevant arguments, and then reach a reasonable position about God's existence. This is a central motivation behind traditional philosophy of religion in focusing on natural theology and its battery of familiar textbook arguments for God's existence. Those arguments, in the judgment even of many theistic philosophers, Kant included, leave much to be desired as a conclusive basis for belief in divine reality (cf. Gale 1991, 2007). In addition, they domesticate God in omitting the inherently authoritative evidence characteristic of a perfectly loving God, in contrast with the spectator evidence typical of natural theology.

This book's alternative to natural theology stems from the idea of purposively available authoritative evidence that includes God's uniquely challenging self-manifestation. The heart of this self-manifestation, as explained in previous chapters, is the noncoercive presence of God's authoritative perfectly loving will in human conscience via the intervening call of God's Spirit. A central aim of this self-manifestation is conciliatory, that is, to offer forgiveness and thereby call willing people into volitional fellowship with a perfectly loving God. Such self-manifestation and fellowship are intended by God to be directly firsthand for humans, and thus not just human talk or belief about such self-manifestation and fellowship. In short, they aim to be *directly interpersonal* between God and willing humans in a way that human personal agents experience God's will directly and then yield to it obediently, for the sake of divine–human volitional fellowship. God's loving purposes are manifested directly to willing humans in conscience, ideally via the Good News of divine redemption in Jesus, in order to bring human purposes in line with divine purposes. The sharing of God's purposes by humans includes their cooperatively building, noncoercively, a Good News community of perfectly loving agents who manifest God's perfect character and will in human action and attitude.

Under the influence of scholasticism, rationalism, and Humean empiricism, modern philosophers and theologians had widely overlooked the centrality of divine–human interpersonal interaction in direct firsthand human knowledge of divine revelation before the work of Kierkegaard (1992 [1846], pp. 45, 55, 66, 77), P. T. Forsyth (1907, 1913), John Oman (1917), Martin Buber (1923), H. H. Farmer (1935), and Emil Brunner (1938). Many philosophers still overlook this key lesson stemming from Jesus and Paul, and the result is epistemological deficiency in philosophy of religion. Forsyth, Oman, and Farmer deserve special credit for bringing the centrality of God's *humanly experienced will* into the modern discussion of divine self-manifestation. (On some of the distinctive epistemological contributions of Oman and Farmer, see Bevans 1992 and Partridge 1998; on Forsyth, see Brown 1952 and Hart 1995.)

Even given a notion of divine–human interpersonal interaction, the category of *purposively available authoritative evidence* needs to be introduced to isolate the kind of self-manifestation to be expected of a noncoercive perfectly loving God. Accordingly, this category has figured centrally in the epistemological position of this book. The corresponding authoritative evidence provides a needed epistemological foundation for the kind of direct experiential knowledge of God suggested by Forsyth, Oman, Farmer, and Brunner. I would add Kierkegaard and Buber to the list, but they tend to be highly elusive regarding issues of traditional epistemology; so, I'll have to settle for identifying what they *should* have said, or would have said if properly pressed, in connection with their subtle approaches to knowledge of divine reality.

Once we open the epistemological door to purposively available authoritative evidence of divine reality, light shines into various parts of our explanatory house. In accordance with Chapter 2, we can then see what underlies some cases of divine hiding: divine redemptive purposes for humans that when unmet by humans call for purportedly corrective divine hiding. One such key redemptive purpose is to have humans renounce their selfishness for the sake of unselfish divine love, given that human selfishness is a central obstacle to divine–human fellowship. Evidence of God's presence can purposively recede upon our languishing in selfishness and in other attitudes patently contrary to God's moral character of unselfish love. This kind of divine hiding, as noted previously, can challenge us to reconsider our motivational attitudes upon seeing their harmful effects, particularly their unrestrained harmful effects given the withdrawal of God's presence. (Paul had such an idea in mind in Rom. 1:21–26; cf. Meadors 2006, chap. 8.)

We may think of some divine hiding as God's allowing a kind of purportedly corrective *human suffering* in connection with evidential restraint in self-manifestation on God's part. A perfectly loving God, quite clearly,

wouldn't be an ethical hedonist regarding sensory pleasure, because the value
of unselfish love in divine–human fellowship could decisively override the
value of sensory pleasure. Human suffering in a context of divine hiding may
be not only an opportunity but also a *needed* purported wake-up call (even in
the divine silence of suffering) to nudge us to attend to otherwise neglected
evidence in conscience of divine expectations for us, including expectations
represented in the divine love commands. In that case, suffering can be cognitively enlightening as a means to our duly appropriating purposively available
authoritative evidence of divine reality. (On some other important ways in
which human suffering can be redeemed by God, see Buttrick 1966 and Jervis
2007; cf. Schneider 2004.)

We might say that God is incognito in the suffering to be redeemed. We
can thus acknowledge that purposively available evidence of God's existence
can be found in ordinary human suffering far removed from any abstruse
evidence proposed by the traditional arguments of natural theology. A person, nonetheless, would still need *willingly to receive* (rather than willingly to
ignore or to dismiss) the divine evidence on offer for it to have its intended significance toward divine redemption of humans in divine–human volitional
fellowship. Paul, accordingly, asks God for the opportunity of "fellowship"
in Christ's sufferings for the sake of being conformed, or attuned, to the
self-giving attitude of his redemptive death (Phil. 3:10). This Pauline attitude makes sense of the otherwise strange early Christian idea of rejoicing in
suffering (cf. Col. 1:24, 1 Pet. 4:14).

In receiving purposively available evidence of God's existence, we don't
thereby remove all of our perplexity about our human situation in the world.
In a case of suffering that awakens a person to firsthand evidence of divine
reality, that person can still be perplexed about the full purposes of God
in allowing such suffering. The suffering may prompt this person, on the
basis of purposively available evidence, to trust in God above all human
resources even in the face of perplexity, frustration, and death. The resulting
evidentially grounded trust may even be resilient, come what may, in this
harsh world, and a perfectly loving God would seek such trust from humans,
for their own good, in divine–human fellowship.

In connection with suffering-resistant trust in God, according to Karl
Rahner, humans may (and should) willingly "fall into the abyss of God's
incomprehensibility" (1983a, p. 161; cf. Rahner 1978, p. 404, Crowley 2005,
p. 132). We shouldn't confuse this abyss with either an empty abyss, an abyss
of chaos, or an abyss lacking evidence of divine reality. The abyss is rather
the mystery of perfect divine love that outstrips human understanding, even
when the Giver of such love offers purposively available evidence of divine

reality to humans. As Rahner puts it, the mystery is "encompassed by the reality of God who is for us" (1983a, p. 161). Contrary to fideism, we should add: encompassed, too, *by purposively available authoritative evidence* of this divine reality who is for us, in redemptive love. The relevant "falling into the abyss" is *volitionally active* in that it includes one's willingly yielding, on the basis of purposively available authoritative evidence, to the divine power of self-giving love that is available even beyond the limits of human power, including the power of human comprehension. This is a *willing, volitional and obedient surrender* to the authoritative God who can show up, with an authoritative call to divine–human volitional fellowship, even in the midst of tragic human darkness, suffering, and death.

A central divine aim of purposively available authoritative evidence of divine reality is to invite humans to recognize (a) the ultimate inadequacy and futility of humanly created and sustained power, including human self-ishness, and (b) the human need of the divine power of authoritative perfect love in redemption. As a result, such evidence of divine reality can emerge and be received for what it is intended to be in *any* context of recognized human limitation where humans are willing to yield to a power of authoritative per-fect love beyond themselves and their own resources. We'll pursue this topic briefly in connection with human death and selfishness, two curses of the ongoing human predicament. We may think of selfishness as a curse we have brought upon ourselves out of habitual fear of loss without counterbalancing gain. In addition, we may regard death as a curse brought or allowed by God in order to manifest the human need of God's power in the face of human selfishness and inadequacy toward life. Even so, as we'll see, a perfectly loving God can bring good out of such curses for willingly receptive humans.

2. DEATH'S GAIN AND LOSS

According to Plato's *Phaedo*, "... those who really apply themselves in the right way to philosophy are directly and of their own accord preparing them-selves for dying and death" (64A). If Plato is right, contemporary philoso-phers have evidently failed to "apply themselves in the right way to philos-ophy." At any rate, in this regard, contemporary philosophers aren't really footnotes to Plato after all. Plato evidently held that dying and death offer an important twofold goal for philosophers, even if we're now inclined to ignore the importance of that goal. We'll try to clarify what the actual goal is. At a minimum, it's doubtful that we can overcome death if we're left to our own meager resources. Evidently, no humans with such power have yet emerged, willingly or unwillingly, even to offer a reliable outline of the needed solution.

According to the previous chapters, the power of lasting life needs to be allowed by us *to find us* and *to know us*, instead of our independently finding it, because our cognitive resources are inadequate on their own to vouchsafe knowledge of divine reality. This grand reversal, as suggested, amounts to a seismic epistemological shift in matters of human knowledge of divine reality, and it seeks to throw cold water on any dogmatic human slumber, pro or con, regarding God's reality. Given this reversal, our needed knowing of divine reality will have to submit willingly to some extent to our *being known* by the personal power in question, if only in terms of our allowing the relevant evidence to emerge for what it is divinely intended to be: an evident authoritative divine call to receive forgiveness and divine–human fellowship. In being thus willingly known, we allow ourselves to be revealed to some extent for who we truly are, by the standard of divine perfect love, agreeably or disagreeably (cf. 2 Cor. 5:11). We thereby begin to know who we really are, relative to this standard, and perhaps even begin to desire to be transformed in the direction of this standard, given recognition of our dire predicament and past failure on our own. Such a change could be painful indeed, especially if we're selfishly fearful and inclined to hide our precarious standing before perfectly loving divine reality. Still, in willingly being known thus, we receive firsthand knowledge of God's reality, even if we respond by ignoring, suppressing, or rejecting it.

We humans typically fear being mastered, and, as acknowledged previously, due caution is certainly in order here, because the potential for abuse surrounds us and towers over us. Even so, our allowing ourselves to be mastered in a certain uniquely rare way may be our only way out of, or at least successfully through, our dire human predicament. With ourselves as masters, we evidently have ultimate trouble, sorrow, and death ahead; so, we evidently need considerable help here, regardless of any human tendency to prefer to help oneself. Previous chapters have suggested that the needed help extends to the area of human knowledge of divine reality. As a result, these chapters have also suggested that the natural assumption of our *achieving* lasting life via self-secured knowledge of divine reality must surrender to good news of our *receiving* such life and such knowledge, based on distinctive purposively available evidence, as a gracious *gift* rather than a human earning intended to obligate God in some way.

A perfectly loving God, as this book explains, seeks to give the gracious gift of lasting fellowship with God, and thus volitional knowledge of divine reality, to all people, because lasting life with a perfectly loving God is eminently good for all concerned. Such a God thus empowers a willing person to seek to *kill* the psychological attitudes and actions of *this* person that devalue or preclude life with God. In this regard, God as life-giving has a *mission to kill* attitudes and actions in the manner noted, for the sake of bringing life into an otherwise dying world. This divine mission, as suggested above, is cognitively significant but *not* in the way Plato thought.

Famously, Plato held that death can contribute to knowing reality (that is, immutable nonphysical forms, or essences) by removing bodily interference from what is ideally, by his rationalist lights, a purely intellectual reality. In contrast, I have contended that volitional knowledge of divine reality calls for renunciation of, or dying to, selfishness and all other attitudes at odds with divine perfect love. Awareness of one's impending physical death can contribute to such renunciation in leading one to recognize the ultimate failure and futility of selfishness in this dying world. It can also highlight human limitations in a way that prompts one, given one's felt need, to be sincerely open to authoritative evidence of a powerful agent who transcends human limitations, namely, God. One must, of course, be willing to receive such distinctive evidence for it to fulfill its redemptive purpose toward lasting divine–human fellowship; otherwise, one will be left in the grips of the tragic human predicament.

A way out of physical death's grave isn't necessarily a way *around* the grave, as if we need only somehow to dance around its edges. A way out could have us go *through* physical death rather than sidestep it, and thus our being saved from physical death could involve our being rescued from it *after undergoing it*. This would be a rescue not on this side of the grave, but on its other side. So, our going to the grave doesn't mean that all is lost, or even that we are lost. Instead, it may offer purposively available evidence indicating that God is authoritatively calling us willingly to undergo physical death (after the Gethsemane example of Jesus) and thereby to experience God's power beyond this physical world. In that case, God is, we might say, incognito in human death. Even though we can't turn back physical death, then, we can yield to it willingly in obedient response to a divine call to surrender physical life at a certain time. Alternatively, some people die without willingly surrendering their wills to death; they struggle valiantly against death until the very end of their earthly lives and wills. So, one's *willingly* surrendering to physical death isn't at all automatic or inevitable among humans.

Given materialism, or physicalism, about all real objects or individuals (the dominant ontology among western philosophers and scientists), theism is false, and human death is an *irreversible* destructive power: there's no coming back from its destruction. If reality is uniformly material, with regard to real objects, then cosmic physical breakdown, or entropy, meets no lasting counterbalance, and human death doesn't either. Our best physics tells us that over the long run the physical universe is destined to break down, in the absence of outside intervention. The energy centers of the physical universe will *naturally* disperse if they aren't counterbalanced by reinforcing energy.

Consider, for instance, how a cube of ice will naturally melt in a heated room. The same ice cube doesn't return from its dispersion. The material world likewise doesn't offer us, as the persons we actually are, a lasting alternative to human death. It leaves us with human dying and death, with the natural dispersing of bodily life. If our existence as persons depends on bodily life, then we too, as persons, will be dispersed forever, given materialism. We can count on this *if* materialism about real objects holds true. (On the prominent species of ontological materialism and of the corresponding methodological naturalism, including reductive, nonreductive, and eliminative species, see Moser and Trout 1995, and Moser and Yandell 2000; for one of the most comprehensive recent statements of (reductive) materialism and naturalism, see Wilson 1998.)

Given materialism, we will no longer be *persons* after our death, even if our bodily remains persist for a while, and thus there is no lasting hope for *us*, regarding our future as persons. In that case, we have no lasting future; so, we have no lasting *good* future. Our destiny, given materialism, is just the abyss of dispersed physical energy. We will then have, in the abyss of dispersed physical energy, no value in ourselves as persons, because *we ourselves* will have ceased to exist *as persons*. People who were once valuable will no longer be valuable as persons. We, in particular, will no longer be important, or worthwhile, as persons, because we will no longer *be* persons. Our existence and value as persons will have ceased, never to be recovered, even if our physical remains and effects have some temporary derivative value. Of course, some people may *remember us* as persons, but mere memories aren't the persons we actually are. We ourselves won't survive in memories, even if thoughts and images of us do remain for a time in memory. We will be gone forever, dispersed and done for, given materialism about real individuals.

The loss of us, even given materialism, will be a real loss, and no mere appearance of loss, because we as persons are now *valuable* – that is, worthwhile – in many ways. We are good in many respects, even if we are bad in various ways too. So, our funerals will be a sad occasion for many people, although not for *us*, of course, if materialism is true; we won't be around to be sad. The sadness in others will come from the loss of us with regard to what *was* valuable about us as persons. Of course, our *effects*, including various projects and accomplishments we had, could still survive and be valuable, but that's not to the point now. People who boldly suppose that death is no loss at all need a reality check from the well-grounded responses of people at typical funerals. One might spin (the interpretation of) the reality of death to fit a far-fetched theory, but the responses of the uninitiated at funerals are telling indeed and are at least as plausible as any opposing theory.

A materialist might go extremist here. The extreme inference is this: if our value as real persons ceases at death (as it will given materialism of any species worthy of the name), then our death isn't important after all, because we as persons aren't truly valuable. We are, according to this line of inference, just insignificant energy centers waiting to be dispersed, entropically so to speak. Such extremism suggests nihilism about human value, and, fortunately, is rare indeed among materialists. At any rate, it shouldn't convince us. The fact that we as persons have no *lasting* value, given materialism, doesn't entail that we have *no* value at all. We can still have *temporary* value, and we do, even though materialism makes our ultimate future as persons bleak indeed. Correspondingly, we can reasonably have *short-term* hope for our temporary well-being, but hope for our lasting well-being as persons would be misplaced, given that materialism offers no basis for such hope. Entropy will leave us all without hope as persons, because it will leave us all dispersed as persons. The final hopelessness of materialism is palpable, since it excludes any lasting meaning, or purpose, among persons, regardless of the short-term future.

Our ultimately hopeless destiny, given materialism, is a reality beyond our power to change, and materialists rarely deny this. We can't save ourselves or anyone else from the abyss of final physical dispersion and destruction. Death will leave us as persons in its cold wake, regardless of our cleverness, drive, or acquaintances. Materialism, then, is less than cheery about the outcome of human death, and materialists should be too, at least as long as they embrace materialism. As a result, a proponent of materialism may understandably want to change the subject to something more hopeful. This would be ill-advised, however, if we aim to understand our deepest needs and the available solutions to urgent problems regarding those needs.

Avoidance and indifference toward human death threaten all of us at times, owing in part perhaps to our fear, insecurity, and weakness in death's presence. Pascal observes:

> ... the fact that there are men indifferent to the loss of their being ... is not natural. They are quite different with regard to everything else: they fear even the most insignificant things, they foresee them, feel them, and the same man who spends so many days and nights in rage over the loss of some [exalted] office or over some imaginary affront to his honor is the very one who, without anxiety or emotion, knows he is going to lose everything through death. It is a monstrous thing to see in the same heart and at the same time both this sensitivity to the slightest things and this strange insensitivity to the greatest (1670, sec. 681).

Avoidance and indifference are undeniably the attitudes toward death among some humans, even if these attitudes seem odd or misplaced to others. One might take these attitudes to suggest that death isn't (deemed as) significant after all. We would do well, however, not to jump to a dubious conclusion about the significance of human death.

Perhaps humans, including philosophers, tend to ignore and become indifferent to human death, because they know that their own resources can't overcome it. We know that death will triumph over us on our own; so, we conclude, let's just resign ourselves to it and look away, to something we can actually handle. We then fail, however, to consider the needed solution in the right way, because we are then looking in the wrong direction. Instead of learning any important lesson human death offers, we have changed the subject. This takes us away from some purposively available evidence of divine reality, in that we are then inattentive to it. We can also become thus inattentive by underestimating, as Bertrand Russell did, the hopelessness for persons in any materialist response to human death. (Although Russell, incidentally, was a Platonist about various abstract entities, particularly those of mathematics and logic, he was a materialist about persons and other temporal individuals.)

Russell properly acknowledges the inadequacy of our own resources for personal survival in the face of death, but he still recommends intentional and courageous "contemplation" of our fate in death. He claims: "it remains only to cherish . . . the lofty thoughts that ennoble [our] little day; . . . to worship at the shrine that [our] own hands have built." He means the shrine that our *minds* have built, particularly human intellectual achievements, including his own considerable achievements in logic, metaphysics, epistemology, and philosophy of language. Russell also recommends that we approach dying people "to give them the pure joy of a never-tiring affection, to strengthen failing courage, *to instill faith* in hours of despair" (1903, p. 18, italics added). It's striking, and nearly incredible, that Russell mentions *faith* in this connection, given his materialism about persons and its implications for the dismal future of persons. The immediate question is just this: faith *in what*? Russell is loudly silent, because he has no hope-conferring *object* of faith to offer. In any case, people rarely portray Russell as an evangelist of faith, and he is, in fact, well known for the opposite. Still, when the chips are down, in the face of death, Russell promotes "faith." From his own ontological perspective, however, this seems to be nothing more than desperate, merely rhetorical behavior. His materialist ontology of persons offers nothing at all for a dying person to have faith *in* regarding the onslaught of death.

Russell's upbeat rhetoric about faith may sound good and even encouraging at first hearing, but he can't deliver on its hopeful suggestion. It's just empty rhetoric, even misleading empty rhetoric, given his uncooperative ontology. The eternal truths he loves passionately, including those of logic and mathematics, offer no real hope to the dying. They can't overcome death for the dying or for anyone, given their lacking the needed *causal power* to control or reverse death. The truths of logic and mathematics, in particular, have no causal power in this regard, given that they are abstract entities, and not agents, individuals, or events. As a result, they supply no reliable basis for us to "instill faith in hours of despair" for dying people. Russell has thus overplayed his weak hand in the face of human death.

Russell deserves some credit for facing human death as an immediate problem even for philosophers, and he at least raises an urgent question or two about death. He has, however, no ontological basis for either his proposed courage, his suggested joy, or his recommended faith. His recommended faith, in particular, can't yield human living through dying, because his faith has no *object* of faith that can overcome death. The mere human *attitude* of faith, being a psychological human state, does nothing whatever to overcome death, given that it has no causal *power* of its own to supply personal survival in the face of death. Human death, at least in Russell's acknowledged world, will always triumph over mere human attitudes. Russell, then, isn't helpful in tempering the tragedy of death in the human predicament, given that he offers no trustworthy basis for his recommended faith or for hope in triumph over death.

3. OUTSIDE HELP

In the face of death, we humans can *reasonably* be hopeful about our future only if we have a conclusive basis for acknowledging outside help. We need help from a power that can overcome death, and this would be *outside* help, because its power would be beyond our own human powers. We clearly lack power of our own to overcome death, and no one has provided a good reason to think otherwise. The help we need is *actual* help, not merely possible help, and it must offer us the actual opportunity to overcome death, to survive the personal destruction brought by human death. The prospect of such help is utterly far-fetched given a materialist ontology, but this doesn't make the prospect implausible all things considered.

A *nonpersonal* power doesn't offer any real hope for saving us from death. This would be a power without plans, intentions, purposes, or goals. By hypothesis, it would enable us to survive destruction by death, but it wouldn't do so intentionally, or purposively. It would happen blindly, in the way the wind, for instance, could blindly form a three-dimensional portrait of

Mother Teresa's face on the sandy shoreline of Lake Michigan. The wind *could* do this, of course, but we can't count on it to do so. If it happened, it would be unpredictable for all cognitively grounded purposes and thus beyond what we can (cognitively) reasonably hope for. Even if it were to happen for Mother Teresa, against all odds and evidence, we couldn't reasonably assume that it will happen for another person too. We thus wouldn't wait on the shoreline for someone's portrait to emerge from the sand, and if we did, many people would plausibly question our sanity, or at least our use of valuable time. Cognitively rational expectation depends on supporting evidence beyond mere possibility that something is, or will be, the case.

Grounded hope in our surviving death requires a cognitively trustworthy basis for supposing that we will overcome death, and this basis can't be the unpredictable vicissitudes of local wind movements. It requires a ground that is cognitively trustworthy by us *in our actual situation*. Specifically, the announced intentions of a reliable, trustworthy personal agent would offer such a ground. We know this from our everyday experience, because we often form a grounded hope on the basis of the announced intentions of trustworthy people. For example, I reasonably hope that my return home from the university campus will be timely, given that a trustworthy friend has promised to drive me home. This hope has a basis different in kind from that of my *wish* that the wind inscribe a human portrait on the shoreline of Lake Michigan just outside my office window. My hope is grounded in a good reason; my wish is not. The two are thus cognitively different in kind.

Chapters 2 and 3 outlined the kind of outside help and corresponding evidence that are purposively available from a trustworthy and perfectly loving personal agent who has the power to overcome death. Still, some people will ask this: if there's outside help from a perfectly loving personal agent, why would that agent allow death to occur *in the first place*? Some people hold that such an agent, *if* real and genuinely helpful, would block human death from the start. Here we have a suggested variation on the so-called "problem of evil" for theism.

Would a perfectly loving God allow us to undergo death even though God seeks to help us to overcome death? If so, why? A noteworthy answer, suggested in Chapter 1, comes from Paul's Epistle to the Romans: "The creation was subjected to futility, not by its own will, but by the will of the One who subjected it, in [that One's] hope that the creation will be freed from its slavery to decay and brought into the glorious freedom of the children of God" (Rom. 8:20–21). Paul's reference to *futility* echoes the following lament from the world-weary author of Ecclesiastes: "Futility of futilities! All is futility." Both writers have in mind what is ultimately pointless, in vain, when left to its own ways and means, apart from a perfectly loving God. Paul thus suggests that God introduced death to show that the ways of creation *on its own*, apart from God, are ultimately futile, pointless, and meaningless. In particular, as part of creation, we humans ultimately come to naught *on our own*, apart from God, and this is the good intention of a perfectly loving God. Human death, in other words, leaves us with a hopeless destiny if we are left to our own resources. All of our own projects, purposes, and achievements, even our intellectual labors, will meet the same fate on their own, apart from God: namely, *futility*. They are, apart from God's sustaining power and authority, all destined for the abyss of destruction, never to be revived. This seems to be nothing but bad news, but there's actually an elusive silver lining, even Good News, we can find on the basis of purposively available evidence.

Paul suggests that a certain "hope" lies behind the apparent futility of death: that is, *God's* hope of freeing people noncoercively from the threat of futility to enter divine–human fellowship in the lasting kingdom family of God. Death is reportedly a means to bring about this hope, and the next section identifies how, on the basis of God's being incognito in human death and accessible via purposively available evidence even in such death. God thus emerges as being in the business of shattering illusions of human independence of the elusive One needed for lastingly good life. The suggestion of lasting hope for humans may initially seem too good to be true, but the actual reality may be that it's too good not to be true, particularly if a perfectly loving God is for us, even if elusively so.

Some people avowedly don't want any divine help to overcome human death. As noted in Chapter 1, Thomas Nagel claims that the existence of God poses a serious "cosmic authority problem" for us, so much so that he hopes that God doesn't exist, as follows: "I want atheism to be true. . . . I hope there is no God! I don't want there to be a God; I don't want the universe to be like that" (1997, p. 130). Contrast Nagel's bold attitude with the tempered attitude of J. J. C. Smart: "I was once a theist and I would still like to be a theist if I could reconcile it with my philosophical and scientific views" (1996, p. 6). An undeniable hardship of life without God is that ultimately it all comes to nought *and* we have definite indications of the futility of such life. Sharing Smart's candid attitude, many atheists rightly feel the ultimate futility of life without God, and candidly express their painful sadness. Somehow, Nagel evidently has overlooked the tragedy of a missed opportunity of a *lastingly* good life with a perfectly loving God, or at least he's playing his cards close to the vest here.

According to Chapter 1, the preeminent status of being a God worthy of worship includes God's having perfectly loving noncoercive authority, or lordship, over humans. Nagel, however, confesses to his having fear of any religion involving God, and such fear seems widespread among humans, including philosophers. It stems typically from human fear of losing our supposed lordship over our decisions and lives. We want to be able to say in effect: "I did it my way." Human adults as well as children are typically proficient in exercising this lordly attitude, so much so that it becomes refined as follows: "It's my way, or no way." This seems to be Nagel's attitude toward any suggestion of divine reality or authority, even if the God in question is perfectly loving and thus after what is lastingly good for us.

Our supposedly self-protective fear, confessed by Nagel, may *seem* to be for our own good, but it actually may block our receiving a lastingly good life as a gracious divine gift. Consider what the previous chapters have argued for on the basis of purposively available evidence: the reality of a perfectly loving authoritative God who sustains, and who alone can sustain, lastingly good life for humans, in divine–human volitional fellowship. The existence of such a God would be genuinely good, all things considered, for us humans, even for such naysayers as Nagel and Russell. In hoping that there is no such God, Nagel actually hopes, with regard to something that would be good, all things considered, for us, that it doesn't exist. (Of course, Nagel doesn't characterize God as "something that would be good, all things considered, for us," but that's beside the point.) Such a hope against the reality of something that would be good for us arises from Nagel's desire to have moral independence, or autonomy, relative to any divine being. At least, no better diagnosis emerges.

Nagel's desire, given the proposed diagnosis, seems willful in a way that flouts good judgment. It rests on this attitude (my language, not Nagel's): "If I can't have my moral independence of God, even though God would be perfectly loving and thus good for me, then I hope that God doesn't exist. I don't want to exist in a universe where God is the moral authority over me and others. I won't accept that kind of moral *dependence*. If I can't be morally independent of God, then I just won't be at all. At least I can then say that I did it *my* way, in the moral domain and elsewhere." Such a willful attitude would yield Nagel's otherwise mysterious remarks, and he has not identified a more likely alternative motivation.

On the diagnosis offered, Nagel seems willing to sacrifice something good for himself and others (namely, lastingly good life with a perfectly loving God and God's redeemed people) for the sake of a desire to be morally independent of God. If, however, God is perfectly loving toward all other persons (as God must be by title), this attitude is dangerously misguided. It invites needless human destruction from suicidal rejection of God in any world graced by

the presence of a perfectly loving God. We thus have a case where a desire
for human independence blocks good and wise judgment, even though this
desire amounts to the trademark for *supposedly* self-protective human fear.
That trademark turns out to be the real danger at hand, even a suicidal killer
of humans. Indeed, we may plausibly regard any final human separation
from a perfectly loving God as ultimately a human suicidal commitment
to proceed without God as authoritative and sustaining Lord. If anything is
"Hell," this is it, and it may be now on earth for some people. Even so, human
opportunity to receive the Good News that God is "for one" wouldn't have to
end with one's earthly life. God's perfectly loving reach need not be limited
in that way, contrary to some unduly harsh theological traditions.

Nagel's position illustrates, if unintentionally, that some human attitudes
toward God's existence aren't purely cognitive in their origin and sustenance,
even if we pretend otherwise in some philosophical discussions. A human
quest for moral independence sometimes looms large behind such important
attitudes, and obstructs purposively available authoritative evidence of divine
reality. Let's consider how the obstruction does damage, but can be overcome
at least for willing persons.

4. DYING TO LIVE

Death, by divine intent, is to be a powerful teacher for us in serving the
redemptive purposes of a perfectly loving God who can overcome death
for willing humans. What might such a divine agent have to teach us with
our (impending) death? We could learn many important things about our
need for a God of perfect love to sustain us through death and its surround-
ing circumstances. In particular, we could all benefit, in terms of a reality
check, from instruction about our desperate situation when left to our own
resources, apart from a perfectly loving God who can overcome death for
willing humans.

We humans do well to learn, sooner rather than later, that all of our best
intentions, efforts, projects, and achievements will ultimately be futile, altogether meaningless, if we are on our own. Human death is, in divine hands,
the intended striking wake-up call to this humbling lesson about our shared
human predicament. It shows, decisively, that we can't think, will, or work
ourselves into lasting satisfaction or even lasting life by our own resources,
because it manifests that we are mortally fragile and even ultimately hopeless
on our own. Death announces, if we listen carefully, that we need outside
help, beyond our own human powers, for lasting satisfaction, meaning, and
life. It solemnly warns us of this: if we stay to ourselves, without outside

power, we are done for, forever. Faced with this warning, we typically change the subject, and look away from death. That, however, profits us nothing in the end.

The reality of human death fits well with the view of humans and divine reality outlined in the previous chapters. That is, we are responsible creatures intended by God to enter into volitional fellowship with God, who has the power needed to overcome death for willing humans. Human life itself readily becomes a harmful idol for humans, and thus an obstacle to our honoring God's supremacy over all created things, including ourselves and our lives. God, in perfect love toward humans, seeks to undermine our treating human life as an idol, and thus uses human death to manifest the ultimate futility of human life apart from God's supreme power of perfect love. Attention to human death can thus reveal purposively available evidence of God's reality, particularly God's authoritative call to have us willingly surrender to God's perfectly loving will and power that can overcome death in lasting fellowship with God. As suggested, God is thus incognito in death, the place of our most serious earthly threat. We do well, then, not to divert attention from our impending death. Instead, we should attend carefully and humbly to our impending death as a context for not only purposively available authoritative evidence of God's reality but also volitional fellowship with God in virtue of our willingly surrendering to, and depending on, God as our redeemer and sustainer.

The needed willing dependence on God is just trust as a dispositional state anchored in an affirmative human response to God's call. This is faith, *not* as guesswork or a leap beyond evidence, but as a receptive response of volitional commitment that includes *willing reliance*, grounded in purposively available authoritative evidence, on the God whom we need to overcome death with lastingly good life. Our trusting God sincerely includes our willingly counting on God as our redeeming, authoritative Lord, in response to God's redemptive intervention in our lives. In counting on God thus, I manifest my having committed to God volitionally as *my* God and *my* Lord. I thereby obediently commit to putting God's will over my own will even with regard to my death, just as Jesus did in praying to God in Gethsemane upon his impending redemptive death by crucifixion: "Not what I will, but what *You* will." In trusting God, I commit to dying to my own selfish ways to live to God's unselfish loving ways, in fellowship with God. In short, I resolve to die to my selfishness to live to God and God's ways of perfect love. This entails a commitment to reject selfishness, in particular, any selfishness that involves exalting my will above God's will of perfect love. The relevant trust, or faith, thus includes my obediently *entrusting myself* to God as God, in response to God's authoritative call that makes a claim on me and my life.

In selfishness, I fail to honor God *as God*, because I put myself and my own ways first, even above the ways of a perfectly loving God. It doesn't follow, however, that I would be selfish in putting God's ways first in order to bring good *to myself*. One's doing something good for oneself isn't necessarily selfish on one's part. *Self-interestedness* and *selfishness* are two different things, and only the latter inevitably conflicts with the will of a perfectly loving God. Selfishness emerges when I seek to fulfill my desires or intentions in ways that knowingly bring harm to others. The divine call to faith in God is, in contrast, a call to die to selfishness in order to live to the God who can empower unselfish love in us and overcome death for us. Whatever else faith is, it is *not* a call to leap beyond or against evidence, as if faith in God were necessarily defective from a cognitive viewpoint. Trust in God can, in principle, be at least as cognitively good as one's trusting in one's best friend. Faith in God, then, need not, and should not, be a cognitive embarrassment. The previous chapters have underwritten this thesis as they reoriented cognitive matters about divine reality.

Why assume that I must die to my ways to live to God? This might seem, at first blush, to be a perversely harsh understanding of what faith in God involves. Even so, it's a needed understanding given a verifiable feature of the human condition: namely, deep-seated selfishness, the antithesis to the unselfish love, including enemy-love, definitive of the morally perfect character of God. Selfishness is the poison inside us that leads us to hoard wealth and resources desperately needed by others. We humans need a powerful antidote, and we gain nothing by denying or soft-pedaling the urgency of the problem. Insofar as we take the problem of selfishness seriously, we apprehend our genuine need of the divine power of perfect love, and in apprehending our need, we should become sincerely open to purposively available evidence of divine reality.

Clearly, if we could rid ourselves of selfishness on our own, we would see much less of it within and around us. For better or worse, we can't reasonably be encouraging about our taking care of this problem on our own. I, for one, am very skilled at hiding my selfish ways from others and even from myself. I tell myself stories of how my selfish ways are commendable, reasonable, and even good. Sometimes my stories convince me, and I become self-deceived. I thus protect and nurture my own selfishness. Unfortunately, I'm not alone in having such a regrettable tendency. Undeniably, our persistent selfishness makes us morally deficient, certainly by the standard of unselfish perfect love, and thus disqualifies us immediately as God. Even so, we humans have the persistent tendency to "play God" in assuming supreme authority in at least some area of our lives. This gets in the way, significantly, of our receiving purposively available authoritative evidence of divine reality. We become inclined to ignore, suppress, or reject the vital evidence in conscience that challenges our wayward tendency.

We often pose as lord over at least part of our lives, particularly in areas we deem vital to our well-being. One such area concerns how we treat our enemies, particularly our acquaintances who clearly threaten our (perceived) well-being. At best, we ignore them; at worst, we seek to destroy them, sometimes with heavy artillery and toxic chemicals and at other times with harm to their reputations. Rarely do we show them unselfish forgiving love, the kind of merciful enemy-love found in the perfectly loving God of the Sermon on the Mount in Matthew's Gospel. The risk of unselfish love is, we suppose, too great, too threatening to *our* comfort and (perceived) well-being. We thereby choose against the ways of a perfectly loving God, because we presume to know better, if only from selfish fear. We thus play God, complete with planned destructive actions against others, particularly our enemies who appear to threaten our own flourishing. Trust in God is, at bottom, the volitional commitment to let God be God in our lives, including the commitment to refuse to play God by going against God's ways of perfect love. Perhaps if we could find a way to trust in God, we could renounce selfishness as ultimately counterproductive and futile. We'll briefly consider some obstacles to trusting in God.

We sometimes play God regarding what is to count as suitable evidence of God's reality. We presume to be in a position to say, on our own, what kind of evidence God *must* supply regarding God's reality. We reason as follows, in agreement with Russell and many other philosophers who have neglected the kind of purposively available authoritative evidence suited to a God of perfect love. If God is real, God would definitely be revealed in way W. For instance, God would show up with considerable heavenly fireworks or at least Pomp and Circumstance. God, however, is definitely not revealed in way W. Hence, according to many casual observers, God is not real. Russell (1970), as Chapter 1 noted, thus anticipated his preferred response if he were to meet God after death: "God, you gave us insufficient evidence." We thereby exalt ourselves as cognitive judge, jury, and executioner over God. God, by our design, is thus left among the dead.

God, we presume, must be revealed on *our* preferred cognitive terms, as if our own terms were cognitively impeccable. In such cognitive idolatry (on which see Chapter 2), we set up our cognitive standards in ways that block so-called "reasonable" acknowledgment of God's reality, without seriously considering that the relevant evidence is purposively available in keeping with God's perfectly loving character and purposes. Our cognitive pride thus goes supreme, and perhaps even suicidal, as we play God even in the cognitive domain, to our own demise. We are, of course, imposters in playing God, because we can't deliver either lasting life in the onslaught of our impending death or unselfish love in the face of our own destructive selfishness. God's power thus contrasts sharply with ours, particularly regarding efficacy in our needed redemption.

By the preeminent standard of a perfectly loving God, we must die to our playing God if we are to live lastingly, in fellowship with God. We do real harm in playing God, in any area of human life, because we offer a weak counterfeit in place of the powerful true article. In our impending physical death, a perfectly loving God calls us to the stark realization that our playing God, including in the cognitive domain, won't last but will instead lead finally to the grave, once and for all. Likewise, this God authoritatively calls us, in the teeth of our impending death, either to yield our selfish wills to God's unselfish ways or to have our selfish wills extinguished altogether, given their destructive tendencies. In its shattering power, human death will eventually lead to the ruin of not only us as supposedly self-made agents but also all of our self-made projects. In the absence of the humbling effects of death, human selfishness and pride would run wild indeed, even beyond their current widespread delusions. Given purposively available authoritative evidence of divine reality, however, we are called to fold now and to welcome divine redeeming power in an alternative mode of living and dying. The life and death of Jesus perfectly model the alternative mode, receptively and obediently under divine authority that is for us, in perfect redemptive love.

Under the power of a perfectly loving God, human death reveals that whatever is lastingly important is not from us humans and our self-made accomplishments. It exposes our core insecurity and impotence about life itself, including about the future of our lives. We know *that* our lives will end, unless we have suppressed the obvious, but we have at best indefinite knowledge of *when* they will end. This indefiniteness makes for insecurity, fear, and anxiety, at least when we honestly attend to the matter, and it can lead to harmful behavior stemming from selfish fear of personal loss in death. Owing to such fear, I put my own importance above that of another person, and the habit of destructive selfishness begins to harden within me. I even seek to *justify* my self-exaltation, and pride then covers my selfishness, even if thinly.

In the selfishness antithetical to divine love, I fear not getting something *I intend to get*, in particular, something I intend to get even at the expense of harming others (say, by blocking them, if with subtlety and rationalization, from good things they need). This "something" could be an object, an opportunity, a relationship, a status, or another kind of thing. The motive at work is self-indulgent fear, and it underwrites greed, covetousness, prejudice, and all other manner of evil. It figures in our natural behavioral tendencies, and explains much of human history, including crimes against people, national wars, racial and ethnic battles, economic injustices, religious violence, and territorial imperialism. We seek certain things even if harm thereby comes to others, as we selfishly fear our missing out on these things without counterbalancing gains. Such fear moves us and drives us, and even captures and binds us, always at the expense of flourishing human relationships, and always contrary to the life-giving ways of a perfectly loving God.

Propositional knowledge by itself won't free us from selfishness, because we need volitional *power* to move beyond selfishness. We can, of course, know what is good but fail to conform to it in our intentions and actions. Knowledge of the good doesn't by itself move our wills, contrary to Plato's puzzling denial of the well-confirmed reality of weakness of will *(akrasia)*. Selfishness, however, is inherently a matter of the will, and thus *cognitive* enlightenment by itself isn't our needed solution. Many philosophers and religious thinkers have somehow missed this vital lesson, to the detriment of many people in need of genuine redemption rather than a tenuous intellectual substitute.

A place of rescue and safe refuge from our selfishness would be a place where we could be set free of selfish fear even in the face of death's onslaught. This is, as suggested, a place of divine–human *interpersonal relationship* where humans are volitionally related, in fellowship, with a personal agent with special *power*: namely, the power of perfect love that can yield good for us, even in suffering, dying, and death, in ways that make selfishness undesirable, ill-advised, and even repugnant. In suffering, dying, and death, we often have a salient opportunity to see that the lasting power of rescue and redemption we need doesn't come from ourselves but must come from God. In particular, God's authoritative power of unselfish lasting love *shows* us (perhaps even without explaining) that we don't need selfishness to receive what is good and vitally necessary for us, and that even physical death can be overcome in resurrection. This is part of the Good News of divine redemption by grace outlined in Chapter 3. In addition, divine perfect love shows us that selfishness opposes what is truly good for us – even when selfishness seems so "reasonable" and "fitting."

We have asked whether we are morally and cognitively *fit* to recognize on our own a personal power of perfect love that could liberate us from our selfishness if we are willing. We may be, as suggested, too deep in the mire of destructive selfishness to see on our own what we truly need to see and to do. This is cognitive pessimism about *our own resources* relative to a perfectly loving God, but it is *not* unqualified pessimism – pessimism about all available resources. The previous chapters have contended that divine resources are purposively available to us if we are suitably willing, in a manner that fits with divine redemptive purposes for us as people in need of volitional transformation, in fellowship with God.

Cognitive blind spots may leave us in the dark even about our own dire human predicament. In that regard, we may be damaged, unreliable measuring instruments relative to our own predicament. People often uncritically, and wishfully, assume that we are cognitively just fine, and thereby neglect blind spots in our cognitive situation. The previous chapters have built a case for holding that our cognitive blind spots can be overcome as we receive and yield obediently to a perfectly loving God on a rescue mission against human death and selfishness – a mission *on God's distinctive terms* rather than on our comfortable terms. We have seen, as part of this case, that we need to think of evidence of God's reality in a new light: in terms of purposively available authoritative evidence suited to divine purposes that seek to transform human purposes toward divine perfect love, in divine–human fellowship. We thus ended up looking for divine reality in places we ordinarily overlook: in human transformation toward unselfish love, including in the context of human suffering, dying, and death where we are invited to see that the authoritative power we need must come from God rather than ourselves.

The twofold curse of selfishness and death upon us will yield, according to the Good News on offer, only as we ourselves yield in certain ways to an ultimate personal Authority, who characteristically is incognito as long as we ourselves insist on playing the role of final authority. Conclusive evidence and knowledge of this Authority's reality, as suggested, follow suit, being purposively available on divine rather than human terms. So, God's being elusive doesn't indicate that God is nonexistent or that it's unreasonable to acknowledge divine reality. On the contrary, we should expect a perfectly loving God to be elusive at times for divine redemptive purposes of challenging and transforming humans in need of challenge and transformation. An epistemology of knowledge of divine reality must accommodate this expectation.

We now have the needed epistemology before us. Even more importantly, we now have a well-founded case for holding, on the basis of purposively available authoritative evidence, that a perfectly loving God is, if elusive, nonetheless real and "for us." We thus have well-founded Good News on offer, despite the history of skeptical misgivings inside and outside philosophy. So, we are now left with a life-defining decision: to entrust ourselves to the Giver of the Good News or to continue with dying business as usual. The stakes couldn't be higher, and the divine gift of fellowship on offer couldn't be more inviting. Upon receiving this gift, we'll be able to appreciate this very rare insight: "Everyone who loves [with perfect love] has been born of God and [even] knows God; the one who doesn't love doesn't know God, because God is love" (1 Jn. 4:7–8). Our knowledge of divine reality will then be anchored in divine *agape*, and our theory and practice will unite under divine authority. In that case, our very lives will become salient evidence of the God who is, if elusive, worthy of our worship.

ભ

Skepticism Undone

On the basis of widely neglected purposively available authoritative evidence, Chapter 1 challenged skeptics about divine reality. It argued that skeptics have no plausible way to recommend their own skeptical doubt about divine reality to people in general. This Appendix further challenges skeptics who invoke a difficult longstanding problem regarding epistemic circularity to support their skepticism. The motivation for this Appendix is straightforward: if skeptics are correct in their view of the pervasive undermining effects of epistemic circularity, the volitional theistic epistemology of this book is in big trouble. We shall see, however, that skeptics aren't correct after all.

Epistemologists have long given special attention, if properly unfriendly attention, to circularity in justification for beliefs. Such attention might stem just from a dislike of circularity, in the way that some people dislike fancy circular shapes in their evergreen bushes. Perhaps some epistemologists simply don't *like* the look of circles in justification. That's a real possibility, of course, but why would these epistemologists then bother to *make a general case* against circles in justification? If they are moved just by a personal dislike of circles, they might as well keep their dislike to themselves. In that case, their dislike wouldn't be relevantly different from my antipathy to eating coconut. It would be unconvincing for me to make a general case against eating coconut on the ground that *I* dislike its taste. You may very well like the taste of coconut, and that would settle that, my personal dislike notwithstanding.

In opposing circles in justification, epistemologists customarily have a *cognitive reason*, not just a dislike. Their reason allegedly has *general* significance, bearing on circularity generally, not just on the circularity in their own doxastic backyard. So, their opposing circularity in justification differs from my disliking the taste of coconut. What, however, underwrites their opposition, and does it underwrite their opposition convincingly? This twofold question has attracted the critical attention of Ernest Sosa in two recent illuminating essays: "Philosophical Scepticism and Epistemic Circularity" (1994) and "Reflective Knowledge in the Best Circles" (1997). In general, Sosa contends that a common species of epistemic circularity isn't automatically vicious, and that therefore some familiar skeptical and relativistic worries are misplaced. I shall argue that the latter worries are surprisingly resilient and troublesome after all, but that skepticism doesn't thereby triumph. In fact, we shall see how skepticism actually becomes undone.

1. EPISTEMIC CIRCLES

William Alston has characterized a common kind of epistemic circularity as involving "a commitment to the conclusion [of a relevant argument] as a presupposition of our supposing ourselves to be *justified* in holding the premises" (1993, p. 15). Skeptics in the tradition of Sextus Empiricus would be uneasy with at least such circularity. They go further, however, in challenging us to secure *non-questionbegging* justification for our beliefs. In securing such justification, we would be able to avoid simply assuming (the truth of) a position under dispute by skeptics. In particular, such justification would free us from merely *presuming* an answer to skeptics' questions that favors our having true, reliable, or well-founded beliefs about a disputed matter.

The demand for non-questionbegging justification exceeds opposition to the kind of epistemic circularity identified by Alston. This demand calls for non-questionbegging justification even in cases where we are neither wielding the premises of an argument nor supposing ourselves to be justified in holding such premises. We can beg questions about truth and reliability even when we don't consider ourselves to be justified in holding an argument's premises. Let's call the key challenge here *the no-questionbegging challenge.* Let's also restrict our talk of skeptics to those who promote this challenge. Skeptics come in many shapes and sizes, but we shall limit our focus to those advancing the no-questionbegging challenge. They are, after all, the most formidable skeptics, as I have explained elsewhere (see Moser 1993, 1998, 2000).

Sooner or later, skeptics raise *comprehensive* questions about the reliability, or truth-yielding character, of our belief-forming sources. Such questions concern our belief-forming sources *altogether*, or *in total.* Specifically, they concern what non-questionbegging justification we have for regarding *any* subset of those sources as reliable, even minimally reliable, for acquiring truth and avoiding error. Such justification would enable one, at least regarding some source, to avoid begging questions against skeptics in virtue of merely presuming the correctness of a disputed view regarding truth or reliability. We thus gain nothing of real value in an exchange with skeptics by trying to have the reliability of one belief-forming source, such as touch, checked for reliability by another source, such as vision. *Any* such source is now under question by skeptics regarding even minimal reliability. These skeptics aren't necessarily obtuse in raising their challenge. They may simply be curious about whether anything speaks convincingly in favor of the reliability of our belief-forming sources *as a group*. We seem to face intelligible questions about the reliability of those sources as a group. So, it seems worthwhile to ask whether non-questionbegging answers to such questions are forthcoming. Once we answer that question, we can assess the significance of the answer for the viability of skepticism.

Suppose we had an answer to the *comprehensive* question of the reliability of our belief-forming sources. Would that answer necessarily rely on input from one of the very sources under question by skeptics? Specifically, would it rely on one of the sources in a way that *presumes* reliability under question? If so, the answer would suffer from question begging. One might find it obvious that we can't test the reliability of our belief-forming sources without relying on (at least one of) them in a way that takes for granted something under dispute by skeptics. In particular, our offering support for the reliability of our belief-forming sources will evidently rely on such sources as perception, introspection, belief, memory, testimony, intuition, and common sense. It evidently will rely on such sources in a way that begs a question about relia-bility against skeptics. *All* such sources are now under question by skeptics, with regard to even their minimal reliability. The problem isn't that we *use* such sources in forming our beliefs by way of reply to skeptics. The problem is rather that in offering support for the reliability of our sources, we evidently rely on those sources *in a questionbegging manner*. We thereby would violate the no-questionbegging challenge. So, reliance on the sources in question evidently won't deliver the kind of evidence of reliability sought by skeptics.

What might deliver the needed non-questionbegging justification? Must we seek a position independent of our own belief-forming sources to deliver a non-questionbegging indication of their reliability? Is such an indepen-dent position possible? If so, how? What exact kind of independence, if any, is available here? Aside from how we answer these questions, the success of the no-questionbegging challenge would entail that we lack the resources for avoiding evidential circularity. This would raise problems in some epistemi-cally relevant areas but not in others. It would *not* preclude our having reliable beliefs, evidence-based beliefs, or even knowledge as either reliably produced true belief or evidence-based true belief. It would, however, undermine our answering comprehensive skeptical challenges in a manner free of the kind of arbitrariness characteristic of circular reasoning. In that case, we wouldn't be able to silence skeptics convincingly. From the standpoint of being judicious truth-seekers, rather than mere knowers, we would be incapable of releasing the sharp bite of skepticism.

Our problem doesn't arise from a demand for certainty (as involving indubitability, infallibility, or incorrigibility in evidence) or even for deductive inference in justification. Skeptics can grant that the epistemic support for (at least contingent) propositions may be fallible and defeasible and fail to yield epistemic certainty, and they can allow for nondeductive inference in cognitively rational belief-transmission. A demand for non-questionbegging evidence isn't a demand for certainty or deductive inferential support, but arises rather from a concern to avoid questionbegging evidential circularity. Such circularity, if exonerated, would make reasoning in debates about skepticism ineffective.

If question begging is generally permissible, one may support *any* position one likes. In that case, one may simply beg the key questions in any dispute regarding the position one happens to like. Given the permissibility of such a *rationally arbitrary* strategy, argument will become ineffective in the way that viciously circular argument is ineffective. Questionbegging strategies, if exonerated, would condone arbitrariness in argument and in philosophical exchange generally. Such strategies are thus rationally ineffective with regard to the questions begged. This position differs from the dubious claim that a particular instance of question begging must be unreliable (that is, not truth-conducive), and skeptics need not endorse that dubious claim. It might be tempting to try to restrict the permissibility of question begging to certain kinds of issues, but arbitrariness is a constant threat to such a ploy.

A natural response is that, with regard to answers to comprehensive skeptical challenges, question begging is *unavoidable*. Sosa comments as follows, in treating a somewhat different topic.

> So far we have been told that we must avoid epistemic circularity because it entails arriving at a generally positive view of one's faculties only by use of those very faculties. But why should that be frustrating when it is the inevitable consequence of its generality? (1997, p. 282).

The no-questionbegging challenge, I have suggested, doesn't oppose epistemic circularity on the ground that "it entails arriving at a generally positive view of one's faculties only by use of those very faculties." It rather opposes relying on those faculties *in a questionbegging manner* in offering support for their reliability.

Regarding circularity as an "inevitable consequence," let's suppose (if only for the sake of argument) that it is indeed such a consequence of generality. We still should withhold an inference from:

(a) the view that we *inevitably* beg questions in the face of a comprehensive skeptical challenge

to:

(b) the view that some questions *rationally may* be begged.

Skeptics properly doubt that any inevitability in our begging comprehensive skeptical questions *rationally entitles* us, as judicious truth-seekers, to beg those questions.

The inevitable, of course, isn't necessarily the rational. At least, we have no compelling reason to hold that inevitability entails rationality, particularly, epistemic rationality. On the contrary, epistemic rationality in truth-seeking (however the details go) seems inherently normative in a way that inevitability is not. That is, what we *inevitably* believe may run afoul of the standard of what is cognitively *valuable* by way of judicious truth-seeking. In fostering arbitrariness (of the kind noted above) in the area of epistemically rational truth-seeking, begging skeptical questions hinders our goal of judiciously, or nonarbitrarily, acquiring truth and avoiding error. It would yield a position that is epistemically arbitrary relative to intelligible skeptical questions about truth or reliability. Arbitrariness here would undermine any convincing recommendation against skepticism, even if we nonetheless have reliable (that is, truth-conducive) belief, evidence-based belief, or knowledge. As epistemologists, we properly inquire about the availability of *skeptic-resistant* judicious truth-seeking. We shouldn't limit our epistemological inquiry to the conditions for reliable belief, evidence-based belief, or knowledge.

Sosa suggests that we are unable to answer skeptics without begging a central question against them, but that nothing important is thereby lost.

> ...in epistemology we want *knowledgeable* understanding, and not just 'understanding by dumb luck'.... But there is no apparent reason why we cannot have it with a theory such as T [A belief X amounts to knowledge if and only if it satisfies conditions C], without compromising the full generality of our account. Of course in explaining how we know theory T... we have to appeal to theory T itself, given the assumptions of correctness and full generality that we are making concerning T. Given those assumptions there seems no way of correctly answering... a sceptic except by 'begging the question' and 'arguing circularly' against him. But, once we understand this, what option is left to us except to go ahead and 'beg' that question

against . . . a sceptic (though 'begging the question' and 'arguing circularly'
may now be misnomers for what we do, since it is surely no fallacy, not if it
constitutes correct and legitimate intellectual procedure) (Sosa 1994, p. 324).

Sosa rightly notes that "it is not just *in virtue of being self-supporting* that our
belief in *T* would acquire its epistemic status required for knowledge. Rather
it would be in virtue of meeting conditions *C*" (1994, p. 324). This is not only
correct but also transparently correct. Even so, the skeptic's challenge, namely
the no-questionbegging challenge, doesn't concern merely "explaining how
we know theory *T*." The challenge concerns, as suggested above, answering
without question begging a shrewd skeptic's comprehensive questions about
the reliability of our belief-forming sources. This challenge isn't met by our
"explaining how we know theory *T*," even if such explaining demands an
appeal to theory *T* itself. So, we aren't out of the woods yet.

Moving a bit closer to the no-questionbegging challenge, Sosa asks whether
epistemically circular arguments enable us to discriminate between reliable
and unreliable belief-forming practices. He proposes that "one can make such
discriminations with epistemically circular arguments (ones with premises
that are in fact true and justified, etc.) even if it is not the circular character
of the reasoning that by itself effects the discrimination" (1994, p. 328, n. 34).
That is certainly true on at least one sense of "discrimination." The key
issue, however, now becomes this: what *kind* of discrimination is relevant to
exchanges with skeptics, particularly when they raise the no-questionbegging
challenge? Some kinds of discrimination will be irrelevant in virtue of failing
to engage *in a non-questionbegging manner* skeptics' comprehensive questions
about the reliability of our belief-forming sources. An appeal to irrelevant
kinds of discrimination would yield our talking past skeptics rather than
effectively answering or challenging them. In particular, such an appeal would
weaken Sosa's desired conclusion that " . . . we have found no good reason to
accept *philosophical scepticism*" (1994, p. 324).

As epistemologists challenged by skeptics, we still have work to do after
separating reliable from unreliable belief-forming practices and even after
identifying and satisfying conditions *C* for knowledge. Beyond the kind(s) of
discrimination needed for those important projects, we need another kind
of discrimination to handle the no-questionbegging challenge. We need a
kind of discrimination that doesn't beg questions against skeptics who raise
comprehensive questions about the reliability of our belief-forming sources.
Otherwise, in settling for question begging, we foster the kind of arbitrariness opposed above. That is, we open the door to one's being permitted
to support *any* arbitrary position one likes, in virtue of the permissibility of
question begging. Condoning such arbitrariness, we in effect make argument

ineffective in the way that viciously circular argument is ineffective. The value of argument in philosophy is thus at stake in our concerns about question begging in reply to skeptics.

Skeptics, we might say, seek a *comprehensive* answer to the issue of whether our belief-forming sources are reliable. Such an answer wouldn't rest on question begging against skeptical questions about reliability or truth. The issue isn't whether we simply *possess* truth or reliability in our beliefs or sources of beliefs. The issue is rather whether we can answer skeptics' intelligible comprehensive questions without begging those questions. Do our reasons (whatever they include) for our beliefs ultimately lack robustness in the teeth of this longstanding skeptical challenge?

Sosa would evidently reply with some considerations about the roles of argument and aptness in knowledge and rational belief concerning reliability. He rightly notes that the validity of an argument delivers at most a restriction on one's available coherent combinations of attitudes regarding premises and conclusions (1994, pp. 318–19). That is, such validity guarantees at most a kind of internal consistency in attitudes towards premises and conclusions. This kind of consistency or coherence doesn't take us very far at all toward answering skeptics without begging questions. Fortunately, we don't have to end the story of epistemic value with the coherence stemming from valid arguments or with any kind of rational coherence. Other factors are equally important.

Sosa explains as follows.

> In order to know that *P*, one's belief must not fail the test of rational, internal coherence. But it must be tested in other ways as well: it must be true for one thing. And, more than that, it must be *apt*: it must be a belief that manifests overall intellectual virtue, and is not flawed essentially by vice. . . . Finally, if it is to amount to knowledge a belief must be such that, in the circumstances it *would* be held by that subject iff it were true, and this in virtue of its being apt in the way that it is apt . . . (1994, p. 320; cf. Sosa 1997, pp. 279, 284).

The use of "test" in this quotation is metaphorical. Nonreflective knowledge, on Sosa's own account, can exist without any testing. Sosa proposes, then, that at least epistemic aptness must be added to proper reasoning to account for epistemic value (or, in his language, "epistemic welfare"). Accordingly, he offers this rhetorical question: " . . . why not distinguish between the [crystal-ball] gazers and the [ordinary] perceivers in that, though both reason properly and attain thereby coherence and justification, only the perceivers' beliefs are epistemically apt and constitute knowledge?" (1997, p. 283).

Reliability of a belief-forming source is evidently a logically *sufficient* condition of epistemic aptness. Sosa claims: "Perception is, of course, reliable while [crystal-ball] gazing is not. Therefore, the perceivers are right and apt both in their particular perceptual beliefs, at least generally, and in their theory of knowledge – for it all rests in large measure on their reliable perception" (1997, p. 283). In addition, reliability is evidently a logically *necessary* condition of epistemic aptness. Sosa remarks: " . . . the [crystal-ball] gazers are wrong and inapt both in their particular gaze-derived beliefs and in their theory of knowledge – for it all rests on their unreliable gazing" (1997, p. 283). Reliability, then, is both necessary and sufficient for epistemic aptness, and this takes epistemic value well beyond rational coherence. For the sake of argument, let's now concede Sosa his aptness approach to epistemic value and to knowledge. Our immediate concerns now lie elsewhere.

We turned to Sosa's notion of epistemic aptness after asking whether we can answer skeptics' intelligible comprehensive questions without begging those questions. How then does epistemic aptness figure in our deliberations about skeptics' no-questionbegging challenge? Let's try this likely question from skeptics: what non-questionbegging reason, if any, have we for thinking that our ordinary perceptual beliefs come from sources that are genuinely apt in Sosa's sense? Sosa has said, as noted, that "perception is, of course, reliable." How can this remark figure in the needed answer to the no-questionbegging challenge? It simply *presumes* something under dispute by skeptics. Notoriously, they dispute whether perception, among other belief-forming sources, is *in fact* reliable, or truth-conducive.

Skeptics don't need to say that perception, or any other belief-forming source, is actually unreliable. They may rest content with asking, in the familiar comprehensive manner, for non-questionbegging justification for endorsing the reliability of perception. An appeal to aptness won't take us very far in reply. It will merely assume something now in question by skeptics. So, skeptics won't be effectively challenged by an aptness approach to epistemic value, even if that approach illuminates the nature of knowledge and epistemic value. Sosa, as suggested, doesn't regard question begging against skeptics as epistemically debilitating. So, he doesn't seek a non-questionbegging reply to skeptics. Even so, it seems implausible as well as ineffective against skeptics to condone question begging at places of the sort just noted. A cogent response to skeptics would supply a deeper, more challenging alternative. Is one actually available?

2. EPISTEMIC BURDENS

The no-questionbegging challenge aims to place a serious epistemic burden on us. Should we accept that burden? Or, alternatively, does the challenge contain a defect that removes its force? Let's consider an application of the challenge, in connection with visual perception. The challenge assigns us the epistemic burden of identifying what non-questionbegging reason, if any, we have for thinking that our ordinary visual beliefs have a reliable source. Do our available epistemic reasons (whatever they actually include) for the truth or the reliability of our visual beliefs crumble in the face of this challenge? Such reasons would evidently have a central role in any answer to the no-questionbegging challenge regarding visual beliefs.

The term "reason" is dangerously slippery, and often suffers from unacknowledged but confusing shifts between "reason," "inference," and "argument." In Sosa's "Philosophical Scepticism and Epistemic Circularity" (1994), epistemic internalism is initially characterized as requiring epistemic backing in "reasons or arguments" (p. 304), but this position shifts to talk of "inference or argument" (p. 306) in a way that may misleadingly suggest that epistemic reasons are an argument's premises. As Chapter 1 suggested, however, epistemic reasons are best understood as (possibly defeasible) truth-indicators that may be nonpropositional (for example, sensory experiences that don't essentially involve either propositions as objects or propositional attitudes) and thus need not be premises of an argument. Sosa has made a major contribution to epistemology, in "The Raft and the Pyramid" (1980) and elsewhere, in clarifying that epistemic justifiers need not be premises of arguments. We should embrace the same view for reasons, particularly epistemic reasons (on which see Moser 1989, and Chapter 1 above).

What concept of "reason" figures in skeptics' demand that we have non-questionbegging *reasons* for thinking that our visual beliefs have reliable sources? (An analogous question bears on my alternative talk of "justification" in the no-questionbegging challenge, but to highlight my evidentialism about justification, we shall speak of "reasons.") Interpretive charity toward skeptics requires that we allow them a plausible concept of epistemic reason. Let's allow them, then, the notion of an epistemic reason as a (possibly defeasible) truth-indicator that may be nondoxastic and even nonpropositional. The no-questionbegging challenge regarding vision thus becomes the demand that we have a non-questionbegging truth-indicator for thinking that our ordinary visual beliefs have a reliable source. Such a non-questionbegging truth-indicator could be nonpropositional; so, it wouldn't have to be a belief. We definitely wouldn't make any progress by offering skeptics the proposition, however confidently, that ordinary vision is reliable. The same point holds, as suggested above, for the proposition that another belief-forming source (say, touch) confirming the reliability of vision is itself reliable. Such propositions are directly under dispute now by skeptics.

Nonskeptics thus need a different kind of truth-indicator to challenge skeptics.

Skeptics who question the reliability of belief-forming sources shouldn't thereby question the reliability of *all* truth-indicators. They shouldn't call for a non-questionbegging truth-indicator for visual beliefs, for example, while calling into question all truth-indicators. That would be to demand with one hand what has already been taken away with the other. A better metaphor is this: that would be to demand that we stand somewhere while we aren't allowed to stand anywhere. Such a demand would suffer from a kind of incoherence: *demand incoherence*, we might say. Skeptics *could* coherently question the reliability of all truth-indicators (available to humans), but then they could *not* coherently demand a non-questionbegging truth-indicator from their interlocutors. Necessarily, if *all* truth-indicators are under question, then *none* will be non-questionbegging. That much is analytically true, and importantly analytically true. The significant lesson is that the no-questionbegging challenge can't coherently proceed with *unrestricted* questioning of truth-indicators. Skeptics, in their skeptical zeal, haven't always taken this lesson to heart. So, we do well to remind them of the real threat of demand incoherence in their skeptical position.

The no-questionbegging challenge can't coherently include the questioning of all truth-indicators, and typically it doesn't. Typically, skeptics wielding this challenge focus on truth-indicators supplied by our familiar belief-forming sources: perception, memory, reason, testimony, and the like. Their comprehensive challenge concerns the reliability of such sources, and it demands a non-questionbegging reason to hold that any such source actually is reliable. Do we have any place to stand, and to answer, without question-begging reliance on the familiar sources in question? This is the crucial, and the most difficult, question arising from the skeptical challenge at hand. If treated aright, it can shed helpful light on the nature of our ultimate epistemic reasons. So, the skeptical challenge can, and does, have important heuristic value in epistemology.

We have just one durable ultimate place to stand against the wide-ranging skeptics under consideration: with our *semantic, concept-forming intentions*. Such intentions give semantic meaning to our terms, including our evidence-related terms (such as "evidence," "justification," "warrant," and "reason"). Consider the key term "epistemic reason." Skeptics and nonskeptics alike use the term, and their uses of the term often overlap in meaning, at least at a level of generality. They can share, as suggested, the general notion of an epistemic reason as a (possibly defeasible) truth-indicator. Many perennial disputes in philosophy, including epistemology, metaphysics, and philosophy of religion, persist as a result of semantic indefiniteness in key terms, but we can't pursue the complex details of this diagnosis here. Analogous points hold for the *concepts* we form as the standards for our use of linguistic terms. Justification, warrant, evidence, reason, and knowledge can still be language-independent *kinds*. Even so, *which* epistemic kinds and *which* specific variants of those kinds figure in our actual aims in inquiry (aims going beyond capturing truth and avoiding error) will depend on our semantic intentions and our wider aims. Still, our intentions and aims should, from a cognitive point of view, be in agreement with the undefeated truth-indicators in our experience. (For the needed details behind this quick sketch, see Moser 1993.)

Ultimately our meaning-forming intentions give semantic content to our talk of an "epistemic reason" and even of "an epistemic reason for a visual belief that *P*." Suppose we form the settled semantic intention to use "truth-indicator" and "epistemic reason" in such a way that a visual experience of an apparent *X* in a situation with no accessible defeaters is a (possibly defeasible) truth-indicator, and thus an epistemic reason, for a visual proposition or belief that *X* exists. This intention, given its meaning-conferring role for us, could then serve as a directly accessible semantic truth-maker for our ascription of an epistemic reason for a visual belief that *X* exists. It would then be *part of what we mean* by "epistemic reason" that *such* an ascription captures an epistemic reason for a visual belief that *X* exists. (People might occasionally haggle over whether a particular ascription is indeed *such* an ascription; that, however, would be a minor empirical squabble rather than a profound philosophical matter.) Our semantic intentions concerning "epistemic reasons" thus serve as ultimate, even if alterable, truth-makers for ascriptions of an epistemic reason. Indeed, they thus serve as nondoxastic truth-makers for a claim that a certain kind of situation includes one's having an epistemic reason for a visual belief. (If the objects of semantic intentions aren't propositions, then semantic intentions are nonpropositional as well as nondoxastic. We need not digress, however, to that ontological topic now.)

The meanings of our evidence-related terms do *not* determine the meanings of our physical-object terms and beliefs, contrary to John Pollock (1974, 1986). The latter aren't person-oriented in the way the former are. So, contrary to Pollock, we have no straightforward semantic refutation of skepticism about physical-object beliefs (on which see Moser 1988). Likewise, the meanings of our evidence-related terms don't determine the meanings of such nonevidential alethic terms as "true" and "reliable." So, we lack a clean meaning-based demonstration of the truth or reliability of ordinary physical-object beliefs. Skepticism doesn't surrender quite so directly, at least on the semantic front.

Skeptics might propose that our semantic intentions can be "mistaken," say in virtue of failing to capture language-independent justification. Just as we can be mistaken about truth, our semantic intentions can yield misrepresentation of such epistemic kinds as evidence and knowledge. So, why should we think that a skeptical challenge regarding epistemic kinds (for example, evidence, or epistemic reason) faces any trouble from *semantic* considerations? In this connection, epistemic kinds seem no safer from skeptical challenges than alethic kinds (for example, truth, reliability). Why then should we assume a relevant difference here? We can't answer skeptical challenges about truth and reliability by semantic means. So, why suppose that skeptical challenges about epistemic kinds are relevantly different?

As but a little reflection shows, reality settles what is true or factual independently of what humans believe or intend regarding that reality. (Dissenters usually end up in either asylums or philosophy departments.) Reality, however, doesn't settle how *in particular* one must seek truth. That is, for better or worse, it doesn't settle which specific variant (or specific concept) of justification, warrant, or knowledge (generally characterized) is binding on a truth-seeker. As a result, we find conceptual variation among philosophers and others with regard to at least specific notions of justification, warrant, and knowledge

Skeptics can properly demand that one seeking to acquire truth and to avoid error accommodate any *necessary* conditions for truth-acquisition and error-avoidance. In addition, as seekers of reliable and justified true belief, we can properly be demanded to accommodate any *necessary* conditions for reliable and justified belief. So, we can't coherently embrace an "anything goes" attitude toward our truth-seeking. Not just *any* concept or procedure can properly guide us as truth-seekers. Our settled objectives in inquiry place real constraints on us, for the good of inquiry. Some semantic variability is allowed, but not just anything goes. Here, as elsewhere, substantive (as opposed to semantic) relativism fails to convince, even if merely semantic relativism obtains, owing to variation in use of concepts at least at a level of specificity.

Skeptics can't convincingly hold nonskeptics to a specific concept or strategy of truth-acquisition that settles the dispute at hand in favor of skepticism. In particular, skeptics can't cogently mandate an epistemic concept or strategy for us that undermines the aforementioned kind of epistemic reason (for visual beliefs) grounded in semantic intentions regarding "epistemic reason." One noteworthy problem for skeptics is that such an epistemic reason is, so far as we can tell, at least as effective for judicious truth-acquisition (and error-avoidance) as anything skeptics offer. In addition, skeptics have no stable foothold to propose that such a semantically grounded epistemic reason is defective as a (possibly defeasible and fallible) truth-indicator.

We can't plausibly be charged with question begging now. Recall that it is now *part of what we mean* by "epistemic reason" that the kind of ascription in question captures an epistemic reason for a visual belief that X exists. A directly analogous point holds regarding an epistemic reason for an experiential belief that a perfectly loving God has intervened authoritatively in human conscience. (See Chapters 1 and 2 on how abductive considerations figure in a challenge to skeptics about divine reality.) So, we may now shift the burden of argument to the skeptic, and we may call this *the skeptic's burden*. This is not just self-serving or arbitrary shifting of the burden of argument. We have, after all, produced a skeptic-resistant truth-indicator grounded in epistemically significant semantic intentions. In addition, we have challenged skeptics to steer clear of demand incoherence in their skepticism. We thus may shift the burden with a clear conscience. As a result, the skeptic's burden is now *properly* the skeptic's, semantically and cognitively properly.

Skeptics (among others) might object that given my proposed sense of "epistemic reason," we will be unable to show that justified, or warranted, beliefs are actually reliable. This may be true in a success-use of "show," but that is no real objection now. It rather highlights a virtue of the approach just sketched. Epistemic reasons (or, truth-indicators) are not "alethic" in my sense of that term, because epistemic reasons logically require neither the truth nor the (objective) reliability of what they support. Semantically grounded truth-indicators constitute epistemic reasons but don't (as a kind) logically entail either the truth or the (objective) reliability of what they justify. For the sake of broad cogency, skeptics must allow for fallibilism and internalism regarding epistemic reasons. So, their no-questionbegging challenge shouldn't require actual truth or reliability in what is epistemically supported. Otherwise, the challenge will be too demanding to be relevant, particularly given the semantic commitments in place among nonskeptics. The skeptical challenge at hand properly concerns the availability of non-questionbegging epistemic reasons.

Notoriously, reliabilists about epistemic justification demand an alethic success-connection of some sort between epistemic justification and truth or reliability. Problems arise, however, from the availability of epistemic justification in cases of massive deception and unreliability (see Pollock 1986 on these and other problems). Propositional knowledge, of course, entails truth, but *if* such knowledge also requires (objective) reliability of some kind (and I doubt that it does), this requirement doesn't arise from the justification condition for knowledge. Some other condition must supply reliability. Even so, nonreliabilists can maintain one kind of "justification-truth" connection. Epistemic reasons for a proposition are reasons for *holding that this proposition is true* rather than false. On this approach, epistemic reasons (at least characteristically) are fallibly and defeasibly truth-indicating, and properly so. Reliabilists go too far in suggesting that this must be a success-connection. The possible massive error of justified beliefs goes against any such reliabilist demand. The "justification-truth" connection fares better in *non*reliabilist garb, where it need not bear the unbearable weight of a success-condition. *Knowledge* can still deliver the success of truth, because knowledge enjoys ingredients (such as a truth-condition) unknown to justification.

What, then, of any lingering demand that we "show" that justified beliefs yield reliability if not truth? Such a demand will be ill-formed in the absence of a well-formed notion of "show." Any demand with a success notion that precludes reliance on fallible sources will inevitably fail. It will fare no better than the aforementioned incoherent demand that we stand somewhere while we aren't allowed to stand anywhere. Until a well-formed notion is supplied, then, we may hold that the demand is ineffective against the view of epistemic reasons just outlined. If "showing" is, however, just a matter of properly relying on justified true beliefs to ground true conclusions, the view outlined here faces no serious threat. Epistemic reasons as characterized can and often do figure in such "showing." So, here again, we may shift a burden with a clear conscience to skeptics.

3. CONCLUSION

Is skepticism, then, finally undone? It is, if being neutralized is sufficient for being undone. Armed with our lessons about (a) demand coherence, (b) the skeptic's burden, and (c) "showing," we may now proceed with the aforementioned kind of semantically grounded truth-indicators, even in the presence of skeptical questions. We may thereby add durable backing to the conclusion, recommended on very different grounds by Sosa, that ". . . we have found no good reason to accept *philosophical scepticism*" (1994, p. 324). We might even claim to have dispensed with skepticism, so long as such dispensing doesn't demand the removal of defeasibility and fallibility in justified beliefs. In any case, it is enough good news for me and my house that skepticism is finally undone. This news is long overdue, but it's better late than never. It fits well with this book's argument that we now have conclusive purposively available evidence to acknowledge the reality of a perfectly loving God who is at times elusive. Skeptics are, then, no longer a serious threat to this book's argument for the reality of the elusive God worthy of worship.

References

Allison, Dale. 2005. *Resurrecting Jesus: The Earliest Christian Tradition and its Interpreters*. London: T&T Clark.

Alston, William P. 1993. *The Reliability of Sense Perception*. Ithaca: Cornell University Press.

Baillie, John. 1962. *The Sense of the Presence of God*. New York: Scribner.

Balentine, Samuel. 1983. *The Hidden God*. Oxford: Clarendon Press.

Banner, Michael C. 1990. *The Justification of Science and the Rationality of Religious Belief*. Oxford: Clarendon Press.

Beasley-Murray, G. R. 1986. *Jesus and the Kingdom of God*. Grand Rapids: Eerdmans.

Bevans, Stephen. 1992. *John Oman and his Doctrine of God*. Cambridge: Cambridge University Press.

Bockmuehl, Markus. 2001. "Resurrection." In Bockmuehl, ed., *The Cambridge Companion to Jesus*, pp. 102–18. Cambridge: Cambridge University Press.

Bonhoeffer, Dietrich. 1978. *Christ the Center*, trans. Edwin Robertson. New York: Harper.

Brondos, David A. 2001. "The Cross and the Curse: Galatians 3:13 and Paul's Doctrine of Redemption." *Journal for the Study of the New Testament* 81, pp. 3–32.

———. 2006. *Paul on the Cross: Reconstructing the Apostle's Story of Redemption*. Minneapolis: Fortress.

Brown, Alexandra R. 1995. *The Cross and Human Transformation: Paul's Apocalyptic Word in 1 Corinthians*. Minneapolis: Fortress.

Brown, Robert McAfee. 1952. *P. T. Forsyth*. Philadelphia: Westminster.

Bruce, F. F. 1977. *Paul: Apostle of the Free Spirit*. Exeter: Paternoster.

Brunner, Emil. 1938. *The Divine-Human Encounter*, trans. A. W. Loos. Philadelphia: Westminster.

———. 1949. *The Christian Doctrine of God*, trans. Olive Wyon. London: Lutterworth.

———. 1953. *The Misunderstanding of the Church*, trans. Harold Knight. Philadelphia: Westminster.

———. 1961. "Easter Certainty." In Brunner, *I Believe in the Living God*, trans. John Holden, pp. 86–97. Philadelphia: Westminster.

Buber, Martin. 1923. *I and Thou*, trans. R. G. Smith. New York: Scribner.

Buckley, Michael J. 1987. *At the Origins of Modern Atheism*. New Haven: Yale University Press.

———. 2004. *Denying and Disclosing God*. New Haven: Yale University Press.

Buttrick, George A. 1966. *God, Pain, and Evil*. Nashville: Abingdon.

Byrnes, Michael. 2003. *Conformation to the Death of Christ and the Hope of Resurrection*. Rome: Gregorian University Press.

Camfield, F. W. 1934. *Revelation and the Holy Spirit*. New York: Scribner.

Cottingham, John. 2005. *The Spiritual Dimension: Religion, Philosophy, and Human Value*. Cambridge: Cambridge University Press.

Crowley, Paul. 2005. *Unwanted Wisdom: Suffering, the Cross, and Hope*. New York: Continuum.

Dales, D. J. 1994. *Living Through Dying*. Cambridge, Eng.: Lutterworth.

Daly, Robert J. 1978. *The Origins of the Christian Doctrine of Sacrifice*. Philadelphia: Fortress.

———. 2003. "Sacrifice Unveiled or Sacrifice Revisited." *Theological Studies* 64, pp. 24–42.

Davis, Caroline Franks. 1989. *The Evidential Force of Religious Experience*. Oxford: Clarendon Press.

Dillistone, F. W. 1977. *C. H. Dodd: Interpreter of the New Testament*. London: Hodder and Stoughton.

Dodd, C. H. 1936. *The Apostolic Preaching and its Developments*. London: Hodder and Stoughton.

Dunn, James. 1975. *Jesus and the Spirit*. London: SCM.

———. 1993. "Christology as an Aspect of Theology." In A. J. Malherbe and W. A. Meeks, eds., *The Future of Christology*, pp. 202–12. Minneapolis: Fortress.

Evans, C. H., and W. R.Herzog, eds. 2002. *The Faith of Fifty Million: Baseball, Religion, and American Culture*. Louisville: Westminster.

Farmer, H. H. 1935. *The World and God*. London: Nisbet.

———. 1942. *Towards Belief in God*. London: SCM.

———. 1946. "The Most Important Question." *Current Religious Thought* 6, pp. 10–13.

———. 1966. *The Word of Reconciliation*. Nashville: Abingdon.

Fee, Gordon D. 2007. *Pauline Christology*. Peabody, MA: Hendrickson.

Fiddes, Paul S. 1988. *The Creative Suffering of God*. Oxford: Clarendon Press.

Filson, Floyd V. 1956. *Jesus Christ the Risen Lord*. Nashville: Abingdon.

Fitzmyer, Joseph A. 1970. "'To Know Him and the Power of His Resurrection' (Phil. 3:10)." In A. Descamps and A. de Halleux, eds., *Mélanges bibliques en hommage au R.P. Béda Rigaux*, pp. 411–25. Reprinted in Fitzmyer, *To Advance the Gospel*, 2nd ed., pp. 202–17. Grand Rapids: Eerdmans, 1998. Page references are to this reprint.

———. 1975. "Reconciliation in Pauline Theology." In J. W. Flanagan and A. W. Robinson, eds., *No Famine in the Land*, pp. 155–77. Missoula, MT: Scholars Press. Reprinted in Fitzmyer, *To Advance the Gospel*, 2nd ed., pp. 162–85. Grand Rapids: Eerdmans, 1998.

———. 1979. "The Gospel in the Theology of Paul." *Interpretation* 33, pp. 339–50. Reprinted in Fitzmyer, *To Advance the Gospel*, 2nd ed., pp. 149–61. Grand Rapids: Eerdmans, 1998.

———. 1985. "*Abba* and Jesus' Relation to God." In R. Gantoy, ed., *À cause de l'Évangile*, pp. 15–38. Paris: Cerf.

Ford, David F. 2007. *Christian Wisdom: Desiring God and Learning in Love.* Cambridge: Cambridge University Press.

Forstman, Jack. 1992. *Christian Faith in Dark Times: Theological Conflicts in the Shadow of Hitler.* Louisville: Westminster.

Forsyth, Peter T. 1907. *Positive Preaching and the Modern Mind.* London: Hodder and Stoughton.

———. 1913. *The Principle of Authority.* London: Hodder and Stoughton.

Fretheim, Terence E. 1984. *The Suffering of God.* Philadelphia: Fortress.

Fry, Christopher. 1961. "A Sleep of Prisoners." In Fry, *Three Plays.* New York: Oxford University Press.

Gale, Richard. 1991. *On the Nature and Existence of God.* Cambridge: Cambridge University Press.

———. 2007. "The Failure of Classical Theistic Arguments." In Michael Martin, ed., *The Cambridge Companion to Atheism,* pp. 86–101. Cambridge: Cambridge University Press.

Gaventa, Beverly Roberts. 1986. *From Darkness to Light: Aspects of Conversion in the New Testament.* Philadelphia: Fortress.

Gorman, Michael J. 2001. *Cruciformity: Paul's Narrative Spirituality of the Cross.* Grand Rapids: Eerdmans.

Grave, S. A. 1989. *Conscience in Newman's Thought.* Oxford: Clarendon Press.

Gundry, Robert H. 1993. *Mark: A Commentary on his Apology for the Cross.* Grand Rapids: Eerdmans.

Gunkel, Hermann. 1979 [1888]. *The Influence of the Holy Spirit,* trans. R. A. Harrisville and P. A. Quanbeck. Philadelphia: Fortress.

Guthrie, Harvey H. 1981. *Theology as Thanksgiving.* New York: Seabury.

Halbertal, Moshe, and Avishai Margalit. 1992. *Idolatry,* trans. Naomi Goldblum. Cambridge, MA: Harvard University Press.

Hallesby, Ole. 1933. *Conscience.* Minneapolis: Augsburg.

Hampton, Jean, and Jeffrie Murphy. 1988. *Forgiveness and Mercy.* Cambridge: Cambridge University Press.

Hanson, N. R. 1971. *What I Do Not Believe and Other Essays.* Dordrecht: Reidel.

Hanson, Paul D. 1982. *The Diversity of Scripture.* Philadelphia: Fortress.

———. 1986. *The People Called: The Growth of Community in the Bible.* San Francisco: Harper.

Hardy, Daniel H., and David F. Ford. 1985. *Praising and Knowing God.* Philadelphia: Westminster.

Hart, Trevor, ed. 1995. *Justice the True and Only Mercy.* Edinburgh: T&T Clark.

Hays, Richard B. 1997. *First Corinthians.* Louisville: John Knox.

Hepburn, Ronald W. 1958. *Christianity and Paradox.* London: Watts.

———. 1963. "From World to God." *Mind* 72, pp. 40–50.

Herberg, Will. 1951. *Judaism and Modern Man.* Philadelphia: Jewish Publication Society.

Heschel, Abraham. 1955. *God in Search of Man.* New York: Jewish Publication Society.

———. 1962. *The Prophets.* New York: Jewish Publication Society.

Howard-Snyder, Daniel. 1996. "The Argument from Inscrutable Evil." In Howard-Snyder, ed., *The Evidential Argument from Evil.* Bloomington, IN: Indiana University Press.

Howard-Snyder, Daniel, and Paul K. Moser, eds. 2002. *Divine Hiddenness.* Cambridge: Cambridge University Press.

Hubbard, Moyer V. 2002. *New Creation in Paul's Letters and Thought.* Cambridge: Cambridge University Press.

Hume, David. 1780. *Dialogues concerning Natural Religion*, ed. N. Kemp Smith. London: Macmillan, 1947.

Hurtado, Larry W. 2003. *Lord Jesus Christ: Devotion to Jesus in Earliest Christianity.* Grand Rapids: Eerdmans.

Jackson, Timothy. 1999. *Love Disconsoled.* Cambridge: Cambridge University Press.

Jeremias, Joachim. 1967. *The Prayers of Jesus.* London: SCM.

———. 2002. *Jesus and the Message of the New Testament*, ed. K. C. Hanson. Minneapolis: Fortress.

Jervis, L. A. 2007. *At the Heart of the Gospel: Suffering in the Earliest Christian Message.* Grand Rapids: Eerdmans.

Johnson, Luke T. 1990. *Faith's Freedom.* Minneapolis: Fortress.

———. 1999. *Living Jesus.* San Francisco: Harper.

Juergensmeyer, Mark. 2003. *Terror in the Mind of God: The Global Rise of Religious Violence*, 3d ed. Berkeley: University of California Press.

Kasser, Tim. 2002. *The High Price of Materialism.* Cambridge, MA: MIT.

Kierkegaard, Søren. 1985 [1844]. *Philosophical Fragments.* trans. H. V. Hong and E. H. Hong. Princeton: Princeton University Press.

———. 1992 [1846]. *Concluding Unscientific Postscript*, trans. H. V. Hong and E. H. Hong. Princeton: Princeton University Press.

Kümmel, W. G. 1973. *The Theology of the New Testament*, trans. J. E. Steely. Nashville: Abingdon.

Lemcio, Eugene E. 1991. "The Unifying Kerygma of the New Testament." In Lemcio, *The Past of Jesus in the Gospels*, pp. 115–31. Cambridge: Cambridge University Press.

———. 2006. "The Gospels within the New Testament Canon." In C. G. Bartholomew, ed., *Canon and Biblical Interpretation*, pp. 123–45. London: Paternoster.

Longenecker, Richard, ed. 1996. *Patterns of Discipleship in the New Testament.* Grand Rapids: Eerdmans.

Lycan, William G. 2002. "Explanation and Epistemology." In Moser 2002a, pp. 408–33.

Mackay, John A. 1969. *Christian Reality and Appearance.* Richmond, VA: Knox.

Martin, Michael, ed. 2007. *The Cambridge Companion to Atheism.* Cambridge: Cambridge University Press.

Martin, Ralph P. 1981. *Reconciliation: A Study of Paul's Theology.* Atlanta: John Knox Press.

Martyn, J. Louis. 1997a. "Epistemology at the Turn of the Ages." In Martyn, *Theological Issues in the Letters of Paul*, pp. 89–110. Edinburgh: T&T Clark.

———. 1997b. "A Law-Observant Mission to Gentiles." In Martyn, *Theological Issues in the Letters of Paul*, pp. 7–24. Edinburgh: T&T Clark.

———. 1997c. *Galatians.* New York: Doubleday.

Meadors, Edward. 2006. *Idolatry and the Hardening of the Heart.* London: T&T Clark.

Meier, John P. 2001. *A Marginal Jew*, Vol. 3: *Companions and Competitors.* New York: Doubleday.

Mele, Alfred R., and Paul K. Moser. 1994. "Intentional Action." *Noûs* 28, pp. 39–68. Reprinted in Alfred R. Mele, ed., *The Philosophy of Action*, pp. 223–55. Oxford: Oxford University Press, 1997.

Michalson, Carl. 1967. "Christianity and the Finality of Faith." In Michalson, *Worldly Theology*, pp. 184–200. New York: Scribner.

Miller, Kenneth R. 1999. *Finding Darwin's God*. New York: HarperCollins.

Moltmann, Jurgen. 1992. *The Spirit of Life*. Minneapolis: Fortress.

Moser, Paul K. 1988. "Meaning, Justification, and Skepticism." *Philosophical Papers* 17, pp. 88–101.

———. 1989. *Knowledge and Evidence*. Cambridge: Cambridge University Press.

———. 1993. *Philosophy after Objectivity*. New York: Oxford University Press.

———. 1998. "Realism, Objectivity, and Skepticism." In John Greco and Ernest Sosa, eds., *The Blackwell Guide to Epistemology*, pp. 70–91. Oxford: Blackwell.

———. 1999. "Jesus on Knowledge of God." *Christian Scholars Review* 28, pp. 586–604.

———. 2000. "Skepticism, Question Begging, and Burden Shifting." In Richard Cobb-Stevens, ed., *The Proceedings of the Twentieth World Congress of Philosophy, Volume 5: Epistemology*, pp. 209–17. Bowling Green, OH: Philosophy Documentation Center.

———. 2001. "Man to Man with *Warranted Christian Belief* and Alvin Plantinga." *Philosophia Christi* 3, pp. 369–77.

———, ed. 2002a. *The Oxford Handbook of Epistemology*. New York: Oxford University Press.

———. 2002b. "Cognitive Idolatry and Divine Hiding." In Daniel Howard-Snyder and Paul Moser, eds., *Divine Hiddenness*, pp. 120–48. Cambridge: Cambridge University Press.

———. 2003. "Cognitive Inspiration and Knowledge of God." In Paul Copan and Paul Moser, eds., *The Rationality of Theism*, pp. 55–71. London: Routledge.

———. 2004a. "Skepticism Undone?" In John Greco, ed., *Ernest Sosa and His Critics*, pp. 135–44. Oxford: Blackwell. (See Appendix.)

———. 2004b. "Divine Hiddenness Does Not Justify Atheism," and "Reply to Schellenberg." In M. L. Peterson and R. J. VanArragon, eds., *Contemporary Debates in Philosophy of Religion*, pp. 42–54, 56–58. Oxford: Blackwell.

———. 2004c. "Philosophy of Religion and Christian Resurrection." *International Journal of Philosophical Studies* 12, pp. 61–69.

———. 2006. Review of *The Resurrection of the Son of God* by N. T. Wright and *The Redemption*, ed. by S. Davis, D. Kendall, and G. O'Collins. *International Journal of Philosophical Studies* 14, pp. 276–82.

Moser, Paul K., and J. D. Trout, eds. 1995. *Contemporary Materialism*. London: Routledge.

Moser, Paul K., and David Yandell. 2000. "Farewell to Philosophical Naturalism." In W. L. Craig and J. P. Moreland, eds., *Naturalism: Critical Essays*, pp. 3–23. London: Routledge.

Murray, M. J. 1993. "Coercion and the Hiddenness of God." *American Philosophical Quarterly* 30, pp. 27–38.

Nagel, Thomas. 1997. *The Last Word*. New York: Oxford University Press.

Niebuhr, Reinhold. 1941. *The Nature and Destiny of Man*, Vol. 1: *Human Nature*. New York: Scribner.

———. 1949. *Faith and History*. New York: Scribner.

Nygren, Anders. 1953. *Agape and Eros*, trans. P.S. Watson. New York: Harper and Row.

Oman, John. 1917. *Grace and Personality*. Cambridge: Cambridge University Press.

Oppy, Graham. 2006. *Arguing about Gods*. Cambridge: Cambridge University Press.

Parsons, Keith. 2007. "Some Theistic Arguments." In Michael Martin, ed., *The Cambridge Companion to Atheism*, pp. 102–17. Cambridge: Cambridge University Press.

Partridge, Christopher. 1998. *H. H. Farmer's Theological Interpretation of Religion*. Lewiston, NY: Mellen.

Pascal, Blaise. 1670. *Pensées*, trans. A. Krailsheimer. London: Penguin, 1966; and trans. H. Levi. New York: Oxford University Press, 1995.

Plantinga, Alvin. 2000. *Warranted Christian Belief*. New York: Oxford University Press.

Plato. 1969. *Phaedo*, trans. H. Tredennick. In *The Last Days of Socrates*. London: Penguin.

Pollock, John. 1974. *Knowledge and Justification*. Princeton: Princeton University Press.

———. 1986. *Contemporary Theories of Knowledge*. Lanham, MD: Rowman & Littlefield. 2nd ed. (with Joseph Cruz), 1999.

Rahner, Karl. 1978. *Foundations of Christian Faith*, trans. W. V. Dych. New York: Crossroad.

———. 1983a. "Christian Pessimism." In Rahner, *Theological Investigations*, Vol. 22, trans. Joseph Donceel, pp. 155–62. New York: Crossroad.

———. 1983b. "Conscience." In Rahner, *Theological Investigations*, Vol. 22, trans. Joseph Donceel, pp. 3–13. New York: Crossroad.

Reiser, Marius. 1997. *Jesus and Judgment*, trans. L. M. Maloney. Minneapolis: Fortress.

Rowe, William L. 2006. "Friendly Atheism, Skeptical Theism, and the Problem of Evil." *International Journal for Philosophy of Religion* 59, pp. 79–92.

Russell, Bertrand. 1903. "A Free Man's Worship." In Russell, *Mysticism and Logic*, pp. 44–54. Garden City, NY: Doubleday, 1957.

———. 1953. "What is an Agnostic?" In Louis Greenspan and Stefan Andersson, eds., *Russell on Religion*, pp. 41–49. London: Routledge, 1999.

———. 1970. "The Talk of the Town," *The New Yorker* (February 21, 1970), p. 29. Cited in Al Seckel, ed., *Bertrand Russell on God and Religion*, p. 11. Buffalo: Prometheus, 1986.

Samra, James G. 2006. *Being Conformed to Christ in Community*. London: T&T Clark.

Savage, Timothy. 1996. *Power Through Weakness*. Cambridge: Cambridge University Press.

Schellenberg, J. L. 1993. *Divine Hiddenness and Human Reason*. Ithaca: Cornell University Press.

———. 2007. *The Wisdom to Doubt: A Justification of Religious Skepticism*. Ithaca: Cornell University Press.

Schneider, John R. 2004. "Seeing God Where the Wild Things Are: An Essay on the Defeat of Horrendous Evil." In Peter Van Inwagen, ed., *Christian Faith and the Problem of Evil*, pp. 226–62. Grand Rapids: Eerdmans.

Schweizer, Eduard 1961. "Spirit of God." In D. M. Barton, P. R. Ackroyd, and A. E. Harvey, eds., *Bible Key Words*, Vol. 3, pp. 1–108. New York: Harper.

———. 1989. "On Distinguishing Between Spirits." *Ecumenical Review* 41, pp. 406–15.

Scott, Ian W. 2006. *Implicit Epistemology in the Letters of Paul*. Tübingen: Mohr Siebeck.

Smart, J. J. C. 1996. "Atheism and Theism." In Smart and J. J. Haldane, *Atheism and Theism*, pp. 6–83. Oxford: Blackwell.

Snodgrass, Klyne. 1994. "The Gospel in Romans: A Theology of Revelation." In L. A. Jervis and Peter Richardson, eds., *Gospel in Paul*, pp. 288–314. Sheffield: Sheffield Academic Press.

———. 2005. "The Gospel of Jesus." In Markus Bockmuehl and Donald Hagner, eds., *The Written Gospel*, pp. 31–44. Cambridge: Cambridge University Press.

Sosa, Ernest. 1980. "The Raft and the Pyramid: Coherence versus Foundations in the Theory of Knowledge." In Peter French et al., eds., *Midwest Studies in Philosophy, Volume 5: Studies in Epistemology*, pp. 3–25. Minneapolis: University of Minnesota Press.

———. 1994. "Philosophical Scepticism and Epistemic Circularity." *Proceedings of the Aristotelian Society, Supplementary Volume 68*, pp. 263–90. Reprinted in Paul K. Moser, ed., *Empirical Knowledge*, 2nd ed., pp. 303–29. Lanham, MD: Rowman & Littlefield, 1996. Page references are to this reprint.

———. 1997. "Reflective Knowledge in the Best Circles." *The Journal of Philosophy* 94, pp. 410–30. Reprinted in Ernest Sosa and Jaegwon Kim, eds., *Epistemology*, pp. 274–85. Oxford: Blackwell, 2000. Page references are to this reprint.

Stanton, Graham. 2004. "Jesus and Gospel." In Stanton, *Jesus and Gospel*, pp. 9–62. Cambridge: Cambridge University Press.

Stuhlmacher, Peter. 1986. *Reconciliation, Law, and Righteousness: Essays in Biblical Theology*, trans. E. R. Kalin. Philadelphia: Fortress.

Swinburne, Richard. 1979. *The Existence of God*. Oxford: Clarendon Press.

———. 1981. *Faith and Reason*. Oxford: Clarendon Press.

———. 1992. *Revelation*. Oxford: Clarendon Press.

———. 2003. *The Resurrection of God Incarnate*. Oxford: Clarendon Press.

Tannehill, Robert C. 1967. *Dying and Rising with Christ*. Berlin: Alfred Töpelmann.

Taylor, Vincent. 1948. "The Creative Element in the Thought of Jesus." In Taylor, *New Testament Essays*, pp. 36–47. London: Epworth.

Terrien, Samuel. 1978. *The Elusive Presence*. San Francisco: Harper.

Thielicke, Helmut. 1966. *Theological Ethics*, Vol. 1: *Foundations*, ed. W. H. Lazareth. Grand Rapids: Eerdmans.

———. 1968. *I Believe*, trans. J. W. Doberstein and H. G. Anderson. Philadelphia: Fortress.

———. 1972. "What Has God to Do with the Meaning of Life?" In Thielicke, *How to Believe Again*, trans. H. G. Anderson, pp. 101–13. Philadelphia: Fortress, 1972.

———. 1974. *The Evangelical Faith*, Vol. 1: *Prolegomena*, trans. G. W. Bromiley. Grand Rapids: Eerdmans.

Thompson, Marianne Meye. 2000. *The Promise of the Father: Jesus and God in the New Testament*. Louisville: Westminster.

Via, Dan O. 2007. *Divine Justice, Divine Judgment: Rethinking the Judgment of Nations*. Minneapolis: Fortress.

von Rad, Gerhard. 1965. *Old Testament Theology*, Vol. 2: *The Theology of Israel's Prophetic Traditions*, trans. D. M. Stalker. New York: Harper.

Wainwright, William J. 1995. *Reason and the Heart*. Ithaca, NY: Cornell University Press.

———. 2002. "Jonathan Edwards and the Hiddenness of God." In Daniel Howard-Snyder and Paul K. Moser, eds., *Divine Hiddenness*, pp. 98–119. Cambridge: Cambridge University Press.

Watts, Rikki E. 1997. *Isaiah's New Exodus and Mark*. Tübingen: Mohr Siebeck.

Wenham, David. 1995. *Paul: Follower of Jesus or Founder of Christianity?* Grand Rapids: Eerdmans.

Westerholm, Stephen. 2004. *Perspectives Old and New on Paul*. Grand Rapids: Eerdmans.

Wiebe, Phillip H. 1997. *Visions of Jesus*. New York: Oxford University Press.

———. 2004. *God and Other Spirits*. New York: Oxford University Press.

Williams, Rowan. 1982. *Resurrection: Interpreting the Easter Gospel*. London: Darton.

———. 2000a. "Between the Cherubim: The Empty Tomb and the Empty Throne." In Williams, *On Christian Theology*, pp. 183–96. Oxford: Blackwell.

———. 2000b. *Christ on Trial: How the Gospel Unsettles our Judgement*. London: Harper-Collins.

Wilson, E. O. 1998. *Consilience: The Unity of Knowledge*. New York: Knopf.

Wright, N. T. 2003. *The Resurrection of the Son of God*. Minneapolis: Fortress.

Yandell, Keith E. 1993. *The Epistemology of Religious Experience*. Cambridge: Cambridge University Press.

Index

Abraham, 83, 164, 221, 225
adequate evidence, 33–35, 55, 106, 107, 199
adoration, 18, 32
agape transformation, 130–132
agnosticism, *see* skepticism
Allison, Dale, 162, 166
Alston, William P., 266
Anselm, 89
Aquinas, Thomas, 1, 176, 202, 205, 236
Aristotle, 11, 37, 201, 202, 209, 219, 220, 235
atonement, 163–165, 216
  manifest-offering approach, 105, 165, 168,
    171, 172, 174, 175, 182, 186, 188, 192, 211,
    226, 230
  see also Jesus and atonement
attunement, 5, 13–14, 17, 26, 82, 101, 104, 113, 114,
    118–123, 142, 147, 157, 231, 241, 246
Augustine, 1, 70, 176, 202, 225
authoritative call of divine love, *see* God,
    authoritative call of
authoritative evidence, 10–12, 16, 46–50, 52, 53,
    55–56, 60–62, 64, 70, 72–74, 77, 79, 81,
    88, 103, 112, 126–128, 134, 138, 142, 152,
    161, 162, 193, 199, 213, 221, 223, 226, 238,
    239, 242, 244–247, 249, 257, 258, 260,
    261, 263–265
authority
  and autonomy, 81, 209, 256
  cognitive, 52, 55, 60, 67, 74–76, 97, 103, 215
  divine, *see* God, authoritative call of
  fear of, 44, 214, 256

Bahaism, 30, 39
Baillie, John, 126
Balentine, Samuel, 106
Banner, Michael, 64
Barth, Karl, 1
Beasley-Murray, G.R., 163
  on an inference to a best available
    explanation, 27, 64, 65, 69, 85–88, 92,
    128, 129, 138, 139, 166, 192
  rational, 33, 47, 68, 85, 92, 244, 271
  reasonableness of, 33, 46, 64, 65, 86, 106

belief
best available explanation, *see* belief
Bevans, Stephen, 245
Bockmuehl, Markus, 160
Bonhoeffer, Dietrich, 1, 75
Brondos, David A., 138, 156, 165, 183, 187, 226
Brown, Alexandra R., 157, 221
Bruce, F. F., 224
Brunner, Emil, 1, 96, 124, 196–197, 231, 245
Buber, Martin, 1, 245
Buckley, Michael J., 35, 84, 193
Buddhism, 30, 39
Buttrick, George A., 245
Byrnes, Michael, 146

Calvin, John (including Calvinism), 70, 109,
    135, 176, 205
Camfield, F. W., 100
church, the, 230–231, 233–237, 239, 240
cognitive grace, 48, 155, 221
cognitive idolatry, *see* idolatry
cognitive inspiration, 155
cognitive modesty, 50, 55
cognitive shift (or cognitive revolution), 4, 7,
    10, 11, 14, 15, 17, 23, 40, 55, 144, 240, 248
cognitive standards, 13, 71, 77, 79, 260
cognitive-volitional disconnect, 71, 77, 79
conclusive evidence, 2, 8, 14, 22–23, 25–28, 38,
    45, 49, 55, 56, 59, 60, 62, 63, 75, 81, 101,
    103–105, 111, 124, 126, 127, 131, 133, 135,
    138, 140–142, 145, 152, 155, 194, 199, 221,
    222, 263, 278
Confucianism, 30, 32
Confucius, 32, 164
conscience, 8, 23, 26, 28, 43, 44, 50, 51, 54, 55,
    65, 66, 69, 93, 97, 99–100, 134, 136, 145,
    148, 154, 195, 197, 204, 218, 234, 244, 277
  and evidence, 6, 24, 62–65, 69, 74, 112, 127,
    134, 138, 149, 150, 217, 238, 243, 246,
    260
corrective judgment, *see* judgment
  see also forgiveness
cosmic authority problem, 80, 102, 214, 255

287